The SCSI Bus and IDE Interface

Protocols, applications and programming

Second edition

Friedhelm Schmidt

 **Addison-Wesley**

Harlow, England • Reading, Massachusetts • Menlo Park, California • New York
Don Mills, Ontario • Amsterdam • Bonn • Sydney • Singapore • Tokyo • Madrid
San Juan • Milan • Mexico City • Seoul • Taipei

Translated from the German edition *SCSI-Bus und IDE-Schnittstelle* published by Addison-Wesley (Deutschland) GmbH.

Addison Wesley Longman Limited
Edinburgh Gate
Harlow
Essex
CM20 2JE
England

and Associated Companies throughout the World.

Translated and typeset by Logotechnics Sales & Marketing Ltd, Sheffield.
Cover designed by Designers and Partners Ltd, Oxford.
Cover figure/photograph by
Typeset in Times 10/12

Printed and bound in the United States of America.

Second edition first printed 1997.
First edition first printed 1995.

ISBN 0-201-17514-2

British Library Cataloguing in Publication Data
A catalogue record for this book is available from the British Library.

The SCSI Bus
and
IDE Interface

Preface

The SCSI bus and IDE interface are without question the two most important interfaces for computer peripherals in use today. The IDE hard disk interface is found
almost exclusively in the world of IBM PC compatibles. The SCSI bus, on the other
hand, is designed not only for hard drives but also for tape drives, CD-ROM, scanners, and printers. Almost all modern computers, from PCs to workstations to
mainframes, are equipped with a SCSI interface.

Both SCSI and IDE are ANSI standards. However, aside from the actual ANSI
documentation, there exists almost no additional reference material to either specification. The purpose of this book is to fill that void with a clear, concise description
of both interfaces. The essential terminology is introduced, while the commands and
protocols are broken down in full. In the interest of economy the less important
details and options have been omitted in certain cases. Often a specific section in the
ANSI documentation will be cited for easy cross-referencing. After reading this
book you should be in the position to easily understand relevant technical documentation, including the ANSI specifications themselves.

First and foremost, a thorough introduction to the terminology is in order.
Especially with respect to SCSI, there is a deluge of terms and definitions that are
used nowhere else or are used differently than in other computer domains. These
keywords, which include signal names and interface commands, are typeset in small
capital letters, for example FORMAT UNIT.

This book is intended for readers with a broad range of technical backgrounds and
interests. Those working on the design of mass storage devices, for example, will find
the protocol descriptions extremely useful. Readers writing software or device drivers
may have other interests. They will find the hardware descriptions, such as that of the
physical organization of a disk drive, very helpful.

This book is not meant to replace the ANSI documentation. On the other hand,
those specifications are not meant to explain the technology, rather to define it. It is
very difficult to find your way around in the original documentation without an
understanding of the subject matter. The book's thorough, in-depth descriptions,
along with index and glossary, make it the perfect tutor for IDE and SCSI, as well
as a helpful guide to the ANSI literature.

Friedhelm Schmidt
February 1993

Preface to the second edition

More than four years have passed since the first edition of this book, but nevertheless the book is still of immediate interest. In the fast-paced computer industry, this is not a matter of course. But even the SCSI bus and the IDE interface go on developing. The current version in the IDE domain is ATA-2, and work on ATA-3 is in progress.

The SCSI-3 standard too is slowly becoming more stable; some parts of it are already implemented in series products. Two examples are the new wide SCSI bus with 16-bit transfers on only one cable and the possibility of having 16 devices on one bus, and the Ultra SCSI bus (Fast-20) with its transmission speed doubled up to 20 mega transfers per second.

The really important change in SCSI-3 is the division of the standard into interface, protocol, device model and command set. This allows the use of SCSI device models and their command sets with different physical interfaces. In particular the Fibre Channel is currently seen as the physical interface of the future. But even with Fast-20, the current parallel SCSI interface too has not yet reached its throughput limit. Developers are already thinking of Fast-40 or even Fast-80.

The contents of this second edition of the book have been slightly rearranged; the structure of the SCSI part is now oriented at the SCSI-3 standard draft. The SCSI-3 architecture model and an introduction to the new physical interfaces have been added. Once again, the time has come to part with well-known techniques and learn something new. Enjoy reading.

Friedhelm Schmidt
May 1997

Contents

Preface   v

Preface to the second edition   vi

Part I Introduction   1

1 Computers and peripherals   **3**
1.1   Mass storage   4
1.2   Peripheral interfaces   5

2 Traditional peripheral interfaces   **7**
2.1   The RS-232 serial interface   7
2.2   The Centronics printer interface   10
2.3   Hard disks and their interfaces   13
2.4   ST506   19

3 Computer buses   **24**
3.1   Characteristics of buses   25
3.2   Specialized buses   27

Part II The IDE interface   29

4 Background   **31**

4.1   The origin of IDE   31
4.2   Overview   32
4.3   Documentation   34

5 The physical IDE interface   **37**
5.1   The electrical interface   37
5.2   Timing specifications   40

6 IDE protocol   **44**
6.1   The register model of the IDE controller   44
6.2   Command execution   49
6.3   Power-up or hardware reset   52

7 The model of an IDE disk drive   **55**
7.1   Organization of the medium   55

7.2	Defect management	58
7.3	The sector buffer	59
7.4	Power conditions	60

8 IDE commands — **61**
| 8.1 | Mandatory commands | 61 |
| 8.2 | Optional commands | 66 |

9 The ATAPI interface — **73**
9.1	ATAPI architecture	74
9.2	ATAPI transport mechanism	75
9.3	ATAPI transport protocol	77
9.4	ATAPI commands	79
9.5	CD-ROM command packets	82

Part III The SCSI bus — **85**

10 Introduction — **87**
10.1	The evolution of SCSI	87
10.2	Overview	90
10.3	Documentation	96

11 SCSI architecture — **101**
11.1	The SCSI architecture model	101
11.2	The SCSI command model	110
11.3	Exceptions and error handling	116
11.4	Task management	118
11.5	Task set management	119

12 SCSI primary commands — **121**
12.1	The SCSI target model	121
12.2	Command structure	123
12.3	Commands for all SCSI devices	127
12.4	Mode parameter pages for all device types	144
12.5	The model of a SCSI processor device	147
12.6	Commands for processor devices	149

13 Block-oriented devices — **152**
13.1	The model of a SCSI disk drive	152
13.2	Hard disk commands	158
13.3	Mode parameter pages for disk drives	168
13.4	The SCSI model of optical storage and WORM drives	175
13.5	Commands for optical storage and WORM drives	176
13.6	Mode parameters for optical storage and WORM drives	181

14 Stream-oriented devices — **183**
14.1	The model of a SCSI tape drive	183
14.2	Commands for tape devices	186
14.3	Mode parameters for tape devices	195
14.4	The model of a SCSI printer	199

14.5   Printer commands   201
14.6   Mode parameters for printers   203
14.7   The model of a SCSI communications device   205
14.8   Commands for SCSI communications devices   206
14.9   Mode parameter pages for communications devices   207

15 Graphics devices   **209**
15.1   The model of a SCSI scanner   209
15.2   SCSI scanner commands   211
15.3   Mode parameters for scanners   213

16 Medium-changer devices   **215**
16.1   The model of a SCSI medium-changer device   215
16.2   Commands for medium-changers   217
16.3   Mode parameter pages for medium-changers   223

17 Storage array controllers   **226**
17.1   The model of the SCSI storage array   226
17.2   Commands for storage array controllers   230
17.3   Mode parameter pages for storage array controllers   233

18 Multi-media devices   **235**
18.1   The model of a SCSI CD-ROM drive   235
18.2   Commands for CD-ROMs   237
18.3   Audio commands for CD-ROMs   241
18.4   Mode parameters for CD-ROMs   243
18.5   CD recorders   245
18.6   Commands for CD recorders   246

19 The parallel SCSI interface   **248**
19.1   Overview   248
19.2   SCSI signals   250
19.3   Cables and connectors   253
19.4   Single-ended SCSI   256
19.5   Differential SCSI   262
19.6   Low voltage differential (LVD)   265
19.7   SCSI expanders   267
19.8   SCSI bus phases   270
19.9   The service model   281
19.10 Synchronous transfers and Fast SCSI   282
19.11 Ultra-SCSI or Fast-20   285
19.12 Ultra-2 SCSI or Fast-40 and more?   285
19.13 Wide SCSI   286
19.14 SCAM   286
19.15 Plug-and-Play SCSI   293

20 SCSI interlock protocol   **296**
20.1   The message system   296
20.2   I/O processes (tasks)   298

20.3   SCSI pointers   301
20.4   Disconnect/reconnect: freeing the bus   302
20.5   Transfer options   303
20.6   Tagged queues   305
20.7   Termination of I/O processes   307
20.8   Error handling in the message system   308
20.9   Asynchronous event notification   309

21 The new SCSI-3 interfaces   **310**
21.1   Fundamental problems of the parallel SCSI interface   311
21.2   Fibre Channel   312
21.3   From Fibre Channel to SCSI-3:
       the Fibre Channel Protocol (FCP)   317
21.4   Fire Wire (IEEE P1394)   318
21.5   From P1394 to SCSI-3:
       the Serial Bus Protocol (SBP)   321
21.6   SSA   322
21.7   From SSA to SCSI-3:
       the Serial Storage Protocol (SSP)   327

22 The ASPI software interface   **329**
22.1   The concept of ASPI   330
22.2   SCSI request blocks   330
22.3   ASPI initialization and function calls   334

23 The SCSI monitor program   **338**

24 Measuring and testing   **344**
24.1   SCSI analyzers   344
24.2   SCSI emulators   345
24.3   Examples from industry   346

25 SCSI chips   **349**
25.1   The NCR 5385   350
25.2   PC host adapters: FUTURE DOMAIN TMC-950   351
25.3   PCI bus to Fast-20: Symbios Logic SYM53C860   353

Appendix A SCSI-2 commands (by opcode)   **357**

Appendix B SCSI-2 commands (alphabetically)   **361**

Appendix C SCSI-2 sense codes   **364**

Appendix D The SCSI bulletin board   **369**

Appendix E Source code for SCANSCSI.PAS   **371**

Appendix F Addresses of manufacturers and organizations **377**

Glossary   **381**

Index   **389**

Part I
Introduction

1   Computers and peripherals
2   Traditional peripheral interfaces
3   Computer buses

1 Computers and peripherals

A computer can be broken down into a number of interdependent functional blocks. The most important of these are the central processing unit (CPU), main memory, input/output (I/O) and mass storage. The CPU executes the instructions of a program, which, along with the necessary data, must reside in main memory at execution time. Therefore, before a program can be run it must be loaded into main memory from mass storage. The data to be processed by the program comes either from mass storage or from an input device such as the keyboard. The CPU accesses memory at least once for each program step in order to read the corresponding machine instructions. In fact, several accesses are usually necessary to read and write data. For this reason the CPU and memory are very tightly coupled: access is uncomplicated and, above all, fast.

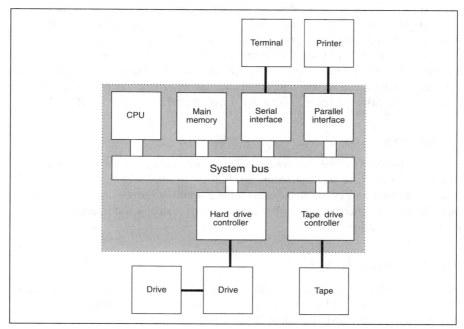

Figure 1.1 Computer system with peripheral devices.

In contrast to memory, I/O devices and mass storage are located further from the CPU, hence the name 'peripherals' (Figure 1.1). Access to such devices is slower and more complicated. Communication with the peripherals is accomplished using an interface such as SCSI or IDE. On the other end of the interface is a controller, which in turn communicates with the CPU and memory.

1.1   Mass storage

A mass storage device is capable of storing data many times the size of main memory. In addition, information stored here is nonvolatile: when the device is turned off the data remains intact.

Hard disks

Disk drives or hard disks store information by writing it onto rotating disks. The information is divided up into blocks of fixed length, each of which can be accessed relatively quickly, typically around 30 milliseconds (ms). For this reason hard disks are also referred to as random access mass storage devices. Among the different types of mass storage devices are hard disks, exchangeable medium drives, diskettes, optical disks and CD-ROM.

Tape devices

In contrast to hard disks, tape devices (or tape drives) write data sequentially onto magnetic tape. The length of time needed to access a specific block of information depends on which position is presently underneath the read/write head. If it is necessary to rewind or fast forward the tape a very long distance, a tape access can take as long as several minutes. Tape drives are also known as sequential mass storage devices. Among these are the traditional reel-to-reel drives, cassette drives, drives that use video cassettes for recording and 4 mm digital audio tape (DAT) drives.

I/O devices

Under the heading I/O devices are the monitor and keyboard used for communication between the user and the computer. Further examples of output devices are printers, plotters and even speakers used for outputting speech. Among the many input devices are mice, analog to digital converters, scanners and microphones used in speech recognition.

Miscellaneous devices

Network connections also fall into this category. This is especially so today where mass storage is often replaced by a file server across a network. Computers with no mass storage of their own are called diskless workstations.

There are many more devices that exchange data with computers, although one hardly refers to a computer controlled lathe or a music synthesizer as a computer peripheral. Nevertheless, they function as peripherals and communicate with the computer using I/O.

1.2   Peripheral interfaces

Peripheral devices are connected to computer systems via interfaces. The abstract model of a peripheral interface is made up of many layers, the boundaries of which are not always clear, especially for older interfaces. It is also true that some layers are omitted in certain interface definitions. In this book I adhere to a model with four layers for the SCSI interface, as was agreed upon by the American National Standards Institute (ANSI) committee for the first time for SCSI-3. The strata of layers are designed bottom up. All low level layers are mandatory for the implementation of an interface. An uppermost layer, however, can be omitted in some cases. A high level interface refers to the case where all possible levels have been implemented.

Among those things defined in the lowest level are cable and connector types. Also defined are the signal voltages and the current requirements of the drivers. Finally, the timing and coordination of all of the signals of the bus are described here. This lowest level is referred to as the physical interface.

Directly above the physical layer resides the protocol layer. The protocol of an interface contains, for example, information about the difference between data bytes and command bytes and about the exchange of messages between devices. If corrupted data is to be corrected through the use of error correction, this is described in the interface protocol.

On top of the protocol layer lies the peripheral device model. Here the behavior of devices to be connected to the interface is described. These descriptions can be very detailed and precise. The SCSI bus is an example of such a detailed model, where in addition to the characteristics of general purpose SCSI devices, those of hard disks, tape drives, printers and so on are defined.

Finally, some interfaces go so far as to define which commands must be understood by the interface devices. The command set builds upon the device model and represents the fourth layer of the interface.

The term 'interface' always refers to all implemented layers in their entirety. There are distinct peripheral interfaces defined using the same physical level but a unique protocol level. It is also possible for a single interface to allow for different options in the physical level.

The interface used for printers is a good example of a four-layer interface. Figure 1.2 makes the relationships among the layers clear. The two lower levels are covered by the Centronics interface. This parallel interface contains the definition of the physical and protocol layers. The particular printer model in Figure 1.2 is a page printer. This means that the printer constructs an entire page in internal memory before printing it. In contrast to line printers, the lines of a page can be sent in any

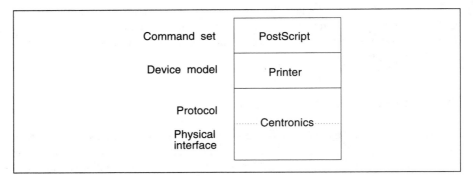

Figure 1.2 Layers of a printer interface.

order as long as a page boundary is not crossed. However, once a page is printed it is impossible to retrieve it in order to make changes.

The page description language PostScript is an excellent example of a large and complex command set. It is built upon the page printer model and makes it possible to output text as well as various graphic elements. These elements can be positioned freely on the current page. Naturally, there are other such page formatting languages written for the page printer model. This makes the division between device model and command set very intuitive.

As you can see, this interface is complete in that it contains all four interface layers. If you purchase a printer with such an interface, it makes no difference which brand name you choose. As long as it is true to the interface specification it will work with any computer also equipped with the printer interface. However, if you were to omit even only the uppermost layer of the specification, then the interface description would be incomplete. It would still be possible to connect up the printer, but whether it would function properly would be a matter of luck.

The IDE interface and the SCSI bus are likewise complete interface definitions. Before getting to these, however, I would like to introduce in Chapter 2 a few classic examples of peripheral interfaces. For the most part their definitions contain only the lower layers of the interface model. This chapter will help to underscore the difference between traditional interfaces on the one hand and the complete IDE and SCSI interfaces on the other.

2 Traditional peripheral interfaces

This chapter will help to familiarize you with several classic peripheral interfaces of the computer industry. As with the printer interface outlined in Chapter 1, these will be described within the framework of the layered interface model. These descriptions are by no means comprehensive; complete specifications would turn this book into several volumes.

I have two goals in mind in presenting these interfaces. First of all, the interfaces are very simple; they will allow you to become acquainted with interface characteristics that are valid for all interfaces, including computer buses. Secondly, to a certain degree these specifications are the forerunners of competition to the IDE and SCSI bus interfaces. A background in the more traditional interfaces will make it much easier to evaluate and understand their modern descendants, the main topic of this book.

2.1 The RS-232 serial interface

RS-232C is the most widely used serial interface. 'Serial' means that the data is transferred one bit at a time across a single connection. RS-232C is used mainly for the connection of computer terminals and printers. Nonetheless, it is also appropriate for the exchange of data between computers. Machine tools and measurement instruments are frequently connected to computers using RS-232C. Understandably, it is not a device specific interface. RS-232C is the responsibility of the Electronic Industries Association (EIA).

The specification for RS-232C contains the physical layer and hardware protocol. In addition, there are software protocols, of which only a few build on top of the RS-232 hardware protocol. This leads to an uncommon situation with RS-232C and other serial interfaces – not all applications use all of the signals. Frequently cables are used that conduct only a few of the defined signals, a situation that would be unthinkable for IDE or SCSI. I concentrate here on a variation of the interface using only three signals, which I call mini-RS-232.

The physical interface

Mini-RS-232 establishes a bidirectional point-to-point connection between equipment. Each direction has its own data signal and a single ground signal is shared. The data signals are called TD (transmit data) and RD (receive data). When two devices are coupled to each other, these signals are crossed such that the TD of one device connects to the RD of the other (Figure 2.1).

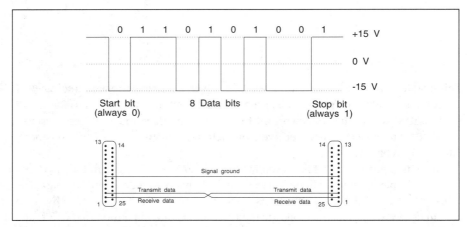

Figure 2.1   Physical interface: mini-RS-232.

The connector chosen by the EIA standard is the 25-pin DB25. Other connectors, however, are frequently employed, such as the DB9 for the IBM AT or the RJ11 telephone connector used in various minicomputers.

On the signal lines, a logical 1 is represented by a voltage between +5 V and +15 V, and the receiver recognizes anything above +3 V as such. Likewise, logical 0 is represented by a signal voltage between −5 V and −15 V. Again, the receiver recognizes any signal below −3 V as such.

Data transfer takes place serially, character by character. The characters are further broken down into bits, which are sent across the line one by one. On the other end, the receiver then assembles the bits back into characters. The number of bits per character lies between five and eight; eight is precisely what is needed to transfer one byte. The data bits are preceded by a start bit and followed by a stop bit. In addition, a parity bit may be sent for error detection. The transfer rate can range between 75 and 115 000 bits per second (baud), and a cable alone cannot compensate for different transfer rates; the devices must be set at the same speed otherwise no exchange of data can take place.

Now comes a rather confusing point: this method of transfer over the serial interface is called asynchronous even though the data is sent and received relative to a clock. Among other serial interfaces the term 'synchronous' is used whenever a clock is involved. For RS-232C, however, the transfer is referred to as asynchronous because the clocks are not tied to each other. The RS-232C specification includes signals that allow the sender and the receiver to use the same clock for data transfer.

When these signals are employed the data transfer is referred to as synchronous. True asynchronous transfer uses control signals to exchange data. This point, among others, will be made clear in Section 2.2.

As a rule of thumb, when thinking about data throughput you can consider a byte or character to be 10 bits (one stop, one start and eight data bits). When the fastest transfer rate possible is employed, namely 115 000 bits per second, the maximum throughput is approximately 11.5 Kbytes per second.

The protocol

Mini-RS-232 has no protocol of its own. However, there is a protocol that is often used with the interface, called the XON/XOFF protocol (Figure 2.2). It works in the following way. When the receiving device is no longer able to take on data from the sender, it sends a special character, an XOFF byte, to indicate this. Later, when it is ready to continue receiving data, it sends an XON byte to tell the sender to proceed. This protocol is in no way error proof – characters are sometimes lost. In addition, the protocol cannot be used for bidirectional transfer of binary data. The reason for this restriction is simple: for text data only a subset of the possible bytes is sent over the interface, those corresponding to letters, numbers, and symbols. This leaves room for a number of special characters, of which XON and XOFF are examples. When, on the other hand, binary data is transferred, the data is not restricted to certain characters; any binary pattern may occur. In this situation there is no room for the special characters and the XON/XOFF protocol is unusable. For connecting terminals and printers, however, the protocol is actually very practical.

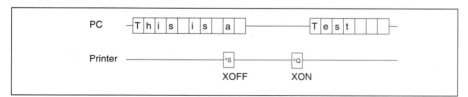

Figure 2.2 XON/XOFF protocol.

An example of a higher level protocol for the transfer of binary data (file transfer) is Kermit. This public domain program can be used at no cost for noncommercial purposes. A number of computer manufacturers have also developed their own internal protocols built on top of RS-232.

Commands

There are no commands special to the RS-232 interface. As RS-232 was developed, commands were designed for specific devices apart from the interface. SCSI is among the first interfaces to define universal command sets for whole device classes.

Nevertheless, some command sets have been designed for use with RS-232. Examples are page formatting languages for printers, such as PostScript.

Summary

As you can see, an interface that builds on top of RS-232 has many possible variations. The complete description of my printer–PC interface would be: RS-232 at 9600 baud, 1 stop bit, no parity, XON/XOFF protocol, PostScript. If I were to change a parameter for only the printer or only the PC, for example by not sending PostScript or starting to use a parity bit, nothing would print. Although mini-RS-232 appears to be simple (only three wires), there are almost an uncountable number of ways in which the connection can fail. What is missing is a protocol that allows the devices to agree upon the available options. Although RS-232 has given a good portion of frustration to just about everyone who has worked with it, it nonetheless has the decided advantage that it exists on every computer and is also device independent.

2.2   The Centronics printer interface

The Centronics interface is a parallel interface developed for printers. It is an industry standard that, to my knowledge, has never been officially approved. As a result there are many variations. This is especially so with respect to the status signals that reflect the printer's current state. Centronics defines the physical interface and the protocol. As a command set, either PostScript or another printer language is used.

Originally developed as a unidirectional interface, the parallel printer link for PCs can also be used bidirectionally. This faster, bidirectional variation, the Bi-Tronics interface, has been standardized as IEEE-1248. It is, however, not our concern here. We are interested in Centronics mostly as another example of the various computer interfaces. However, it is also a good idea to know this interface in order to understand the difference from SCSI printers (see Figure 2.3).

The physical interface

Centronics uses a shielded twisted-pair cable with 36 signals, of maximum length 5 meters (about 16 feet). A 36-pin amphenol connector is used on the printer end, which most people have come to refer to as a Centronics connector. The computer end of the cable has either a corresponding female Centronics or a female DB25.

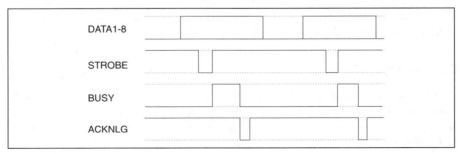

Figure 2.3   Centronics interface timing.

Table 2.1 The signals of the Centronics interface.

Pin (Cen)	Pin (DB25)	Signal	Source	Description
1	1	STROBE	Host	Indicates valid data on DATA1–8
2	2	DATA1	Host	Data bit 0
3	3	DATA2	Host	Data bit 1
4	4	DATA3	Host	Data bit 2
5	5	DATA4	Host	Data bit 3
6	6	DATA5	Host	Data bit 4
7	7	DATA6	Host	Data bit 5
7	8	DATA7	Host	Data bit 6
9	9	DATA8	Host	Data bit 7
10	10	ACKNLG	Printer	Indicates printer has accepted DATA1–8
11	11	BUSY	Printer	Indicates printer is not ready for new data
12	12	PE	Printer	Paper error
13	13	SELECT	Printer	Printer is online
14	14	AUTOFEED	Host	The printer should add a carriage return to each line feed
16		SIGNAL GROUND		0 V reference point for the signals
17		CHASSIS GROUND		Protective ground
18		+5V	Printer	+5 V power (50 mA maximum)
19–30	18–25	SIGNAL GROUND		Grounds of the twisted signal wires
31	16	INIT	Host	Initialize printer
32	15	ERROR	Printer	General error
36	17	SLCT IN	Host	Select printer

Electrical specifications

The signal voltages correspond to those for transistor–transistor logic (TTL). A 0 is recognized from 0 V to +0.8 V, a 1 from +2.4 V to +5.0 V. Table 2.1 lists the signals of the Centronics interface. Note that I have described the data signals starting with 0; that is, using the logical names. The actual signal names, however, are data1 to data8.

Data transfer takes place in parallel across signals DATA1 to DATA8. The signals STROBE, BUSY and ACKNLG control the sequencing, which is shown in Figure 2.3. The term 'protocol' does not apply completely here. Relative to our layer model, this timing belongs to the definition of the physical interface.

Request/acknowledge handshake

The transfer of a byte begins when the computer sets the 8 bits on signals data1 to data8. After waiting for at least a microsecond, it then activates a pulse across strobe, which indicates that there is valid data on the data lines. In response, the printer sets busy and reads the data byte. As soon as the byte has been successfully read and the printer is ready to receive the next byte, it clears the busy signal and sends a pulse across the acknlg line. Now the computer may change the data signals and send the next strobe for the next byte. This method of data transfer, where a signal is used to indicate a request (here strobe) and another to acknowledge that request (here acknlg), is called asynchronous. The mechanism itself is termed request/acknowledge handshake.

Throughput

Throughput, or the amount of data transferred per second, is dependent upon how long the printer leaves its busy signal active for each byte. The other signals involved in the handshake need at least 4 microseconds (μs) in total. If a printer were exceptionally fast, it could accept a byte in around 10 μs. This would correspond to a data rate of 100 Kbytes per second. The handbook for my old laser printer reports a value of approximately 100 μs for the length of busy, which allows for a rate no faster than 10 Kbytes per second. More recent printers with Bi-Tronics interface reach up to 400 Kbytes per second.

The protocol

The Centronics interface protocol is very simple. The flow of data is solely the responsibility of the physical layer. When the printer is not able to receive data it simply holds BUSY active. There are, however, a couple of status signals that reflect the printer's status. These fall under the category of message exchange, which places them in the protocol layer. These signals are PE, SELECT, and ERROR. In addition to these are the control signals AUTOFEED, INIT, and SLCT IN. All of these signals are described in Table 2.1.

Summary

The Centronics printer interface is our first example of a device specific interface. The method of data transfer is very similar to many parallel interfaces. Nevertheless, the status signals for end of paper and carriage return pertain strictly to printers. Although this is the case, devices have been developed that use Centronics as a general purpose parallel interface simply by ignoring the printer specific signals. Examples of these include SCSI adapters, network adapters and disk drives.

The data transfer is parallel and asynchronous, controlled by the handshaking signals STROBE/ACKNLG. The transfer rate is dependent on the speed of the printer: the faster the printer is able to activate its ACKNLG signal, the higher the transfer rate. This characteristic of asynchronous transfer will appear again when we look at the SCSI bus.

As in the case of RS-232, the Centronics interface itself contains neither a device model nor a command set. As shown in Figure 1.2, all components are necessary in order to define a complete printer interface. On the other hand, the interface as it stands is flexible, and there are actually PC solutions for connecting peripheral devices via the Centronics interface.

Centronics, like RS-232, establishes a point-to-point connection between devices. This means that only a single printer can be used for each interface because the ability to address different devices is lacking. This new feature belongs to the next interface we will discuss.

2.3 Hard disks and their interfaces

This section and the following section on ST506 delve more deeply into details than previous sections, because it is here that the foundation for understanding IDE and SCSI is laid. If you are not well acquainted with the internals and workings of hard disks, you will find this section especially interesting. Here, you will learn the terminology of the disk drive domain.

A little history

Disk drive interfaces were standardized early on. Beginning in 1975, drives with a diameter of 14 inches and then 8 inches were shipped with the SMD interface. The name comes from the Storage Module Drives of the company, CDC. CDC has since sold its drive production to Seagate. During the late 1980s, as a result of steady improvements, SMD became the favorite interface for 8 inch high performance drives. SMD-E, the final version, had a transfer rate of 24 MHz or about 3 Mbytes per second. The interface, however, could not survive the transition to 5.25 inch drives, primarily because of the very wide cable. As a result SMD died along with 8 inch drives in about 1990.

Five years after the arrival of SMD, Seagate introduced a 5.25 inch drive with a storage capacity of 5 Mbytes. This economical disk drive, at the lower end of the performance scale, used a new interface called ST506. You will often hear ST506/ST412 being used to refer to the same interface. ST506 was not developed from scratch, but evolved from the floppy interface. The transfer rate was increased to 5 MHz (about 625 Kbytes per second) but the method of moving the heads by sending step pulses remained the same. In the past few years, advances have allowed the transfer rate to be doubled once again. However, the demands of modern PCs have finally exceeded the interface's capabilities: ST506 has been steadily losing ground to IDE and SCSI since around 1991.

It was apparent early on that 5.25 inch drives would be capable of performance that ST506 could not support. SMD could have fitted the bill but it was too big and too expensive. In 1983 the disk drive manufacturer Maxtor came out with the Enhanced Small Device Interface (ESDI) to remedy this situation. The ESDI used the same cables as ST506 but allowed transfer rates of up to 20 MHz (2.4 Mbytes per second). In addition, ESDI had commands, for example, seek to track. Today, 1997, the ESDI interface is practically dead and has completely been crowded out by the SCSI interface.

The disk drive model

On our way to understanding IDE we will make a stop to examine its predecessor, the ST506 interface. Before we do this, however, we need to become acquainted with the basic model of a disk drive. A hard disk drive stores information on a set of rotating disks. The information can be written and read any number of times and the data remains intact even after the drive is turned off.

The term 'hard disk' most often refers to a drive with nonremovable media although some removable media drives do use hard disks. A hard disk contrasts with the flexible media used in floppy drives.

This model of a disk drive will say nothing about the exact method of writing to the medium. This means that it will be valid for magnetic disk drives as well as magneto-optical, diskettes, and removable media drives. CD-ROM and WORM drives, however, do not fall into this category; these formats lack the ability to rewrite information.

Organization of the medium

The disk assembly of a drive usually consists of a number of writable surfaces, each of which stores data on concentric rings called tracks. The tracks are further divided into sectors, which are the smallest readable/writable unit. A sector is accessed by first positioning the read/write head above the proper track. The drive then waits until the desired sector rotates underneath the head and reads the data. Writing and reading the sector is done serially bit by bit.

A drive usually contains somewhere between two and eight disks, and both sides of a disk can be utilized for storage. Each surface has its own read/write head although only one track can be written to or read at a given time. The heads are positioned collectively over the tracks. A set of tracks that can be accessed by the heads from a single position is called a cylinder. A consequence of this organization is that every sector of the drive can be uniquely addressed by its cylinder, head and sector numbers. This is referred to as the drive geometry (Figure 2.4).

Sector format

In order to identify the beginning of a track there is an interface signal called INDEX, which issues a pulse at the precise moment when the heads reach this position. This is where the first sector of the track begins. At the start of the other sectors another

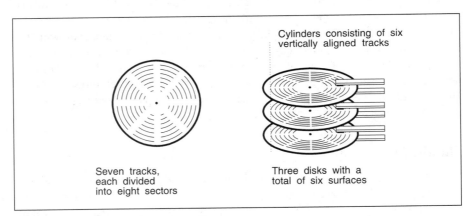

Figure 2.4   Structure of disk medium.

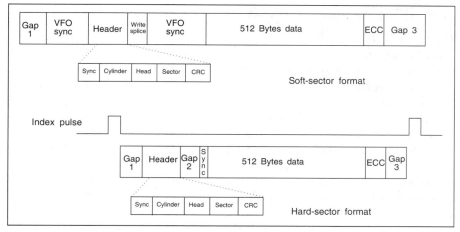

Figure 2.5 Typical sector format.

interface signal, SECTOR, issues a pulse. If the sector pulse is generated by special circuitry that senses the relative angular position of the disks, the drive is said to be hard sectored. The drive is soft sectored if the beginning of the sector is actually read off the medium by the heads.

A computer uses data in parallel; that is, bytes not bits. The disk formatter is a chip, which in addition to identifying sectors by their sector number also takes the serial data from the heads and groups it properly into bytes. The data separator sits between the heads and the formatter chip. When data is read from the drive it generates an accompanying clock. Finally, the read/write amplifier circuitry amplifies the analog signals to and from the heads. The electronics that pertain to actual reading and writing of information are collectively referred to as the data channel.

A sector is made up of a number of different fields which are together referred to as the sector format. Sector formats differ from interface to interface but a typical format can be described as follows: first comes a field for synchronizing the data separator followed by the address field. The address field contains the cylinder, head, and sector numbers. With this information the controller verifies that it is reading or writing the correct sector. After the address field comes the cyclic redundancy code (CRC) checksum, which is used to check whether the address was read properly. All fields up to this point are collectively referred to as the header. Now comes the data. Here too a synchronization field is used, followed by the actual data of the sector. In the place where the address field has a CRC checksum, the data has a number of error correction code (ECC) bytes. The ECC allows the controller to test whether the data has been correctly written or read. In addition a certain number of incorrectly read bits can actually be corrected using this code. The sector ends with a gap used to even out small differences in motor speed. The number of data bytes in a sector corresponds to its formatted capacity. Typical formatted sector sizes are 512, 1024 and 4096 bytes. The header, ECC and gaps use up space for between 40 and 100 bytes, depending on the sector format (Figure 2.5).

Formatting, reading, and writing

Only after the drive's medium has been formatted is it usable for data storage. This procedure involves writing not only the headers but also the data field. An arbitrary data pattern is usually written along with the correct ECC. Normally the entire drive is formatted at one time although soft sectoring allows a single track and hard sectoring a single sector to be formatted.

The reading of a sector is relatively simple. As soon as the head is positioned at the correct cylinder, the desired head is chosen and the formatter chip reads headers until the proper address comes by. The data directly following this header is the data required.

Writing a sector is a bit more complicated. A write looks just like a read until the proper header is found, then the amplifier circuitry switches from reading to writing, and the new data, along with ECC, is written. A write-splice is located between the header and the data field to allow time to turn on the write current.

Format characteristics

It is not necessarily the case that two sectors with adjacent addresses are adjacent to one another on the medium. The limited throughput of early drive controllers made it necessary to employ certain techniques in the format design. The techniques discussed here are pertinent to IDE as well as SCSI.

Interleave

Early drive controllers had a very small local buffer which held at most a sector's worth of data. This situation forces the controller to pass the data on to the computer before reading the next sector. If this cannot be accomplished in the time it takes the head to pass over the short gap between sectors, the controller must wait for a complete revolution of the disk for the sector to come around again. For drives of this era, this meant waiting 17 ms for the next sector. In order to avoid this delay, the format of the track can employ an interleave to insure that there is enough time to get ready for the next sector. With an interleave of two, for example, the sector with the next adjacent address is two physical sectors away. This makes it possible to read all sectors of a track with only two rotations of the disk while insuring that there is ample time to pass the data to the computer. Older devices employed even larger interleaves. An interleave of three means that two physical sectors lie between adjacent sector addresses. Modern controllers no longer use interleaving; they have data buffers, which accommodate at least an entire track.

Track and cylinder skew

To obtain the highest throughput for transferring large blocks of data the controller or operating system will place the data on a single track. If the data occupies more than a single track then the track of the next head in this same cylinder is used, and

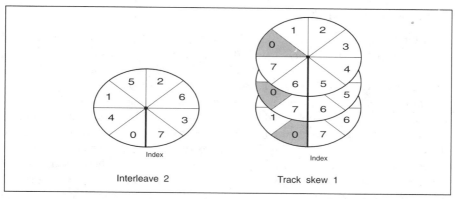

Figure 2.6   Interleave and track skew.

so on, until the cylinder is full. The reason for this organization is that the time needed to change heads is much shorter than the time needed to change tracks. Only after the entire cylinder has been used must the heads be repositioned to the next cylinder, where the procedure can begin again.

Even switching the heads, which is done electronically, can cause enough of a delay to miss a sector. When the last sector of a track is read and the heads are switched to begin a new track, the resulting lag may prevent the first sector of the track being read. Waiting for an additional revolution (called 'missing a rev') can be avoided by offsetting the first sector address by one or several physical sectors. This feature is called track skew (spiral offset). Modern controllers, however, are usually capable of a track skew of zero with the help of very fast data channel electronics.

The delay resulting from a seek from one cylinder to the next adjacent cylinder is of the order of 2 ms. In this case as well, an offset can be employed to avoid missing a rev. However, transfers of this size, across cylinder boundaries, rarely occur. Therefore, the implementation of a cylinder skew is often forgone (see Figure 2.6).

Technical specifications

The physical drive model described above is the basis for the technical specifications cited for disk drives. The most important of these are the capacity, transfer rate, and average seek time.

Capacity

Two capacities are usually given for a drive. The unformatted net capacity is the product of the number of bits per track, the number of cylinders, and the number of heads. Its value is usually given in bytes and is independent of the sector format. The formatted capacity, on the other hand, is directly dependent on the sector format employed. Its value is the product of the sector size, the number of sectors per track, and the number of heads.

Transfer rate and throughput

Transfer rate refers to the speed at which bits are serially read and written to the drive by the heads. It is simply the product of the number of bits on a track and the number of rotations of the disk per second. The units are actually megabits per second, but MHz is often used, which corresponds to one bit per Hz.

Throughput, the amount of data the drive can deliver or accept at the interface on a sustained basis, can be estimated fairly accurately in the following way. Divide the transfer rate by eight (giving the number of bytes per second). Take this result and divide it by the interleave (in this context think of interleave as the number of revolutions needed to read a track). Take off 10% of this value (for headers and so on), and you are left with the approximate throughput of the drive in bytes per second. Throughput, then, is a function of how quickly the medium can be written to and read, plus formatting factors. A drive's peak transfer rate, which is an instantaneous rate, will be higher.

Average access time

The average access time has two components. The average seek time is the mean time it takes to position the heads to a specific cylinder. In addition to this is the time it takes for the desired sector to rotate under the heads. On average this is the time for half a revolution. This second component, called the rotational latency, is by no means insignificant. For a disk that rotates at 5400 rotations per minute it takes 11 ms for a complete revolution. This translates to an average rotational latency of 5.5 ms. The same drive may have an average seek time of 11 ms which means that rotational latency accounts for about 30% of the average access time.

Where to put the interface

A hard disk is actually a subsystem of many components. First of all is the drive mechanism, consisting of the medium, the heads, the analog data electronics, and the head positioning electronics. This group is called the head disk assembly (HDA). Next comes the data separator to digitize the analog signal data, followed by the formatter for parallelization of the data. The controller is in charge of orchestrating reading and writing, along with positioning the heads. Finally, a host adapter is the link between the controller and the host system (Figure 2.7).

Physically, the interface is the cable that connects the unit built by the drive manufacturer to the computer. There are a number different possible locations along the data channel where this cable can be placed in the design of a drive. The trend, as SCSI's success indicates, is to incorporate more and more functionality in the drive itself. This moves the cable further from the heads, so to speak.

The ST506 interface lies between the analog data electronics and the data separator. One result of this is that the controller determines the analog method of writing data to the drive. In practice, two techniques are employed – modified frequency modulation (MFM) and run length limited (RLL) – across the ST506 interface. The ESDI interface moves one step from ST506 and incorporates the data separator into

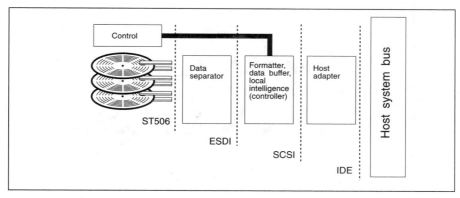

Figure 2.7　Various drive interfaces.

the drive. Next in line, SCSI packs the formatter and controller into the drive as well. Finally, IDE integrates almost the entire host adapter onto its circuit board. This final step has its disadvantages: by integrating the host adapter, the drive is compatible with only one type of host system, in this case IBM PC compatibles. This approach makes sense in the PC market due to sheer volume.

Summary

When we finally reach the SCSI standard later in the book, you will be introduced to a model of a type of peripherals known as logical devices. In principle, any interface, for instance any of those discussed so far, could be used with such a device. For example, a RAM disk could be equipped with an ST506 interface. Of course, in order for the RAM disk to simulate an ST506 device it would have to simulate sectors with track, head, and sector number. In addition, a strategy would be needed to prevent the data being lost when the device is turned off.

2.4　ST506

The ST506 interface lies between the read/write amplifier and the data separator. The data separator is the component that generates a clock and a data signal from the pulses stored on the medium.

Physical interface

ST506 can address up to four drives (Figure 2.8). Two cables, named A and B, are used to make the connections. The A cable, which is a single cable, contains control signals, and runs from drive to drive in what is called a daisy chain. The last drive in the chain must contain terminating resistance. The B cable carries the analog read/write data. Each drive has its own B cable. You can recognize a controller that supports four drives by the connectors for a single A cable and four B cables. The maximum cable length for ST506 is 3 meters.

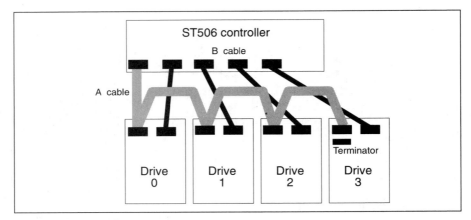

Figure 2.8   ST506 configuration.

Cables, connectors, and electrical specifications

The A cable is a ribbon cable with 34 connections. On the controller end of the cable is a ribbon connector. The drives are attached using edge connectors. The signals are single ended; 7438/7414 open collector drivers and receivers are used (Figure 2.9).

For the first time, we meet the need for terminating resistors in an interface. The signals of the A cable must be connected to +5 V across a 150 ohm resistor. The resistors for all signals are usually incorporated in a single dual in-line package. Since only the last drive may have termination, terminators are mounted in a socket for easy removal.

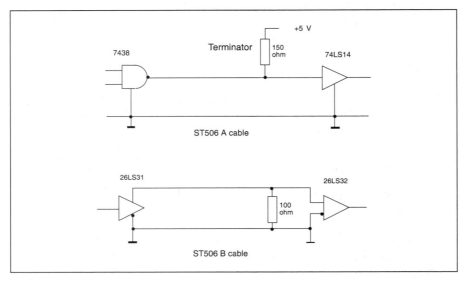

Figure 2.9   ST506 drivers and receivers.

Table 2.2 ST506 A cable signals.

Pin	Name	Signal source	Description
1, 3, 5, 7, 9, 11, 13, 15, 17, 19, 21, 23, 25, 27, 29, 31, 33	GROUND		
2	REDUCED WRITE CURRENT/HEAD SELECT 3	Controller	Once used to reduce write current, now bit 3 of head number
4	HEAD SELECT 2	Controller	Bit 2 of head number
6	WRITE GATE	Controller	Activates write current
8	SEEK COMPLETE	Drive	Indicates cylinder has been reached
10	TRACK 00	Drive	Indicates heads are on cylinder zero
12	WRITE FAULT	Controller	Write error
14	HEAD SELECT 0	Controller	Bit 0 of the head number
16	ERROR RECOVERY	Controller	
18	HEAD SELECT 1	Controller	Bit 1 of the head number
20	INDEX	Drive	Indicates beginning of track
22	READY	Drive	The drive is up to speed and ready for read/write
24	STEP	Controller	The heads are to be moved by one cylinder
26	DRIVE SELECT 1	Controller	Drive 1 selected
26	DRIVE SELECT 2	Controller	Drive 2 selected
26	DRIVE SELECT 3	Controller	Drive 3 selected
26	DRIVE SELECT 4	Controller	Drive 4 selected
34	DIRECTION IN	Controller	Selects direction for head movement

The B cable is a ribbon cable with 25 connections. Like the A cable, there is a ribbon cable connector on the controller end and an edge connector on the drive end. The signals here are differential. A 26LS31 and 26LS32 pair is recommended as driver and receiver. Since each drive has its own B cable there is no need to make termination for these signals removable.

Signals

Tables 2.2 and 2.3 show the signal assignments for the ST506 cables. Every other signal is ground, which acts as shielding.

Addressing

In order to choose a specific sector for reading or writing, the head, cylinder, and sector number of the proper drive must be selected. There are four signals for addressing drives on the ST506 interface labeled DRIVE SELECT 1–4. This means that each drive has a dedicated select line.

In contrast to this, the four signals HEAD SELECT 0–3 select the track under one of 16 possible heads. HEAD SELECT 3 did not exist in the original specification; originally, this connection was used to control the amount of write current. The inner

Table 2.3 ST506 B cable signals.

Pin	Name	Signal source	Description
1	DRIVE SELECTED	Drive	Drive is selected
2	GROUND		Ground
3	RESERVED		Reserved
4	GROUND		Ground
5	RESERVED		Reserved
6	GROUND		Ground
7	RESERVED		Reserved
8	GROUND		Ground
9	NOT USED		Not used
10	NOT USED		Not used
11	GROUND		Ground
12	GROUND		Ground
13	+ MFM/RLL WRITE DATA	Controller	Differential write data
14	− MFM/RLL WRITE DATA	Controller	Differential write data
15	GROUND		Ground
16	GROUND		Ground
17	+ MFM/RLL READ DATA	Drive	Differential read data
18	− MFM/RLL READ DATA	Drive	Differential read data
19	GROUND		Ground
20	GROUND		Ground

tracks of a disk need less write current than the outer tracks. This signal became unnecessary as disk drives themselves controlled the amount of write current.

The method for choosing a cylinder using the ST506 interface is identical to that for floppy drives. A pulse on the STEP signal causes the heads to move one cylinder in the direction indicated by the signal DIRECTION IN. The status signal SEEK COMPLETE indicates that this positioning of the heads has been completed. Another status signal, TRACK 00, reflects whether or not the heads are on track 0, the outermost cylinder. Using this signal the controller can find track 0 by sending STEP pulses until TRACK 00 is true.

The ST506 interface supports only soft sectoring. For this reason there is no sector pulse among the signals; the desired sector is found by the address information in the header. The INDEX signal is generated by the drive and indicates the beginning of the first sector. It is used during formatting to align the sectors of the different heads.

Clearly, an ST506 controller has a lot of responsibility in controlling the drive. The method of positioning the heads is primitive and slow. The only advantage of the step pulse approach is that the number of cylinders is unlimited.

Data encoding

In principle, many methods of data encoding can be used with the ST506 interface. The encoding of the data results in pulses that can be written to the actual drive medium. Originally, MFM encoding was used and more recently RLL encoding. Not all ST506 drives can accommodate RLL, however, because typically a drive's data channel electronics are optimized for MFM.

The data rate for MFM encoding is 5 MHz, which corresponds to 625 kilobytes per second. MFM drives have 17 sectors per track, each of 512 bytes. RLL allows a data rate of 7.5 MHz. Here a track can hold 22 512-byte sectors. Therefore, the use of RLL encoding increases the capacity of the drive by 50%.

Summary

A well-defined protocol layer or command set is not defined for the ST506 interface. The bus timing definitions belong solely to the physical layer. ST506 is undeniably device specific; it makes no sense to use it for anything other than a disk drive.

ST506 has its weak points. The low data transfer rate makes it nearly unusable for higher performance drives. Other low performance characteristics include its lack of commands and step impulse positioning.

Despite its shortcomings the ST506 used to be incorporated into systems far beyond the PC domain. Even the IDE and SCSI interfaces show signs of their ST506 origins – you still see, for instance, a parameter to reduce the write current.

3 Computer buses

In contrast to the peripheral interfaces discussed so far, a computer bus is designed to connect the various components within the computer. All computers utilize a number of internal buses. These buses transport information between the system components like the nervous system of an organism. The more complex a computer system, the more exotic its buses can become (Figure 3.1).

The boundary between a bus and an interface is blurred at best. I consider it an important characteristic of a bus to connect various devices of equal authority. By this measure the IDE interface is excluded, as are all computer memory buses, for that matter. The SCSI bus, on the other hand, clearly matches this definition of a bus. Of course, the discussion of such border cases is purely academic.

The layer model for interfaces can also be applied to computer buses. It is defined by the physical interface, bus protocol and optional device model along with a command set.

A computer bus is built from three basic functional blocks: addressing, data transfer and control. In the literature you will frequently see block diagrams depicting the

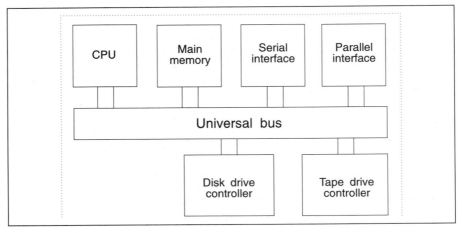

Figure 3.1 Universal bus.

address, data, and control bus as separate paths. However, since all three of these components depend on the others we will always refer to a computer bus in its entirety.

3.1 Characteristics of buses

There are a number of characteristics that make a bus well suited for a particular application. The most important of these are the throughput, the address space, the real-time performance, the electrical and mechanical characteristics, and the production costs. The following sections examine these in closer detail.

Data throughput

Data throughput, also known as bandwidth, is the amount of information the bus can transport per unit of time. It is measured in Mbytes per second. Two parameters come into play in order to calculate the net throughput: the clock speed and the data width. The clock speed tells how many data words are transferred per second. The data width is the number of bits in one data word and usually corresponds to the width of the bus. The net throughput is the product of the clock speed and the data width. It is reduced by an appreciable amount by the bus protocol, otherwise known as the protocol overhead.

For example, SCSI-1 supports a synchronous clock speed of 5 MHz; the bus width is 1 byte. The resulting throughput is 5 Mbytes per second. Under SCSI-2, fast-SCSI allows 10 MHz clock speed; the Wide-SCSI option allows a 4 byte bus width. Together they contribute to a 40 Mbyte per second throughput.

Address space

In order to transfer data in a meaningful manner, a method is needed to uniquely identify the source and destination of the transfer. The identification is made using an address, and the scheme is called addressing. The address space of a bus is dependent upon the width of the address; that is, the number of bits in the address. A bus with an address width of 16 bits uniquely identifies 2^{16} or exactly 65 536 locations.

For example, the Q-22 bus of a PDP-11 has an address width of 22 bits. It can therefore address 4 Mbytes of memory. The ISA bus of IBM PC compatibles has 24 address bits and is able to address 16 Mbytes. Modern systems with 32 bit data buses also have 32 bit address buses, corresponding to an address space of 4 Gbytes.

Real-time capabilities

Real-time systems are distinguished from other systems by their ability to react to an external event within a given amount of time. This external event may occur at any time. In addition the system may not be able to anticipate the exact moment. A real-time system does not necessarily have to be very fast; however, its reaction time must be predictable and, of course, adequate for the application. This predictability usually means that a mechanism has been implemented to interrupt running processes. A real-time capable I/O bus must allow, for example, interruption of a lengthy data transfer from disk to tape for an event with higher priority. A bus without this capability could also be used for real-time applications, but only when used for a single device.

Electrical characteristics

Two important attributes result directly from the electrical characteristics of a bus: the maximum length of the bus and the integrity of the data. While the bus inside a PC is only a few inches long, I/O buses more than 30 feet in length are often used to connect computers and peripherals. When many such cables are in close proximity to each other, as is often the case, data integrity is a major issue. A bus in a cable duct needs to be less sensitive to electromagnetic interference than a bus that resides inside a metal enclosure.

Mechanical characteristics

There are two basic ways to implement a bus physically. Internally, the individual signals are usually part of a printed circuit board. Insertable boards use edge connectors to link to the main bus of a system. The mother board of a computer sometimes has a number of slots that are nothing other than bus connections for such boards. Another type of board, referred to as a backplane, has no other circuitry than that to connect together bus slots. Backplanes are common for the VME and ECB buses. Recently entire PC systems have come on the market that reside on an insertable board. These are inserted along with other boards into a backplane to form a system.

The other type of physical bus is the cable. A bus cable is defined with regard to its maximum length, resistance, whether it is shielded or unshielded and other less important details. The bus cable connector is also very precisely standardized.

Production costs

An important factor in the mass production of PCs, workstations, and mass storage devices is the associated production costs of the bus. As a rule of thumb, the more signals a bus has, the more costly it becomes; the more sophisticated the control logic, the more costly; the fewer items produced, the more costly. The success of SCSI and IDE can be attributed above all to the availability of economical bus interface components and the fact that a simple ribbon cable can be used to interconnect devices. Moreover, peripheral manufacturers need to equip devices with at most two connector types. Cost is also the reason why SCSI and IDE can coexist in the marketplace: IDE costs slightly less to manufacture than SCSI. In fact, this is often reflected in the price of the IDE and SCSI versions of a particular drive model.

3.2   Specialized buses

The ideal bus, then, would have a large address space, a maximal throughput, and excellent real-time capabilities. There would be no constraints on its length and it would be simple and inexpensive to produce. Unfortunately, such a bus is not even theoretically possible, as the following example shows. A real-time system is characterized by its reaction time to a particular event. This time is independent of, among other things, the length of system buses. Since electrical signals travel with finite speed, as the length of a bus increases so does the reaction time to any signal on the bus. Therefore, it is impossible to design a bus of unconstrained length, which at the same time guarantees an arbitrary reaction time.

For this reason a wide range of buses with differing characteristics have come into existence, each for a particular application.

Memory bus

A memory bus connects the CPU or memory controller to memory. The main requirement of this bus is high bandwidth since every CPU instruction and all data must travel over this path. To meet this constraint, most memory buses are very short. The address space of a memory bus is the physical address space of the computer system.

The CPU of a MicroVAX, for example, has an address width of 32 bits. While this corresponds to an address space of 4 Gbytes, the system physically accommodates only 16 Mbytes. Consequently, the memory bus could be implemented using only 24 address lines.

A memory bus need not implement any real-time or interrupt capabilities. The division of labor is well defined among system components: the CPU makes a request, the memory reads or writes the information. By my definition of a bus at the beginning of this chapter, the memory bus is not a bus at all since in this case the devices do not have equal authority over one another.

I/O bus

An I/O bus connects the CPU with the I/O devices. Here the requirements are somewhat different. The I/O bus must be able to support a variety of devices. It must be able to handle slow as well as fast devices. In addition, there must be a method for determining which device may use the bus when more than one requests use of it. This mechanism is called arbitration. Depending on the application, an I/O bus must also be capable of near real-time performance. This can be extremely important in the area of computer controlled systems. One need only look at the example of a nuclear reactor: it is imperative that the CPU be informed the moment some particular event occurs. All other I/O processes must be suspendable. An I/O bus that allows this must employ interrupt and event priority mechanisms.

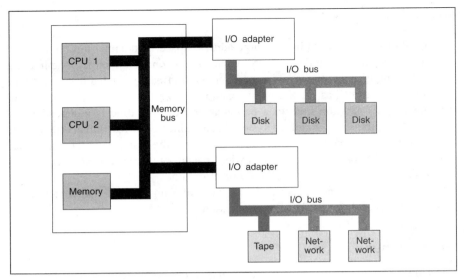

Figure 3.2 Computer system with multiple buses.

Universal bus

Many less sophisticated computer systems use a universal bus to link together the CPU, memory and I/O devices. The goal here is to find the best compromise between bandwidth, real-time capability, and production cost. Examples of universal buses include the ECB bus, VME bus and the ISA bus of IBM AT compatibles. The older PDP 11/73 with its Q-22 bus is another example. In this light, Figure 1.1 can be viewed as a simplified block diagram of an IBM AT. Figure 3.2 shows the structure of a more complex system, the VAX 8800, with several specialized buses.

Part II
The IDE interface

4   Background
5   The physical IDE interface
6   IDE protocol
7   The model of an IDE disk drive
8   IDE commands
9   The ATAPI interface

4 Background

Several common expressions for the IDE interface are currently in use. IDE stands for Integrated Disk Electronics. Another popular name is the AT bus interface, which refers to the fact that the integrated electronics within the drive emulate the hard disk controller of an IBM AT computer. However, when used out of context, this name can be confusing, since the term 'AT bus' is also used for the system bus of the IBM AT. The official name for the IDE interface is AT-Attachment (ATA).

In this book, the name IDE will be used when discussing interfaces in general. When the ANSI standard is meant, the term ATA will be used. The system bus of IBM AT compatible computers will always be referred to as the ISA bus.

ATA is administered by the X3T9.2 ANSI working group, the same group that is responsible for the SCSI standard.

4.1 The origin of IDE

The development of the IDE interface began in 1984, stimulated by the Texan computer manufacturer, Compaq. The idea was to embed the hard disk controller of an IBM AT compatible on the disk drive. Compaq contacted the controller manufacturer, Western Digital, in California. They were to produce an ST506 controller that could be mounted directly on the disk drive and connected to the system bus via a 40 pin cable. In 1985, the disk manufacturer, Imprimis (CDC), integrated this controller into its hard disk drives. Thus, the first IDE disk drive was built and installed in a Compaq computer system.

Other hard disk and computer manufacturers recognized the advantage of IDE. Not only was the increase in the cost of the disk drive negligible, but there was a great saving on the hard disk controller. Gradually, more and more IDE implementations were developed, and with them, the various deviations of the industry standard.

ATA

As a consequence, a committee of the X3T9.2 working group of ANSI began to deal with the problem in October 1988. As its first project, the common access method

31

(CAM) committee put forward a suggestion for the normalization of the IDE interface. The new name for the IDE interface was ATA. This standard has now been approved under the name of X3.221-1994.

ATA-2

However, development did not stand still. The ATA-2 standard was approved in autumn 1995. It offers higher transfer rates and some new commands. This book is based on the ATA-2 standard. Differences against the original ATA (which will be called ATA-1 when differentiation is needed) are shown in the appropriate places.

ATAPI

Parallel to the development of ATA-2, a completely different development took place: ATAPI. This was developed with the aim of operating devices other than hard disks at the IDE interface. ATAPI uses IDE as a physical interface, but the commands used are SCSI commands. Today, the ATAPI interface is mainly used with CD-ROM drives.

ATAPI development is led by Western Digital. Meanwhile, two standardizing institutions have made proposals for a standard: the Small Form Factor committee has proposed SFF8020, and the ATA working group of ANSI is preparing a proposal too.

ATA-3

The latest development in the domain of the IDE interface is the ATA-3 proposal of ANSI. ATA-3 does not offer a further increase in speed, but offers new commands and more precisely defined procedures. Integration of ATAPI into ATA-3 is under discussion.

EIDE

At the time of writing (summer 1995), there is much confusion about EIDE (Enhanced IDE). One cannot really talk about a standard; actually, it is a combination of various features in different variations. Some manufacturers use EIDE to denote the faster transfer modes which have, however, partly been already specified in ATA-1, and then completely in ATA-2. Others call EIDE the capability of addressing more than 504 Mbytes with its own PC BIOS. This too is contained in ATA-1. Others again call their ATAPI CD-ROMs EIDE drives. Finally, there are controllers with two IDE channels. They can be used to attach a total of four drives and are also marketed under the EIDE label. As you can see, when you are faced with EIDE, you had better look carefully at what you are offered.

4.2   Overview

The essential functions of the IDE interface have already been described in Part I. Nevertheless, much new ground will be covered in this part. Figure 2.7 shows the

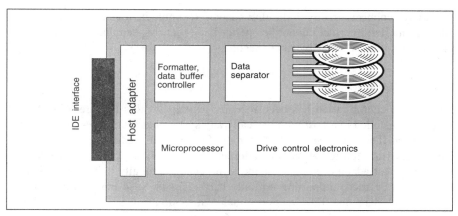

Figure 4.1 IDE drive block diagram.

fundamental shift in the function of IDE, from serving the host to serving the peripherals. Also shown is how the IDE controller has been embedded physically into the peripheral unit. The only components left from the IDE bus adaptor in the IBM AT are a few driver and decoder components. It is this aspect where the IDE resembles a system bus more than a peripheral interface. The similarity between the IDE and a system bus will be described in more detail when the physical interface is discussed (Figure 4.1).

Despite its similarity to a system bus, IDE is not referred to as an I/O bus, because the universal addressing required to access various different units is lacking. IDE can only serve one or two hard disks, and allows only one host access to the disks.

IDE adapter

In this section two possible configurations for the IDE bus are introduced. The first (Figure 4.2) is the standard configuration of IDE, consisting of an interface board, also called an IDE adapter, installed in a host with an ISA or EISA bus. Two IDE

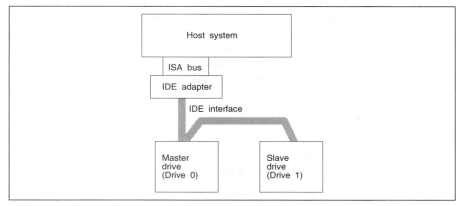

Figure 4.2 IDE configuration for AT compatibles with ISA bus.

disk drives connect directly to the IDE adapter. It should be noted that with such an adapter, the IDE interface cannot be operated at a higher speed than that allowed by the ISA bus, that is, 8.3 Mbytes per second.

IDE controller

The second configuration has been recently gaining success (Figure 4.3). A host adapter is installed in a host with basically any system bus that serves the hard disk through the IDE interface. Products for the PCI bus fall under this configuration. However, in this configuration, the major advantage of the IDE bus, not needing an expensive host adapter, is lost. For the same cost, an equally effective SCSI host adapter can be used, supporting not only hard disks but also many other types of devices. The hard disk IDE version remains an option only because of the price, which at present is slightly less than the SCSI version.

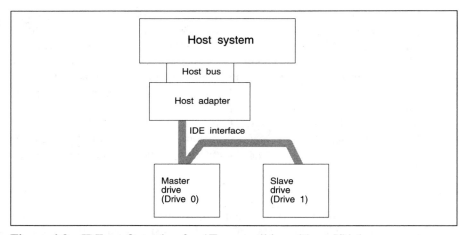

Figure 4.3   IDE configuration for AT compatibles without ISA bus.

The drive with address 0 is the master drive; the drive with address 1 is the slave drive. In normal operation the two drives operate independently of each other. The master/slave relation only comes into play, for example, at system start-up, or after a reset. Since both connected drives contain a complete controller, commands arrive simultaneously at both controllers which, on the basis of the drive addressing bit of the drive register, decide which of them is actually addressed.

4.3 Documentation

The draft for the ANSI standard ATA is called X3.221-1994. It is available, like the SCSI standard, either in printed form or electronically through the SCSI mailbox.

The addresses and telephone numbers, including a short description of the mailbox, can be found in Appendix D. A short summary of the contents and an example from the proposed ANSI standard are given in Figures 4.4 and 4.5.

```
1.      Scope
1.1         Description of Clauses
2.      References
3.      General Description
3.1         Structure
4.      Definitions and Conventions
4.1         Definitions
4.2         Conventions
5.      Interface Cabling Requirements
5.1         Configuration
5.2         Addressing Considerations
5.3         DC Cable and Connector
5.4         I/O Connector
5.5         I/O Cable
6.      Physical Interface
6.1         Signal Conventions
6.2         Signal Summary
6.3         Signal Descriptions
7.      Logical Interface
7.1         General
7.2         I/O Register Descriptions
8.      Programming Requirements
8.1         Reset Response
8.2         Translate Mode
8.3         Power Conditions
8.4         Error Posting
9.      Command Descriptions
9.1         Acknowledge Media Change (Removable)
... etc. ...
9.32        Write Verify
10.     Protocol Overview
10.1        PIO Data In Commands
10.2        PIO Data Out Commands
10.3        Non-Data Commands
10.4        Miscellaneous Commands
10.5        DMA Data Transfer Commands (Optional)
11.     Timing
11.1        Deskewing
11.2        Symbols
11.3        Terms
11.4        Data Transfers
11.5        Power On and Hard Reset
```

Figure 4.4   Contents of the ANSI proposal for ATA.

```
10.1  PIO Data In Commands
This class includes:
 - Identify Drive
 - Read Buffer
 - Read Long
 - Read Sector(s)
Execution includes the transfer of one or more 512 byte (512 bytes on Read
Long) sectors of data from the drive to the host.
  a) The host writes any required parameters to the Features, Sector Count,
     Sector Number, Cylinder and Drive/Head registers.
  b) The host writes the command code to the Command Register.
  c) The drive sets BSY and prepares for data transfer.
  d) When a sector of data is available, the drive sets DRQ and clears BSY
     prior to asserting INTRQ.
  e) After detecting INTRQ, the host reads the Status Register, then reads one
     sector of data via the Data Register. In response to the Status Register
     being read, the drive negates INTRQ.
  f) The drive clears DRQ. If transfer of another sector is required, the drive
     also sets BSY and the above sequence is repeated from d).
10.1.1  PIO Read Command
 +- a) -+- b) --+        +- e) -+--------+        +- e) -+--------+
 |Setup | Issue |        | Read |Transfer|        | Read |Transfer|
 |      |Command|        |Status|  Data  |::::::::|Status|  Data  |
 +------+-------+        +------+--------+        +------+--------+
 |BSY=0 |      |BSY=1    |BSY=0 |        |BSY=1   |BSY=0 |        |BSY=1
        |DRDY=1          |      |        |        |      |        |
                         |DRQ=1 |        |DRQ=0   |DRQ=1 |        |DRQ=0
                         |Assert|Negate  |        |Assert|Negate
                         |INTRQ |INTRQ   |        |INTRQ |INTRQ
If Error Status is presented, the drive is prepared to transfer data, and it
is at the host's discretion that the data is transferred.
10.1.2  PIO Read Aborted Command
 +- a) -+- b) --+        +- e) -+
 |Setup | Issue |        | Read |
 |      |Command|        |Status|
 +------+-------+        +------+
 |BSY=0 |      |BSY=1    |BSY=0 |
        |DRDY=1          |      |
                         |DRQ=1 |DRQ=0
                         |Assert|Negate
                         |INTRQ |INTRQ
Although DRQ=1, there is no data to be transferred under this condition.
10.2  PIO Data Out Commands
This class includes:
 - Format
 - Write Buffer
 - Write Long
 - Write Sector(s)
Execution includes the transfer of one or more 512 byte (512 bytes on Write
Long) sectors of data from the drive to the host.
  a) The host writes any required parameters to the Features, Sector Count,
     Sector Number, Cylinder and Drive/Head registers.
  b) The host writes the command code to the Command Register.
  c) The drive sets DRQ when it is ready to accept the first sector of data.
```

Figure 4.5   Sample page from the ANSI proposal for ATA.

5 The physical IDE interface

5.1 The electrical interface

The ATA standard for the IDE interface encompasses both the signal cable and the power supply leads.

Signal cable and connectors

The IDE interface uses a 40-pin ribbon cable. The length of the cable may not normally exceed 46 cm (18 inches). Cable connectors, which are crimped on, are used both at the host end and at the disk drive end of the cable. Table 5.1 gives the most important specifications for ATA-2. Almost all signal lines use TTL drivers and receivers, except for the signals DASP, PDIAG, IOCS16 and SPSYNC:PSEL.

For 2.5-inch hard disks, a 44-pin cable is used which carries both the signals and the power supply voltages. The disk drive end uses a 50-pin Dupont connector. Two of the six additional pins are removed for coding; the remaining two can be used by the manufacturer as jumpers for setting the drive number. In Table 5.3, the additional pins are marked by an underlying dark gray shade. Please note that pins A–F are present only on the connector, not on the cable.

Finally, since ATA-2, a 68-pin plug-in connection is defined which uses the same connections as the PCMCIA interface. The signals are arranged in such a way that they mostly correspond to the PCMCIA assignments. Although these two interfaces are not identical, a PCMCIA device in an ATA slot must not be damaged and vice versa. Up to now, I am not aware of any product that uses this pin assignment. But since it is also contained in the ATA-3 proposal, the industry must believe that it will make its way.

Table 5.1 Cable parameters for 0.5 m cable length.

Parameter	Minimum	Maximum
Drive sink current at +5 V	12 mA	
Driver leakage current for logical 1		−400 µA
Capacitive load		25 pF

Table 5.2   Supply voltages for IDE drives (AMP connector).

Pin	Signal
1	+12 V
2	Ground
3	Ground
4	+5 V

Supply voltages

The power supply to the disk drives is also covered by the ATA standard. Provision is made for the 4-pin AMP connector familiar to users of 5.25-inch disk drives. The ATA-1 standard also mentions a 3-pin Molex connector which is, however, no longer present in ATA-2. Table 5.2 shows the specifications for the power supply.

Signals

The ATA standard specifies signals by their names as well as by their abbreviations. Both the signal name and its abbreviation are written in capital letters. As elsewhere in this book, I use small capital letters when referring to names and signals specified by the standard. The signals are listed in Table 5.3. Signals that are low active are indicated by a bar over the name of the signal. The direction of data flow is given with respect to the disk drive: IN means to the drive, and OUT means from the drive. Bidirectional data lines are designated I/O.

- $\overline{\text{CS0}}$: This signal selects the command register block. It is generated from the ISA bus addresses by the IDE bus adapter and is active when an I/O port address between 1F0h and 1FFh is being accessed. In ATA-1, this signal is called $\overline{\text{CS1FX}}$.

- $\overline{\text{CS1}}$: This signal selects the control register block. It is generated from the ISA bus addresses by the IDE bus adapter and is active when an I/O port address between 3F0h und 3FFh is being accessed. In ATA-1, this signal is called $\overline{\text{CS3FX}}$.

These two signals are the reason why an IDE disk drive still requires an adapter to interface with the ISA bus. Of course, it would also have been possible to reproduce the address lines of the ISA bus on the IDE cable, but this would have caused it to exceed the capacity of a 40-pin cable. The solution to this problem is thus a compromise between the desire to achieve full integration of the disk drive with the controller and the desire to use the smallest and least expensive cable possible.

- DA0 through DA2: These signals are taken directly from the ISA bus addresses. They select one of the registers from the command or control register block.

- $\overline{\text{DASP}}$: This signal fulfills two distinct functions. Immediately after the system is powered up, or after a reset, disk drive 1 should assert this signal to indicate that it is present. This process is described in more detail in Chapter 6. In normal operation, this signal indicates that the selected disk drive is active, and is used for the disk drive activity display.

Table 5.3 IDE interface pin assignments.

Name	Source	Signal	Pin	Pin	Signal	Source	Name
Vendor-specific			A	B			Vendor-specific
Vendor-specific			C	D			Vendor-specific
N.C. (Coding Pin)			E	F			N.C. (Coding Pin)
RESET	I	$\overline{\text{RESET}}$	1	2	Ground		Ground
DATA BUS BIT 7	I/O	DD7	3	4	DD8	I/O	DATA BUS BIT 8
DATA BUS BIT 6	I/O	DD6	5	6	DD9	I/O	DATA BUS BIT 9
DATA BUS BIT 5	I/O	DD5	7	8	DD10	I/O	DATA BUS BIT 10
DATA BUS BIT 4	I/O	DD4	9	10	DD11	I/O	DATA BUS BIT 11
DATA BUS BIT 3	I/O	DD3	11	12	DD12	I/O	DATA BUS BIT 12
DATA BUS BIT 2	I/O	DD2	13	14	DD13	I/O	DATA BUS BIT 13
DATA BUS BIT 1	I/O	DD1	15	16	DD14	I/O	DATA BUS BIT 14
DATA BUS BIT 0	I/O	DD0	17	18	DD15	I/O	DATA BUS BIT 15
Ground		Ground	19	20	N.C.		(Coding Pin)
DMA REQUEST	O	DMARQ	21	22	Ground		Ground
I/O WRITE	I	$\overline{\text{DIOW}}$	23	24	Ground		Ground
I/O READ	I	$\overline{\text{DIOR}}$	25	26	Ground		Ground
I/O CHANNEL READY	O	IORDY	27	28	SPSYNC: CSEL		SPINDLE SYNC or CABLE SELECT
DMA ACKNOWLEDGE	I	$\overline{\text{DMACK}}$	29	30	Ground		Ground
INTERRUPT REQUEST	O	INTRQ	31	32	IOCS16	O	16 BIT I/O
ADDRESS BIT 1	I	DA1	33	34	PDIAG		PASSED DIAGNOSTIC
ADDRESS BIT 0	I	DA0	35	36	DA2	I	ADDRESS BIT 2
CHIP SELECT 0	I	$\overline{\text{CS0}}$ ($\overline{\text{CS1FX}}$)	37	38	$\overline{\text{CS1}}$ ($\overline{\text{CS3FX}}$)	I	CHIP SELECT 1
DRIVE ACTIVE/ DRIVE 1 PRESENT	O	$\overline{\text{DASP}}$	39	40	Ground		Ground
+5V (Logic)			41	42			+5V (Motor)
Circuit Voltage Ground			43	44	$\overline{\text{TYPE}}$		TYPE

- DD0 through DD15: These signals are taken directly from the ISA bus data lines. They are used in the transfer of data to the register block and to the disk drive.

- $\overline{\text{DIOR}}$ and $\overline{\text{DIOW}}$: Handshake request for read or write access to the disk drive register.

- DMARQ and $\overline{\text{DMACK}}$: Handshake signals for the transfer of data between host and disk drive. Since DMA is an optional feature, so are these signals. In ATA-2, the electrical implementation of $\overline{\text{DMACK}}$ has changed with respect to ATA-1 (ATA-2: 5.2.9).

- INTRQ: This signal triggers an interrupt in the host.

- $\overline{\text{IOCS16}}$: This signal tells the host that a 16-bit data transfer is occurring; otherwise the transfer is 8-bit using the data lines DD0 to DD7. However, it only applies to register accesses to the data register, not to other registers and also not to DMA. If 8-bit DMA is implemented, this is specified in the feature register.

- IORDY: This signal is optional. When it is not implemented, it should be set to high impedance. If it is implemented, a low level indicates that the controller is momentarily denying access to the registers, and that the host must delay its access cycle.

- PDIAG: This signal is part of the power-up protocol. It indicates to the master drive that the slave drive has completed its self-test.
- $\overline{\text{RESET}}$: This signal from the host resets both disk drives. It forces an initialization to occur identical to that after power-up.

The signal SPSYNC shares a line with the signal CSEL. The implementation of both signals is optional, but only one of the two can be used. Both drives must be using the signal for the same purpose, otherwise drive behavior is unpredictable. This is a potential source of errors.

- SPSYNC: This signal is vendor specific since drive synchronization only makes sense if the two disk drives that are communicating are identical. The only specification for this signal is that the master drive is the signal source and the slave is the receiver.
- CSEL: This optional signal allows a disk drive to change its number. If it is attached to the disk drive interface, the disk drive is the master drive and has the number 0; otherwise it is the slave drive and has the number 1. In this way it is possible for both drives to modify their numbers without anything needing to be changed on the drives themselves.

5.2   Timing specifications

Data can be transferred over the IDE interface in one of two ways: via programmed I/O (PIO) or via direct memory access (DMA). In this chapter on the physical interface only the timing of these transfer methods is discussed. The higher level description of the interface, for instance how the host sets up the transfer, is considered as part of the protocol level and is discussed in Chapter 6.

A preliminary remark about the timings listed: the ATA standard defines three operating modes for PIO and DMA. Mode 0 is the normal mode, and is also the slowest. The parameter list of the command IDENTIFY DRIVE tells which operating mode the controller has implemented. The exact timings of all operating modes have not been listed in this book. These are necessary only if you wish to build an IDE controller, in which case the newest version of the ATA standard should be obtained. Table 5.4 lists cycle times and achievable data rates of the different modes.

Two important facts can be seen from this table: firstly, DMA is not necessarily faster than PIO. All depends on the currently selected mode. In multi-tasking systems, however, the processor could perform other tasks during a multi-word DMA. If the device driver is written in such a way, DMA is advantageous at least in heavily loaded systems. Secondly – as shown by Detlef Grell in his article 'Geschwindigkeitsrausch' [Speed ecstasy] in *c't* (August 1995 issue) – the 8.3 MB/sec that can be reached with PIO mode 2 is still sufficient to serve the fastest disks currently available. These supply a sustained transfer rate of about 6 MB/sec.

Table 5.4   Cycle times and data rates of different DMA modes.

Mode	0	1	2	3	4
PIO cycle time	600 ns	383 ns	240 ns	180 ns	120 ns
Data rate	3.3 MB/sec	5.2 MB/sec	8.3 MB/sec	11.1 MB/sec	16.6 MB/sec
Single-DMA cycle	960 ns	480 ns	240 ns		
Data rate	2 MB/sec	4.1 MB/sec	8.3 MB/sec		
Multi-DMA cycle	480 ns	150 ns	120 ns		
Data rate	4.1 MB/sec	13.3 MB/sec	16.6 MB/sec		

The data rates are taken from the article 'Quellen und Senken' [Sources and sinks] by Andreas Stiller, *c't* (August 1995). The gray-shaded boxes are already defined in ATA-1.

You may be wondering about PIO modes 4 and 5. They transmit faster than the ISA bus from which IDE is derived. Thus, these modes cannot be used with simple ISA bus adapters. They are reserved for ISA controllers for faster host bus systems, such as PCI.

PIO data transfer

All accesses to the controller register are executed via PIO. This includes the reading of status and error information, the setting of parameters and the writing of commands. However, even read and write operations can be carried out via the data register using PIO or DMA. It is called PIO because, in contrast to DMA, every access must be individually programmed. A simplified timing diagram for a PIO access is given in Figure 5.1.

For a PIO data transfer, the host first puts the addresses on the address lines. These are the signals CS1FX, CS3FX and DA0–DA2. After 70 nanoseconds (ns), it asserts the signal $\overline{\text{DIOR}}$ for read access or the signal $\overline{\text{DIOW}}$ for write access. Simultaneously, it indicates with the signal $\overline{\text{IOCS16}}$ whether it wants an 8-bit or a 16-bit transfer. For a write access, the host places the data on the data lines; for a read access, the controller supplies the data. This data must be valid by the time $\overline{\text{DIOR}}$ (in the case of a read) or $\overline{\text{DIOW}}$ (in the case of a write) is negated. The data is then read in by the host

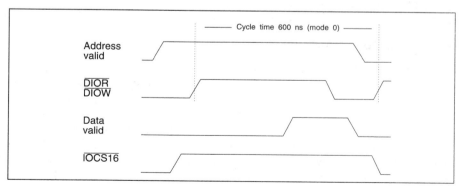

Figure 5.1   Timing diagram for PIO data transfer.

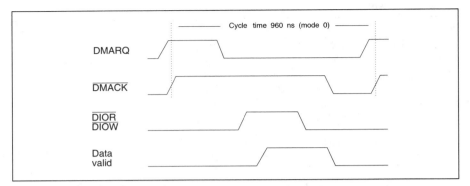

Figure 5.2 Timing diagram for single-word DMA.

or the controller, depending on the direction of the transfer. Shortly thereafter, the address, data and $\overline{\text{IOCS16}}$ lines must be released, and the cycle is complete. This entire cycle normally lasts 600 ns, but the specification also includes faster modes with cycle times as fast as 240 ns.

Single-word DMA

Apart from the initial request, DMA transfers take place without intervention by the CPU. This is advantageous above all in multi-tasking systems; while one process waits for its I/O access to be completed, the CPU is free to do computations for other processes. Figure 5.2 shows the simplified timing diagram for a single-word DMA.

In what follows, the sequence of events involved in a read access is described; a write access works in an analogous way. The host asserts the DMARQ signal to initiate a DMA transfer. The IDE controller replies by asserting DMACK. Within 200 ns, the host releases the DMARQ signal and asserts DIOR for 480 ns. The controller must then immediately set the data signals because data is gated on the falling edge of $\overline{\text{DIOR}}$. At the same time, the controller may remove its DMACK signal. After 50 ns, the data bus is released and the host can begin the next cycle. A cycle takes between 240 and 960 ns, depending on the operating mode used.

Multiple DMA transfers

DMA really begins to pay off only with multiple DMA. This is the case because the CPU need issue only one transfer request to initiate a sequence of many data accesses. Figure 5.3 shows the simplified timing diagram for multiple DMA. Once again, a read access is used as an example. The cycle begins in exactly the same way as with a single-word DMA, up to the point where the transfer of the first word is complete and the data lines are once again free. Unlike in the single-word case, however, the host does not stop asserting the DMARQ signal, and in response the DMACK signal also remains high. About 200 ns after the host negates DIOR, it asserts it again, and the next transfer begins. During the transfer of the last data word, while DIOR is asserted, the host removes the DMARQ signal. The transfer request is over when this last transfer is completed.

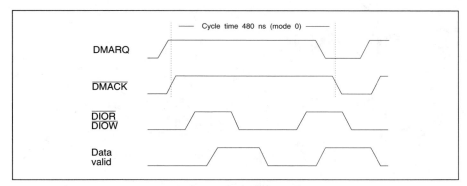

Figure 5.3 Timing diagram for multiple DMA transfers.

6 IDE protocol

6.1 The register model of the IDE controller

The register model of the IDE controller describes how the controller appears to the host system. The IDE interface mediates between the host and the controller. The controller belongs to the description of the interface and the ATA standard. I have included the register model in this chapter on protocol because the status bits play a very important role in the protocol.

To the host system, the IDE controller essentially looks like the ST506 controller of the original IBM AT. There are, however, a few additional features. The host sees an IDE controller as two blocks of I/O registers. They lie in the I/O space of the ISA bus rather than in the memory address space. Here they could occupy addresses between 0 and FFFFh but PC compatible computers restrict the I/O space to 0 to 3FFh. The command register block is used to send commands to the disk drive and to exchange data. The control register block is used for disk control. The command register block is often called the AT task file, although I avoid this terminology.

The two register blocks are differentiated by the lines $\overline{CS0}$ and $\overline{CS1}$ (ATA-1: $\overline{CS1FX}$ and $\overline{CS3FX}$). $\overline{CS0}$ is derived from the ISA bus and, as its former name suggests, is active when an address in the range 1F0–1FF is accessed. Analogously, $\overline{CS1}$ is active when an address in the range 3F0–3FF is accessed. Whether the signals are actually decoded in this way, however, is up to the IDE adapter card. It is often possible to choose an alternative address range for the two register blocks using a jumper. In this way, it is possible to have more than one IDE interface in a single computer.

In some cases the same address is used to access multiple registers in order to save I/O address space; during a read the address refers to one register, during a write to a different register. Table 6.1 gives an overview of both register blocks.

The data register (1F0h, read/write)

The data register is used to exchange 8- or 16-bit data words between the host and the disk drive buffer. The signal IOCS16 indicates a 16-bit access. Transfer of data using this register is called PIO because the computer must retrieve each word of data individually. Data transfers may also be accomplished using DMA.

Table 6.1 IDE command and control register.

	Addresses				Name and function	
CS1FX	CS3FX	DA2	DA1	DA0	Read access	Write access
Command register block						
1	0	0	0	0	Data register	Data register
1	0	0	0	1	Error register	Feature register
1	0	0	1	0	Sector count register	Sector count register
1	0	0	1	1	Sector number register	Sector number register
					Sector number or block address 0–7	Sector number or block address 0–7
1	0	1	0	0	Cylinder register 0	Cylinder register 0
					Cylinder 0–7 or	Cylinder 0–7 or
					Block address 8–15	Block address 8–15
1	0	1	0	1	Cylinder register 1	Cylinder register 1
					Cylinder 8–15 or	Cylinder 8–15 or
					Block address 16–23	Block address 16–23
1	0	1	1	0	Drive/head register	Drive/head register
					Drive/head number or block address 24–27	Drive/head number or block address 14–31
1	0	1	1	1	Status register	Command register
Control register block						
0	1	0	0	0	Not used	Not used
0	1	0	0	1	Not used	Not used
0	1	0	1	0	Not used	Not used
0	1	0	1	1	Not used	Not used
0	1	1	0	0	Not used	Not used
0	1	1	0	1	Not used	Not used
0	1	1	1	0	Alternate status register	Control register
0	1	1	1	1	Reserved	Not used
0	1	1	1	1	(ATA-1: Address register)	

The error register (1F1h, read)

After power-up, reset or the execution of the command EXECUTE DRIVE DIAGNOSTICS, this register contains a diagnostic code. The diagnostic codes are listed in Chapter 8 together with the command EXECUTE DRIVE DIAGNOSTICS.

If the ERR bit in the status register is set, then this register contains the error code of the last executed command. In this case, the contents of the register are as follows (Table 6.2):

- ATA1: BBK (bad block detected): Set if an error mark is detected in the header of the requested sector. In ATA-2, this bit is reserved.

Table 6.2 IDE error register.

7	6	5	4	3	2	1	0
BBK	UNC	MC	IDNF	MCR	ABRT	TK0NF	AMNF

- UNC (uncorrectable data error): Set if an error was detected in the data field of the requested sector and this error could not be corrected by the ECC. The data is unusable.

- MC (media change): A replaceable medium was changed since the last access. This is not an error but a signal to the host to take appropriate measures (for example, to reset the software cache) so that the new medium can be used.

- IDNF (ID not found): The controller could not find the address field of the requested sector. Either it is damaged or a sector was requested that does not exist.

- MCR (media change requested): Signals to the host that the user has pressed the button that initiates a change of medium. It is now up to the host to take the necessary steps (such as completing any pending I/O requests) and then to issue a MEDIA EJECT or DOOR UNLOCK command.

- ABRT (aborted command): The command was interrupted because it was illegal or because of a disk drive error.

- TK0NF (track 0 not found): Track 0 could not be found during the execution of a RECALIBRATE command. This is usually a fatal error.

- AMNF (address mark not found): The data region of the requested sector could not be found.

The feature register (1F1h, write)

This register is not used with all disk drives. In accordance with the ATA standard, it is used to set certain features of the interface using the command SET FEATURES.

In the case of a normal ST506 controller for the IBM AT, this register contains the cylinder number divided by four, indicating where the write precompensation begins. A few older IDE controllers, which do not conform to the ATA standard, expect to find this number here as well.

The sector count register (1F2h, read/write)

This register contains the number of sectors to be read or written. The value 0 is interpreted as 256. If an error occurs, this register contains the number of sectors yet to be transferred.

A few commands use this register for other purposes. Refer to the description of commands INITIALIZE DRIVE PARAMETERS, FORMAT TRACK and WRITE SAME in Chapter 8.

The media address registers

The following registers, sector number register, cylinder number register and drive register, contain the media address of the block to be processed. In this book, I refer to this group of registers collectively as the media address registers. Their importance varies depending on whether the system uses physical or logical addressing (see Chapter 7).

In ATA-1, the address registers contain the constantly updated media address. In ATA-2, this is no longer the case. Only when an error has occurred do the media address registers contain the address of the block where the error occurred.

The sector number register (1F3h, read/write)

This register contains the number of the first sector to be transferred. In logical block address (LBA) mode it contains byte 0 of the logical block number.

The cylinder number register (cylinder low register, 1F4h, cylinder high register, 1F5h, read/write)

This pair of registers contains the cylinder number. The ATA standard allows 65 536 cylinders to be addressed. Earlier IDE controllers use only bits 0 and 1 from the high byte of the cylinder address (1F5h), which limits the number of addressable cylinders to 1024. In LBA mode, the register holds bytes 1 and 2 of the logical block number.

The drive/head register (1F6h, read/write)

This register contains the drive number, head number and addressing mode. It is broken down as follows (Table 6.3):

Table 6.3 IDE drive/head register.

7	6	5	4	3	2	1	0
1	L	1	DEV (DRV)	HS3	HS2	HS1	HS0

- HS0–HS3 (head select 0–3): Head number. In LBA mode these bits represent the low four bits of byte 3 of the logical block address. The high four bits are always 0.
- DEV (device): Device number. Device 0 is always the master device. ATA-1: DRV (drive): same meaning.
- L (LBA mode): When this bit is set LBA addressing is being used; otherwise the usual cylinder/head/sector (CHS) method is being used (see Chapter 7).

The status register (1F7h, read)

The status register contains the status of the disk drive as of the last command. A read access to this register clears pending interrupt requests (see protocol). To avoid this, one can read the alternate status register (3F6h, read). Both status registers consist of the following fields (Table 6.4):

- BSY (busy): If BSY is set, no other bits in the status register are valid. BSY is always set when the controller itself is accessing the command register block. During this

Table 6.4   IDE status register.

7	6	5	4	3	2	1	0
BSY	DRDY	DF	DSC	DRQ	CORR	IDX	ERR

time the host may not access any of the other registers in the command register block.

- DRDY (drive ready): Indicates that the drive is ready to accept a command. When the drive is first switched on, DRDY remains clear until the drive is ready for operation.

- DF (drive fault): Indicates an error on the drive. (ATA-1: DWF (drive write fault): write error.)

- DSC (drive seek complete): Indicates that the heads are positioned over the desired cylinder.

After a command resulting in an error, BSY, DF and DSC remain unchanged until the status register is read. Afterwards they will reflect the drive's current status.

- DRQ (data request): This bit is set when the drive wants to exchange a byte with the host via the data register.

- CORR (corrected data): This bit is set if a correctable read error has occurred. The data transfer continues uninterrupted.

- IDX (index): This bit is set once per rotation of the medium, when the index mark passes under the read/write head.

- ERR (error): Indicates an error has occurred in the process of executing the previous command. The error register contains further information.

The command register (1F7h, write)

This register receives the commands that are sent to the controller. Execution of the command is started immediately after writing the command register. The commands and their parameters are part of the command level of the interface model and are described in Chapter 8.

The alternate status register (3F6h, read)

This register contains the same information as the status register. However, a read from this register has no effect on pending interrupt requests (see the IDE protocol). Thus you can read this register at any time without having to worry about side effects.

The device control register (3F6h, write)

Two bits are defined in this register (Table 6.5):

- SRST (software reset): As long as this bit is set, the attached disk drives are in the RESET state. When this bit changes to 0, the drives are executing a start-up procedure.

Table 6.5 IDE control register.

7	6	5	4	3	2	1	0
–	–	–	–	1	SRST	$\overline{\text{IEN}}$	0

- $\overline{\text{IEN}}$ (interrupt enable): This bit is negative true. A 0 signifies that interrupts are allowed; a 1 blocks them.

The drive address register (3F7h, read)

This register is no longer defined in ATA-2; it should not answer when accessed. In ATA-1, it contains constantly updated information about the execution of the current command. The head-number information is not always correct for drives using caching and mapping. All bits in this register are negative true (Table 6.6):

Table 6.6 IDE address register.

7	6	5	4	3	2	1	0
–	$\overline{\text{WTG}}$	$\overline{\text{HS3}}$	$\overline{\text{HS2}}$	$\overline{\text{HS1}}$	$\overline{\text{HS0}}$	$\overline{\text{DS1}}$	$\overline{\text{DS0}}$

- $\overline{\text{WTG}}$ (write gate): If this bit is clear then a write access is currently taking place on the selected drive.
- $\overline{\text{HS3}}$–$\overline{\text{HS0}}$ (head select 3–0): Inverted current head number of the selected disk drive.
- $\overline{\text{DS1}}$ (drive 1 selected): When this bit is 0 the slave drive is selected.
- $\overline{\text{DS0}}$ (drive 0 selected): When this bit is 0 the master drive is selected.

6.2 Command execution

There are five protocols for the execution of IDE commands. In ATA-1, these were called command classes 1–5.

PI protocol (class 1): read commands with PIO

Read commands are commands that involve the reading of the sector buffer one or more times. A PI (PIO In) protocol command is executed in the following way. The host first writes any required parameters to the address and feature registers. It then writes the opcode to the command register to begin execution (Figure 6.1).

The drive sets the BSY bit in the status register and puts data for the transfer into the sector buffer (see Chapter 7). When the sector buffer is ready, the drive sets the DRQ bit and clears the BSY bit. It simultaneously asserts the signal INTRQ.

The host then reads the status register, whereupon the drive negates INTRQ. The DRQ bit tells the host that it may now read 512 bytes (or more in the case of the READ

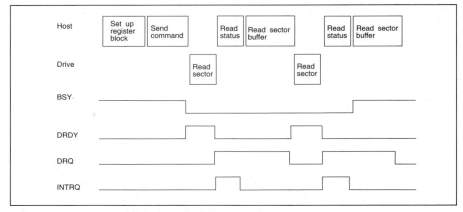

Figure 6.1 Timing of a PI protocol command.

LONG command) from the sector buffer. This read is then performed according to the timing specifications described in Chapter 5.

As soon as all the data in the buffer has been read, the drive resets the DRQ bit. After all of the requested sectors have been read the command is complete. Otherwise, the drive again sets the BSY bit and prepares the next sector for transfer.

In the event of an error, the drive still attempts to prepare the sector buffer for a read but also sets the corresponding error bit in the status register. It is then up to the host to decide whether or not to read the sector buffer despite the error.

Things are different when a command is aborted. In this case, the drive resets the DRQ bit immediately after the host has read the status register, and no data is transferred.

PO protocol (class 2): write commands with PIO

PO (PIO Out) commands are write commands. Thus the first thing that must happen is that the sector buffer must be filled with 512 bytes of data (or more in the case of WRITE LONG). Figure 6.2 shows the sequence of steps involved in executing this command. In this example, two sectors are being written.

First, the host places the necessary parameters in the appropriate registers of the command register block. It then waits until the DRDY bit is set and writes the opcode to the command register.

At this point, the drive sets the DRQ bit in the status register and thereby signals that it is waiting to receive data. The host writes the data via the data register to the sector buffer. When the sector buffer is full the disk drive sets the BSY bit and clears DRQ.

As soon as the data in the buffer has been processed (for example, been written to the medium), the drive clears the BSY bit and sets INTRQ. This signals to the host that it should read the status register. Once this has happened, the drive resets INTRQ.

If only one sector is to be written the command is now complete. Otherwise, if the write involves multiple sectors, the drive again sets DRQ and the next sector is processed.

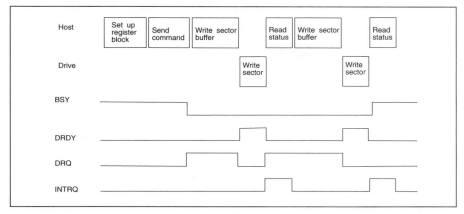

Figure 6.2   Timing of a PO protocol command.

In the event of an illegal command the drive does not set DRQ after the command has been written, but instead indicates that status is to be read by setting INTRQ. The host can then examine the error bits of the status register.

ND protocol (class 3): commands without data transfer

Commands not involving data transfer (ND: No Data) do not use the sector buffer. Nevertheless, such commands may involve an exchange of information between drive and host. This exchange of information is accomplished by reading and writing registers.

Here the sequence of steps is more simple. The host writes the necessary parameters to the controller registers and writes the opcode to the command register. The drive sets BSY and executes the command. When it finishes it writes status to the status register, resets BSY and sets INTRQ. The host then reads the status, the drive clears INTRQ and the command is complete.

DM protocol (class 4): commands with DMA data transfer

This class is comprised of only two optional commands, one for reading and the other for writing. Although DMA transfers involve more work for the processor before and after each transfer, the processor is completely free during the transfer. Also, during the transfer of multiple sectors, an interrupt occurs only at the end of the entire transfer, not after each sector. This is especially advantageous in multi-tasking systems where the processor can utilize the time it gains through DMA. The execution of DMA commands can be broken down into three phases (Figure 6.3).

In the command phase the host first initializes a DMA channel. It then writes the parameters and opcode to the controller registers, just as in the PIO case. The drive sets BSY and executes the command.

In the data phase the DMA channel transfers the data using the DMARQ handshake sequence. The contents of the controller's registers are not valid during the data phase.

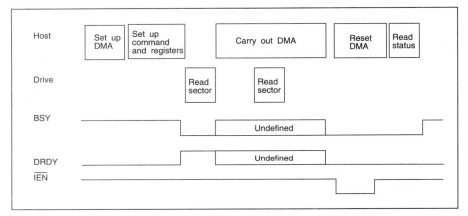

Figure 6.3 Timing of a DM protocol command.

The drive then begins the status phase by triggering an interrupt. In response the host resets the DMA channel and reads the status and (if necessary) the error register.

In case of error the status phase may occur before the data phase or interrupt it, since the drive requests an interrupt the moment the error occurs.

VS protocol (class 5): vendor-specific protocol

There are a few commands that do not fit neatly into the above classifications because their execution protocols differ slightly from those described above. These differences are explained together with the commands in Chapter 8.

6.3 Power-up or hardware reset

The same sequence of steps is executed after both power-up and a hardware reset. The procedure varies slightly depending on whether one or two disk drives are present.

The timing diagrams require a few words of explanation. All signals are represented as active high even when they are marked as inverted by a bar above their names. This makes the diagrams simpler to understand. In reality, that is, on an oscilloscope or a logic analyzer, these signals would appear inverted.

The timing diagrams are not drawn to scale. Thus, it is possible that an event lasting 400 ns might appear to be as long as one lasting 450 ms. Important times are also included in the diagram. For complete specifications consult the most recent ATA standard.

Reset in a single-drive system

The host activates the signal $\overline{\text{RESET}}$ for at least 25 μs. It should be noted that the host is responsible for a $\overline{\text{RESET}}$ after the system first powers on and all system voltages

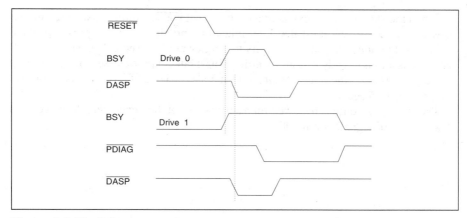

Figure 6.4 Timing at power-up or RESET.

have stabilized. At most 400 ns after $\overline{\text{RESET}}$ goes low again the master drive sets the BSY bit in the status register. At most 1 ms after that, the drive negates $\overline{\text{DASP}}$ and carries out its self-test. Simultaneously, it observes DASP for 450 ms to see if a slave drive is present. Since a slave will not be found the master is able to use $\overline{\text{DASP}}$ to indicate drive activity. As soon as the master drive has completed its self-test and is ready to accept commands it resets the BSY bit. All of this must occur within 31 seconds.

Reset in a two-drive system

Before the ATA standard there was no standard way of determining whether a slave drive was present or not. Often the master drive was equipped with a special jumper for this purpose. Such drives may be incompatible with drives using the ATA protocol described here.

Both ATA compliant drives negate $\overline{\text{DASP}}$ at most 1 ms after $\overline{\text{RESET}}$ is negated. The master drive detects the existence of a slave within 400 ms after $\overline{\text{RESET}}$ by examining $\overline{\text{DASP}}$. Prior to this the slave negates $\overline{\text{PDIAG}}$ thereby indicating that it has begun its self-test.

When the self-test is finished and the slave drive is ready to accept commands it asserts $\overline{\text{PDIAG}}$. This must occur no more than 30 seconds after the reset. If the master drive does not recognize the slave within 31 seconds it concludes that an error has occurred and sets bit 7 in the error register.

The slave drive should negate $\overline{\text{DASP}}$ within 30 seconds of receiving the first valid command (Figure 6.4).

The Conner protocol

Many drive manufacturers use special protocols for detecting a slave drive, which differ from the ATA protocol sketched above. One such protocol, that used by Conner Peripherals, is discussed here.

When the slave powers up it activates the signal $\overline{\text{PDIAG}}$ within 1 ms. (If the master does not see PDIAG within 4 ms, it assumes that no slave drive is present.) $\overline{\text{PDIAG}}$ remains active until the slave clears its BSY bit or until 14 seconds have elapsed. If the slave is still not ready it stops asserting $\overline{\text{PDIAG}}$ but continues asserting BSY. Before clearing its BSY bit, the master waits until the slave clears $\overline{\text{PDIAG}}$, but does not wait longer than 14.5 seconds.

The same procedure is followed for a software reset; however, here the slave must clear the $\overline{\text{PDIAG}}$ signal within 400 ms.

7 The model of an IDE disk drive

When examined briefly, the model of an IDE disk drive corresponds to that of an ST506 drive. This is not at all surprising given that IDE is a direct descendant of ST506. However, the IDE model of the ATA standard contains a number of significant improvements over its predecessor.

7.1 Organization of the medium

The medium of an IDE drive is organized by head (surface), cylinder and sector. An IDE drive can have 16 heads, 1024 cylinders and 256 sectors. The ATA standard even permits up to 65 636 cylinders. A sector normally contains 512 bytes of usable data. These sectors are addressed in one of two ways.

What is a megabyte?

Before we go on, a brief remark on the definition of megabyte and gigabyte. In principle, two different indications are used. A kilobyte is 1024 bytes; thus, a megabyte should be 1024 kilobytes, that is, 1 048 576 bytes. Similarly, a gigabyte should be 1024 megabytes. For the specification of disk capacities, however, it has become common practice to use the 'decimal' mega and giga. A 'decimal' megabyte is 1000 kilobytes, and a 'decimal' gigabyte 1000 megabytes. To comply with majority rule, in this chapter we will use the 'decimal' notation and indicate the correct values in parentheses.

Physical addressing (CHS mode)

In CHS mode the cylinder, head and sector number uniquely identify a given sector. IDE comes from ST506, which always has 17 sectors of 512 bytes each per track. For this reason many IDE drives with more than 17 sectors utilize either a native or translated mode of addressing. In the native mode the drive geometry is presented as it physically exists to the host. In the translated mode the physical geometry is mapped to a logical one. The logical geometry has 17 sectors but with a greater number of logical heads so that the total capacity is the same.

IDE drives use a linear mapping for physical addressing. This means that consecutive sectors begin at cylinder 0, head 0, sector 0. This track is used first, then head 1 of the same cylinder and so on until the entire cylinder is used. This is then repeated for the next cylinder number with head 0. This mapping must be known to the host since the IDE interface has commands that transfer as many as 256 sectors at one time.

Another aspect of IDE that perhaps belongs to the drive model is that average access time within a given track is shorter than when a head switch must occur. A head switch, on the other hand, takes less time than a change of cylinders. This is not necessarily true in translation mode. Here a head switch may take place within a logical track access.

In CHS mode, a disk can have a maximum of 65 535 cylinders, 16 heads and 256 sectors. With a sector size of 512 bytes, this corresponds to a capacity of 136 (127) gigabytes.

Logical addressing (LBA mode)

In this mode the drive presents itself as a continuous sequence of blocks which are addressed by their logical block number. In this case the drive's physical geometry need not be known to the host.

In LBA mode, 28 bits can be used for the logical block address. Thus, 2^{28} blocks can be addressed. As with CHS addressing, this results in a theoretical upper limit of 136 (127) gigabytes per IDE medium.

The ATA standard specifies that the mapping from physical geometry to logical block numbers should be accomplished in the following manner:

```
LBA := (CylinderNumber * HeadCount + HeadNumber) *
SectorCount + SectorNumber - 1
```

This mapping assures that the time needed to access from LBA n to LBA $n + 1$ is shorter than from LBA n to LBA $n + 2$. In other words, the logical blocks are also in sequential order in terms of access time. This is important for the host because it means that large blocks of data will be written and read in the shortest possible time if the logical blocks are continuous.

Zone-bit recording

Using such a mapping, be it translated physical or logical addressing, it is now possible to employ drives that do not have the same number of sectors per cylinder for the entire surface of the medium.

This leads to a recording technique that makes possible an increase of up to 50% in capacity without special heads or medium. In order to describe this technique, known as zone-bit recording, we need to talk a bit about disk recording in general. The composition of the magnetic surface of the disk and the type of the heads used determine the maximum recording density in flux changes per millimeter. For the purpose of our discussion here, we can think of a flux change as corresponding to a bit written to the disk. Using traditional recording methods, it is the innermost track that determines the maximum number of flux changes per track, but since the circumferences of the tracks increase as one moves away from the center, the number of flux changes that can be accommodated also increases. Zone-bit recording makes it possible to take advantage of this by increasing the number of flux changes in outer tracks. This is done by dividing the medium into several regions, in each of which the number of sectors per track is constant. The innermost region has the least number of sectors per track while the outermost region has the greatest. The regions in between bridge the two extremes. In this way the ideal of maximal flux density is approached and the capacity is significantly increased. A side effect of this is that the data rate of the medium increases from the inner tracks to the outer tracks. This, however, is an aspect that only the drive electronics has to deal with, not the IDE interface. The ST506 cannot accommodate zone-bit recording since the data comes directly from the heads and would therefore come at varying rates.

Capacity limits

It has already been mentioned twice that the IDE interface can physically handle disk drives of up to 136 (127) gigabytes. However, in the PC and MS-DOS world, there are several restrictions to this.

The 528-Mbyte limit

The first restriction comes from the PC BIOS and applies to disks that are to be used without a special software driver. The BIOS allows 1024 cylinders, 16 heads and 63 sectors. With 512 bytes per sector, this results in a capacity of 528 (504) Mbytes. In order to use a disk drive with more than 1024 cylinders, an adapter can map the addresses and make the host see exactly 1024 cylinders, but more sectors. Surmounting the 528-Mbyte limit with special drivers or an adapter-specific BIOS is often perceived as a part of EIDE. In practice, however, this possibility has always been there.

The 8-Gbyte limit

A second capacity limit is introduced by the disk interrupt INT 13h and the partition tables of FAT-based operating systems. This also applies to disks which are not addressed by the BIOS but by special drivers. INT 13h and the partition tables can manage 1024 cylinders, 256 heads and 63 sectors. This results in a capacity of 8.4 (7.7) GBytes. The small number of only 1024 cylinders, together with the high number of 265 heads will often need mapping. The 8-Gbyte limit applies not only to IDE disks, but also to SCSI disks. It is, however, limited to operating systems such as DOS, Windows 3.x and Windows 95. UNIX, OS/2 and Windows NT use different media structures and therefore have other (higher) capacity limits.

7.2 Defect management

The definition of the IDE interface and also the ATA standard specify no precise rules for dealing with errors. There are, however, two basic approaches that may be employed.

Defective sectors may be marked as such during formatting. Exactly how this is to be done is left up to the manufacturer. When the sectors are read they are recognized as defective and dealt with appropriately.

The second approach reallocates defective sectors. This is possible with translated physical addressing or logical addressing only. Here a specific area of the drive is reserved for replacement sectors. When a sector is identified as defective, it is formatted in a particular way. Multiple copies of the replacement sector's address are written in that defective sector, so that it can be read in any case. In this way it is possible to present the host with an apparently defect free medium at all times.

Care must be taken in order to keep the access time of a reallocated sector to a minimum. Bear in mind the relevant time relationships: a revolution takes 11 ms, a track-to-track seek about 2 ms, the average seek time is 11 ms, and a head switch takes approximately 1 ms. Since a seek is most costly, it makes sense for each cylinder to contain several replacement sectors for that cylinder. This approach avoids seeks altogether.

Better still is the approach where each track has a sector for defect management. However, if the defective sector is simply reallocated to the reserve sector this is still not optimal. Figure 7.1 describes the situation. In order to read sectors 0 through 2, one must first read sector 0 and then wait almost an entire revolution until the replaced sector 1 is reached. Afterwards one must wait until sector 2 finally revolves underneath the heads to be read. The entire procedure takes 1¼ revolutions although only ¼ of a revolution is needed for reading; in other words, an entire revolution is lost.

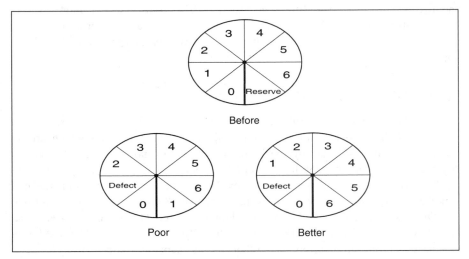

Figure 7.1 Strategies for sector reallocation.

The following is an approach that minimizes the access time to reallocated sectors. A replacement sector is reserved for defect management for each track. When a defective sector is found it is marked as such, and all subsequent sectors of the track are shifted by one. In this way even after the reallocation access to a continuous sequence of sectors can take place without losing a revolution. In addition, a number of replacement cylinders are also reserved for reallocation purposes. In the event that a track is found to have more than a single defective sector then the entire track can be reallocated.

7.3 The sector buffer

The sector buffer is used as a temporary storage for all read and write operations. This decouples the rate at which data is exchanged with the host and the rate at which data is written and read from the medium. This is necessary since a sector must always be written or read as a whole.

In the simplest case the sector buffer is an area of RAM on the IDE controller. If the buffer can only be used to exchange data with the medium or the host, one speaks of a single ported buffer. A buffer that is able to receive data from the host and write data to the disk simultaneously is referred to as a double ported buffer (Figure 7.2).

A double ported buffer must be able to hold more than a single sector. Only after an entire sector has been received will the controller begin to write the data to the medium. If during that time the buffer is able to receive additional data from the host the throughput of the system is significantly improved.

As a further example, assume that we are reading a number of sequential sectors. A drive with a single ported buffer is forced to use an interleave, otherwise a subsequent

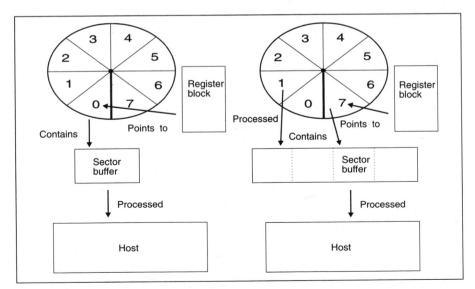

Figure 7.2 Single and double ported sectors.

sector will be lost by the time the host reads the first sector. This approximately halves the throughput of a double ported buffer, where the host can read the first sector during the time the second sector is read from the medium.

A double ported buffer looks like a sector buffer to the host in that it contains the data of the current sector. In a sense the sector buffer is a window through which the host and medium exchange data. The window is constantly shifted so that the data always corresponds to the current contents of the address register. Figure 7.2 makes these relationships clear.

The communication between the sector buffer and the host takes place either byte- or word-wise via the data register of the controller (PIO). Optionally, direct memory transfers are possible using DMA.

7.4 Power conditions

The ATA model of an IDE disk drive includes various power conditions. An IDE drive can be put into energy saving states of differing levels. This is an important capability in view of the increasing number of notebook and portable computers. Table 7.1 shows the possible states and the corresponding status bits. The status bits have already been explained in Chapter 6. In ATA-1, there used to be an additional REST state which no longer exists in ATA-2.

In the SLEEP state the drive is turned on, but uses as little power as possible. Only through a RESET can the drive be brought into the active state again. Since in this state the motor may be turned off, a medium access may take as long as 30 seconds.

In the STANDBY state the IDE interface is capable of accepting commands. Here too the motor may be turned off, so a medium access may take up to 30 seconds.

In the IDLE state the motor is on and the drive is able to react to commands immediately. However, certain portions of the drive electronics may be turned off for power savings if this will cause only minimal delay for a medium access.

Finally, the ACTIVE mode is the normal state of the drive. Commands are executed in the shortest possible time in this state.

Table 7.1 Power conditions for IDE drives.

Power condition	BSY	DRDY	Interface	Medium
SLEEP	X	X	no	no
STANDBY	0	1	yes	no
IDLE	0	1	yes	yes
ACTIVE	X	X	yes	yes

The standby timer

With the standby timer, the drive can decide at its own discretion to switch from the IDLE state or the ACTIVE state to the STANDBY state. Using CHECK POWER MODE the host can determine in which of the two states the drive currently resides.

8 IDE commands

In this chapter, all the key IDE commands defined in the ATA standard are introduced briefly. The commands are listed in Table 8.1. Among these, ten are mandatory. The others may be optionally implemented, but then only in accordance with the ATA standard. There are a couple of differences between ATA-1 and ATA-2. Some mandatory commands of ATA-1 are now optional, and some valid commands of ATA-1 are now reserved as obsolete. These differences are shown in the ATA-1 and ATA-2 columns which use the codes R for reserved, O for optional, V for vendor-specific and M for mandatory.

The table gives the command name, followed by the opcode. The mandatory commands of ATA-2 are shown on a gray-shaded background, and the column labeled Prot. designates the command protocol used. The last five columns show which control register is used for parameters. Included are FR (feature register), SC (sector count register), SN (sector number register), CN (cylinder number register), and DH (drive/head register). D in the DH column means that only the disk drive number is used; D* means that disk drive 0 is addressed, but both disk drives execute the command.

Some commands have a second opcode in parentheses. These opcodes were established by the industry prior to the ATA standard and are still in use. Conner drives use these earlier opcodes.

In addition, some manufacturers implement optional commands that are often very useful. A good example of this would be a command to read the defect list. In any case, it is always a good idea to consult the drive handbook when planning a large project.

8.1 Mandatory commands

EXECUTE DRIVE DIAGNOSTICS (90h)

This command is always issued to disk drive 0, but initiates the internal diagnostics of both disk drives. After the diagnostics have run, the BSY bit is cleared and an interrupt given. The results can then be retrieved from the error register. However, the contents must be interpreted with the aid of the special error codes listed in Table 8.2. Please note that under ATA-1, this command was executed in a different way.

Table 8.1   IDE commands of the ATA standard.

Command name	Opcode	ATA-1	ATA-2	Prot.	FR	SC	SN	CN	DH
ACKNOWLEDGE MEDIA CHANGE	DBh	O	O	VS					D
BOOT POST-BOOT	DCh	O	O	VS					D
BOOT PRE-BOOT	DDh	O	O	VS					D
CHECK POWER MODE	98h (E5h)	O	O	ND		*			D
DOOR LOCK	DEh	O	O	VS					D
DOOR UNLOCK	DFh	O	O	VS					D
DOWNLOAD MICROCODE	92h	R	O	PO	*	*	*	*	D
EXECUTE DRIVE DIAGNOSTICS	90h	M	M	ND					D*
FORMAT TRACK	50h	M	V	VS					
IDENTIFY DEVICE	ECh	O	M	PI					D
IDLE	97h (E3h)	O	O	ND		*			D
IDLE IMMEDIATE	95h (E1h)	O	O	ND					D
INITIALIZE DEVICE PARAMETERS	91h	M	M	ND		*			*
MEDIA EJECT	EDh	R	O	ND					D
NOP	00h	R	O	ND					*
READ BUFFER	E4h	O	O	PI					D
READ DMA (with and without retries)	C8h, C9h	O	O	DM		*	*	*	*
(READ DRIVE STATE)	E9h	O	R	ND	*				
READ LONG (with and without retries)	22h, 23h	M	O	PI		*	*	*	*
READ MULTIPLE	C4h	O	O	PI		*	*	*	*
READ SECTORS (with and without retries)	20h, 21h	M	M	PI		*	*	*	*
READ VERIFY SECTORS (with and without retries)	40h, 41h	M	M	ND		*	*	*	*
RECALIBRATE	1xh	M	O	ND					D
(REST)	E7h	O	R	VS	*				
(RESTORE DRIVE STATE)	EAh	O	R	VS	*				
SEEK	7xh	M	M	ND			*	*	*
SET FEATURES	EFh	O	O	ND	*				D
SET MULTIPLE MODE	C6h	O	O	ND		*			D
SLEEP	99h (E6h)	O	O	ND					D
STANDBY	96h (E2h)	O	O	ND		*			D
STANDBY IMMEDIATE	94h (E0h)	O	O	ND					D
WRITE BUFFER	E8h	O	O	PO					D
WRITE DMA (with and without retries)	CAh, CBh	O	O	DM		*	*	*	*
WRITE LONG (with and without retries)	32h, 33h	M	O	PO	*	*	*	*	*
WRITE MULTIPLE	C5h	O	O	PO	*	*	*	*	*
WRITE SAME	E9h	O	O	PO	*	*	*	*	*
WRITE SECTORS (with and without retries)	30h, 31h	M	M	PO	*	*	*	*	*
WRITE VERIFY	3Ch	O	O	PO	*	*	*	*	*

Table 8.2   Error codes for EXECUTE DRIVE DIAGNOSTICS.

Code	Device 0	Device 1
01h	OK	OK or not connected
00h, 02h–7Fh	defective	OK or not connected
81h	OK	defective
80h, 82h–FFh	defective	defective

IDENTIFY DEVICE (ECh)

The command IDENTIFY DEVICE is of special interest. After receiving this command, the drive writes a parameter block with information about the drive in the sector buffer. This parameter block is sometimes called configuration sector. It is read in the normal way from the sector buffer by the host.

This command has changed in many regards from ATA-1 to ATA-2. First of all, in ATA-1 it is still called IDENTIFY DRIVE. Then there are a number of parameters in the parameter list which have a meaning in ATA-1, but are marked as obsolete in ATA-2. However, since there are still large numbers of devices around that conform to ATA-1, I have put both standards next to each other.

Table 8.3 shows the structure of the parameter block. It consists of 255 16-bit words. The parameter words used in ATA-2 are shown on a gray background. Column 3 shows the ATA-1 meaning and, in parentheses, the changes made in ATA-2. Reserved parameter words must be filled with 00h. The parameter words that are marked as obsolete in ATA-2 are considered vendor-specific. Thus, they may contain a value.

Table 8.3 Parameter list of the IDENTIFY command.

Word	ATA-2	ATA-1 contents (changes in ATA-2)
0	Yes, changed	Configuration word (see Table 8.4)
1	Yes	Number of (logical) cylinders
2	Reserved	Reserved
3	Yes	Number of (logical) heads
4	Obsolete	Bytes per track unformatted
5	Obsolete	Bytes per sector unformatted
6	Yes	(Logical) sectors per track
7–9	Vendor-specific	Vendor-specific
10–19	Yes	Serial number in ASCII
20	Obsolete	Buffer type
21	Obsolete	Buffer size in 512-byte segments
22	Yes	Number of vendor-specific ECC bytes for READ and WRITE LONG
23–26	Yes	Firmware revision in ASCII
27–46	Yes	Model name in ASCII
47	Yes	Bits 7–0: sectors per interrupt for READ and WRITE MULTIPLE
48	Reserved	Bit 0: double word I/O possible
49	Yes, changed	Capabilities (see Table 8.5)
50	Reserved	Reserved
51	Yes	Bits 15–8: timing mode for PIO data transfers
52	Yes	Bits 15–8: timing mode for DMA data transfers
53	New	Reserved (bit 0: words 54–58; bit 1: words 64–70 apply)
54	Yes	Apparent (current) number of cylinders
55	Yes	Apparent (current) number of heads
56	Yes	Apparent (current) number of sectors per track
57–58	Yes	Apparent (current) capacity in sectors
59	Yes, changed	Bits 7–0: (current) number of sectors per interrupt (bit 8: values in bit 0–7 apply)
60–61	Yes	Total number of addressable sectors in LBA mode
62	Yes	Bits 15–8: active mode for single DMA
		Bits 7–0: supported modes for single DMA

Table 8.3 Parameter list of the IDENTIFY command *(cont.)*.

Word	ATA-2	ATA-1 contents (chages in ATA-2)
63	Yes	Bits 15–8: active mode for multiple DMA
		Bits 7–0: supported modes for multiple DMA
64	New	Bits 15–8: reserved
		Bits 7–0: reserved (supported modes for advanced PIO)
65	New	Reserved (minimum cycle time for multi-word DMA in ns)
66	New	Reserved (recommended cycle time for multi-word DMA in ns)
67	New	Reserved (minimum PIO cycle time without flow control)
68	New	Reserved (minimum PIO cycle time with IORDY flow control)
69–127	Reserved	Reserved
128–159	Vendor-specific	Vendor-specific
160–255	Reserved	Reserved

Some of the fields require further explanation. First, word 0 is a bitwise-coded word with configuration parameters. Table 8.4 illustrates the meaning of the individual bits. In ATA-2, of all these specifications, only the distinction between hard disk and changeable media in bits 6 and 7 has remained. All other specifications are obsolete. They are a hangover from ST506: drive internals that an IDE driver does not have to be concerned with.

The geometry values given in words 1 to 6 refer to the default mapping, which is usually physical addressing without translation. The current geometry of the disk drive is found in words 54 to 58.

A new item in ATA-2 is a configuration word which contains coded information on different capabilities of the drive. This field is explained in Table 8.5.

The following values are defined for the buffer type *only in ATA-1*: 0001h stands for a one-way buffer implemented for a single sector, 0002h stands for a two-way buffer of several sectors, and 0003h indicates a read cache. In ATA-2, this word is obsolete.

Table 8.4 Configuration bits for IDENTIFY data.

ATA-2	Bit	Meaning
–	0	Reserved
–	1	Hard-sectored drive
–	2	Soft-sectored drive
–	3	Encoding other than MFM
–	4	Head switching time 15 µs
–	5	Spindle motor control implemented
Yes	6	Hard drive
Yes	7	Changeable medium
–	8	Data rate to 5 MHz
–	9	Data rate between 5 and 10 MHz
–	10	Data rate above 10 MHz
–	11	Motor speed tolerance above 0.5%
–	12	Data clock offset available
–	13	Track offset available
–	14	Speed tolerance gap necessary
–	15	Reserved

Table 8.5 Capability word for IDENTIFY data.

Bit	Meaning
0–7	Vendor-specific
8	DMA commands supported
9	LBA mode supported
10	IORDY may be deactivated
11	IORDY is supported
12	Reserved
13	Standby timer available
14	Reserved
15	Reserved

INITIALIZE DEVICE PARAMETERS (91h)

Using this command, the disk drive geometry can be configured. This is accomplished by loading the number of sectors in the sector count register and the disk drive number and number of heads in the drive/head register.

This command also allows a drive to be switched from native to translated physical addressing. According to the ATA-1 standard, the parameters do not have to be checked. If they are incorrect, the next disk access will result in an error. However, many drives use the default values when incorrect parameters are given for this command. In ATA-2 an ABORTED COMMAND error must be reported.

READ SECTORS (20h with and 21h without retries)

This command reads the number of sectors given in the sector count register. A value of 0 means 256 sectors. The address of the first sector is given in the address register. An interrupt follows each sector that is read. If the heads are not over the desired track, they are positioned automatically. After the command is executed, the address register holds the address of the last sector read.

In case of error the action taken depends on whether the command was issued with or without retries. Without retries the command will be aborted and the IDNF bit set in the error register if the correct sector is not found in two revolutions. Otherwise repeated attempts will be made to read the proper sector. The number of repeated attempts is vendor-specific.

When the sector is found, the start of the data field is expected within a given number of bits. If it is not found, the command is aborted with an AMNF bit in the error register.

If a correctable ECC error occurs, the corresponding bit is set in the error register, but the command is not aborted. Only uncorrectable ECC errors lead to a command being aborted.

After a command is aborted, the address register contains the address of the sector in which the error occurred. The sector buffer could contain damaged data.

READ VERIFY SECTORS (40h with and 41h without retries)

This command reads the requested sectors, but no data is transferred. It only verifies (hence the name) whether or not the sectors are readable. The response to an error is identical to that of the READ SECTORS command.

SEEK (7xh)

Under ATA-1 this command instructs the drive to position the heads over the cylinder given in the address register, and to switch to that head. Under ATA-2, it is vendor-dependent whether any actions are triggered by this command and, if this is the case, which ones. Since the READ and WRITE commands explicitly position the head, the SEEK command is rarely needed.

WRITE SECTORS (30h with and 31h without retries)

This command behaves exactly like READ SECTORS, except that the data are written instead of read.

8.2   Optional commands

ACKNOWLEDGE MEDIA CHANGE (DBh)

This command applies only to changeable media. In ATA-1 it clears the MC bit in the error register. The operating system uses this to acknowledge that the media change has been recognized. In ATA-2 the action triggered by the command is vendor-specific.

BOOT – POST-BOOT (DCh)

This command applies only to changeable media. In ATA-2 the action triggered by the command is vendor-specific.

BOOT – PRE-BOOT (DDh)

This command applies only to changeable media. In ATA-2 the action triggered by the command is vendor-specific.

CHECK POWER MODE (98h, E5h)

With this command, the host can determine whether the drive is in an IDLE or STANDBY state. This is necessary since the drive can go to STANDBY on its own, which, under certain circumstances, can cause a delay of up to 30 seconds for the first command.

If the drive is in STANDBY or transitioning to this state, it replies with the value 00h in the sector count register. In the IDLE state, the drive replies with FFh in the sector count register.

DOOR LOCK (DEh) and DOOR UNLOCK (DFh)

These commands, which are for removable media drives, close and lock, and unlock and open the door. New in ATA-2: when the door is closed, the DOOR LOCK command returns a GOOD state if the button for manual door opening has not been operated. Otherwise, an error with the MCR bit set must be reported.

DOWNLOAD MICROCODE (92h)

This command is new in ATA-2. It allows you to modify the firmware of the device. The number of transferred bytes is a multiple of the sector length. The sector count register contains the upper bits, the sector number register the lower bits of the 16-bit data length counter. Thus, between 0 and 33 Mbytes (approximately) of firmware can be transferred. The feature register specifies how the new firmware is to be used: a value of 01h means that the firmware is to be used immediately and up to the next reset. A value of 07h specifies that the new firmware is used immediately and forever.

FORMAT TRACK (50h)

In ATA-2 this command is vendor-specific; no further assertions are made with regard to its implementation. Therefore I describe how it is implemented in ATA-1.

Although in ATA-1 the command is mandatory it is left to the manufacturer exactly what will be performed. Some drives format the track from scratch, others initialize only the data area of the sectors, others do nothing at all. The ATA standard recommends that drives should at least write the sector with a data pattern. In this way formatting will always erase all data, which is desirable for security reasons.

The command formats an entire track. The sector count register, the cylinder number register, and the drive/head register must be loaded with the address of the track, then 256 16-bit words must be transferred to the sector buffer. Afterwards, the drive sets BSY and executes the command.

The codes written to the sector buffer have the meaning shown in Table 8.3. Whether or not the drive uses these or instead uses its default parameters is up to the manufacturer.

A data word should be written to the sector buffer for each sector, with the remainder filled with 0s. Each data word contains the sector number in the upper byte. If an interleave is called for, it is suppressed. The lower byte holds the code that indicates how the sector should be formatted. Table 8.6 lists the possible codes.

Table 8.6 Codes for FORMAT TRACK.

Code	Format
00h	Format good sector
20h	Suspend reallocation
40h	Reallocate sector
80h	Mark sector defective

IDLE (97h, E3h)

This command is used to set the drive's standby timer. A timeout value can be provided in the sector count register. Its meaning is shown in Table 8.7. In ATA-1 the meaning was always value × 5 seconds.

Table 8.7 Values for the standby timer.

Sector count register	Timeout value
00h	Standby timer deactivated; pass directly into IDLE state
01h–F0h	Value × 5 seconds
F1h–FBh	(Value – F0h) × 30 minutes
FCh	21 minutes
FDh	Vendor-specific value between 8 and 12 hours
FEh	Reserved
FFh	21 minutes and 15 seconds

IDLE IMMEDIATE (95h, E1h)

This command puts the drive immediately into the IDLE state.

MEDIA EJECT (EDh)

This command is new in ATA-2. The drive terminates the current operation, spins down the medium and opens the door to allow access to the medium.

NOP (00h)

This command is new in ATA-2. It is needed to allow hosts that perform only 16-bit transfers to write the head register, since a 16-bit access automatically also writes the command register. The device must react to the NOP command as to any other unknown command, by aborting the command with an ABORTED COMMAND bit in the error register.

READ BUFFER (E4h)

This command functions differently to the READ command. It reads 512 bytes from the sector buffer without a disk access. The address register is therefore not used. Whatever is in the sector buffer will be read.

READ DMA (C8h with and C9h without retries)

This command functions like the other READ commands, except that the contents of the sector buffer will be read using DMA. It is therefore necessary for the host to set up the proper DMA channel.

READ DRIVE STATE (E9h)

This command exists only under ATA-1; it has been eliminated in ATA-2. Using this command the host can read the current status of the drive after a REST command. This status can then be sent back to the drive using the RESTORE DRIVE STATE command when the REST state is over.

READ LONG (22h with and 23h without retries)

Unlike the READ SECTORS command, READ LONG always reads only one sector. Not only is the data transferred, but also the ECC bytes of the sector. The ECC is not checked. In all other respects, including errors, the command executes identically to the READ SECTORS command. The format of the ECC bytes is vendor-specific. Some drives have difficulties with the transfer of ECC bytes. Therefore the slow PIO mode 0 must be used for this command.

READ MULTIPLE (C4h)

This command fuctions similarly to the READ SECTORS command. The difference is that instead of a single sector, blocks of several sectors are transferred without an interrupt occurring in between. The number of the sector must be given in the sector count register. Just how many sectors are to be included in a block is determined by the SET MULTIPLE MODE command. If the required sectors do not fit into the block size, an additional block (not fully used) will be transferred containing the remaining sectors.

RECALIBRATE (1xh)

All opcodes between 10h and 1Fh are interpreted as a RECALIBRATE command, whereupon the disk drive seeks track 0. If it is not found, TK0NF will be set in the error register. In ATA-1 RECALIBRATE was still a mandatory command. With modern drives, however, it has lost importance.

RECALIBRATE is often used when trying to recover from an error situation. For example, when a sector cannot be found, a RECALIBRATE should be tried. If this works, a sector access can be tried again. Otherwise, it is fatal disk error.

REST (E7h)

This command only exists in ATA-1; in ATA-2 it has been eliminated. The disk drive is put into the REST state which also no longer exists in ATA-2. It then waits for a READ DRIVE STATE command to be informed of its state before the execution of the last command. After this command is executed only the READ DRIVE STATE command will be accepted; all others will be rejected. If two drives are installed, first the slave drive then the master drive will be put into the REST state.

RESTORE DRIVE STATE (EAh)

This command only exists in ATA-1; in ATA-2 it has been eliminated. If a drive's status is collected and the drive is put into the REST state before being turned off this prior state can be restored at power-up using this command, assuming that it is the first command received after turning on. Bear in mind that the head position and the status of the controller are restored but that the contents of the sector buffer and cache are lost.

Table 8.8 Opcodes for SET FEATURES.

Opcode	Meaning
01h	Enable 8-bit data transfers
02h	Enable write cache
03h	Set transfer mode according to sector count register value (only ATA-2, 3)
(22h	Only ATA-1: WRITE SAME to write the specified area)
33h	Disable retries
44h	Vendor-specific ECC length for READ LONG and WRITE LONG
54h	Place number of cache segments in sector number register
55h	Disable read ahead
66h	Maintain parameters after software reset
77h	Disable ECC
81h	Disable 8-bit data transfers
82h	Disable write cache
88h	Enable ECC
99h	Enable retries
AAh	Enable read ahead
ABh	Use the value in the sector count register as the number of sectors to be read ahead
(ACh	Only ATA-1: allow REST mode)
BBh	4 bytes of ECC for READ LONG and WRITE LONG
CCh	Software reset loads default features
(DDh	Only ATA-1: WRITE SAME to write entire medium)

SET FEATURES (EFh)

This command enables the setting of various characteristics of the drive by writing a specific opcode in the feature register. Opcodes higher than 80h represent the default values after booting or a reset. Table 8.8 lists the opcodes. All unlisted opcodes are considered reserved. In ATA-2 all opcodes except the ones shown on a gray background are vendor-specific.

Opcode 03h which is new in ATA-2 is of particular interest. It is used to set the transfer mode by providing the sector count register with a parameter. The upper five bits specify the mode to be set and the lower three bits the value it assumes. The transfer mode parameters are listed in Table 8.9.

SET MULTIPLE MODE (C6h)

The block sizes for the commands READ MULTIPLE and WRITE MULTIPLE are given to the disk drive via the sector count register using this command. If the block size is not supported, or if it is 0, the multiple commands will be turned off.

Table 8.9 Transfer mode parameters for the SET FEATURES command.

Mode	Value	
PIO default transfer mode	00000	000
PIO default transfer mode, without IORDY	00000	001
PIO transfer mode with flow control, mode nnn	00001	nnn
Single-word DMA, mode nnn	00010	nnn
Multiple DMA, mode nnn	00100	nnn

In ATA-1, disk drives that have at least 8 KByte buffer must support at least block sizes 2, 4, 8, and 16. In ATA-2, disk drives must support the block size parameter word 47 of the IDENTIFY DEVICE command.

SLEEP (99h, E6h)

This command puts the drive in the SLEEP state. The motor will also be switched off. Only a hardware or software reset will end the SLEEP state.

STANDBY (96h, E2h) and STANDBY IMMEDIATE (94h, E0h)

This command puts the drive into STANDBY state. The STANDBY IMMEDIATE command is executed immediately. If the sector count register has a value other than 0 when the STANDBY command is issued, the standby timer is enabled.

WRITE BUFFER (E8h)

This command writes the sector buffer of the drive with a data pattern. No writing to the medium will occur.

WRITE DMA (CAh with and CBh without retries)

This command functions like the other WRITE commands except that the contents of the sector buffer are written using DMA. The host must initialize the proper DMA channel beforehand.

WRITE LONG (32h with and 33h without retries)

This command behaves exactly like the READ LONG command, except that the data are written instead of read. Here, the ECC must also be written to the sector buffer.

This is not trivial, since the ATA standard does not specify the sector format or how the ECC polynomial is to be computed. This command may be used when running system tests in order to produce an ECC error. A sector can be read using READ LONG, the data and ECC modified so as to reflect an ECC error, and the falsified sector rewritten using WRITE LONG. In this way, the error handling can be tested.

WRITE MULTIPLE (C5h)

This command functions analogously to the READ MULTIPLE command.

WRITE SAME (E9h)

Depending upon the mode set in the feature register, this command will write all or part of the medium with the same data. The feature register must previously be loaded with either 22h (for part of the medium) or DDh (for the entire medium) using the SET FEATURES command. Otherwise, the command will be rejected. The

ATA-2 standard discourages use of this command. (And it is no longer contained in the current ATA-3 proposal.)

WRITE VERIFY (3Ch)

This command functions like the WRITE SECTORS command, with the exception that the sectors are subsequently verified. During verification only the ECC is checked without a transfer of data. Any read errors are reported.

9 The ATAPI interface

You will probably be familiar with the ATAPI interface in connection with CD-ROM drives. However, although this interface is mainly used with CD-ROM drives, it is not limited to this application. Practically, ATAPI is a mixture of SCSI and IDE (ATA). The IDE interface and its protocol are used for transmission of both ATA and SCSI commands. Thus, in principle this extension allows you to control all devices for which a SCSI command set exists. For this purpose, the SCSI commands are wrapped into an ATA command; hence the name of the interface: ATA Packet Interface (ATAPI).

SFF

The ATAPI document is not elaborated and maintained directly by ANSI, but by the SFF (Small Form Factor) industry committee. The ATAPI document bears the number SFF-8020 and consists of parts SFF-8021 to SFF-8029.

The SFF committee calls itself an ad hoc group. Its declared goal is to define and document industry standards faster than the established organizations. However, SFF will hand over its finished documents to established organizations such as ANSI or EIA in order to have them published as separate standards or as parts of a superior standard. Currently incorporation of ATAPI into the SCSI-3 standard is under discussion.

About this chapter

The fact that ATAPI mainly employs the SCSI CD-ROM command set leads to a slight problem in the structure of this book. On the one hand, the SCSI chapter on device model, command set and parameters of SCSI CD-ROM drives appears later on in the book; on the other hand, I would like to spare you a double description of more or less the same issues. Therefore, in this chapter, I will put the emphasis on how the ATA mechanisms are used to transmit SCSI data. At the same time, I would like to ask you to refer to Chapters 12 on SCSI commands and 18 on multi-media devices during your reading of this chapter. Even if you do not wish to go into SCSI to the very last detail, you should read these chapters to gain an overview of those aspects that are relevant for understanding ATAPI.

9.1   ATAPI architecture

The ATAPI document quotes a number of goals underlying the ATAPI standard. The two most important ones are that a CD-ROM with ATAPI connection must not affect existing IDE disks and that it must be ensured that neither a PC BIOS nor any operating system recognize an ATAPI CD-ROM as a hard disk. CD-ROM and IDE disk must be able to coexist on one cable, and the IDE master/slave protocol must be supported.

Architecture

Figure 9.1 shows a good overview of how ATAPI fits into the ATA standards. ATAPI itself consists of the transport mechanism (TM), the transport protocol (TP) and the CD-ROM commands (CP).

ATAPI and ATA

ATAPI uses the same signals and the same timing as ATA-2. However, the ATAPI devices support a different command set; some commands are added and many ATA commands are omitted.

The most important new command is the ATAPI PACKET command which is used to transmit the SCSI-like command packets. These commands consist of the command packet, the command parameters, the command response and the status information. The command packet contains the command itself together with embedded flags and parameters. The command parameters are additional parameters, such as data to

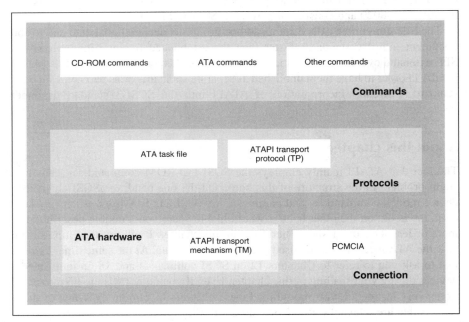

Figure 9.1 Block diagram of ATA and ATAPI standards.

be written. The command response consists of read user data or parameter information. The status information indicates whether the command has been executed successfully.

ATAPI and SCSI

Those of you who have already been concerned with SCSI will certainly find a summary of similarities and differences between ATAPI and SCSI quite interesting.

First of all, ATAPI uses many SCSI commands, the device model of the SCSI CD-ROM and its parameter pages. However, this is where the similarities end. The ATAPI version of the SCSI command has no LUN field and no control byte. Furthermore, the commands are always filled up to 12 bytes length, even if the corresponding SCSI command is a 6-byte or 10-byte command.

There are no bus phases and no messages. The status is not transmitted as a SCSI status byte, but is ATAPI specific. There is no arbitration, and the ATAPI device is always the slave device. There are no disconnect/reselect mechanisms, no command chains and no contingent allegiance status.

For some functions, both the ATA-2 and the SCSI command are allowed, because they offer slightly different possibilities. This applies to the ATA-2 commands DOOR LOCK and DOOR UNLOCK and their SCSI counterparts PREVENT/ALLOW MEDIA REMOVAL. The ATA-2 command IDENTIFY DRIVE supplies low level information, whereas the SCSI command INQUIRY supplies information on a higher level. The ATA-2 command SET FEATURES allows access to the ATA-specific properties. The SCSI commands MODE SENSE and MODE SELECT allow access to the parameters at device level.

9.2 ATAPI transport mechanism

The physical interface, that is signals, drivers and cable, are the same in ATAPI and ATA-2. The essential difference lies in the way in which the command register block (task file) is used in ATAPI commands.

Configuration

For the interplay of ATA-2 Enhanced IDE and ATAPI devices, the ATAPI standard proposes some preferred configurations which are listed in Table 9.1.

Table 9.1   Preferred ATAPI configurations.

Primary cable		Secondary cable (with E-IDE)		
Drive 0	*Drive 1*	*Drive 0*	*Drive 1*	*Remark*
ATA				Standard
ATA		ATAPI		Disk and CD-ROM in E-IDE
ATA	ATAPI			Disk and CD-ROM in IDE
ATA		ATAPI	ATAPI	Disk and 2 ATAPI devices in E-IDE

Table 9.2   ATAPI task file.

					Command register block	
	Addresses				*Name and function*	
CS0	CS1	DA2	DA1	DA0	*Read access*	*Write access*
1	0	0	0	0	Data register	
1	0	0	0	1	ATAPI error register	ATAPI feature register
1	0	0	1	0	ATAPI cause of interrupt	Not used
1	0	0	1	1	Reserved	
1	0	1	0	0	ATAPI byte count register (bits 0–7)	
1	0	1	0	1	ATAPI byte count register (bits 8–15)	
1	0	1	1	0	Drive select register	
1	0	1	1	1	ATAPI status register	Command register

					Control register block	
	Addresses				*Name and function*	
CS0	CS1	DA2	DA1	DA0	*Read access*	*Write access*
0	1	0	0	0	Not used	Not used
0	1	0	0	1	Not used	Not used
0	1	0	1	0	Not used	Not used
0	1	0	1	1	Not used	Not used
0	1	1	0	0	Not used	Not used
0	1	1	0	1	Not used	Not used
0	1	1	1	0	Alternative ATAPI Status register	Control register
0	1	1	1	1	Reserved	Not used

ATAPI task file

Register usage in the command register block (ATAPI task file) differs quite considerably between ATAPI and ATA. Table 9.2 shows the modified task file. The modified registers are described below. Please note that for normal ATA-2 commands, ATAPI devices too use the command register block as ATA task file.

The ATAPI status register

Essentially, the ATAPI status register corresponds to the ATA-2 status register. Only during overlapping ATAPI functions does the meaning of bit 5 and bit 6 change. Bit 5 becomes DMA READY and indicates that the device is ready to begin a DMA transfer. Bit 6 becomes SERVICE and indicates that the device is waiting for a SERVICE command.

The ATAPI error register

The ATAPI error register is shown in Table 9.3. The sense key field contains the SCSI sense key. The MCR and ABRT bits are used in the same way as in the ATA standard. EOM means that the end of the medium was detected. Finally, ILI indicates an illegal length.

The ATAPI feature register

The ATAPI feature register serves two purposes. In the ATA set features command it contains the feature code, whereas in the other commands it is used to set the

Table 9.3 ATAPI error register.

Bit	7	6	5	4	3	2	1	0
	Sense key				MCR	ABRT	EOM	ILI

ATAPI command features. Currently two bits are defined. Bit 0 is the DMA bit and means that the data for this command (not the command packet) is transmitted via DMA. Bit 1 is the OVERLAP bit which says that the device can release the interface before the command is terminated. Both ATAPI features are optional.

The cause of interrupt register

This register contains the cause of an interrupt, together with the DRQ bit of the status register. If the DRQ bit is not set, the status register contains a status. Otherwise, bits 0 and 1 have the following meaning: bit 0 is the COD bit (command or data). If it is set, a command is transmitted, otherwise data is transmitted. Bit 1 is the IO bit. If it is set, the information transfer goes to the host, otherwise it goes to the device. Bit 2 is the RELEASE bit which indicates that the device has released the IDE interface before the command was terminated.

The drive select register

The drive select register is structured in ATAPI in the same way as in ATA-2, except that bits 0–3 (ATA head select) are reserved. They might eventually be used in ATAPI to indicate the SCSI LUN number.

The ATAPI byte count register

This 16-bit register is used to specify the data length of command packets.

9.3 ATAPI transport protocol

The ATAPI transport protocol is all about the ATAPI PACKET command. As a matter of fact, this command functions in the same way as any other ATA-2 command insofar as it initializes the command register block, sets the drive bit and writes the command register. However, while in a normal ATA command data would be written with the first DRQ, here the command packet is written instead.

This command packet contains a SCSI-like command. After this, the procedure continues as with any other normal ATA command. The command packet is always written in PIO mode. The way the command packet is structured will be described further below in Section 9.4.

The ATAPI PACKET command (A0h)

The exact timing is shown in Figure 9.2 for a sample command with PIO-IN transfer. The other transfer modes function analogously.

● The host waits until BSY and DRQ are 0 and subsequently initializes the ATAPI task file. Then it writes the ATAPI PACKET opcode (A0h) into the command register.

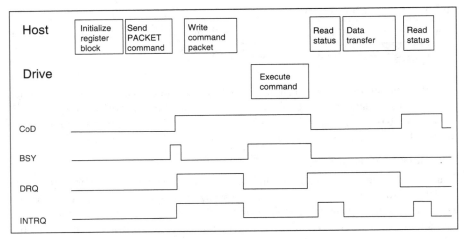

Figure 9.2 Timing of an ATAPI PACKET command.

- The device sets BSY and prepares to accept the command packet proper. When it is ready it sets COD and cancels IO. Then it sets DRQ and cancels BSY.

- As soon as it sees DRQ, the host writes the 12 command bytes into the data register. After having received the 12th byte, the device cancels DRQ, sets BSY and reads the features and the byte count from the task file.

- Let us now assume that we are dealing with a command packet which entails a data transfer to the host. The device executes the command and prepares for the data transfer.

- The device loads the byte count register, sets IO and cancels COD, sets DRQ and cancels BSY, and finally sets INTRQ.

- As soon as the host sees DRQ, it reads the status register. As a reaction, the device cancels INTRQ. The host reads the data register as many times as specified in the byte count register. When all data are read, the device negates DRQ.

- The device writes the final status into the status register, sets COD, IO and DRDY and cancels BSY and DRQ. Then it sets INTRQ.

- This is the signal for the host to read the final status and, if necessary, the error register.

Immediate commands

Immediate commands return a status immediately after command transmission, while the command is still being executed (hence their name). This kind of command, for example, is used to play CD audio tracks.

If during execution of an immediate command a new ATA command arrives, the immediate command is terminated and the new command is aborted with an ABRT error message in the error register. If a new ATAPI packet arrives while the previous one is still processed, both commands are aborted with a CHECK CONDITION status.

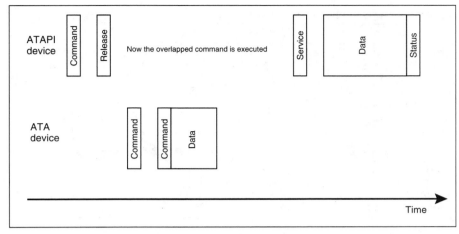

Figure 9.3 Example of overlapping ATAPI commands.

Overlapping commands

ATAPI can optionally support overlapping commands. A device that supports overlapping commands can release the IDE interface and the command register block after receiving an ATAPI command packet. While this device processes the command, the second device on the IDE interface can execute a command. The overlap mode is set via the feature register for each individual command packet. An ATAPI device may or may not release the interface at its discretion. The exact process is as follows (see Figure 9.3):

● The ATAPI device releases the interface after receiving an ATAPI command packet. It sets the RELEASE bit in the status and optionally triggers an interrupt.

● While the ATAPI device processes its command, the controller issues commands to the other connected drive.

● Since only the selected drive can generate interrupts, the controller must always select the ATAPI drive, provided the other device is not currently executing an overlapping command.

● The ATAPI device uses the SERVICE status and triggers an interrupt when it needs the interface again.

● Via a SERVICE command the driver returns control over interface and task file to the ATAPI device.

9.4 ATAPI commands

ATAPI CD-ROM drives support only part of the ATA-2 commands. These commands are listed in Table 9.4. Commands which do not exist in ATA-2 are shaded gray.

Table 9.4   ATA commands for ATAPI.

Command name	Opcode	ATAPI	ATA-2
ATAPI IDENTIFY DEVICE	A1h	M	–
ATAPI PACKET	A0h	M	–
ATAPI SOFT RESET	08h	M	–
CHECK POWER MODE	E5h	M	O
EXECUTE DRIVE DIAGNOSTIC	90h	M	M
IDLE	E3h	O	O
IDLE IMMEDIATE	E1h	M	O
NOP	00h	M	O
SERVICE	A2h	O	–
SET FEATURES	EFh	M	O
SLEEP	E6h	M	O
STANDBY	E2h	O	O
STANDBY IMMEDIATE	E0h	M	O

Table 9.5   ATAPI IDENTIFY parameters.

Word	ATAPI	ATAPI contents
0	M	Configuration word (see Table 9.6)
1–9	No	Reserved
10–19	O	Serial number (ASCII)
20–22	No	Reserved
23–26	M	Firmware revision (ASCII)
27–46	M	Model name (ASCII)
47–48	No	Reserved
49	M	Capabilities (see Table 9.7)
50	No	Reserved
51	M	Bits 15–8: timing mode for PIO data transfers
52	M	Bits 15–8: timing mode for DMA data transfers
53	M	Bit 0: words 54–58; bit 1: words 64–70 apply
54–61	No	Reserved
62	M	Bits 15–8: active mode for single DMA
		Bits 7–0: supported modes for single DMA
63	M	Bits 15–8: active mode for multiple DMA
		Bits 7–0: supported modes for multiple DMA
64	M	Bits 15–8: reserved
		Bits 7–0: reserved (supported modes for advanced PIO)
65	M	Minimum cycle time for multi-word DMA in ns
66	O	Recommended cycle time for multi-word DMA in ns
67	O	Minimum PIO cycle time without flow control
68	O	Minimum PIO cycle time with IORDY flow control
69–70	No	Reserved
71	O	Typical time in μs for interface release with an overlapping command
72	O	Typical time in μs for interface release with a SERVICE command
73	O	Revision number
74	O	Version number
75–255	No	Reserved

ATAPI IDENTIFY DEVICE (A1h)

This command functions in the same way as identify device in ATA-2, with the exception that only few parameter bytes are used from the parameter block and that their meaning sometimes differs from that in ATA-2. These bytes are shaded gray in Table 9.5.

The ATAPI configuration word is substantially different from the one of ATA-2. Bit 15 therefore indicates the format. If it is set, the configuration word is in ATAPI format, otherwise it is in ATA format.

Bits 0 and 1 specify the length of the command packet. A value of 00b means that the command packets are 12 bytes long. This is the case with all ATAPI CD-ROMs. A value of 01b stands for 16 byte long command packets. These packets are reserved for other device types.

Bits 5 and 6 indicate the DRQ mode. A value of 00b means that the device should set DRQ and fetch the command packet within 3 ms from receiving an ATAPI PACKET command. If the value is 10b, the same must happen within 50 µs. A value of 01b allows for 10 ms, but in this case the device must trigger an interrupt.

Bits 8 to 12 contain the device type as defined for the SCSI command inquiry. For a CD-ROM, this value must be 5h.

Table 9.6 ATAPI configuration word.

	7	6	5	4	3	2	1	0
0	Rem	DRQ type		Reserved			Packet size	
1	Protocol		Res.	Device type				

The capability word

The capability word differs only in one bit from the ATA-2 standard. Table 9.7 shows the capability word 49.

Table 9.7 ATAPI parameter word for device capabilities.

Bit	Meaning
0–7	Vendor-specific
8	DMA commands supported
9	LBA mode supported
10	IORDY may be deactivated
11	IORDY is supported
12	Reserved
13	Overlapping operations are supported
14	Reserved for proxy interrupt
15	Reserved for embedded DMA

ATAPI PACKET (A0h)

The ATAPI PACKET command functions in the same way as any other ATA-2 command. It initializes the command register block, sets the drive bit and writes the command register. However, whereas in a normal ATA command data would be written with the first DRQ, now a command packet is written. After this, processing continues as with any normal ATA command. The command packet is always written in PIO mode. The structure of the command will be described in Section 9.5.

ATAPI SOFT RESET (08h)

For CD-ROM drives, a reset is occasionally used to force recalibration and find a lost track. However, the ATA reset cannot be used for this purpose, since it would equally affect a hard disk connected to the same adapter. For this reason, the ATAPI SOFT RESET was introduced.

SERVICE (A2h)

The SERVICE command is used to restore the command register block of a device that had released the ATA interface.

SET FEATURES (EFh)

The SET FEATURES command works in the same way as in ATA-2. Only the codes that are used have a different meaning. They are listed in Table 9.8.

Table 9.8   Opcodes for ATAPI SET FEATURES.

Opcode	Meaning
03h	Set transfer mode according to sector count register value
5Dh	Allow interrupt after overlapping command
5Eh	Allow interrupt after SERVICE command
66h	Maintain parameters after software reset
CCh	Software reset loads default features
DDh	Prohibit interrupt after overlapping command
DEh	Prohibit interrupt after SERVICE command

9.5   CD-ROM command packets

This section should contain the description of the CD-ROM device model, all CD-ROM command packets and the parameter pages. You will, however, find extensive descriptions of these issues in Chapter 18 on multi-media devices.

At this point, we are only introducing a list of the commands (see Table 9.9) and present an example of how a SCSI command is converted into an ATAPI command packet.

Table 9.9 CD-ROM commands.

Opcode	Name	Type	Page	SCSI-2	ATAPI	Description
00h	TEST UNIT READY	M	131	7.2.16	10.8.26	Reflects whether or not the LUN is ready to accept a command
03h	REQUEST SENSE	M	132	7.2.14	10.8.20	Returns detailed error information
12h	INQUIRY	M	128	7.2.5	10.8.1	Returns LUN specific information
1Bh	START/STOP UNIT	M		8.2.17	10.8.25	Load/unload medium
1Eh	PREVENT/ALLOW MEDIUM REMOVAL	M		8.2.4	10.8.11	Lock/unlock door
25h	READ CD-ROM CAPACITY	M	239	13.2.8	10.8.14	Read number of logical blocks
28h	READ(10)	M	159	8.2.6	10.8.12	Read
2Bh	SEEK(10)	M		8.2.15	10.8.22	Seek LBN
42h	READ SUBCHANNEL	M		13.2.10	10.8.18	Read subchannel data and status
43h	READ TOC	M		13.2.11	10.8.19	Read contents table
45h	PLAY AUDIO(10)	O*	241	13.2.2	10.8.8	Audio playback
47h	PLAY AUDIO MSF	O*	241	13.2.4	10.8.9	Audio playback
4Bh	PAUSE/RESUME	O*		13.2.1	10.8.7	'Pause' button
4Eh	STOP/PLAY SCAN	M		–	10.8.24	Stop audio playback
55h	MODE SELECT(10)	M		7.2.9	10.8.4	Set device parameters
5Ah	MODE SENSE(10)	M		7.2.10	10.8.5	Read device parameters
A6h	LOAD/UNLOAD	O			10.8.2	Load/unload CD changer
A8h	READ(12)	M		15.2.4	10.8.13	Read data
B8h	SET CD-ROM SPEED	O		–	10.8.23	Set data rate
B9h	READ CD MSF	M		–	10.8.16	Read CD information (all formats, MFS addresses)
BAh	SCAN	O			10.8.23	Fast audio playback
BCh	PLAY CD	O			10.8.10	Play CD (universal)
BDh	MECHANISM STATUS	M			10.8.3	CD changer status
BEh	READ CD	M		–	10.8.15	Read CD information (all formats, LBN addresses)

Note: Commands included in this command set with SCSI-3 are shaded light gray; mandatory commands are marked dark gray. O* marks a play command; either all or none of these commands must be implemented.

The INQUIRY command

The INQUIRY command returns a complex data structure which supplies detailed information about a device. This data structure is extensively described in Section 12.3. Here we are only interested in the different command structures of the ATAPI command packet and the SCSI INQUIRY command (see Tables 9.10 and 9.11). This difference is characteristic of all commands.

The SCSI INQUIRY command is a 6-byte command. Since ATAPI command packets are always 12 bytes long, bytes 6 to 11 are filled with the value 'reserved' which, in practice, is 00h.

In SCSI, byte 5 is the control byte. In ATAPI it is omitted and equally reserved. The three higher order bits in byte 1 specify the LUN number in SCSI-1. They too are reserved, because LUNs do not (yet) exist in ATAPI.

The remainder of the command is the same for both ATAPI and SCSI.

Table 9.10   SCSI version of the INQUIRY command.

	7	6	5	4	3	2	1	0
0	INQUIRY(12h)							
1	(LUN)			Reserved				EVDP
2	Page code							
3	Reserved							
4	Data length							
5	Control byte							

Table 9.11   ATAPI version of the INQUIRY command.

	7	6	5	4	3	2	1	0
0	INQUIRY(12h)							
1	Reserved							EVDP
2	Page code							
3	Reserved							
4	Data length							
5	Reserved							
6								
7								
8								
9								
10								
11								

General rule

By following this rule – removing control byte and LUN number and filling the command up to 12 bytes – you can roughly convert any supported SCSI command into an ATAPI command. However, minor differences are possible. Some ATAPI commands do not support all options offered by SCSI. Thus, if you need to be really sure, you should consult the original document.

Part III
The SCSI bus

10   Introduction
11   SCSI architecture
12   SCSI primary commands
13   Block-oriented devices
14   Stream-oriented devices
15   Graphics devices
16   Medium-changer devices
17   Storage array controllers
18   Multi-media devices
19   The parallel SCSI interface
20   SCSI interlock protocol
21   The new SCSI-3 interfaces
22   The ASPI software interface
23   The SCSI monitor program
24   Measuring and testing
25   SCSI chips

10 Introduction

10.1 The evolution of SCSI

SCSI, which the entire industry affectionately pronounces as 'scuzzy', stands for Small Computer Systems Interface. SCSI can trace its beginnings back to 1979, when the disk drive manufacturer Shugart began work on a new interface. The goal was to develop a drive interface that supported logical addressing of data blocks instead of physical addressing of cylinders, heads and sectors. Moreover, the interface would present data byte-wise instead of serially. Such an interface could end the compatibility problems associated with bringing new drive technologies to market. In the past it took a long time for computer companies to support the new drives. The new interface would allow computer manufacturers to develop hard disk drivers that were able to recognize the properties of the connected disk drives themselves. This interface was originally called SASI (Shugart Associates Systems Interface), and the specification totaled 20 pages.

SASI

SASI is the forerunner of the modern SCSI. The interface specification, which included some 6-byte commands and defined single-ended drivers and receivers, was made public to encourage companies to build SASI controllers. Companies such as OMTI and DTC became involved in these early days. In 1980, Shugart's first attempt to make SASI an ANSI standard failed. At that time ANSI preferred the more sophisticated IPI interface.

Progress began in 1981, but not before a failed agreement between NCR and Shugart to work together on further development of SASI. NCR wanted 10-byte commands and a differential interface, features Shugart considered unnecessary. Most likely Shugart believed that these options would make the interface too complicated. At this point the company Optimem came on the scene. A subsidiary of Shugart, Optimem manufactured optical disks. They needed to be able to address more than 2^{21} logical blocks for their optical drives. Moreover, the 6 meter cables then in use were too short. These were precisely the reasons why Shugart had declined to work with NCR in the first place. In December 1981, Shugart, together with NCR, requested that an ANSI committee be formed for SASI.

SCSI-1

In April 1982 ANSI committee X3T9.2 met for the first time and began the work that has evolved into SCSI. In the following years a draft proposal was prepared, which was presented to ANSI for approval in 1984. However, even before final approval had been given, manufacturers began producing SCSI host adapters and device controllers. The first protocol chip, the NCR 5385, came on the market in 1983. The interface had become an industry standard long before it received approval from ANSI. In June 1986, SCSI-1 became official as ANSI X3.131-1986.

The growing number of SCSI products exposed weak points in the definition. In defining commands, too much room for variation was given for vendor unique options. For example, format parameters for disk drives were not standardized. In addition, although a SCSI drive should present a virtual defect free medium to the host – by having medium defects managed transparently by the device – defect management was left undefined. Consequently, each manufacturer implemented these things as they saw fit, which basically meant that a new device driver had to be written for each new SCSI device. The goal of a device independent interface was definitely lacking on the software side. At that time it was fair to say that SCSI was not necessarily SCSI compatible.

CCS

Looking for a solution to this problem, the drive specialists in the committee began defining a Common Command Set (CCS) for disk drives in 1985. The main purpose of the command set was to nail down some of the many options for disk drives. Among the features introduced in the CCS was the defect list format, and the introduction of the mode parameter listing. The CCS was a big step forward and once again the manufacturers began implementing it before it became official. However, CCS was only a solution for disk drives; tape drive manufacturers had to make do with SCSI-1 the way it was.

SCSI-2

In 1986, even before SCSI-1 had become an official standard, work on SCSI-2 began. In addition to further development of the CCS and the other device classes, the committee worked on numerous modifications in protocol and hardware. Many features were developed, only to be discarded in the end. The option to support more than eight devices is an example of this. On the other hand, 10 MHz synchronous transfers were incorporated along with a 32-bit wide data bus. Of course, the real challenge in the implementation of these options lay in maintaining compatibility among the different devices. As a protocol option, a device could inform a host 'unsolicited' of change in device status. This is important, for example, when a cassette is removed from a tape drive.

The formal approval procedure for SCSI-2 began in February 1989. As usual, there were dozens of devices already equipped with SCSI-2 before it became a standard. These early releases, incidentally, were never a problem. During the final phases of development the standard had become so stable that only minor changes were being discussed. Above all, tape drive manufacturers were anxious to implement SCSI-2 for their devices. However, organizational changes in ANSI caused the early 1992 delivery date to be postponed several times. In January 1994, SCSI-2 became official as ANSI X3.131-1994.

Presently (1997) SCSI-2 has reached its climax, with general support from both peripherals and computer manufacturers. The only serious competitor is the IDE interface for disk drives in PCs. Both for its functionality and its throughput, SCSI-2 is suited to cover the demands of the next few years.

SCSI-3

However, for several years now, the ANSI SCSI committee has been working on SCSI-3. Following the tradition, SCSI-3 will be compatible with SCSI-2. Amongst others, SCSI-3 provides a more clearly structured documentation and a modular structure. Figure 10.1 shows this new structure which is also reflected in the structure of this book. The shaded modules are already present in SCSI-2.

In the physical and protocol area, SCSI-3 defines in particular the new Fibre Channel, SSA and IEEE P1394 interfaces. The idea to use the SCSI protocol to communicate across any regular serial interface has been removed from the standard proposal. It is now documented in a technical report.

The present parallel interface has been further developed so that SCSI-3 now allows transfer rates of up to 20 megatransfers per second and up to 32 SCSI devices with 32-bit wide SCSI. The new P cable allows you to employ 16-bit wide SCSI with only one cable. These changes have been impatiently expected by industry and users alike. Thus, once again before a standard has become official, there are already many devices on the market that support one or more of these new features.

The principal change with regard to the commands is the structuring of the documentation. In particular, the command sets for 'exotic' SCSI devices are becoming more complete. Furthermore, at least one new device type is added: the controller devices for RAID controllers.

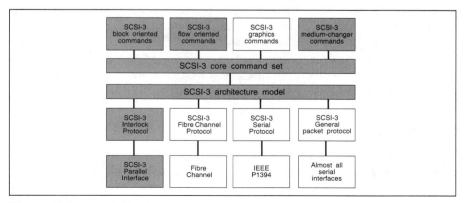

Figure 10.1   The SCSI-3 architecture.

To summarize, SCSI-3 introduces a new view of SCSI. Emphasis is no longer put on the physical connection via the parallel interface and its protocol, but on the device type and its command set. Maybe the new serial interfaces will eventually supersede today's SCSI interface. This will, however, only have minimal effects on operating system software and applications. The market penetration and functionality presently reached by SCSI device types and command sets will ensure SCSI's survival for many years to come.

In 1991, Dal Allan, a SCSI industry specialist, wrote in an article for the magazine *Computer Technology Review*:

> No technical rationale can be offered as to why SCSI-1 ended and SCSI-2 began, or as to why SCSI-2 ended and SCSI-3 began. The justification is much more simple – you have to stop sometime and get a standard printed. Popular interfaces never stop evolving, adapting, and expanding to meet more uses than originally envisaged.

10.2   Overview

I begin with a broad overview of SCSI. Everything discussed here will be gone over in greater detail later in the book. If you are only interested in particular aspects of SCSI, read this section first, then use the index to find specific topics.

SCSI is a device-independent I/O subsystem

SCSI is a device-independent I/O subsystem, allowing a variety of devices to be linked to a computer system. The electrical characteristics and protocol of the SCSI bus were designed with the requirements of peripheral devices in mind. Device-independent means that in order to connect such devices, no specific knowledge of the properties of the devices is needed. SCSI makes available a number of commands for querying a device about necessary parameters. This makes it possible to write device drivers for a device without knowing device-specific details.

SCSI offers high-level functionality. The entire device-specific intelligence resides in the SCSI peripheral device, especially in the case of disk drives. Firstly, data is addressed via logical block numbers. The host need not concern itself with the exact physical organization of the drive. Complex operations, such as formatting the entire disk, are triggered by a single SCSI command. Moreover, a SCSI drive can manage defects autonomously, making it possible to present a virtually defect-free medium to the host.

SCSI devices

Up to eight devices can be addressed using the parallel SCSI-2 bus. With SCSI-3 this number can be greater depending on the physical interface. The SCSI bus address of a device is referred to as the SCSI ID. These devices play the role of either an initiator or a target.

Initiator and target

An initiator is a device that triggers a task on the SCSI bus. A target is a device that carries out the task. The SCSI host adapter of a computer is a typical initiator; a disk drive is a typical target. The specification does not specify the number of initiators and targets that can be installed in a SCSI configuration. Only the total number is limited depending on the SCSI version. Obviously, a minimal sensible configuration must contain at least one initiator and one target. It is worth noting that some devices can play the role of both a target and an initiator. However, for each individual I/O process, it is clearly defined which is the initiator and which is the target.

Host adapter and SCSI controller

Figure 10.2 introduces two more terms that have a particular meaning in the SCSI world. A computer system is connected to the SCSI bus through a host adapter. For a peripheral device the corresponding role is played by a controller. This SCSI specific terminology can be confusing because in other computer domains – for example, the IDE interface – a controller often connects a peripheral directly to a computer. Both controllers and host adapters can be either implemented as a separate board or integrated into the device or system. Host adapters often reside directly on the mother board of workstations and modern personal computers, in which case they are referred to as embedded host adapters. PC compatibles use the insertable card variation. SCSI controllers are usually embedded in the drive electronics of disk drives.

Bridge controller

When the controller is implemented on a separate board and the physical devices are connected to it via a device-specific interface, it is referred to as a bridge controller. Bridge controllers were often used with new peripheral devices which were not yet

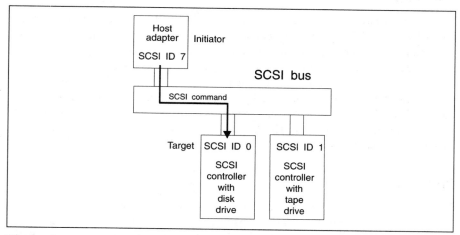

Figure 10.2   A simple SCSI configuration.

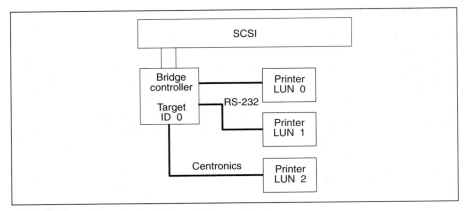

Figure 10.3 Bridge controller with logical units.

available with SCSI. Today intelligent bridge controllers are used in applications such as RAID arrays, which make several drives act as one powerful SCSI drive. In this case, SCSI is often also used as the interface between the bridge controller and the drives of the array.

LUNs

Figure 10.3 shows a bridge controller connecting a Centronics printer to the SCSI bus. Yet another application of bridge controllers takes advantage of the eight logical units (LUNs) that SCSI allows for each device. In this case each LUN can represent a separate peripheral device. Such a controller must possess a number of device specific interfaces, one for each LUN.

The parallel SCSI bus

Up to now we have focused on SCSI devices, not on the bus itself. The parallel SCSI bus is from 8 to 32 bits wide, depending on configuration. A simple 50-pin ribbon cable can be used for the 8-bit bus, including all other necessary control signals. The 16- and 32-bit variations introduced with SCSI-2 are called Wide SCSI and call for an additional cable. Naturally, any device that supports Wide SCSI must also have a second connector. With SCSI-3 the 68-pin P cable was introduced which also allows 16-bit Wide SCSI on a single cable. Wide SCSI is optional and is ever more prevailing with hard disk drives. The advantages are evident; using the same clock frequency, the bandwidth of 16-bit SCSI is twice that of 8-bit SCSI.

Protocol

Commands, messages and data are sent across the parallel SCSI bus exclusively using asynchronous transfers. This means that the sender and receiver exchange data using a request/acknowledge handshake. This allows devices that process the SCSI protocol at different speeds to use the same bus. Asynchronous transfers can reach a

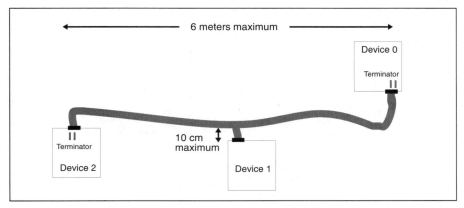

Figure 10.4 SCSI cable.

maximum of approximately 3 MHz. Additionally, there exists the option to transfer data synchronously, which under SCSI-2 allows devices to exchange data at speeds of up to 10 MHz. With SCSI-3 the Fast-20 mode with a 20 MHz clock frequency was introduced. It is, however, subject to restrictions in cable length. Whether or not and at which speed synchronous transfers will be used is negotiated by the two devices beforehand. This allows SCSI-1, SCSI-2 and SCSI-3 devices to operate on the same bus without compatibility problems.

Cabling

Currently, there are a large number of different cables for connecting SCSI devices. The most widely used cable is still the 50-pin ribbon cable. It is also called internal SCSI cable because it is only designed for connections inside a computer cabinet. It runs from device to device and must not have any derivations. This is important to mention since in the schematic drawings, including those in this book, it always looks as though the connections of the individual devices were branching off a main SCSI cable. Since most SCSI devices have only a single SCSI connector, a cable is used that has the appropriate number of connectors crimped along its length (see Figure 10.4).

Termination

The devices on the extreme ends of the bus – and no other devices – must have terminating resistors. On internal SCSI buses, these terminators are usually socketed inside the devices in question.

Single-ended or differential

There are two fundamentally different variations on the type of electrical signals used for the bus: single-ended and differential. These variations are not compatible with each other. Devices with single-ended and differential interfaces cannot be used

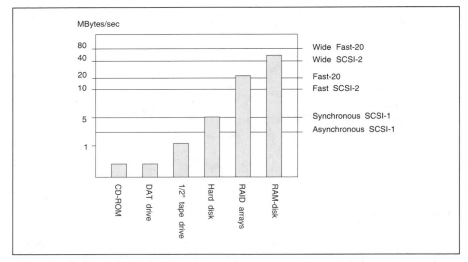

Figure 10.5 SCSI transfer rates.

on the same bus, although they can use the same type of cable. Before configuring a system, the decision must be made as to what type of interface will be used. This choice is made somewhat easier by the fact that most devices are only available with single-ended SCSI.

Single-ended SCSI uses open-collector drivers to power the bus. One advantage of this is that the drivers can usually withstand an improperly inserted connector. There is no reason to panic if you accidentally insert a connector the wrong way: I've done this a number of times and haven't damaged a device yet! The pin assignments are such that a ground is opposite every signal. In addition to flat cable, twisted-pair cables can also be used.

Differential drivers allow cable lengths beyond the 6 meters of the single-ended drivers, up to 25 meters. Since so few devices come with a differential interface, single-ended to differential converters have appeared on the market.

Summary of hardware options

Many terms have been introduced in the preceding section. Here they are brought together in one place. These are the terms that you will find in SCSI product manuals (Figure 10.5):

- **Asynchronous SCSI:** This method of data transfer is basic to all SCSI devices. The transfer rate is normally around 1.5 MHz although modern chips are capable of 3–4 MHz.

- **Synchronous SCSI:** This optional method of data transfer makes possible rates of 5 MHz. Since commands and other protocol related information are sent asynchronously, devices are able to negotiate which method will be used. Devices that use this option and those that do not can function side by side on the same bus. The synchronous option is found on most high performance devices.

- **Fast SCSI:** An improvement to synchronous transfers for SCSI-2 devices allowing a data rate up to 10 MHz. Today, fast SCSI has become the standard for disk drives.

- **Wide SCSI:** 16- or 32-bit transfers are made possible with an additional cable (B cable) or with the new SCSI-3 P cable. The resulting data rate is double or quadruple the previous rate. This SCSI-2 option also allows a mix of device types on a single bus. 8-bit devices are simply not connected to the additional signal lines. With the new P cable, 16-bit wide SCSI is becoming ever more popular particularly for disk drives.

- **Single-ended/differential:** These two variations on the implementation of the electrical signals were already part of the original SCSI definition. The vast majority of devices employ a single-ended interface. Here the maximum cable length is 6 meters. The differential option allows cable lengths up to 25 meters. Single-ended and differential devices cannot be used together on the same bus.

Device types and commands

A well-defined command set is an important element of a device independent I/O subsystem. With respect to SCSI, device independence takes on two dimensions. On the one hand, there are the ten SCSI device types, of which hard disks and tape drives are two examples. Each type defines a specific model and command set for the devices of that type. On the other hand, a number of different physical devices can be supported by a single device type. One component of a device model is a set of parameters that allows you to define or specify the exact features of the individual device. For example, the maximum storage capacity of a disk drive is fixed, whereas the length of a data block can be individually specified.

In principle, transactions take place on the SCSI bus in the following manner: an initiator sends a command to a target, and the target carries out the command and afterwards informs the initiator of the outcome. The nature of SCSI commands gives a great deal of autonomy to the device carrying out the command. In this way an initiator can send a SCSI floppy drive a FORMAT UNIT command and relinquish complete control to the drive. When the formatting is finished, the initiator is merely informed of success or failure.

Another example of device autonomy is the READ command for disk drives. The initiator instructs the target to fetch a certain number of blocks starting at a particular block number. The target calculates a physical address of cylinder, head, and sector number from the logical block number and sends the data to the initiator. An important difference with the SCSI interface is that this data is strictly usable information – no headers, no ECC, no gaps. All of these ancillary fields are managed by the target alone. This is important because different devices use completely different formats to store information on the medium. This also explains how it is possible to produce a very inexpensive host adapter capable of controlling up to seven different devices. The intelligence is located in the devices, not in the host adapter.

SCSI makes available a number of commands for general interrogation of devices on the SCSI bus. A possible scenario could begin with a host looking to see which

SCSI IDs are occupied. Afterwards, the host can determine what types of devices are located at those IDs. Finally, device specific commands can be used to gather detailed information about each device. A device driver can be written in just this way without knowing the specific details of the device.

Evolution of the command sets

- **SCSI-1**   The SCSI-1 standard originally contained many commands that have remained unchanged in SCSI-2. SCSI-1 also left many parameters vendor unique or unspecified, which sidestepped the original intent of the standard. The result was that practically every device needed its own slightly different device driver. This complicated the goal of device independent software. It was at this point that many people felt that SCSI simply was not SCSI compatible, a feeling that today has rightly disappeared.

- **CCS**   The CCS supplement to SCSI-1, which became an official part of SCSI-2, had the aim of further standardizing the hard disk command set. The CCS introduced the concept of mode parameter pages for the MODE SELECT command and defined a set of defect list formats. Tape drives and other device types, however, were not included in the CCS. These had to make do with SCSI-1 as it was originally formulated.

- **SCSI-2**   Finally, a very significant step forward was made in the definition of SCSI-2. In SCSI-2, a model is defined for every device type. Moreover, the same level of detail used in the CCS for disk drives was used in defining the other device types. It is worth noting that the first SCSI implementations were for streamer tape devices. It is fair to say that the goal of a device independent I/O subsystem was reached with SCSI-2.

- **SCSI-3**   At command level, SCSI-3 will not provide too many novelties. However, the documentation has been completely restructured. One important new feature will probably be a command set for RAID controllers.

To conclude, SCSI-1 no longer plays a role with new devices; thus, you should watch out for a SCSI-2 implementation in all devices. SCSI-3 is still under development and is not supposed to bring dramatic changes in the command sets of most devices.

10.3   Documentation

One goal of this book, in addition to providing a thorough overview of SCSI, is to give enough detailed information to make possible the undertaking of simple SCSI projects without the need of additional documentation. Naturally, if you wish to take advantage of the vendor specific features of a certain device, you will need that device's SCSI manual. For example, the optional commands and parameter pages can be found there.

If you are interested in working with SCSI at a professional level, you cannot avoid getting a copy of the original ANSI documentation in addition to this book. A project involving writing firmware for a SCSI target or host adapter would be of this magnitude, as would writing a software driver that used more than simply READ and WRITE commands. Copies of the standard may be ordered from:

Global Engineering Documents,
2805 McGaw,
Irvine, CA 92714, USA
Telephone: 1-800-854-7179

The SCSI-2 document is called X3.131-1994. If you still need a copy of the SCSI-1 standard, the name is X3.131-1986.

You can also download the SCSI documentation from the SCSI Bulletin Board. The telephone number and the procedure are described in detail in Appendix D.

The organization of the SCSI-2 standard

The SCSI-2 standard is a document of about 600 pages, which is organized in the following way:

1 Scope
2 Reference standards and organizations
3 Glossary and conventions
4 Physical characteristics
    4.1   Physical description
    4.2   Cable requirements
    4.3   Connector requirements
    4.4   Electrical description
    4.5   SCSI bus
    4.6   SCSI bus signals
    4.7   SCSI bus timing
    4.8   Fast synchronous transfer option
5 Logical characteristics
    5.1   SCSI bus phases
    5.2   SCSI bus conditions
    5.3   SCSI phase sequences
    5.4   SCSI pointers
    5.5   Message system description
    5.6   SCSI messages
6 SCSI commands and status
    6.1   Command implementation requirements
    6.2   Command descriptor block
    6.3   Status
    6.4   Command examples
    6.5   Command processing considerations and exception conditions
    6.6   Contingent allegiance condition

6.7	Extended contingent allegiance condition
6.8	Queued I/O processes
6.9	Unit attention condition

Sections 7 to 17 of the standard deal with the individual device types. They are all organized in the same way: first comes a description of the device model of the type, followed by a summary of commands, and finally the MODE parameters for the type.

7	All device types
8	Direct-access devices
9	Sequential-access devices
10	Printers
11	Processor devices
12	WORM
13	CD-ROM
14	Scanners
15	Optical memory devices
16	Medium-changer devices
17	Communication devices
A–J	Appendices

Figure 10.6 shows a page from the actual SCSI documentation. Many drive manufacturers organize their own manuals in a similar manner, including, naturally, only those chapters which are relevant for a given device. The result is that once you are familiar with the ANSI specification, it is very easy to find your way around in SCSI manuals in general. If you know one – you know them all. This makes it easy to concentrate on important things, namely, implementation details.

The organization of the SCSI-3 standard

As shown in Figure 10.1, the SCSI-3 standard is divided into many individual documents, in particular:

- SCSI-3 Architecture Model   SAM   [X3T10/994-D]
- SCSI-3 Block Commands   SBC   [X3T10/996-D]
- SCSI-3 Stream Commands   SSC   [X3T10/997-D]
- SCSI-3 Graphics Commands   SGC   [X3T10/998-D]
- SCSI-3 Medium Changer Commands   SMC   [X3T10/999-D]
- SCSI-3 Controller Commands   SCC   [X3T10/1047-D]
- SCSI-3 Multimedia Commands   MMC   [X3T10/1048-D]
- SCSI-3 Primary Commands   SPC   [X3T10/995-D]
- SCSI-3 Parallel Interface   SPI   [X3T10/855-D]
- SCSI-3 Interlocked Protocol   SIP   [X3T10/856-D]
- SCSI-3 Serial Bus Protocol   SBP   [X3T10/992-D]
- SCSI-3 Fibre Channel Protocol   FCP   [X3T10/993-D]

```
 All Device Types                                          3/9/90

 7.2.5 INQUIRY Command

                    Table 7-14: INQUIRY Command

 ================================================================
 | Bit|  7    |  6    |  5    |  4    |  3    |  2    |  1    |  0  |
 |Byte|       |       |       |       |       |       |       |     |
 ================================================================
 |0   |                     Operation Code (12h)                 |

 |1   |  Logical Unit Number  |         Reserved          |EVPD|

 |2   |                        Page Code                        |

 |3   |                        Reserved                         |

 |4   |                    Allocation Length                    |

 |5   |                        Control                          |
 ================================================================
```

> The INQUIRY command (Table 7-14) requests that information re-
> garding parameters of the target and its attached peripheral de-
> vice(s) be sent to the initiator. An option allows the initiator
> to request additional information about the target or logical unit
> (see 7.2.5.2).
>   An enable vital product data (EVPD) bit of one specifies that
> the target shall return the optional vital product data specified by
> the page code field. If the target does not support vital product
> data and this bit is set to one, the target shall return
> CHECK CONDITION status with the sense key set to ILLEGAL REQUEST
> and an additional sense code of INVALID FIELD IN CDB.
>   An EVPD bit of zero specifies that the target shall return the
> standard INQUIRY data. If the page code field is not zero, the tar-
> get shall return CHECK CONDITION status with the sense key set to
> ILLEGAL REQUEST and an additional sense code of INVALID FIELD
> IN CDB.
>   The page code field specifies which page of vital product data
> information the target shall return (see 7.3.4).
>   The INQUIRY command shall return CHECK CONDITION status only
> when the target cannot return the requested INQUIRY data.

Figure 10.6   Sample page from the SCSI-2 standard.

These documents are associated with three layers. The link layer describes the physical interface, and the protocol layer describes the corresponding protocol. There is a 1:1 correspondence between the interfaces defined up to now and their protocols. The command layer describes the device models and the commands for the different device types.

SAM

The SCSI-3 Architecture Model is the basis for all other SCSI documents. People who already know the SCSI-2 standard may have some problems in getting used to the SAM document because it is entirely written in an object-oriented notation. It describes well-known SCSI terms such as initiator and target, but also new ones such as the SCSI domain. Many old terms have been generalized and extended. Also the properties of certain elements have been dimensioned for the future: counters such as SCSI ID and LUN are now 64 bits wide. Only the individual protocols then limit these values in various ways.

SPC

The SCSI-3 primary commands (SPC) set defines the behavior and the commands that are common to all SCSI-3 devices.

SBC, SSC, ...

Currently, the SCSI-3 standard has six different command sets. The most important ones are the block-oriented commands (SBC) for hard disks and similar devices, and the stream-oriented commands (SSC) for magnetic tapes and printers.

SIP and SPI

The parallel SCSI-3 interface is described by the interlock protocol (SIP) and the parallel interface (SPI). It is both an improvement and an extension of the well-known SCSI-2 interface. The Fast-20 standard which allows transfer rates of up to 20 Megatransfers per second is currently described in a separate document (X3T10/1071-D).

FCP and FCP-PH

This pair of documents describes SCSI via Fibre Channel. The Fibre Channel protocol (FCP) is a document of the X3T10 committee. The FCP-PH document describes the physical level of Fibre Channel and is issued by the ANSI X3T11 committee.

SBP and 1394

IEEE 1394 is the official name of 'Fire Wire', a serial bus favored amongst others by Apple. This standard is managed and maintained by the IEEE. Only the serial bus protocol (SBP) belongs to the SCSI committee.

SSP and SSA

These two documents describe a further approach of a serial interface which is favored mainly by IBM.

Until now, the parallel interface is the only tangible alternative. SCSI over Fibre Channel, Fire Wire and SSA are all at project stage. Whether or not they will be finalized and which of the three is going to succeed is a completely open question.

11 SCSI architecture

11.1 The SCSI architecture model

The present chapter on SCSI architecture is new in the second edition of this book. This may seem surprising since SCSI has always had something like an architecture. True, but only since SCSI-3 is this architecture explicitly described.

On the other hand, you can currently buy practically no SCSI-3 products. This may change very quickly, but this edition of the book is quite rightly still based on the SCSI-2 standard. However, the changes SCSI-3 will bring are extensively described in many places.

Thus, in this chapter I will try to be a contortionist, because I will be describing the architecture of SCSI-2 in terms that are used in the SCSI-3 architecture. This will facilitate the understanding of the following chapters, because the SCSI-3 architecture is very clear. Furthermore, it will make the transition to SCSI-3 much easier. SCSI-3 mostly presents issues already known from SCSI-2, but from a different point of view; however, where new extensions are introduced, they too will be extensively discussed in this chapter.

The SCSI-3 documentation contains a separate document which describes the architecture of SCSI-3. The *SCSI-3 Architecture Model* (SAM) X3T9.2/994D is the basis of all other SCSI-3 documents.

Why do we need an architecture model?

The SCSI architecture is an abstract model of a SCSI I/O system. A real-life implementation will not necessarily look like this model. On the other hand, however, each SCSI implementation must be realized in such a way that the rules of this model are not violated.

The SAM document itself defines its task as follows: SAM defines the functional groups and specifies a model of the behavior of SCSI-3 I/O systems and devices which applies to all SCSI interfaces, protocols, access methods and devices.

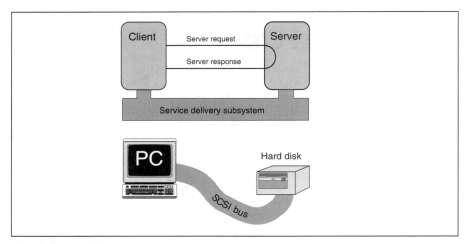

Figure 11.1   Client–server model.

Client–server model

The client–server model is a good way to represent a SCSI system. The client sends a request to the server. The server answers with a response. Both use the Service Delivery Subsystem (SDS) as a transport medium.

Thus, in the personal computer world, a PC is the client and its SCSI hard disk the server. The PC sends a read request to the disk; the disk carries it out and returns the data. As SDS, both use the parallel SCSI-2 bus.

For example, a PC might issue the request 'Send me 10 blocks of data starting with block number 312'.

The disk first converts the block number into a physical address of cylinder, head and sector numbers. Then it checks whether this address is legal. Furthermore, it checks whether the other requested blocks lie inside the capacity limits. Then it starts moving the read/write head. When this is positioned over the correct cylinder, it waits until the required sector passes. Then it starts the reading process, separating header information, CRC and ECC from the data proper. If needed, several reading attempts are made. Only after the first block has been completely read, the disk starts to transmit it to the client.

The client must only know how to communicate via the SCSI bus and which commands are understood by a block-oriented device. These details are specified in the SCSI standard.

All device-dependent information – where a logical block can be physically found on the disk, how the data is coded on the medium, what has to be done in case of error and so on – is known by the server, that is, the SCSI disk drive. This information is manufacturer-dependent, frequently even model-dependent. Thus, SCSI separates device-specific from general issues, offering the user the freedom to employ his/her favorite peripheral devices. Device manufacturers, on the other hand, can implement the functionality in the way they deem to be the best. This allows

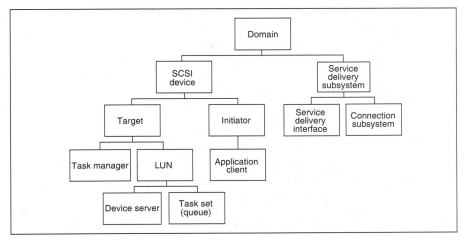

Figure 11.2   SCSI object hierarchy.

easy introduction of technological progress, for example a new recording method for magnetic disks, without causing changes for the end-user.

Structural model

The SCSI-3 structural model consists of a hierarchy of objects. At the top stands the domain which represents the I/O system. A SCSI domain structural model consists of SCSI devices linked by an abstract service delivery subsystem. Figure 11.2 shows the complete SCSI-3 object hierarchy. All components already exist in SCSI-2. The following section will discuss the individual function groups in more detail.

You may find this structural model rather complicated, particularly if you already know something about SCSI-2. But if you find yourself in the situation where you are writing firmware for a SCSI target, this structural model relieves you from a lot of planning work. You simply implement all objects of this structural model as modules into your firmware. Task and task set are data structures; the task manager manages these structures; and the device server executes the SCSI commands.

Obviously, you can also represent all elements of SCSI-2 in this model. Thus, if you use this model now to implement a SCSI-2 target, the transition to SCSI-3 will be relatively easy.

The SCSI domain

A SCSI domain is a self-contained SCSI I/O system, for example a SCSI-2 bus connected to a host adapter and two hard disks. The correct definition of the SCSI domain is: a SCSI domain is an I/O system consisting of several SCSI devices which communicate with each other via a service delivery subsystem.

You will certainly have an intuitive idea of a SCSI device. It is a host or an I/O device that uses SCSI commands.

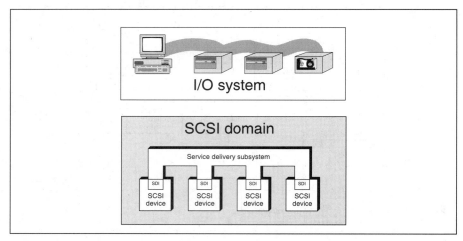

Figure 11.3   SCSI domain.

The service delivery subsystem

In the narrower sense of SCSI-2, the service delivery subsystem (SDS) is the SCSI bus. The SAM generalizes this to a system that consists of a connection subsystem and at least two service delivery interfaces (SDI). Its task is the error-free transmission of requests and responses between client and server. The connection subsystem is the physical bus with its cables, connectors and electrical properties. The service delivery interfaces represent the corresponding protocol.

The SCSI-2 bus

The SCSI-2 bus allows you to connect up to eight different SCSI devices. At any point in time, only two of these devices can communicate with each other. Each SCSI device is uniquely identified by its SCSI ID which thus represents its address. At the same time, the SCSI ID also defines the priority of the associated device. SCSI ID 0 has the lowest priority, SCSI ID 7 the highest priority.

These are the sober facts as set out in Chapter 4.5 of the SCSI-2 standard. Some explanation may be useful. If at any time only two devices can communicate with each other, this also means that messages cannot be sent to all connected devices. The only method for influencing all connected devices at a time is a SCSI reset which has its own dedicated signal line. Furthermore, no third device can interrupt a running communication. No matter how high the priority, each device must wait until the two communicating devices terminate their communication themselves.

Most SCSI devices will do this as often as possible. As soon as the command has been transmitted, the device which is to execute the command releases the bus for use by other devices. After the command has been executed, the device reconnects to the device that issued the command. This disconnect/reconnect mechanism is extensively described in Chapter 20 on the SCSI bus protocol.

On each SCSI device the SCSI ID must be set in such a way that it is unique for the bus to which the device is connected. The priority plays a minor role. It is only of importance when more than one SCSI device at a time requires the free bus. As soon as the connection between two devices is established or when only a short delay (2.4 µs) lies between the bus requests of two devices, priority plays no role.

The parallel SCSI-3 bus

Under certain hardware conditions, the parallel SCSI-3 bus can address up to 32 devices. Otherwise, with regard to the aspects relevant for this description, it corresponds to the SCSI-2 bus.

SCSI devices

The definition of host adapter and SCSI controller is not part of the SAM. It is, however, important and fits well into this position.

Host adapters

A host adapter is the connection of a computer to the SCSI bus. This host adapter can be realized as a separate plug-in board, as is the case with most PC systems. It can, however, also be integrated into the mother board, as is the case particularly with home computers and workstations.

A computer can also have several SCSI host adapters. These are used to connect more than one SCSI bus to a computer. Then, these different SCSI buses are separate SCSI domains. Therefore, the same SCSI IDs can be used on both buses.

SCSI controllers

The connection of peripheral devices to the SCSI bus is called the SCSI controller. In most cases, the SCSI controller is integrated into the peripheral device (embedded

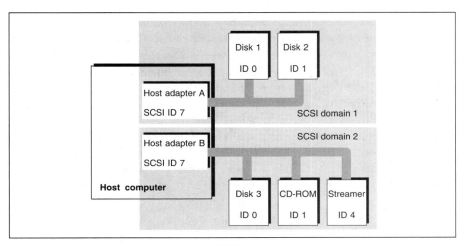

Figure 11.4 Computer with several SCSI domains.

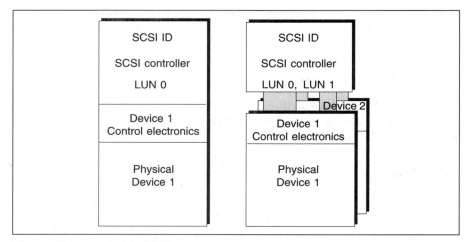

Figure 11.5   Embedded SCSI and bridge controllers.

controller). Controllers housed on a separate board are called bridge controllers. Figures 10.3 and 11.5 show SCSI controllers.

Although priority plays only a minor role in SCSI, the following convention has been generally adopted: the first host adapter gets SCSI ID 7 and IDs for additional host adapters are given in descending order. The first SCSI controller gets SCSI ID 0, and additional SCSI controllers are given ascending IDs. This convention is, however, neither written nor even mentioned anywhere in the SCSI standard. All properly written software must be able to cope with any other assignments as well.

Initiator and target

SCSI devices can assume either the role of an initiator or that of a target. This is principally independent of whether the device is a host adapter or a SCSI controller. Originally, most devices were set up to be either an initiator or a target. In such a constellation, the host adapters were initiators and the SCSI controllers were targets. Today, an ever increasing number of devices is capable of assuming either role. Nearly all hard disks and tape devices can become initiators in the context of the COPY command and copy data from other devices to themselves. Only many host adapters find it difficult to adapt to the target role or can still only be initiators.

The initiator triggers an action on the SCSI bus by selecting a target and sending a command. But as soon as the command is transmitted, the target takes over control of the bus protocol. It decides whether to release the bus and, after having released the bus, when to reconnect to the initiator. My former colleague Michael Schultz, who translated the first edition of this book into English, coined the phrase: 'The initiator is the master in function and the slave in protocol.'

The definition of the SAM is: An initiator is a SCSI device that can send out SCSI commands and task management requests. A target is a SCSI device that can execute SCSI commands and task management requests.

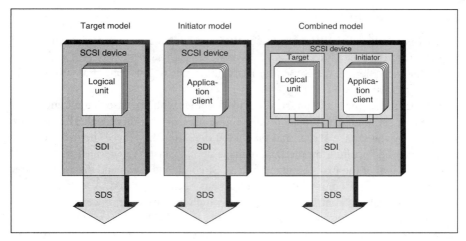

Figure 11.6   SCSI device model.

Initiator

An initiator is a fairly simple device. For most purposes it is sufficient to know that it has an ID and generates SCSI requests.

According to the abstract SAM, it consists of an identifier and as many application clients as it has outstanding tasks. The identifier is its address, which is 64 bits long. Its contents depends on the employed SDS. Thus, in SCSI-2, it can only lie between 0 and 7, in the parallel SCSI-3 protocol between 0 and 31. Other protocols might allow larger addresses.

An application client is an abstract object which generates exactly one SCSI command or one task management request. Thus, there is a separate application client for each individual command.

Target

A SCSI target is significantly more complicated than an initiator. The easy definition is: A target has an ID, accepts SCSI commands and forwards them to the corresponding LUN for execution. A LUN represents the physical peripheral device and the logics needed for the execution of SCSI commands.

According to the SAM, the SCSI target consists of an identifier, one or more LUNs and a task management.

For the target identifier, the same applies as for the initiator identifier. It is also 64 bits long, but its true value range is limited by the current SDS.

Task

The task management controls the execution of one or more tasks and reacts to task management requests. A task is defined as the set of actions needed to carry out a SCSI command or a sequence of linked SCSI commands.

LUN (logical unit)

A LUN is a rather complex thing. It consists of a LUN number, a device server and a queue for tasks, the task set.

As the identifiers in the SAM, the LUN number is 64 bits long, but is limited in its value range by the SDS.

The device server is the physical device together with the associated logics.

The task set, finally, is the queue containing the tasks for this LUN. The tasks are managed by the device server and processed one after the other. The order of processing can be specified by the task management. A task is generated in the LUN with the arrival of the first command of a SCSI command chain and disappears after execution of the last command of this chain has been terminated. A task set can be ordered. This allows control of the order in which the tasks are processed.

Each SCSI target has at least one LUN. This so-called base device also processes the SCSI commands that are addressed to the target as such. These are mainly commands that supply information on the configuration of the target.

SCSI configurations for the parallel SCSI bus

A parallel SCSI bus supports every combination of initiators and targets, provided that they contain at least one initiator and one target each. Practically all publications on the subject of SCSI-2 present three basic configurations with different requirements for the implemented SCSI options. These configurations are not part of the SAM. They are presented here because this is a point in the description into which they fit.

Single initiator, single target

This is the simplest and maybe most frequent configuration. One initiator, the host adapter, communicates with one target, the peripheral device. You will often read that in this configuration bus release via disconnect/reconnect is superfluous. This is not entirely correct. At least in multitasking operating systems, such as UNIX, Novell Netware or OS/2, the host can issue further write or read requests to the hard disk when it is still busy processing the first one. This fills the task set and allows the device server to sort the requests in such a way that the minimum number of head movements is required. This can significantly improve the overall throughput.

Single initiator, multiple target

This configuration is more interesting. It fulfills one of SCSI's promises, namely to operate different types of peripheral devices on one I/O bus. Here, it is of enormous importance that all SCSI devices release the bus when they do not need it. Otherwise, slow devices block all other I/O activities. Bus release via connect/reconnect is optional in SCSI-1 and SCSI-2. In practice, however, all current devices support this option. Should you have to employ an older device that does not yet

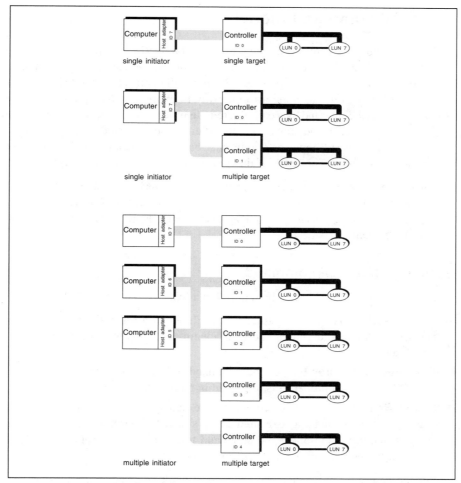

Figure 11.7   SCSI configurations.

support this option, you ought to plan a separate SCSI bus for that particular device, if at all possible.

Multiple initiator, multiple target

In this configuration it is generally necessary that the initiators reserve the SCSI devices they access. This obviously depends on the device type. Almost no operating system can cope with the fact that more than one host computer requires write access to the same disk drive. Multiple access to CD-ROMs, which can only be read anyway, might, however, be possible without problems. Personally, I would recommend that devices are reserved also in configurations with only a single initiator. The additional effort is not excessive, but when eventually a further initiator is added to the system, you will not have to change your software drivers.

11.2   The SCSI command model

SCSI commands are sent by an initiator to a target. More precisely, they are addressed to the LUN of a target. This LUN's device server executes the command and returns a status. This was true in SCSI-1 and still applies today to SCSI-3.

The SAM, however, has quite a formal way to express this simple matter. The SAM sees a SCSI command as a call of a remote procedure. This procedure has the task identifier, a command block and the status byte as mandatory parameters. Optional parameters are input or output data buffer, command length, auto sense request and sense data. The result of this procedure is the service response.

```
Service Response = Execute Command(Task Identifier, Command
Descriptor Block, [Task Attribute], [Data Output Buffer], [Data
Input Buffer], [Command Length], [Autosense Request], [Sense
Data], Status)
```

Structure of a SCSI command

The following components must be realized in a SCSI command:

- **Task identifier**: The task identifier is constituted by a set of 64-bit numbers. It consists of the initiator, target and LUN identifiers. Ordered tasks have an additional tag.

- **Command descriptor block**: The command descriptor block (CDB) contains the SCSI command proper. It is described in more detail below.

- **Status byte**: After the end of a command, the status byte supplies information on whether the command was executed successfully. Furthermore, it carries some additional information about the command termination. The status byte too is described in more detail in a dedicated section.

Command descriptor block and status byte exist in all SCSI versions; only the task identifier is new in SCSI-3.

Optionally, a SCSI command can also contain a data area. This is either an input or an output data buffer. The data direction is viewed from the initiator – the input data buffer contains data directed from the LUN to the application client.

A single SCSI command can only either send or fetch data to or from the target. For read–modify–write operations in which the initiator reads data, modifies it and then writes it back, linked commands are used to ensure that no-one else modifies the data in the meantime.

- **Data input buffer**: The data input buffer contains command-specific data supplied by the LUN before command termination. The data is only valid when the status byte contains the status GOOD, INTERMEDIATE or INTERMEDIATE CONDITION MET.

- **Data output buffer**: The data output buffer contains command-specific data that is sent to the LUN. It can be user data or, for example, parameter lists.

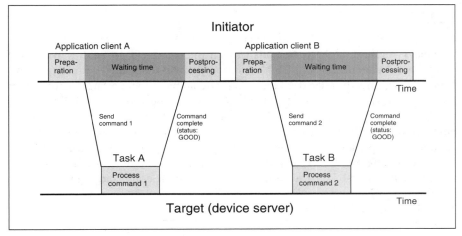

Figure 11.8   SCSI command execution.

A further optional element in this formal model is the task attribute. In SCSI-2 and in the parallel SCSI-3 protocol, it is realized by means of SCSI messages.

- **Task attribute**: The task attribute specifies how the task is to be handled by the task management. A simple task bearing the SIMPLE attribute cannot be inserted into a queue. This can only be done with an ordered task bearing the ORDERED or HEAD OF QUEUE attribute. This is explained in more detail in Section 11.4.

- **Command length**: The command length specifies the maximum number of bytes that can be transmitted by the command.

- **Autosense request**: New in SCSI-3 is the autosense mechanism which allows, in case of error, detailed information on the error to be transmitted automatically to the initiator. In SCSI-2 a REQUEST SENSE command must be explicitly specified for this purpose. The **sense data** parameter contains the data supplied by the autosense mechanism.

The command descriptor block

Table 11.1 shows the structure of a typical SCSI command descriptor block.

Table 11.1   SCSI command descriptor block.

	7	6	5	4	3	2	1	0
0	Opcode							
1								
...			Command-specific parameters						
...								
n–1								
n	Control byte							

Opcode

Byte 0 of each command is the opcode which defines type and length of the command. Its three higher order bits contain the command group, the five lower order bits the command itself. Each command group is associated with a command length. Thus, directly after decoding the first command byte, a target knows how many bytes it still has to expect. Table 11.2 shows the opcode structure. Depending on the device type, the same opcode can denote different commands which, however, usually show at least some similarity. Thus, the opcode 0Ah means WRITE for disk and tape devices, whereas it means SEND for processor devices. Also the structure is different; therefore you cannot deduce the command from the opcode alone – you must also know to which kind of device the command is addressed.

Table 11.2   Opcode structure.

Bit	7	6	5	4	3	2	1	0
	Group			Command				

Command group

The three bits of the command group allow for eight different groups. Reserved groups must not be used. These commands are kept free by the SCSI committee for future versions of the standard. In SCSI-2, group 4 was still reserved. In SCSI-3 this is where the 16-byte commands are added. When manufacturers want to implement proprietary standards, they must use group 6 or 7. In practice, however, this seldom occurs.

Table 11.3   SCSI command groups.

Group	Opcodes	Description
0	00h – 1Fh	Six-byte commands
1	20h – 3Fh	Ten-byte commands
2	40h – 5Fh	Ten-byte commands
3	60h – 7Fh	Reserved
4	80h – 9Fh	Sixteen-byte commands
5	A0h – BFh	Twelve-byte commands
6	C0h – DFh	Vendor-specific
7	E0h – FFh	Vendor-specific

Control byte

In SCSI-2, the control byte contains only two bits defined in the standard. Both are optional.

The **link** bit allows you to chain a linked I/O process across several commands. This is used to prevent a command of a further I/O process being inserted between two commands of the linked I/O process, due to optimization in the target. This is, for example, useful when a block is to be read, modified and written back. Furthermore, linked commands allow the use of relative addressing of the logical blocks.

Table 11.4 The control byte.

Bit	7	6	5	4	3	2	1	0
	Manufacturer-specific		Reserved			ACA	Flag	Link

The **flag** bit must only be used with linked commands. This causes the service response LINKED COMMAND COMPLETE (WITH FLAG) (0Bh) to be sent after termination of the linked command instead of the service response LINKED COMMAND COMPLETE (0Ah). Thus you can mark a determined command inside a command chain.

New in SCSI-3 is the **ACA** bit. ACA stands for auto contingent allegiance, a status assumed by a LUN in case an error has occurred during command execution. If the ACA bit is not set, the error status is canceled as soon as the next command arrives from the same initiator. A set ACA bit prevents this and maintains the error condition.

Linked commands

Figure 11.9 shows an example of the execution of two linked commands. An application client is generated in the initiator, and a task is generated in the task set of the target LUN. This task is executed by the device server of the LUN.

First, the initiator generates an application client, sends the first command to the target LUN and goes into a waiting state. This command has the link bit set. The target LUN generates a task and inserts it into the task set. When this task's turn arrives, the device server of the target LUN executes this first command. When it is ready, the target sends a service response LINKED COMMAND COMPLETE with an INTERMEDIATE status. The task remains in existence and goes into a waiting state. Now, the application client in the initiator continues its work, preparing the second command and sending it to the target. In our example, the second command has not set the link bit; thus it is the last of the command chain. The application client goes again into a

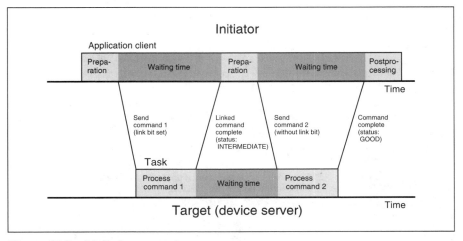

Figure 11.9 Linked commands.

Table 11.5 Service response.

COMMAND COMPLETE	The task is terminated. The status parameter contains a valid value.
LINKED COMMAND COMPLETE	A linked command is terminated.
LINKED COMMAND COMPLETE (WITH FLAG)	A linked command is terminated with a set flag bit in the control byte.
SERVICE DELIVERY OR TARGET FAILURE	The task was aborted through an error in the target or in the SDS. All parameter values, including the status, may be invalid.

waiting state. Now the task in the target LUN wakes up again and executes the second command. This time, the target returns a service response COMMAND COMPLETE with a GOOD status. The task is terminated and ceases to exist. With the reception of the service response, the existence of the application client too comes to an end.

Status

All SCSI commands are normally terminated with a status. The only exception is when a command was aborted by unforeseen circumstances. Table 11.6 shows all possible status codes.

In practice, mainly three status codes occur, GOOD (00h), BUSY (08h) and CHECK CONDITION (02h). The first two are self-explanatory. You will meet the CHECK CONDITION status at the latest when you carry out your own tests with the SCSI monitor

Table 11.6 Status codes.

Status byte	Status	Meaning
00h	GOOD	The command was terminated successfully.
02h	CHECK CONDITION	The command was not terminated successfully. Now the LUN is in the ACA state. You should now use a REQUEST-SENSE command to find out the exact cause.
04h	CONDITION MET	This code is used instead of GOOD, for example with a SEARCH-DATA command, to indicate the success of the search.
08h	BUSY	The LUN can currently not accept any further command. Try again later.
10h	INTERMEDIATE	Used instead of GOOD by commands inside a command chain.
14h	INTERMEDIATE CONDITION MET	Used instead of CONDITION MET by commands inside a command chain.
18h	RESERVATION CONFLICT	The LUN is currently reserved for another initiator. Try again later.
22h	COMMAND TERMINATED	The target device has aborted the command because of a TERMINATE I/O PROCESS message.
28h	TASK SET FULL (QUEUE FULL)	The command should be associated with a task set, but this cannot accept any further tasks.
30h	ACA ACTIVE	The command was not inserted into the task set because of an auto contingent allegiance state.

program. This is the status used by a target to indicate, amongst others, all erroneous commands, when either the command itself or the parameters are incorrect. When this status has occurred, the target is ready to supply additional information on the precise cause of the error. This information can be called up with a special command, namely REQUEST SENSE. In SCSI-3 there is the additional possibility of having the sense data automatically transmitted to the initiator.

Two changes have been made between SCSI-2 and SCSI-3. They are shaded gray in the table. The first one is only editorial: code 28h is now called TASK SET FULL instead of the former QUEUE FULL. Furthermore, code 30h has been added.

The service response

The service response contains the result of the execution of a SCSI command. For those readers already familiar with SCSI-2 it should be mentioned that the service response corresponds to the message phase during command termination. This will be explained in more detail in Chapter 20. A list of all possible values a service response can assume is given in Table 11.5.

After these highly theoretical arguments, we will get down to earth again with a detailed presentation of the most significant elements.

Task and command

For each SCSI command that an initiator addresses to a target, the device server in the addressed LUN generates a task. This task exists until the command or (in case the first command had the link bit set) the entire command chain has been executed. From the points of view of the target (device server) and the initiator (application client) this life span looks different because they have different sources of information.

The target sees the following: as soon as it receives a command, the device server generates a task. This task normally exists until the device server sends the service response COMMAND COMPLETE. Furthermore, a task dies with a power-on, when the target performs a hard reset, or when the task management executes one of the functions TARGET RESET, ABORT TASK or ABORT TASK SET.

From the target's point of view, a command is normally considered pending as long as the task exists. Only a linked command is terminated with an additional service response LINKED COMMAND COMPLETE or LINKED COMMAND COMPLETE (WITH FLAG).

The initiator cannot look inside the target. It must therefore rely on assumptions. An application client assumes that a task exists as soon as it has sent the command. It normally assumes the task's existence until it receives the service response COMMAND COMPLETE. Furthermore, a unit attention state with determined causes or the service response SERVICE DELIVERY OR TARGET FAILURE convinces the client that its task has died. If it has itself terminated the task by means of a task management request, it assumes that the task is terminated when it has received the service response FUNCTION COMPLETE.

11.3   Exceptions and error handling

Up to now we have discussed the normal execution of SCSI commands and tasks. Things become slightly more complicated when for whatever reason a command cannot be processed normally. Here too the structured model of SCSI-3 is of great help because it divides errors and exceptions into groups which can usually be associated with a determined function block of the SCSI subsystem.

Sense data

When a SCSI device, usually a LUN, finds itself in an exception state, it refuses execution of the next command and returns a CHECK CONDITION status. It also holds at its disposal a data record at least 18 bytes long with coded information on the error, the so-called sense data. This sense data can be transmitted to the initiator by means of a REQUEST SENSE command, an asynchronous message or an autosense request. All these mechanisms will be explained in more detail later in this book.

Meaning and format of the sense codes are not part of the SAM. They are described in the primary command set. In this book, you will find the description together with the REQUEST SENSE command and the sense code tables in Appendix C.

Auto contingent allegiance

Auto contingent allegiance (ACA) is a state assumed by a task set when the LUN detects an error. It then sends a CHECK CONDITION or COMMAND TERMINATED status to the initiator. In the ACA state, further execution of commands and insertion of new commands into the task set are very restricted. This is necessary to preserve the sense data, because there is only one sense data memory area per LUN which would be overwritten if a further command were executed.

In SCSI-2 there is a contingent allegiance and an extended auto contingent allegiance state. In SCSI-3, these have been united into the ACA state. The differences are not dramatic. A precise definition of the contingent allegiance states of SCSI-2 can be found in the Glossary.

As long as the ACA state exists, all tasks of the affected task set are in a waiting state. States that a task can assume are described in Section 11.4. Tasks that come from the initiator that caused the error are inserted into the task set. Tasks coming from other initiators are refused with an ACA ACTIVE status.

When a task set passes into the ACA state, the initiator that caused it should fetch the sense data with a REQUEST SENSE command. Otherwise they will get lost, because the first command that is accepted in the ACA state deletes the sense data and terminates the ACA state. This applies to all SCSI versions.

SCSI-3 offers the additional possibility of sending the sense data automatically to the initiator that caused the unsuccessful command. However, this auto sense mechanism is not mandatory. Here, the command that causes the ACA state must have the ACA bit set. Then the affected task set accepts only a command with ACA attribute even from the causing initiator. With this command, the sense data are returned and the ACA state for this task set is terminated.

Thus, an ACA state ends either with the next command or with the transmission of the autosense data. Furthermore, it ends with a power-on or a hard reset. In addition, in SCSI-3 the ACA state can also be terminated by means of the task management functions TARGET RESET and CLEAR ACA.

Unit attention state

A UNIT ATTENTION state occurs when a change happens on a LUN that the initiator should know of, for example a media change on a removable disk or tape unit. In such a case there are two possibilities for notifying the initiator. The most elegant one is to send an asynchronous message (AEN, see below) to the initiator. This possibility is already present in SCSI-2, but it is supported only by few initiators and targets.

Thus, as a standard solution for SCSI-2 only the second possibility remains. A LUN in UNIT ATTENTION state passes into the ACA state and aborts the next command with a CHECK CONDITION status. Then the initiator finds out what happened by means of a REQUEST SENSE command.

After power-on or a reset, each target goes into the UNIT ATTENTION state as soon as it has finished initialization. Thus, a CHECK CONDITION status will be present when the first command is sent to the target. When you try this out with the SCSI monitor program, however, you must consider that your host adapter might probably have checked all targets after power-on and therefore reset the UNIT ATTENTION state.

In SCSI-3 the list of events that trigger a UNIT ATTENTION state has been enriched with several interesting variations. Thus, for example, modification of device settings (the mode parameters described in Chapter 12) by another initiator or reloading of firmware too trigger a UNIT ATTENTION state. Furthermore, LUNs can now store several UNIT ATTENTION states in a queue and assume them one after the other.

The UNIT ATTENTION state ends with the sending of the asynchronous message or the termination of the ACA state.

Overlapping commands

Overlapping commands can occur in SCSI-2 in tagged queues and generally in SCSI-3. They occur when a command is to be inserted into a task set in which a command with the same identifier already exists. Whether the LUN must consider this state or not is specified in the corresponding SCSI-3 protocol.

Incorrect LUN selection

A LUN may not be available for the most varied reasons. In particular, it may not be accessible. The wide majority of SCSI devices support only LUN 0. When a bridge controller is employed, it may happen that the LUN is supported, but not connected or switched on. In all cases, each command to this LUN is aborted with a CHECK CONDITION status, that is, an ACA status. The sense data will then give precise information on the exact cause.

11.4   Task management

In the SCSI architecture model, task management is a formal description of functions for aborting task sets and individual tasks. The functions are implemented in each of the SCSI-3 protocols. In the parallel SCSI-3 protocol and in SCSI-2, they are realized by means of the message system.

In the client–server model, the task management functions are represented as a function call of the following form:

```
Service Response = Function(Object Identifier)
```

The service response can assume the values FUNCTION COMPLETE, FUNCTION REJECTED or SERVICE DELIVERY OR TARGET FAILURE.

Task management functions are generated by an application client in the initiator and executed by the task manager as a function of the target. A list of task management functions follows below.

Task management functions

ABORT TASK SET

Aborts all tasks in the task set that belong to the specified initiator. This function must be implemented in SCSI-3 when ordered tasks are implemented in the LUN. In SCSI-2, this corresponds to the ABORT TAG message.

ABORT TASK

Aborts the specified task. This function must be implemented in all SCSI-3 LUNs. In SCSI-2 there is no exact correspondence because there are no task identifiers. Here, the ABORT TAG message aborts the currently active task.

CLEAR ACA

Aborts all tasks in the task set. This function must be implemented in SCSI-3 when ordered tasks are implemented in the LUN. In SCSI-2, this corresponds to the CLEAR QUEUE message.

TARGET RESET

Resets the target and terminates all tasks in all task sets. This function must be implemented in all SCSI-3 devices. In SCSI-2, this corresponds to the BUS DEVICE RESET message.

TERMINATE TASK

Terminates the specified task as soon as possible. This 'soft' abortion of a task allows, for example, the hard disk to finish writing the current sector. This function is a SCSI-3 option. In SCSI-2, there is no exact correspondence because there are no task identifiers. Here, the message TERMINATE I/O PROCESS aborts the currently active task in a similar way.

Results

As a result of task management functions, the service responses FUNCTION COMPLETE, FUNCTION REJECTED and SERVICE DELIVERY OR TARGET FAILURE can occur. FUNCTION COMPLETE means that the function was executed correctly. FUNCTION REJECTED is returned when the LUN does not support the task management function. SERVICE DELIVERY OR TARGET FAILURE means that an error has occurred in the target or in the transmission system. It is not clear whether the task management function has been executed or not.

11.5   Task set management

The task set is the SCSI-3 equivalent of tagged queues in SCSI-2. Task set management is carried out by means of the task management functions listed in the previous section. You will meet these elements again in their actual implementation in Chapter 20 in the sections on the SCSI-2 message system and the parallel SCSI-3 bus.

The task set management deals with task states, task attributes and events that cause changes in task states. Task set management only refers to tasks previously inserted into a task set. Task are not inserted into a task set only when they are immediately aborted with a BUSY, RESERVATION CONFLICT, TASK SET FULL, ACA ACTIVE or CHECK CONDITION status.

Task states

The current task is the task that currently has access to the resources of the target, that is, the physical device or the bus interface. Whether a task of a task set can become the current task depends on its state. A task can assume one of four states, as shown in Table 11.7.

Figure 11.10 shows the possible transitions between task states.

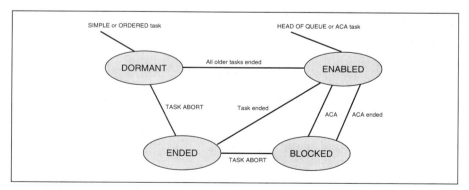

Figure 11.10   State transitions between tasks.

Table 11.7 Task states.

DORMANT	A task that cannot be terminated because other tasks in the task set occupy the necessary resources.
ENABLED	A task that satisfies all requirements for becoming the current task.
BLOCKED	A task that cannot become the current task because of an ACA state.
ENDED	This task waits to be removed from the task set.

Task attributes

At the server request call the task is assigned an attribute. This attribute determines the task state with which it is inserted into the task set.

Table 11.8 Task attributes.

SIMPLE	A task with the simple attribute is inserted into the task set as DORMANT. It is only ENABLED when all older tasks with ORDERED or HEAD OF QUEUE attributes are terminated.
ORDERED	A task with the ORDERED attribute is inserted into the task set as DORMANT. It is only ENABLED when all older tasks are terminated.
HEAD OF QUEUE	This task is inserted into the task set as ENABLED.
ACA	An ACA task is inserted into the task set as ENABLED. There can only be one ACA task in a task set at any one time.

12 SCSI primary commands

You have seen the basic flow of phases of SCSI command execution in Chapter 11. The initiator sends the command to the target as part of a service request. The device server of the corresponding LUN processes the command. The command is terminated with a COMMAND COMPLETE service response and returns at least the status as a parameter.

This chapter describes the basic SCSI commands, that is, the commands which can be found in the SCSI-3 primary command set. The description starts from the SCSI-2 standard, explaining the minor changes brought by SCSI-3 in the individual context.

12.1 The SCSI target model

A basic model for a SCSI-3 target was introduced in Section 11.1. At this point, we slightly modify the model and take a look at the SCSI-2 target in greater detail (Figure 12.1). A SCSI target is addressed using its SCSI ID. Within a single SCSI-2 target up to seven LUNs and seven target routines are accessible. A target must implement at least one LUN. Target routines are optional. Each SCSI command is executed by the particular LUN or target routine identified within the command.

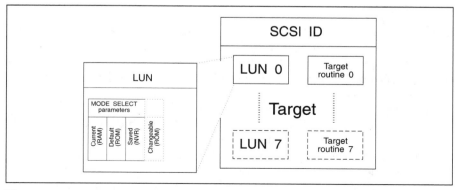

Figure 12.1 Model of a target.

LUNs

LUNs have already been introduced in the previous chapter on SCSI architecture. A LUN is a part of the target accessible from outside that implements a SCSI device type. Most commonly a target will consist of a single LUN; however, it is left to the target whether it wants to combine more than one physical device to a LUN. This is the case, for example, in RAID disk arrays. From a SCSI point of view, however, a LUN is seen as one device. Thus, a LUN is associated with a device type and has a set of parameters and states. The various LUNs of a target may belong to different device types.

Target routines

Target routines are processes that run on the target itself. These were added with SCSI-2, but are no longer present in SCSI-3. They were supposed to be used, amongst other things, for diagnostic and test purposes. Target routines are always vendor specific; there is no model or command set defined in SCSI-2. They are at most of secondary importance and I know of no SCSI target that implements them.

Device types

SCSI supports a variety of device types, from disk drives to printers to scanners. While disk drives are a source as well as a destination of information, printers only receive and scanners only send data. Data is exchanged with disk drives in a block format. Printers accept an unstructured stream of data. For these reasons SCSI defines a number of device types. Table 12.1 shows an example of the codes returned by an INQUIRY command.

For each device type SCSI defines a model, a command set and specific parameter pages. The center column of the table indicates in which SCSI-3 document the corresponding device type is described. This chapter covers the commands and parameter pages that are common to all device types, together with processor devices. The following chapters cover each device type in detail, together with their specific commands and mode parameter pages.

Parameter pages

Every LUN contains a set of parameters that configure its operation. These parameters can be written with MODE SELECT and read with MODE SENSE. Collectively, they are typically referred to as mode parameters. The parameters are sent across the bus in blocks called pages. Here, as with commands, some pages pertain to all devices, while some are only for specific types.

One thing that all device types have in common is the way in which the parameters are organized and maintained by the LUN. A LUN has three copies or sets of its parameters: the current, the default, and the saved parameters. The current parameters are those with which the device is currently functioning. These reside in RAM on the target and are lost when the device powers down. The saved values are kept in some type of non-volatile memory. On a disk drive this might be the medium

Table 12.1   List of device classes.

Code	SCSI-3 document	Device types
00h	SBC	Disk drives
01h	SBC	Tape drives
02h	SSC	Printers
03h	SPC (here)	Processor devices
04h	SBC	WORM drives
05h	MMC	CD-ROM drives
06h	SGC	Scanners
07h	SBC	Optical disks
08h	SMC	Media changers
09h	SSC	Communication devices
0Ah–0Bh		(Reserved in SCSI-2; SCSI-3: printer preprocessing devices)
0Ch	SCC	Reserved in SCSI-2; SCSI-3: array controllers (RAID)
0Dh–1Eh		Reserved
1Fh		Unknown device

itself, otherwise NOVRAM is frequently employed. At power-on time all devices copy the saved values to the current parameters. The default values are set by the manufacturer into PROM. The saved values reflect default settings when the device is purchased. A SCSI command allows the default to be copied to the saved values.

There is actually a fourth set of parameters, though somewhat different from the others, that the target can access. These changeable parameters are also hard-coded into the firmware. This set tells an initiator which individual parameters may be manipulated and to what extent. In this way a diagnostic program or device driver can determine, for example, which sector sizes a disk drive will allow before blindly attempting to set the value and running into a CHECK CONDITION status.

Parameter rounding

A new feature in SCSI-3 is that a target may round a parameter value that it does not support precisely to a value that it does support. When a target rounds a parameter, it must return a CHECK CONDITION status. The sense key (see the REQUEST SENSE command) should be RECOVERED ERROR. The extended sense code finally reports ROUNDED PARAMETER.

12.2   Command structure

All SCSI commands consist of at least a command descriptor block and a status byte. Many commands also include additional parameter lists. Parameter lists are transmitted by the SDS in the same way as pay data. SCSI commands process logical blocks, that is, pay data, or they work with parameter lists. Parameter-oriented commands can, for example, read and also modify the properties of devices. There are also commands that deliver no information at all except in the status byte that concludes all commands. SCSI-2 commands can be 6, 10, or 12 bytes long. SCSI-3 defines an additional 16-byte command.

Table 12.2   Template for 6-byte commands.

	7	6	5	4	3	2	1	0
0	Opcode							
1	(LUN)			(MSB)				
2	Logical block							
3								(LSB)
4	Data length							
5	Control byte							

6-byte commands

The fundamental structure of a SCSI command has already been introduced in Chapter 11, where you will also find a list of all command groups and an explanation of the structure of opcode and control byte. Table 12.2 shows the structure of a typical 6-byte command. Depending on whether the command uses logical blocks, parameter lists or status information, each field will have a different interpretation or perhaps no function at all.

LUN

In SCSI-2 this field exists for reasons of compatibility with SCSI-1. In SCSI-3 it is reserved. Byte 1 contains the number of the logical unit to be addressed in the three most significant bits. All SCSI-2 devices I am familiar with use the IDENTIFY message as well as the LUN field. The target routines in SCSI-2 are addressable only using the IDENTIFY message.

Logical blocks

Six-byte commands that operate on logical blocks spread the logical block number (LBN) over three bytes, as shown in Table 12.2. In total, 21 bits are available to address the LBN, which corresponds to approximately 2 million logical blocks. Since a logical block is usually 512 bytes long this represents about a gigabyte of addressable storage. Therefore, 6-byte commands must not be used with devices with more than a gigabyte of storage. Since the original SASI standard only had 6-byte commands, there exist both 6-byte and 10-byte versions of many commands. New initiators, however, should only use the 10-byte versions.

Transfer length

This byte reflects the amount that should be transferred. Depending on the command itself, this field is interpreted differently. Some commands transfer no data at all and here the byte is meaningless. If the command uses a parameter list (which I will refer to as a parameter oriented command) then the data length byte contains the parameter list length in bytes. If there are fewer parameter bytes available than requested, a target will simply send what is there without complaining. For commands that operate on logical blocks (what I call block oriented commands) transfer length represents the number of logical blocks starting at the LBN to be transferred.

The 6-byte commands but also some 10- and 12-byte commands use a single byte for the transfer length. For such commands that are block oriented a transfer length of 0 means that 256 blocks should be sent. For parameter oriented commands 0 means that no data should be transferred.

10-, 12- and 16-byte commands

The 10-, 12- and 16-byte commands are very much the same as the 6-byte commands (Tables 12.3, 12.4 and 12.5). The only difference is the number of bytes available for the LBN and the transfer length.

Table 12.3 Template for 10-byte commands.

	7	6	5	4	3	2	1	0
0	Opcode							
1	(LUN)			Reserved				
2	(MSB)							
3	Logical							
4	block							
5	(LSB)							
6	Reserved							
7	(MSB)	Data length						
8	(LSB)							
9	Control byte							

Table 12.4 Template for 12-byte commands.

	7	6	5	4	3	2	1	0
0	Opcode							
1	(LUN)			Reserved				
2	(MSB)							
3	Logical							
4	block							
5	(LSB)							
6	(MSB)							
7	Data length							
8								
9	(LSB)							
10	Reserved							
11	Control byte							

Table 12.5 Template for 16-byte commands.

	7	6	5	4	3	2	1	0
0	Opcode							
1	Reserved							
2	(MSB)							
3	Logical							
4	block							
5								(LSB)
6	(MSB)							
7	Additional							
8	command data							
9								(LSB)
10	(MSB)							
11	Data length							
12								
13								(LSB)
14	Reserved							
15	Control byte							

A 10-byte command contains a 32-bit block address or an address space of approximately 2 terabytes. The transfer length field is 16 bits long. In SCSI-2 the 12-byte command extends this field to 32 bits.

The 16-byte command has been added in SCSI-3. In bytes 6 to 9 it contains room for additional data. Both logical block address and data length field are 32 bits long.

Command implementation

There are four different types of command implementation (Table 12.6). These determine how and whether a command must be implemented.

Table 12.6 Command types.

Symbol	Meaning
M	Mandatory: these commands must be implemented
O	Optional: these commands may or may not be implemented. When implemented, they must adhere to the standard
V	Only in SCSI-2: vendor specific: these opcodes are reserved for manufacturers to implement their own commands
Z	New in SCSI-3: device type specific: mandatory with some device types, optional with others
R	Reserved: these opcodes may not be used. The SCSI committee may assign commands at a later date

12.3 Commands for all SCSI devices

There are a number of commands that are common to all device types (Table 12.7). The most important of these will be introduced here. We begin with those commands whose implementation is mandatory.

Compared with SCSI-2, six more commands have been added in SCSI-3 to the list of commands for all devices. However, these commands are not new commands, but were previously associated with other device types. On the other hand, the MODE SELECT(6) and MODE SENSE(6) commands are no longer mandatory in SCSI-3. Thus, there are only four commands left in SCSI-3 which every SCSI target must be able to handle.

Table 12.7 Commands for all SCSI devices.

Opcode	Name	Type	Page	SCSI-2	SCSI-3 (SPC)	Description
00h	TEST UNIT READY	M	131	7.2.16	7.22	Reflects whether or not the LUN is ready to accept a command
03h	REQUEST SENSE	M	128	7.2.14	7.18	Returns detailed error information
12h	INQUIRY	M	132	7.2.5	7.5	Returns LUN specific information
15h	MODE SELECT(6)	Z	140	7.2.8(M)	7.8(Z)	Set device parameters
16h	RESERVE(6)	Z	136	16.2.8	7.19	Make LUN accessible only to certain initiators
17h	RELEASE(6)	Z	136	16.2.6	7.16	Make LUN accessible to other initiators
18h	COPY	O		7.2.3	7.3	Autonomous copy from/to another device
1Ah	MODE SENSE(6)	Z	140	7.2.10(M)	7.10(Z)	Read device parameters
1Ch	RECEIVE DIAGNOSTIC RESULTS	O		7.2.13	7.15	Read self-test results
1Dh	SEND DIAGNOSTIC	M	138	7.2.1	7.21	Initiate self-test
39h	COMPARE	O		7.2.2	7.2	Compare data
3Ah	COPY AND VERIFY	O		7.2.4	7.4	Autonomous copy from/to another device, verify success
3Bh	WRITE BUFFER	O		7.2.17	7.23	Write the data buffer
3Ch	READ BUFFER	O		7.2.12	7.13	Read the data buffer
40h	CHANGE DEFINITION	O	139	7.2.1	7.1	Set SCSI version
4Ch	LOG SELECT	O		7.2.6	7.6	Read statistics
4Dh	LOG SENSE	O		7.2.7	7.7	Read statistics
55h	MODE SELECT(10)	O		7.2.9	7.9	Set device parameters
56h	RESERVE(10)	Z			7.20	Make LUN accessible only to certain initiators
57h	RELEASE(10)	Z			7.17	Make LUN accessible to other initiators
5Ah	MODE SENSE(10)	O		7.2.11	7.11	Read device parameters
A7h	MOVE MEDIUM	Z		16.2.3	SMC	Move medium
B4h	READ ELEMENT STATUS	Z		16.2.5	SMC	Read element status

Note: Commands that have been added to this command set in SCSI-3 are shaded light gray. Mandatory commands are shaded dark gray. (M) means that the command is classified differently in SCSI-2 and SCSI-3. The corresponding classification is indicated after the reference to the standard.

Attached medium changer

It should be noted that two commands have been added for handling recording media. SCSI-3 now supports devices with attached medium changer. This medium changer is no LUN on its own, but the main device, for example a CD-ROM drive, understands these two commands and controls the media changer.

INQUIRY (12h)

The INQUIRY command tells us about a LUN, giving us a list of specific details in a concise format. This command can be used to learn, among other things, which SCSI options have been implemented, the SCSI version number, the device type and the name of the device. This command will function even if the LUN is not able to accept other types of commands. In fact, INQUIRY will only return CHECK CONDITION if the target is unable to return the requested inquiry data. INQUIRY is the only command that does not reply with CHECK CONDITION when a non-existent LUN is addressed. Instead, this fact is reflected in the data returned.

It is most common to see this command with a transfer length of FFh, with all other bytes set to zero (Table 12.8). This represents a request for standard INQUIRY data, where 255 bytes or less are expected.

Standard inquiry data can only be obtained when neither the EVDP nor the CmdDt bit is set.

- **EVDP** (enable vital product data): When this bit is set the page code determines the type of information returned by the target. Implementation of this bit is optional. Additional information can be found in Chapter 7.3.4 of the SCSI-2 standard document.

- **CmdDt** (command support data): This feature is new in SCSI-3. When this bit is set, byte 2 must contain an opcode. Then the LUN returns a data structure which explains whether a command with this opcode is supported and how. Further details can be found in Chapter 7.4.4 of the SCSI-3 SPC document.

- **Page code/opcode**: This byte is valid only when the EVDP or the CmdDt bit is set. It specifies that more detailed information concerning the target be returned as INQUIRY data.

Table 12.8 The INQUIRY command.

	7	6	5	4	3	2	1	0
0	INQUIRY (12h)							
1	(LUN)			Reserved			CmdDt	EVDP
2	Page code							
3	Reserved							
4	Data length							
5	Control byte							

Table 12.9   Standard INQUIRY data format.

	7	6	5	4	3	2	1	0
0	Peripheral qualifier			Device class				
1	RMB	Reserved (SCSI-1)						
2	ISO		ECMA			ANSI		
3	AEN	TIO (TrmTsk)	Reserved (NACA)	Reserved	Data format			
4	Additional length							
5	Reserved							
6	Reserved		Reserved (Port)	Reserved (DualP)	Reserved (MChngr)	Reserved (ARQ)	Reserved (Adr32)	Reserved (Adr16)
7	Rel	W32	W16	Sync	Link	Res. (TrnDis)	Que	SftR
8–15	Manufacturer (8 bytes)							
16–31	Product (16 bytes)							
32–35	Revision (4 bytes)							
36–55	Vendor unique (20 bytes)							
56–95	Reserved (40 bytes)							
96–n	Vendor unique							

Note: The fields shaded in light gray have changed in SCSI-3. The fields shaded in dark gray only apply to the SCSI-3 SIP, that is, the parallel interface.

- **Allocation length**: The number of bytes the initiator has reserved for the INQUIRY data. Normally this byte will be set to FFh, thus allocating 256 bytes. In response to this the target will send as much data as it has, up to FFh in total.

The standard INQUIRY data

The standard INQUIRY data is structured in the following manner (Table 12.9):

- **Peripheral qualifier** (Table 12.10): These three bits reflect whether a physical device can be supported under this LUN and whether or not it is connected, but say nothing about whether the device is ready.
- **Peripheral device type**: These five bits indicate the peripheral device type, or class, to which the logical unit belongs. A list of the device types can be found in Table 12.1 on page 123.

Table 12.10   Peripheral qualifier.

Status	Description
000b	The device described is connected to the LUN
001b	The target supports such a device, but none is connected
011b	The target does not support a physical device for this LUN

Table 12.11   ANSI version.

Status	Meaning
0h	The device supports the SCSI-1 standard
1h	The device supports the CCS
2h	The device supports SCSI-2
3h	The device supports SCSI-3

- **RMB** (removable bit): A 1 indicates that the medium is removable. For example, this bit is always set for diskette drives and tape units.

- **ISO version, ECMA version**: Indicates that the device supports the ISO IS-9316 or the ECMA-111 versions of the SCSI standard.

- **ANSI version**: see Table 12.11.

- **AEN** (asynchronous event notification capability): In SCSI-2 this bit is defined only for processor devices and indicates that the device supports asynchronous event notification. Thus, such a device will accept a SEND command from another target. In SCSI-3 this bit is called AERC (asynchronous event reporting capability) and means that the device supports asynchronous messages as defined in the SAM architecture model.

- **TIO/TrmTsk**: The device supports the message TERMINATE I/O PROCESS. In SCSI-3 the bit is called TrmTsk (terminate task) and indicates that the device supports the task management function TERMINATE TASK of the SAM architecture model.

- **Data format**: Indicates the response format of the following standard INQUIRY data. Interpreted in the same way as the ANSI version field.

- **Additional length**: Indicates how many additional bytes of information follow.

- **Port**: This bit is new in SCSI-3. It only applies if the DualP bit is set as well. It is not set when the command was received on port A and set when the command arrived on port B.

- **Dualport** (DualP): This bit is new in SCSI-3. It indicates that the device supports dual ports.

- **Media Changer** (MChngr): This bit is new in SCSI-3. It indicates that the device has an attached media changer and supports the MOVE MEDIUM and READ ELEMENT STATUS commands.

- **Rel**: The device supports relative addressing. Relative addressing means that it is not the absolute LBN to be specified, but the offset to the current LBN. This is only supported when linked commands are supported as well.

- **W32**: The device supports 32-bit wide SCSI.

- **W16**: The device supports 16-bit wide SCSI.

- **Sync**: The device supports synchronous transfers.

- **Link**: The device supports linked commands.

- **Transfer Disable** (TrnDis): This bit is new in SCSI-3. It indicates that the device supports the SCSI messages CONTINUE I/O PROCESS and TARGET TRANSFER DISABLE.

- **Que**: The device supports tagged commands.

```
        SCSI Monitor V1.0 rev 024 11.3.93 (fs)
                                                       Id Lu St LN nX
        SCSI command 00: 12 00 00 00 FF 00 00 00 00 00 00 00  03 00 00 00 FF

        SCSI data buffer No. 00:

        0000: 01 80 02 02 26 00 00 18 48 50 20 20 20 20 20 20  C&HP
        0010: 48 50 33 35 34 38 30 41 20 20 20 20 20 20 20 20  HP35480A
        0020: 41 20 20 20 30 30 30 2F 00 00 02 00 00 00 00 00  A   000/
        0030: 00 00 00 00 00 00 00 00 00 00 00 00 00 00 00 00
        0040: 00 00 00 00 00 00 00 00 00 00 00 00 00 00 00 00
        0050: 00 00 00 00 00 00 00 00 00 00 00 00 00 00 00 00
        0060: 00 00 00 00 00 00 00 00 00 00 00 00 00 00 00 00
        0070: 00 00 00 00 00 00 00 00 00 00 00 00 00 00 00 00
        0080: 00 00 00 00 00 00 00 00 00 00 00 00 00 00 00 00
        0090: 00 00 00 00 00 00 00 00 00 00 00 00 00 00 00 00
        00A0: 00 00 00 00 00 00 00 00 00 00 00 00 00 00 00 00
        00B0: 00 00 00 00 00 00 00 00 00 00 00 00 00 00 00 00
        00C0: 00 00 00 00 00 00 00 00 00 00 00 00 00 00 00 00
        00D0: 00 00 00 00 00 00 00 00 00 00 00 00 00 00 00 00
        00E0: 00 00 00 00 00 00 00 00 00 00 00 00 00 00 00 00
        00F0: 00 00 00 00 00 00 00 00 00 00 00 00 00 00 00 00

        Command: G
```

Figure 12.2   Example of an INQUIRY command.

- **SftR**: The device supports soft reset capability. Otherwise the device performs a hard reset to a RESET condition.
- **Manufacturer**: Manufacturer's name in ASCII.
- **Product**: Product's name in ASCII.
- **Revision**: Product's version number in ASCII.

As you can see, the INQUIRY command is capable of delivering a wide variety of useful information. An example of INQUIRY data as the SCSI monitor program presents it on the screen is shown in Figure 12.2. This particular command is inquiring about LUN 0 of SCSI ID 3. A total of 256 bytes (0FFh) have been requested.

In order to simplify interpretation of the INQUIRY data, in Table 12.12 I have placed it in a frame corresponding to Table 12.9.

The peripheral qualifier is 000b, meaning that a physical device is addressable under this LUN. The peripheral device type is 00001b, which according to the list on page 123 specifies a tape device. The RMB bit is set in byte 1 indicating removable medium. The ANSI field in byte 2 shows that the device is SCSI-2 compliant. This is also reflected in the response data format of byte 3. Byte 4 tells us that 38 (26h) additional bytes of data follow. The link and sync options are set in byte 5, meaning that the device supports synchronous transfers and linked commands but not, however, tagged queues.

TEST UNIT READY (00h)

The command TEST UNIT READY determines whether the LUN in question will allow access to the medium (Table 12.13). This means, for example, for a removable medium drive that the medium is present and READY for access. Depending on the

Table 12.12   Evaluation of INQUIRY data.

	7	6	5	4	3	2	1	0
0	0	0	0	0	0	0	0	1
1					0			
2	0	0	0	0	0	0	1	0
3	0	0	0	0	0	0	1	0
4				26h				
5–6			00h		00h			
7	0	0	0	0	0	0	0	0
8–15				HP				
16–31				HP35480A				
32–35				A				
36–55								
56–95								
96–n								

device, it can take tens of seconds before the READY condition is reached. If you are only interested in finding out whether a certain LUN exists then the INQUIRY command should be used instead.

TEST UNIT READY is an unusual command because no information transfer takes place. No parameters are sent and no data is returned. When the physical device is ready this command simply returns a GOOD status, otherwise CHECK CONDITION is returned. The precise reason for the CHECK CONDITION status is stored in the LUN's sense data. In SPC section 7.22 the SCSI-3 standard contains a list of recommended sense codes. You should adhere to this list when you implement a target.

REQUEST SENSE (03h)

The REQUEST SENSE command (Table 12.14) is always used in response to a status CHECK CONDITION status in order to read the sense data. This data gives information concerning the reason why the preceding command ended abnormally. The sense data is also updated when a command ends with COMMAND TERMINATED status.

Table 12.13   The TEST UNIT READY command.

	7	6	5	4	3	2	1	0
0	TEST UNIT READY (00h)							
1	(LUN)			Reserved				
2								
3								
4	Reserved							
5	Control byte							

Table 12.14 The REQUEST SENSE command.

	7	6	5	4	3	2	1	0
0	REQUEST SENSE (03h)							
1	(LUN)			Reserved				
2								
3	Reserved							
4	Data length							
5	Control byte							

It is important to remember that sense data always reflects the state of the previous command. It is the initiator's responsibility to follow up on a CHECK CONDITION status immediately with REQUEST SENSE. An intervening command will cause sense data to be overwritten.

The command itself looks similar to the INQUIRY command. Here too the allocation length is in general set to FFh in order to receive all of the data that the target has available.

Sense data

Since interpreting sense data can be complicated, to say the least, we divide the task into four steps:

(1) Determine validity of sense data

(2) Evaluation of the sense key

(3) Evaluation of sense key specific information

(4) Evaluation of the sense code

It is often the case that the sense key alone is enough information, making subsequent steps unnecessary.

I explain here only the most important fields, which are shaded gray in Table 12.15; the meaning of the less important fields can be found in the standard:

- **Error code**: An error code of 70h is the normal case. This means that the sense data refers to the current command. An error code of 71h, on the other hand, means that the sense data refers to an earlier command.

   Such a deferred error can occur, for example, with disk drives using write cache. Here the disk drive will send a GOOD status immediately after receiving the data of a WRITE command. To the host the write appears to be complete, but in reality the data merely resides in the drive's write cache waiting to be written to the medium. We find ourselves in a critical situation if during the actual write to the medium an unrecoverable data error occurs. We will discuss caching and its ramifications in more detail in Chapter 13. Fortunately, such errors occur extremely infrequently.

   Error codes 00h to 6Fh are not assigned, codes 72h to 7Eh are reserved, and code 7Fh can be used for manufacturer-specific sense data formats.

Table 12.15 Structure of sense data.

	7	6	5	4	3	2	1	0
0	Valid	Error code (70h or 71h)						
1	Segment number							
2	FilMrk	EOM	ILI	Reserved	Sense key			
3–6	Information							
7	Additional data length							
8–11	Command-specific information							
12	Sense code							
13	Extended sense code							
14	FRU							
15–17	SKSV	Sense key specific						
18–n	Additional sense bytes							

- **Sense key**: The sense key is the principal information concerning the reason for a CHECK CONDITION. Table 12.16 lists the keys with their corresponding meanings.

- **Sense code**: After deciphering the sense key, we may or may not need to look for more information concerning the error (Table 12.17). For the sense key NOT READY, for example, we look to the sense code for further explanation. This byte tells of possible hardware and medium errors, among others.

ILLEGAL REQUEST is a sense key that occurs often while testing a device with the SCSI monitor. The sense key specific field contains more detailed information.

Table 12.16 The most important sense keys.

Sense key	Description	
0h	NO SENSE	There is no sense information
1h	RECOVERED ERROR	The last command completed successfully but used error correction in the process
2h	NOT READY	The addressed LUN is not ready to be accessed
3h	MEDIUM ERROR	The target detected a data error on the medium
4h	HARDWARE ERROR	The target detected a hardware error during a command or a self-test
5h	ILLEGAL REQUEST	Either the command or the parameter list contains an error
6h	UNIT ATTENTION	The LUN has been reset, for example through SCSI reset or a medium change
7h	DATA PROTECT	Access to the data is blocked
8h	BLANK CHECK	Reached unexpected written or unwritten region of the medium
9h		Vendor specific
Ah	COPY ABORTED	COPY, COMPARE or COPY AND VERIFY was aborted
Bh	ABORTED COMMAND	The target aborted the command
Ch	EQUAL	Comparison for SEARCH DATA successful
Dh	VOLUME OVERFLOW	The medium is full
Eh	MISCOMPARE	Source data and data on the medium do not agree

Table 12.17 Sample sense codes.

Sense code 13 14	Description
04 00	LUN not ready, reason unknown
04 01	LUN is in transition to become ready
04 02	LUN not ready, waiting for initialization command
04 03	LUN not ready, operator action necessary
04 04	LUN not ready, medium being formatted
24 00	Error in command block

Table 12.18 The sense key specific information.

	7	6	5	4	3	2	1	0
15	SKSV	C/D	Reserved		BPV	Bit position		
16	(MSB)		Error position					
17								(LSB)

Table 12.18 lists the possibilities for this field for the sense key ILLEGAL REQUEST. Look to the standard for the description of other sense keys. If the SKSV bit is set, this shows that the sense key specific data is valid. Afterwards, the C/D bit should be examined. When set the error lies in the command, otherwise the error lies in the parameter list. The position of the first byte in error is contained in the error position field. The field for bit position only has meaning for other sense keys.

It should be apparent that the REQUEST SENSE command provides a great deal of useful information. The following example, which can easily be duplicated using the SCSI monitor, will bring this point home (Figure 12.3). My first step was to send an

```
SCSI Monitor V1.0 rev 024 11.3.93 (fs)
                                                      Id Lu St LN nX
SCSI command 01: 03 00 00 00 FF 00 00 00 00 00 00 00  03 00 00 00 FF

SCSI data buffer No. 00:

0000: 70 00 05 00 00 00 00 0B 00 00 00 00 24 00 00 CF  p$
0010: 00 03 00 00 00 00 00 00 00 00 00 00 00 00 00 00
0020: 00 00 00 00 00 00 00 00 00 00 00 00 00 00 00 00
0030: 00 00 00 00 00 00 00 00 00 00 00 00 00 00 00 00
0040: 00 00 00 00 00 00 00 00 00 00 00 00 00 00 00 00
0050: 00 00 00 00 00 00 00 00 00 00 00 00 00 00 00 00
0060: 00 00 00 00 00 00 00 00 00 00 00 00 00 00 00 00
0070: 00 00 00 00 00 00 00 00 00 00 00 00 00 00 00 00
0080: 00 00 00 00 00 00 00 00 00 00 00 00 00 00 00 00
0090: 00 00 00 00 00 00 00 00 00 00 00 00 00 00 00 00
00A0: 00 00 00 00 00 00 00 00 00 00 00 00 00 00 00 00
00B0: 00 00 00 00 00 00 00 00 00 00 00 00 00 00 00 00
00C0: 00 00 00 00 00 00 00 00 00 00 00 00 00 00 00 00
00D0: 00 00 00 00 00 00 00 00 00 00 00 00 00 00 00 00
00E0: 00 00 00 00 00 00 00 00 00 00 00 00 00 00 00 00
00F0: 00 00 00 00 00 00 00 00 00 00 00 00 00 00 00 00

Command: G
```

Figure 12.3 SCSI monitor with REQUEST SENSE command.

Table 12.19 Interpretation of the sense data.

	7	6	5	4	3	2	1	0	
0	0	1	1	1	0	0	0	0	◄— Error code
1	0	0	0	0	0	0	0	0	
2	0	0	0	0	1	0	1	0	◄— Sense key
3–6									
7	0	0	0	0	1	0	1	1	
8–11									
12	0	0	1	0	1	0	0	0	◄— Sense code
13	0	0	0	0	0	0	0	0	
14	0	0	0	0	0	0	0	0	
15	1	1	0	0	0	1	1	1	
16	0	0	0	0	0	0	0	0	◄— Byte 3

SKSV — (points to row 15, bit 7)
C/D — (points to row 15, bit 6)

INQUIRY command, 12 00 00 FF 00 00, to which the target responded with CHECK CONDITION. I then sent a REQUEST SENSE allocating 255 bytes for sense data. In the status field for this command is 00h, meaning that the REQUEST SENSE was successful. If you do not have much experience in interpreting hexadecimal numbers it helps to write out each byte in binary on a piece of paper, then, using Table 12.19, draw in the boundaries of the individual fields. Byte 0 of the sense data is error code 70h; that is, this data refers to the previous command. In byte 2 is the sense key 05h: ILLEGAL REQUEST. The sense code is 24h, meaning that a field in the previous command was invalid. Looking at the sense key specific information, byte 15 is C0h; the valid bit is set, indicating that there is useful information here. The C/D bit is also set, meaning that the error is in the command itself. Bytes 16 and 17 contain 00h and 03h; in other words, the error is in the third byte of the INQUIRY command. A look at the definition shows that byte 3 of an INQUIRY command must be zero. The FFh belonged not in byte 3 but in byte 4 as the allocation length. Thus, the correct command should have been 12 00 00 00 FF 00.

RESERVE (16h) and RELEASE (17h)

This pair of commands makes it possible to reserve a LUN for a particular initiator and then to free it for use by others. These commands are common to all device types. There are special versions of the commands for disk drives.

What happens when a LUN reserved for a certain initiator receives a command from another initiator? This LUN will end each such command with a RESERVATION CONFLICT status and ignore the command. This reservation mechanism provides a degree of protection, albeit somewhat unsophisticated, in multi-initiator environments. Many operating systems do not allow, for example, two hosts to access a single disk drive. In such situations, however, it is possible to use RESERVE and RELEASE to share drives between two hosts. As soon as one system brings a drive

Table 12.20 The RESERVE command.

	7	6	5	4	3	2	1	0
0	RESERVE (16h)							
1	(LUN)			3rdPty	3rdPty ID			Reserved (Xtnt)
2	Reserved (SCSI-3: Reservation ID)							
3	Reserved							
4	(SCSI-3: Extent list length)							
5	Control byte							

online it reserves that LUN. Should the system go down for any reason, a simple SCSI reset is all that is needed to make the drive accessible for the other host.

The reserve command itself looks standard (Table 12.20). Only two fields call for any explanation; these make it possible for an initiator to reserve a device for a third party:

- **3rdPty**: Third party reservation. When clear, this bit calls for the reservation to be made for the initiator sending the command. When set, the reservation should hold for the initiator whose ID is contained in the third-party device ID field.

- **3rdPty ID**: When third party is set this field holds the ID of the device for which the reservation holds.

The extent reservation mechanism is new in SCSI-3. An extent is part of a storage device. The term is described in detail in the model of the SCSI hard disk. In short, extent reservation means that an initiator does not always have to reserve a complete LUN, but also individual extents. Furthermore it allows explicit reservation for determined access modes (read, write, and so on). Both the implementation of extents and the extent reservation are optional.

- **Xtnt** (extent): When this bit is set, only the extents in the extent list are to be reserved.

- **Reservation ID**: This is used to identify the initiator responsible for an extent reservation.

- **Extent list length**: This must be valid when the Xtnt bit is set. The extent list is passed as a command parameter during the data phase. The format of the extent list can be found in Section 7.19 of the SCSI-3 SPC standard document.

It is possible for an initiator to modify its own reservation. It can, for example, first reserve a device for itself, followed later by a reservation for a third device. In this way a device always remains protected. One application for third-party reservation is the COPY command.

A reservation can be dissolved in a number of different ways: by SCSI reset, a DEVICE RESET from any initiator, or by a RELEASE command from the initiator which made the reservation. The RELEASE command looks almost identical to the RESERVE command (Table 12.21).

Table 12.21   The RELEASE command.

	7	6	5	4	3	2	1	0
0	RELEASE (17h)							
1	(LUN)			3rdPty	3rdPty ID			Reserved (Xtnt)
2	Reserved (SCSI-3: Reservation ID)							
3	Reserved							
4								
5	Control byte							

SEND DIAGNOSTIC (1Dh)

The SEND DIAGNOSTIC command causes the target to run certain diagnostic programs (Table 12.22). In the most simple case, when the ST bit is set, the device will run a self-test. If the self-test discovers no problems then the status returned is 00h (GOOD). If, on the other hand, a problem is detected a CHECK CONDITION status, 02h, is returned. A follow-up REQUEST SENSE will reveal a sense key of 04h (HARDWARE ERROR). Only this implementation of the command is mandatory. The optional bits of byte 1 are:

- **PF** (page format): When this bit is set the page format conforms to SCSI-2 and SCSI-3. In SCSI-1 the page format was vendor specific.

- **DevO** (device offline): When set, this bit allows the target to run diagnostics that may affect all LUNs and possibly change their state. If clear no such operations will take place.

- **UniO** (unit offline): This bit plays the same role as DevO but for protecting individual LUNs.

Optionally, various diagnostics can be run using diagnostic pages sent as parameter lists. Diagnostic pages have been defined for each device type. Some pages may be vendor specific. For example, a frequently implemented page is the TRANSLATE ADDRESS page. This page makes it possible to find out the physical address of a logical block. The results are collected from the target using the RECEIVE DIAGNOSTIC RESULTS command. Table 12.23 shows the basic structure of a diagnostic page.

Table 12.22   The SEND DIAGNOSTIC command.

	7	6	5	4	3	2	1	0
0	SEND DIAGNOSTIC (1Dh)							
1	(LUN)			PF	Reserved	ST	DevO	UniO
2	Reserved							
3	(MSB)			Data length				
4								(LSB)
5	Control byte							

Table 12.23 Diagnostic page.

	7	6	5	4	3	2	1	0
0	Page code							
1	Reserved							
2	(MSB)			Page length (n–3)				
3								(LSB)
4	Diagnostic							
n	parameter							

Several such pages can be sent together in a single parameter list. The page code and basic structure of the pages are the same for SEND and RECEIVE DIAGNOSTIC. The actual parameters, however, usually differ somewhat.

CHANGE DEFINITION (40h)

This command allows an initiator to configure a SCSI-2 target to behave like an earlier SCSI version (Table 12.24). The following values are allowed in the version field:

- 00h: No change
- 01h: SCSI-1 (SCSI-3: Reserved)
- 02h: SCSI-1 with CCS (SCSI-3: Reserved)
- 03h: SCSI-2
- 04h: (SCSI-3: SCSI-3)
- 3Fh: (SCSI-3: Manufacturer default value)

The Save bit causes the target to save the change permanently. At the next power-up cycle the change will be in force. The Data length indicates the size of the

Table 12.24 The CHANGE DEFINITION command.

	7	6	5	4	3	2	1	0
0	CHANGE DEFINITION (40h)							
1	(LUN)			Reserved				
2	Reserved							Save
3	Reserved	SCSI version						
4								
5								
6								
7								
8	Data length							
9	Control byte							

Table 12.25   The MODE SELECT command.

	7	6	5	4	3	2	1	0
0	MODE SELECT(6) (15h)							
1	(LUN)		PF	Reserved				SP
2	Reserved							
3								
4	Data length							
5	Control byte							

	7	6	5	4	3	2	1	0
0	MODE SELECT(10) (55h)							
1	(LUN)			Reserved				
2	Reserved							
3								
4								
5								
6								
7	(MSB)	Data length						
8								(LSB)
9	Control byte							

parameter list that the initiator intends to send to the target. Such lists, however, are vendor unique and in general are seldom used.

MODE SELECT(6) (15h) and MODE SENSE(6) (1Ah)

MODE SELECT and MODE SENSE are a pair of optional commands that use the same parameter lists. These allow an initiator to configure a device and also to determine its configuration. They are the same for all devices; however, the parameter lists used can be very device type dependent. Relative to a typical SCSI command, MODE SENSE and MODE SELECT are complex, with many parameters and fields. Both commands are essential, implemented for virtually all devices. They are covered here in great detail.

There are 6-byte and 10-byte versions of both MODE SELECT and MODE SENSE. Only the 6-byte version is discussed here. The 10-byte version is identical except for the parameter list length, which is two bytes instead of one.

MODE SELECT(6) allows an initiator to set the internal configuration of a LUN (Table 12.25). The command itself is typical. Byte 4 contains the parameter list length, which can be up to 255 bytes long. If this byte is zero no list is sent. In byte 1 there are two bits of interest:

- **PF** (page format): When this bit is set the parameter pages conform to SCSI-2; that is, as they are described in this book. Otherwise the parameter pages are SCSI-1 compliant.

- **SP** (save pages): When this bit is clear changes affect only the current parameters. If the bit is set then changes will also be written to the saved parameters and will be valid at the next power-up cycle.

The MODE SENSE command is used to read the mode parameter lists from a device (Table 12.26). Like the MODE SELECT command, there is a 10-byte version for working with lists longer than 255 bytes:

Table 12.26   The MODE SENSE command.

	7	6	5	4	3	2	1	0
0	MODE SENSE(6) (1Ah)							
1	(LUN)		Res.	DBD	Reserved			
2	PCF		Page					
3	Reserved							
4	Data length							
5	Control byte							

	7	6	5	4	3	2	1	0
0	MODE SENSE(10) (5Ah)							
1	(LUN)		Res.	DBD	Reserved			
2	PCF		Page					
3	Reserved							
4								
5								
6								
7	(MSB)	Data length						
8								(LSB)
9	Control byte							

- **DBD** (disable block descriptors): When this bit is set no block descriptors are sent before the pages.
- **PCF** (page control field):
  - 00b: Current values
  - 01b: Changeable values
  - 10b: Default values
  - 11b: Saved values
- **Page code**: The number of the desired parameter page.

The parameter lists for MODE SELECT and MODE SENSE are basically the same. This is useful in that one can read the parameters from the device with MODE SENSE, edit them in memory, and write them back with MODE SENSE. A parameter list consists of three elements: the mode parameter header (Table 12.27), the block descriptors, and the parameter pages. Each element has a pointer to the beginning of the subsequent one. Figure 12.4 shows a typical mode parameter list. This one has a header, two block descriptors, and two parameter pages. The arrows on the right-hand side represent the pointers within the elements. You will need to refer to this figure as we discuss the individual elements.

Table 12.27   Mode parameter header.

(6)	(10)	7	6	5	4	3	2	1	0
0	0–1	Data length							
1	2	Media type							
2	3	Device specific							
–	4–5	Reserved							
3	6–7	Block descriptor length							

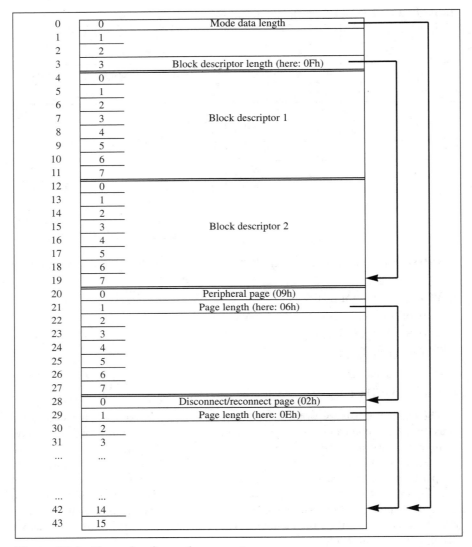

Figure 12.4   Example of a mode parameter page.

Mode parameter header

The header of the 6-byte MODE commands is four bytes long:

- **Mode data length**: The length of the entire parameter list in bytes.

- **Block descriptor length**: The total length of the block descriptors. Since a block descriptor is always eight bytes long this field is either zero or a multiple of eight.

Block descriptor

Zero or more block descriptors (Table 12.28) may follow a mode parameter header. The block descriptor defines the logical block length of all or part of the medium.

Table 12.28 Block descriptor.

0	Write density	
1	(MSB)	
2	Number of blocks	
3		(LSB)
4	Reserved	
5	(MSB)	
6	Block length	
7		(LSB)

Theoretically, one could use this feature to divide a drive into several partitions of differing logical block sizes. However, in the vast majority of cases a single block descriptor is employed with a block size defined for the entire medium.

- **Write density**: This field is dependent on device type. For floppy drives there are codes for the popular densities. For disk drives this field has no meaning.

- **Number of blocks**: The number of blocks that this descriptor defines.

- **Block length**: The number of bytes per logical block for the blocks defined by this descriptor. For tape drives a block length of zero means that it is variable and is determined by the WRITE command. The block descriptor does not contain a pointer to the next element since the descriptor is of a fixed length (8 bytes).

Mode parameter pages

The third, final, and most important element is the parameter page itself (Table 12.29). A parameter page begins with the page code in the lowest 6 bits of byte 0. It follows that the largest page code is 3Fh. The next byte contains the page length. Parameter pages vary in length but are at most 255 bytes long.

The PS (parameter savable) bit of byte 0 is only defined for MODE SENSE. When set it indicates that the target is able to save these parameters.

The page length specifies the number of parameter bytes of the page, that is, two bytes less than the total length of the page.

There are three parameter pages, which are defined for all device types. These are the control mode page (0Ah), the disconnect/reconnect page (02h), and the peripheral device page (09h).

Most parameter pages are device type specific. These pages are defined in the SCSI literature included with the device. Table 12.30 gives an overview of parameter

Table 12.29 Mode parameter page.

	7	6	5	4	3	2	1	0
0	PS	Reserved	Page code					
1	Page length (n–1)							
2 ...	Mode							
... n	parameter							

Table 12.30 List of parameter pages.

Code	Name	Device
00h	Vendor specific	DTPRSOMC
01h	Read/write error page	DTRO
02h	Disconnect/reconnect page	DTPRSOMC
03h	Format page	D
03h	Parallel interface page	P
03h	Measurement units page	S
04h	Rigid disk geometry page	D
04h	Serial interface page	P
05h	Flexible disk page	D
05h	Printer options page	P
06h	Optical memory page	O
07h	Verification error page	DRO
08h	Cache page	DRO
09h	Peripheral device page	DTPRSOMC
0Ah	Control mode page	DTPRSOMC
0Bh	Medium type page	DRO
0Ch	Notch partitions page	D
0Dh	CD-ROM page	R
0Eh	CD-ROM audio page	R
0Fh	Data compression page	T
10h	Device configuration page	T
11h	Medium partitions page 1	T
12h	Medium partitions page 2	T
13h	Medium partitions page 3	T
14h	Medium partitions page 4	T
1Ch	Informal exception page	DTPRSOMC
1Dh	Element address assignment page	M
1Eh	Transport geometry page	M
1Fh	Device capabilities page	M
3Fh	All available pages	DTPRSOMC

pages defined in the SCSI standard. Of special interest is page code 3Fh, which allows MODE SENSE to read all of the pages maintained by a device. The device column indicates the device types for which a parameter page is defined. The abbreviations are defined as follows: D, disk drives; T, tape drives; P, printers; R, CD-ROMs; S, scanners; O, optical storage; M, medium changers; and C, communications devices.

12.4 Mode parameter pages for all device types

The following parameter pages are defined for all device types.

Table 12.31 Mode parameter pages for all device types.

Page code	Name	Page	SCSI-2	SCSI-3 (SPC)
02h	Disconnect/reconnect page	145	7.3.3.2	8.3.2
09h	Peripheral device page	146	7.3.3.3	8.3.4
0Ah	Control mode page	147	7.3.3.1	8.3.1
1Ch	Informal exception page		–	8.3.3

Disconnect/reconnect page (02h)

The parameters of this page (Table 12.32) determine the behavior of the target with respect to freeing the bus. Whether or not the target is allowed to free the bus at all is a function of the DiscPriv bit in the IDENTIFY message of every I/O process.

The parameter DTDC (data transfer disconnect) in byte 12 also determines the general behavior of the target. It has the following effect:

- **00b**: Disconnection from the bus is allowed.

- **01b**: No disconnection should take place once the data transfer has begun until all data has been sent. The time parameters of this page are ignored in this case.

- **10b**: Reserved.

- **11b**: No disconnection should take place once the data transfer has begun until the command is complete. Time parameters are also ignored in this case.

The maximum burst length cannot be specified when the DTDC is non-zero. The following parameters affect the target's disconnect/reconnect behavior when DTDC is zero.

The EMDP and DImm bits are new in SCSI-3. The EMDP (enable modify data pointers) bit is only meaningful in connection with the parallel protocol (SIP). When it is set, the target is allowed to send a MODIFY DATA POINTERS message.

Table 12.32   The disconnect/reconnect page.

	7	6	5	4	3	2	1	0
0	PS	Reserved	Disconnect/reconnect page (02h)					
1	Page length (0Eh)							
2	Buffer full condition							
3	Buffer empty condition							
4	(MSB)	Maximum bus						
5	inactivity time							(LSB)
6	(MSB)	Maximum						
7	bus free time							(LSB)
8	(MSB)	Maximum						
9	connection time							(LSB)
10	(MSB)	Maximum						
11	burst length							(LSB)
12	SCSI-3: EMDP	Reserved			SCSI-3: DImm		DTDC	
13	Reserved							
14								
15								

The DImm (disconnect immediate) bit tells the target to release the bus immediately after a command was received.

- The buffer full ratio determines, for read operations, how full the data buffer should be before the target attempts a reconnect to the initiator. The value is in units of 1/256 times the number of buffers. The buffer empty ratio works the same way for write operations. It determines how empty the buffer should be before attempting to reconnect to the initiator.

- The bus inactivity limit specifies the maximum amount of time in 100 μs increments that a target may occupy the bus without sending or receiving data. If the limit is exceeded the target must free the bus.

- The disconnect time limit specifies the minimum amount of time in 100 μs increments that a target must wait after freeing the bus before it attempts a reselection.

- The connect time limit specifies in 100 μs increments the maximum amount of time that a target may occupy the bus.

- The maximum burst size specifies the maximum number of data bytes (in 512 byte increments) that the target may transfer before relinquishing the bus.

Peripheral device page (09h)

This parameter page does not allow many settings and is more or less vendor specific (Table 12.33). The interface identifier describes a physical interface. This is meaningful for bridge controllers; otherwise a zero stands for SCSI. A few values are defined in the standard:

- 0000h: SCSI
- 0001h: SMD
- 0002h: ESDI
- 0003h: IPI-2
- 0004h: IPI-3

Table 12.33 The peripheral device page.

	7	6	5	4	3	2	1	0
0	PS	Reserved	Peripheral device page (09h)					
1	Page length (n–1)							
2	(MSB)	Interface						
3								(LSB)
4	Reserved							
5	Reserved							
6	Reserved							
7	Reserved							
8 ...n	Manufacturer specific							

Table 12.34 The control mode page.

	7	6	5	4	3	2	1	0
0	PS	Reserved		Control mode page (0Ah)				
1	Page length (06h)							
2	Reserved						GLTSD	RLEC
3	Queue algorithm				Reserved		QErr	DQue
4	EECA	Reserved			RAENP	UAAENP	EAENP
SCSI-3	Reserved	RAC	ByprtM	BybthS	Reserved	RAERP	UUAERP	EAERP
5	Reserved							
6	(MSB)	AEN waiting time						
7	after initialization							
8	(MSB)	Busy timeout in 100 ms						
9	SCSI-3 only							

Control mode page (0Ah)

The control mode page contains parameters for controlling various SCSI-2 characteristics (Table 12.34). I mention here only a few of the more important ones and refer the reader to the standard for more details.

The queue algorithm modifier pertains to SIMPLE QUEUE TAG commands. It takes on two values: a value of 0 specifies that the target must order commands in such a way that data integrity is guaranteed across the entire medium for all initiators. A value of 1 allows the target to re-order commands without restrictions. A drive can often achieve a substantial increase in throughput by optimizing the order in which logical blocks are accessed.

The DQue bit allows tagged queuing to be disabled. When set all queue messages are replied to with MESSAGE REJECT. The three bits RAENP, UAAENP and EAENP allow AEN in certain situations. If none of these bits is set AEN is disabled.

RAENP (ready AEN permission) specifies that the target should use AEN to notify initiators of an initialization instead of responding with UNIT ATTENTION for the first command. UAAENP (unit attention AEN) allows AEN instead of UNIT ATTENTION during normal operation. EAENP (error AEN permission) allows a target to use AEN for deferred errors again instead of relying on a UNIT ATTENTION response to the next command. In SCSI-3 the denomination AEN (asynchronous event notification) is replaced by AER (asynchronous event reporting).

12.5 The model of a SCSI processor device

Processor devices are a very general device type. Although such devices only send and receive data across the bus, they are capable of a wide variety of very useful general tasks. Processors that offload a main processor or a data acquisition system are two examples of such devices.

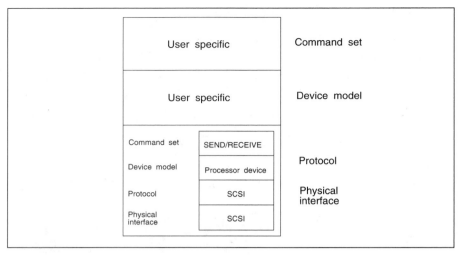

Figure 12.5   User defined protocol.

SCSI processor devices are also indispensable for the asynchronous notification mechanism. In order to be able to receive an asynchronous notification, the initiator must also be capable of handling the target role. For this reason, the processor device commands have been included in the kernel command set.

Asynchronous notification was introduced in SCSI-2 as AEN (asynchronous event notification), but seldom used. In SCSI-3 asynchronous notification plays an important role in different protocols as AER (asynchronous event reporting.

From the SCSI perspective, a processor device simply exchanges data over the bus with the initiator (Figure 12.5). The kind of data sent is left completely unspecified. Here SCSI simply acts as a physical interface between devices. The protocol above that is left up to the designers.

A processor device, like all SCSI targets, can support up to eight logical units. If a LUN is momentarily incapable of receiving or sending data it can either return a CHECK CONDITION status or it can disconnect and reconnect at a later time.

In a way, a SCSI processor device resembles the SCSI communication device (see Section 14.7), with the difference that the SCSI processor processes its data locally whereas a communication device forwards its data to other devices.

Thus, the most important application in SCSI-3 is AER. Assume that an unexpected event occurs in a LUN, for example, a user removes a changeable medium. Without AER, the LUN would abort the next command with a CHECK CONDITION status, and the initiator would try to determine the cause of the problem with a REQUEST SENSE. With AER, the LUN itself can send a SEND command with the sense data to all known initiators. For this purpose, a special data format has been defined which is described together with the SEND command.

What follows are descriptions of two applications for SCSI processor devices. The first consists of two coupled processors, which together act as a redundant file server. Both servers are identical and contain the same data. The servers use the

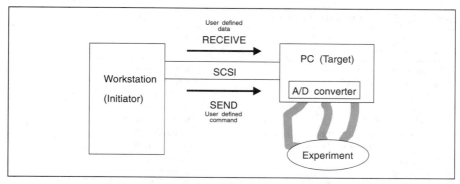

Figure 12.6 Example of a SCSI processor.

SCSI bus for communicating with each other and for insuring that they each contain the same data. If one system should fail the other system remains fully functional.

The second application is a PC equipped with an A/D converter, which together function as a data acquisition system. The PC collects all of the necessary data and is even capable of preprocessing. It plays the role of a SCSI target and delivers the preprocessed data to a workstation.

There are countless other possible applications for processor devices (Figure 12.6). It should also be noted that it suffices to implement the SEND command in order to allow communication between two processor devices. SCSI is powerful in this area because it allows customized hardware to be controlled using an industry standard interface.

SCSI host adapters for PCs that also function as targets are, however, still hardly available. Above all, adequate support is often lacking. This is a point that you should carefully check before you decide which hardware you buy.

12.6 Commands for processor devices

Table 12.35 lists all of the commands defined for processor devices.

Table 12.35 Commands for processor devices.

Op-code	Name	Type	Page	SCSI-2	SCSI-3 (SPC)	Description
00h	TEST UNIT READY	M	131	7.2.16	7.22	Reflects whether or not the LUN is ready to accept a command
03h	REQUEST SENSE	M	132	7.2.14	7.18	Returns detailed error information
08h	RECEIVE	M	149	11.2.1	9.1	Like read
0Ah	SEND	M	149	11.2.2	9.2	Like write
12h	INQUIRY	M	128	7.2.5	7.5	Returns LUN specific information
16h	RESERVE(6)	O	136	16.2.8	7.19	Reserve LUN
17h	RELEASE(6)	O	136	16.2.6	7.16	Release reservation
18h	COPY	O		7.2.3		Autonomous copy from/to another device
1Ch	RECEIVE DIAGNOSTIC RESULTS	O		7.2.13		Read self-test results

Table 12.35   Commands for processor devices (*continued*).

Op-code	Name	Type	Page	SCSI-2	SCSI-3 (SPC)	Description
1Dh	SEND DIAGNOSTIC	M	138	7.2.1		Initiate self-test
39h	COMPARE	O		7.2.2		Compare data
3Ah	COPY AND VERIFY	O		7.2.4		Autonomous copy from/to another device, verify success
3Bh	WRITE BUFFER	O		7.2.17		Write the data buffer
3Ch	READ BUFFER	O		7.2.12		Read the data buffer
40h	CHANGE DEFINITION	O	139	7.2.1		Set SCSI version
4Ch	LOG SELECT	O		7.2.6		Read statistics
4Dh	LOG SENSE	O		7.2.7		Read statistics
56h	RESERVE(10)	O			7.20	Reserve LUN
57h	RELEASE(10)	O			7.17	Release reservation

Note: Commands added in SCSI-3 are shaded light gray, mandatory commands dark gray.

RECEIVE (08h)

The RECEIVE command (relative to the initiator) instructs the target to send data to the initiator (Table 12.36). The direction of the transfer can be confusing. Remember that the direction is the same as that for READ, with which RECEIVE shares an opcode.

SEND (0Ah)

The SEND command instructs the target to receive data from the initiator (Table 12.37). The transfer length indicates the amount of data to be sent. The AEN bit indicates that the data packet is in AEN format. This is used to send sense data to a processor device.

AEN data format (SCSI-2)

The workings of AEN are explained in detail in Chapter 20. Byte 0 of an AEN data packet contains in the lowest three bits the value LUNTRN. When the LUNTAR bit is set then LUNTRN reflects the target routine to which the data pertain. Otherwise the data pertain to the LUN specified in this field (Table 12.38).

Table 12.36   The RECEIVE command.

	7	6	5	4	3	2	1	0
0	RECEIVE (08h)							
1	(LUN)			Reserved				
2	(MSB)							
3	Data length							
4								(LSB)
5	Control byte							

Table 12.37 The SEND command.

	7	6	5	4	3	2	1	0
0	SEND (0Ah)							
1	(LUN)			Reserved				AEN
2	(MSB)							
3	Data length							
4								(LSB)
5	Control byte							

Table 12.38 Data format for asynchronous events (AEN/SCSI-2).

	7	6	5	4	3	2	1	0
0	Reserved		LUNTAR	Reserved		LUNTRN		
1	Reserved							
2								
3								
4 to	Sense data, byte 0							
n + 4	Sense data, byte n							

AER data format (SCSI-3)

The AER data format (Table 12.39) is slightly different from the AEN format of SCSI-2. In particular, room has been made for the 64-bit LUN number as defined in the SAM architecture model. On the other hand, there is no more support for target routines. When set, the SCSI-3 bit indicates that the data is in AER format.

Table 12.39 Data format for asynchronous events (AER/SCSI-3).

	7	6	5	4	3	2	1	0
0	SCSI-3							
1	Reserved							
2								
3								
4	LUN							
...								
11								
12 to	Sense data, byte 0							
n + 12	Sense data, byte n							

13 Block-oriented devices

The SCSI-3 standard unites the three device types, disk drives, WORM disks and optical storage devices in the SBC (SCSI Block Devices) document. For each of these device types, the device model is described first, followed by the command set and finally by the parameters.

This classification is also reflected in the current edition of this book. However, this book is based on the SCSI-2 standard. Changes introduced with SCSI-3 are added where necessary. You will find that in SCSI-3 there is not much change in the domain of block-oriented devices.

13.1 The model of a SCSI disk drive

I have chosen the term 'disk drive' for this device type because it is very widely used. To be precise, this class does not only include magnetic disk drives, but it also includes all devices that allow direct access to any logical block, such as disk drives, magneto-optical drives, diskettes and RAM disks. The ANSI standard knows this device type as 'direct access devices'.

The basic physical design of disk drives and the organization of data on the medium were described in Part I. Refer to Chapter 2 before continuing if any of the following terms are unclear: read/write head, sector, cylinder, logical block, ECC, CRC, mapping, interleave, track skew, and zone-bit recording

Logical blocks

A SCSI disk drive presents the user with a sequence of logical blocks for storing information (Figure 13.1). These blocks can be written to and read any number of times. They are uniquely identified by their logical block number (LBN). The first logical block has the number 0, the last block has the number n−1. The value of n−1 can be determined by means of the READ CAPACITY command.

In contrast to tape drives, the logical blocks of a disk drive allow direct access to any block. The actual fetching of the data is completely transparent to the host. In general the host has no idea where on the medium a logical block is located.

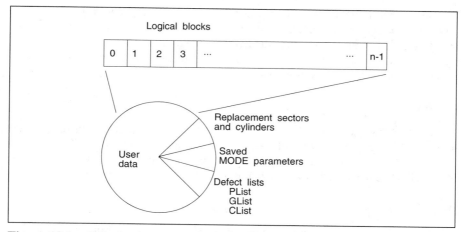

Figure 13.1   Organization of the SCSI medium.

Normally, a logical block contains user information exclusively. However, there are optional commands that allow limited access to format information such as ECC or CRC.

The size of a logical block can vary between 1 byte and 64 Kbytes. The most widely used size is 512 bytes, as is the case for the DOS operating system. In the UNIX world there are also blocks of 4 Kbytes. A SCSI drive can accommodate more than one block size on a single medium. Theoretically, each block may be a different size.

Mapping

The mapping of logical blocks to physical sectors is not specified in the SCSI standard (Table 13.1). However, it should be implemented in such a way that the time needed to access adjacent blocks is minimized. Most drives use a linear mapping, where adjacent logical blocks come from adjacent physical sectors.

Table 13.1   Mapping of logical blocks.

LBN	Cylinder	Head	Sector
0	0	0	0
1	0	0	1
⋮			
24	0	0	24
Head switch			
25	0	1	0
⋮			
49	0	1	24
Adjacent track seek and head switch			
50	1	0	0
⋮			
19999	399	1	24

The following example will help to make this clear. Assume a drive with 400 cylinders (tracks), 2 heads, and 25 sectors. A state-of-the-art disk drive can switch heads within the time it takes to rotate from one sector to another. A change of tracks typically takes around 2 ms. A linear mapping minimizes delays by switching heads before calling for a change of tracks.

Extents

A continuous sequence of blocks of the same size is called an extent. Extents are defined using the parameter list of a MODE SELECT command (see page 140). However, this optional feature is seldom employed. For most applications all blocks of a SCSI drive will have the same block size; that is, they will belong to a single extent.

Notches

Modern disk drives use zone-bit recording (ZBR). Zone-bit recording has to do with how the information is stored on the medium. Here the outer tracks contain more sectors than the inner tracks (see Figure 13.2). This becomes possible because the outer tracks are longer and therefore allow more sectors to be fitted on a track while maintaining the same recording density (bits per cm). The resulting regions of the drive that employ the same number of sectors per track are called notches. Notches are defined via notch pages in the mode parameters. In real terms, the existence of notches has almost no effect. However, in ZBR disks, the sustained data rate is higher in the outer zone than in the inner zone.

Removable medium drives

The medium of a SCSI drive may or may not be removable. Diskette drives, magneto-optical drives and removable cartridge drives are examples of removable medium drives. The medium is said to be 'mounted' when it is loaded into the unit and is ready to read or write. A SCSI drive in this state is said to be in condition ready. Any attempt to access a drive that is not ready leads to a CHECK CONDITION with the sense key NOT READY. You may use the TEST UNIT READY command to check whether a changeable medium is mounted or not.

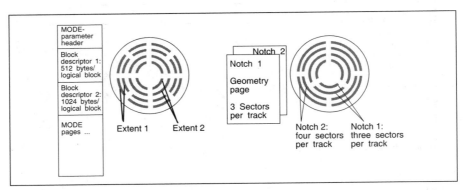

Figure 13.2   SCSI extents and notches.

Attached media changers

New in SCSI-3 are the so-called attached media changers. Already in SCSI-2, but also in SCSI-3, there is a separate device type for media changers. These devices, which are often called juke boxes, allow remote-controlled transport of changeable media from a storage magazine into a drive and are regarded by SCSI as self-contained devices with their own SCSI ID. They have their own, quite substantial set of commands.

Attached media changers, instead, are integrated into the disk drive and thus have no SCSI ID of their own. Their command set is added to the command set of the drive. Attached media changers have only two commands, MOVE MEDIUM and READ ELEMENT STATUS. Whether a device has an attached media changer can be recognized by a set MChngr bit in the standard inquiry data.

RAM disks

The model of a SCSI disk drive does not specify that information must be stored in a nonvolatile manner. This allows for the implementation of a 'disk drive' out of RAM (hence RAM disk). The result is lightning fast storage that loses information when the power is removed.

Medium defects

A medium defect prevents information from being written and read correctly. Such a defect renders an entire sector unusable. Defects are an unavoidable outcome of the plating process of rigid disks but can also result from a fingerprint on a diskette. Section 7.2 goes into more detail concerning medium defects as they actually occur.

SCSI makes it possible for a target to present a virtually defect-free medium to the outside world. This is done by replacing defective logical blocks with replacement blocks set aside solely for this purpose. It does not concern an initiator whether or not a logical block has been replaced. The defect management is carried out by the drive alone. Replaceable medium drives like diskettes, however, cannot accommodate such an approach because here the physical format of the medium plays an important role. If SCSI defect management were employed then a diskette written on a SCSI drive could not be read by a standard PC floppy drive.

There are a number of methods of defect management. A target using automatic reallocation replaces a block automatically as soon as a defect is detected. This sounds very attractive but brings with it certain disadvantages as well. If the data in a logical block can no longer be read successfully the block will be replaced with a good one. However, the data in this block is obviously not what was written to the original defective block but rather the format pattern. For this reason the target should inform the host of such an action; it can do this using the message system. Automatic reallocation during writing, on the other hand, is not a problem. Here either the data is still in the write buffer and the target can write it to the new block or the target can respond to the host with a write error. Because of the inherent differences SCSI allows these features to be enabled and disabled separately.

In addition to the above method where the drive autonomously manages defects is the more standard approach where the host is in charge. Here defective blocks are replaced using the command REASSIGN BLOCK. This method is preferred because the operating system has full control.

Defect lists

There are four different types of defect lists used with SCSI drives. The primary defect list (PList) contains the defects discovered by the manufacturer using analog testing equipment. Such equipment can find positions that might not cause errors until the medium ages. The PList is permanent and never changes after the drive leaves the factory. The grown defect list (GList) contains additional defects that were discovered during the operation of the drive. These are defective blocks discovered during formatting or reallocated either automatically or using REASSIGN BLOCK. The certification list (CList) contains defects that were discovered during the certification procedure of formatting. The defects of the CList belong to the GList as well. Finally, there are the defects that an initiator sends to the target. Called the DList, this list is sent to the target before formatting takes place, at which time it becomes part of the GList. The PList and GList together contain all medium defects.

Data buffers and cache

Every SCSI disk controller has a built-in memory buffer with at least enough room to store a sector's worth of data. A physical sector is written or read in entirety at one time, therefore the data must be processed in real time. Since SCSI cannot guarantee real-time performance a sector's worth of data is first collected in the buffer before writing it to the medium.

Pre-fetch

When the data buffer is large enough to accommodate an entire track it is possible to implement speed enhancing options like read pre-fetch. Here a controller will assume that whenever a logical block X is to be read, block $X+1$ will be requested next. The validity of this assumption depends on the operating system of the host. Nevertheless, when the controller reads a sector it reads the rest of the track into the buffer as well. This extra work costs practically no time since it is merely a DMA transfer to the buffer. In the event that the subsequent blocks are called for the transfer can take place immediately. Otherwise, the data can simply be ignored with no penalty.

Another method of optimization is possible when a large enough buffer is available. Assume that a large number of continuous blocks is requested from the drive. After the seek to the proper track is complete it is probably the case that the head is located somewhere in the middle of the set of requested blocks. Normally, the controller would wait until the first block rotates underneath the heads before starting to read. However, when the buffer is large enough the controller can begin to read the sectors into memory immediately. Afterwards the controller simply rearranges the order in which the data is sent to the host. This method can save many milliseconds of time.

Writing optimization

Other methods of optimization are available when writing data to the drive. Consider the point in time just after the data has been collected into the controller's write buffer. Normally, the seek takes place and the data is written to the medium before COMMAND COMPLETE is sent to the initiator. However, if the controller responds immediately with GOOD status and COMMAND COMPLETE the access time is effectively eliminated. This approach brings with it an element of risk. If the actual write to the medium should fail the host must be notified of the error. In SCSI-2 this is possible using AEN. Here the target informs the host that the WRITE command that originally terminated with GOOD status was, in fact, unsuccessful. More difficult is the situation where power is lost. Drives are normally built so that once writing a sector has begun it can be completed, thus maintaining the integrity of the medium even when power is interrupted. However, implementing a feature whereby the entire data buffer could be saved would be much too costly.

An operating system assumes that everything written to a drive is secure. If this is not, in fact, the case the results can be catastrophic. More than just data is at stake here: if configuration information or other operating system specific data is lost it may necessitate reinstallation of the entire system. However, as with any mechanical device, failures do occur no matter what precautions are taken. In this case the increase in performance must be weighed against such risks.

For these reasons this write feature is configurable using the cache page of MODE SELECT. When enabled, writes are extremely fast but data integrity is at risk; when disabled data integrity is maintained but with a degradation in performance.

Caching

Caching goes one step further with the data buffer than the techniques described above. Since SCSI-2 provides a mode parameter page especially for configuring the cache we will look at caching here in greater detail. Certain aspects of drive performance as well as the definition of average access time can be found in Section 2.3.

In general a cache is fast storage which contains copies of certain portions of another slower storage medium. The cache can be accessed usually at least an order of magnitude faster than the slower storage but is much smaller in capacity. A cache directory is used to determine whether a specific piece of data is resident in the cache. When the desired data is in the cache we speak of a cache hit; otherwise it is called a cache miss.

Caches were first employed in the main memory of mainframe computers. Here very expensive, very fast RAM is used to cache the slower, less expensive, but very large main memory of the system. Even though such a cache is typically only a fraction of the size of main memory it is not uncommon to reach a hit quota of over 90%. Such success is due largely to the fact that much of computer programs are loops.

The situation for mass storage is completely different. The effectiveness of a mass storage cache is very dependent on the operating system and application. At least in multi-user systems, disk accesses are distributed over the entire medium. There are, however, areas that are more frequently accessed, for example, directories and tables that the operating system manages. This makes designing an effective disk cache very challenging.

The hit quota of a disk cache usually lies under 50%. Nevertheless, the increase in performance can be quite high. A cache hit can turn a 17 ms disk access into a 500 ns cache read.

The effectiveness of a disk cache is strongly influenced by the way in which it is configured. The cache fills as read data is copied there. This can happen in parallel to the data transfer so that no loss in performance occurs. When write data is written first into the cache and then onto the disk it is referred to as write-through cache. Here the same potential problems can occur as earlier with the simple memory buffer. If the device waits until the data is written to the medium before responding with GOOD status there is no speed advantage. If GOOD status is returned upon receiving data into the cache, data may be lost. These two features – whether write-through cache is used and when status should be returned – can be controlled using the cache page parameters. A third option is read pre-fetch. Several parameters are used to set how many more blocks than requested should be read into the cache.

The next issue relevant to cache management is determining which blocks should be overwritten when the cache is full. The most simple and most commonly used approach displaces the data that has not been accessed for the longest time. This method can be enhanced by allowing certain areas in the cache to be exempt from being displaced. Additionally, it can be specified that pre-fetch data should be sacrificed first.

13.2   Hard disk commands

Table 13.2 shows a list of commands for disk drives. The most important of these are discussed here.

Table 13.2   Hard disk commands.

Op-code	Name	Type	Page	SCSI-2	SCSI-3 (SBC)	Description
00h	TEST UNIT READY	M	131	7.2.16	SPC	Reflects whether or not the LUN is ready to accept a command
01h	REZERO UNIT	O	–		6.1.13	Seek track 0
03h	REQUEST SENSE	M	132	7.2.14	SPC	Returns detailed error information
04h	FORMAT UNIT	M	163	8.2.1	6.1.1	Format the medium
07h	REASSIGN BLOCKS	O		8.2.10	6.1.10	Defective blocks reassigned
08h	READ(6)	M	159	8.2.5	6.1.5	Read. Limited addressing
0Ah	WRITE(6)	(M)	159	8.2.5 M	6.1.20 O	Write. Limited addressing
0Bh	SEEK(6)	O		8.2.15	6.1.15	Seek to a logical block
12h	INQUIRY	M	128	7.2.5	SPC	Returns LUN specific information
15h	MODE SELECT(6)	(M)	140	7.2.8 M	SPC O	Set device parameters
16h	RESERVE UNIT	M	136	8.2.12	6.1.12	Make LUN accessible only to certain initiators
17h	RELEASE UNIT	M	136	8.2.11	6.1.11	Make LUN accessible to other initiators
18h	COPY	O		7.2.3	SPC	Autonomous copy from/to another device

Table 13.2 Hard disk commands (*continued*).

Op-code	Name	Type	Page	SCSI-2	SCSI-3 (SBC)	Description
1Ah	MODE SENSE(6)	(M)	140	7.2.10 M	SPC O	Read device specific parameters
1Bh	START/STOP UNIT	O		8.2.17	6.1.17	Load/unload medium
1Ch	RECEIVE DIAGNOSTIC RESULTS	O		7.2.13	SPC	Read self-test results
1Dh	SEND DIAGNOSTIC	M	138	7.2.1	SPC	Initiate self-test
1Eh	PREVENT/ALLOW MEDIUM REMOVAL	O		8.2.4	6.1.4	Lock/unlock medium
25h	READ CAPACITY	M	162	8.2.7	6.1.7	Read number of logical blocks
28h	READ(10)	M	159	8.2.6	6.1.6	Read logical block
2Ah	WRITE(10)	(M)	159	8.2.6 M	6.1.21 O	Write logical block
2Bh	SEEK(10)	O		8.2.15	6.1.15	Seek to a logical block
2Eh	WRITE AND VERIFY	O		8.2.22	6.1.22	Write logical block, verify success
2Fh	VERIFY	O		15.2.11	6.1.19	Verify
30h	SEARCH DATA HIGH	O		8.2.14	6.1.14	Search logical blocks for data pattern
31h	SEARCH DATA EQUAL	O		8.2.14	6.1.14	Search logical blocks for data pattern
32h	SEARCH DATA LOW	O		8.2.14	6.1.14	Search logical blocks for data pattern
33h	SET LIMITS	O		8.2.16	6.1.16	Define logical block boundaries
34h	PRE-FETCH	O		8.2.3	6.1.3	Read data into buffer
35h	SYNCHRONIZE CACHE	O		8.2.8	6.1.18	Write cache to medium
36h	LOCK/UNLOCK CACHE	O		8.2.2	6.1.2	Hold data in cache
37h	READ DEFECT DATA	O		8.2.8	6.1.8	Read list of defective blocks
39h	COMPARE	O		7.2.2	SPC	Compare data
3Ah	COPY AND VERIFY	O		7.2.4	SPC	Autonomous copy from/to another device, verify success
3Bh	WRITE BUFFER	O		7.2.17	SPC	Write the data buffer
3Ch	READ BUFFER	O		7.2.12	SPC	Read the data buffer
3Eh	READ LONG	O	161	8.2.9	6.1.9	Read data and ECC
3Fh	WRITE LONG	O	161	8.2.23	6.1.23	Write data and ECC
40h	CHANGE DEFINITION	O	139	7.2.1	SPC	Set SCSI version
41h	WRITE SAME	O		8.2.24	6.1.24	Write data pattern
4Ch	LOG SELECT	O		7.2.6	SPC	Read statistics
4Dh	LOG SENSE	O		7.2.7	SPC	Read statistics
55h	MODE SELECT(10)	O	140	7.2.9	SPC	Set device parameters
5Ah	MODE SENSE(10)	O	140	7.2.10	SPC	Read device parameters
A5h	MOVE MEDIUM	O	218	16.2.3	SMC	Move medium
B8h	READ ELEMENT STATUS	O	220	16.2.5	SMC	Read element status

Note: Commands added to this command set in SCSI-3 are shaded light gray; mandatory commands are shaded dark gray. (M) means that the command is classified differently in SCSI-2 and SCSI-3. The corresponding classification is indicated after the reference to the standard.

READ(6) (08h) and WRITE(6) (0Ah); READ(10) (28h) and WRITE(10) (2Ah)

The READ command requests a certain number of logical blocks from a target. The WRITE command provides a target with a number of logical blocks to be written to the medium. The structure of these commands is identical (Table 13.3). Each contains the start address and the transfer length expressed in logical blocks.

Table 13.3 READ and WRITE commands.

	7	6	5	4	3	2	1	0
0	READ(6) (08h) or WRITE(6) (0Ah)							
1	(LUN)			(MSB)				
2	Logical block							
3								(LSB)
4	Data length							
5	Control byte							

	7	6	5	4	3	2	1	0
0	READ(10) (28h) or WRITE(10) (2Ah)							
1	(LUN)			DPO	FUA	Res.		Rel
2	(MSB)							
3								
4	Logical block							
5								(LSB)
6	Reserved							
7	(MSB)	Data length						
8								(LSB)
9	Control byte							

There is a 6-byte as well as a 10-byte version of both the READ and WRITE commands. Implementation of the READ commands is mandatory in both SCSI-2 and SCSI-3, whereas the WRITE command is only mandatory in SCSI-2.

The 6-byte version stems from SCSI's predecessor SASI. It has the disadvantage that only 21 bits are provided for the logical block address. Assuming a block length of 512 bytes, this allows a little more than a gigabyte to be addressed. For many modern drives this is simply not adequate.

The 6-byte demon

It is hard to believe but at one time there existed software drivers and firmware that used the 6-byte READ and WRITE commands. At the same time these adapters were capable of recognizing and using the full capacity of drives of more than a gigabyte. When a block above the magical 21-bit boundary was addressed, the host adapter would simply ignore the uppermost bits. Of course, this would address and write the wrong logical block on the drive. You can imagine what happened. An operating system would gradually fill a drive starting with the lowermost logical blocks. The system would operate normally until the 21-bit address was reached, at which time logical block 0 would be overwritten. This mistake would wipe out the boot block, the internal medium tables, and the directories (in this order). The drive would mysteriously become unusable without even a hardware error having been detected. For this reason it is highly recommended to avoid the 6-byte READ and WRITE commands, and if you ever find yourself the victim of unexplainable data corruption be sure to investigate whether or not the 6-byte demon is to blame.

Parameters

Other than the start address and transfer length, the 6-byte versions have no parameters. As with all block oriented 6-byte commands, a transfer length of zero actually means that 256 are requested. In contrast, zero transfer length means just that for the 10-byte commands and no data is sent. In the 10-byte version there are a number of additional control bits:

- **DPO** (disable page output): This bit helps the target to manage the cache. If it is set, it tells the target that the host does not intend to read the data again in the near future. The target may decide not to keep this data in the cache.

- **FUA** (force unit access): When this bit is set the target is forced to read the data from the medium even if it resides in the cache. If the cache contains a newer version of the data then it must first be written to the medium and then re-read. In the case of a WRITE command the target must wait until the data is on the medium before responding with GOOD status. This affects drives with cache as well as with buffer memory.

- **Rel** (relative addressing): This bit, which is valid only in conjunction with linked commands, causes the start address to be interpreted as an offset to the start address of the last command.

READ LONG (3Eh) and WRITE LONG (3Fh)

The most important variants to the READ and WRITE commands are READ LONG and WRITE LONG. Both are 10-byte commands, which operate not only on the user data but also on the ECC. Moreover, these commands operate on strictly one block at a time (Figure 13.3). The transfer length is interpreted as the number of bytes to transfer. There are also some differences in byte 1. The DPO and FUA bits do not exist, whereas bit 1 of a READ LONG command is the COOR control bit. Only if COOR is set will data correction be attempted in the event of a read error. Otherwise the data will be transferred just as it comes from the medium.

The type of encoding used to write data onto the medium as well as the ECC polynomial is vendor specific. However, the ECC polynomial must be known if we wish to write a valid ECC along with the data. Unfortunately, this makes it necessary to

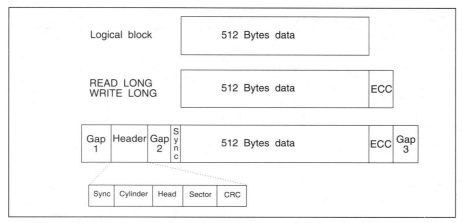

Figure 13.3   Physical layout of a logical block.

know device specific information when using READ LONG or WRITE LONG, which is at odds with the vendor independent philosophy of SCSI.

A very practical application of these commands is in the testing of a system's response to a data error. To accomplish this the drive is first connected to a PC running the SCSI monitor and a logical block is read using READ LONG. After modifying a few bytes the data is written back to the drive using WRITE LONG. Now in the system, the first access to this block will result in an ECC error. With a little practice it is possible to produce correctable as well as uncorrectable data errors.

Other variants of READ and WRITE

Two additional commands remain to be mentioned: WRITE AND VERIFY writes data to the medium and then reads it back while comparing it to the original data. The data is only transferred once across the SCSI bus. Another way to insure absolute data integrity from host memory to the medium is to link together a standard READ and WRITE command and then compare the data in host memory. Finally, the command WRITE SAME allows one to write the same block several times to the medium.

READ CAPACITY (25h)

Also mandatory for disk drives is the command READ CAPACITY (Table 13.4). It has the standard structure of 10-byte commands and returns eight bytes of information: four bytes reflect the last LBN of the drive while the remaining four reflect the block length.

The PMI (partial medium indicator) control bit, byte 8, bit 0, plays an important role. When clear, the command returns the LBN of the last logical block of the medium as described above. In this case the block number in the command block must be zero.

When PMI is set the command returns something completely different. Now the LBN in the command is interpreted and the target returns the next LBN, after which

Table 13.4   The READ CAPACITY command.

	7	6	5	4	3	2	1	0
0	READ CAPACITY (25h)							
1	(LUN)			Reserved				Rel
2	(MSB)							
3	Logical							
4	block							
5								(LSB)
6	Reserved							
7								
8								PMI
9	Control byte							

Table 13.5 The FORMAT UNIT command.

	7	6	5	4	3	2	1	0
0	FORMAT UNIT (04h)							
1	(LUN)			Fmt	Cmpl	Defect list format		
2	Vendor specific							
3	(MSB)	Interleave						
4								(LSB)
5	Control byte							

a noticeable delay in access will occur. Delays in access occur, for example, at cylinder boundaries. Using this command the operating system can determine whether a certain area of frequently accessed storage is ideally located.

FORMAT UNIT (04h)

The FORMAT UNIT command instructs the target to format the medium of a specific LUN (Table 13.5). In its simplest form no parameters are sent and the target formats using default settings. The actual formatting procedure has two phases. First the physical medium is formatted, meaning that each sector is written with header, data, and ECC information. Afterwards, the mapping from physical blocks to logical blocks takes place. Finally, during a second pass over the medium defective blocks are reallocated; that is, replaced with reserve blocks. The target will also accept a list of additional medium defects to be reallocated in a parameter block. Since format parameters are set using the MODE SELECT command it is imperative to first use MODE SELECT, then the FORMAT command. Only in this way will the drive configuration reflect the desired mode parameters (see Figure 13.4).

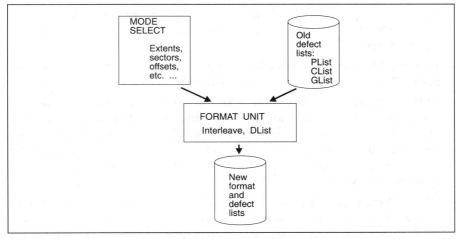

Figure 13.4   Influences on formatting.

The following parameters are contained in the command itself:

- **Fmt** (format data): This bit must be set when a parameter list follows the FORMAT UNIT command.

- **Cmpl** (complete): This bit may only be set when Fmt is set. It indicates that the defect list in the parameter list is exhaustive. All defect lists except the PList are deleted and newly constructed.

- **Defect list format**: This field indicates one of three defect list formats: block format (000b), index format (100b), or sector format (101b). Only one format type is allowed in a single parameter list. The formats are described in detail later in this section under the heading 'Defect descriptors'.

- **Interleave**: The term 'interleave' is explained in Chapter 2. This field indicates the interleave that should be employed. A value of 00h means that the target should use its default values. To assure a one-to-one interleave a value of 01h must be used.

Parameter lists

Figure 13.5 describes by way of example the structure of the FORMAT UNIT parameter list. Bytes 0 to 3 contain the header. Next comes the optional initialization pattern descriptor. This has a variable length, which in this example spans from byte 4 to byte 8. This is followed by optional defect descriptors. Thus, a parameter list is necessary when sending either an initialization pattern or defect lists with the FORMAT command. Any other pertinent format information is found in the MODE parameter pages, especially the format page.

In addition to the control bits in byte 1, the header of the parameter list contains the length of the defect lists in bytes 2 and 3. This length may be zero. The number of defects can be inferred from the list length together with the list format in byte 1 of the command itself. A description of the control bits follows:

- **FOV** (format option valid): Only when this bit is set are the bits DPR, DCR, STP, IP and DSP valid. Otherwise, these bits must be set to zero and the target will use its default values.

- **DPR** (disable primary): When this bit is set a PList will not be transferred to the target. The PList constructed by the manufacturer, however, remains intact.

- **STP** (stop format): This bit controls what should happen when the target does, in fact, accept a PList or GList to use in formatting, but the list cannot be found or read. In both cases the command terminates with CHECK CONDITION status. When STP is set, the target will abort formatting and prepare the sense key MEDIUM ERROR. Otherwise, the formatting will take place and the sense key RECOVERED ERROR will be available.

- **IP** (initialization pattern): When set this bit indicates that the parameter list contains a descriptor for the initialization pattern.

- **DSP** (disable saving parameters): Normally all mode parameters are saved during the formatting process. This action is inhibited when DSP is set.

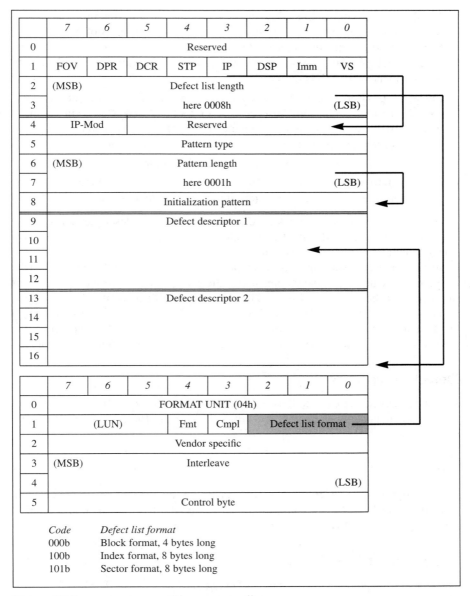

Figure 13.5   FORMAT UNIT with parameter list.

- **Imm** (immediate): The setting of this bit causes status to be returned as soon as the parameter list has been received. Otherwise the status is sent after completion of the task as usual.
- **VS:** (vendor specific)

If IP is set then an initialization pattern descriptor follows the parameter list header. This pattern is a sequence of bytes that are written as data to each block of the drive.

- **IP-Mod**: These control bits allow the target to modify a portion of the initialization pattern for each block. 01b means that the first four bytes of every logical block should contain the logical block number. 10b means that each physical block should contain the logical block number. 00b leaves the initialization pattern unchanged. 11b is reserved.

- **Pattern type**: Here 00h means that the target should use its default pattern. In this case the pattern length must also be zero or a CHECK CONDITION will result. A value of 01h causes the supplied pattern to be used. The remaining values are reserved or vendor specific.

- **Pattern length**: Indicates the length of the initialization pattern.

- **Initialization pattern**: This pattern is written to each logical block during the formatting process. The pattern is repeated until the block is filled.

The rest of the parameter block is comprised of the defect descriptors. The defect descriptors that are used with FORMAT UNIT as well as other commands receive special attention in their own section.

In conclusion, consider again the example in Figure 13.5. An arrow points from the IP bit to the beginning of the initialization pattern descriptor because only when this bit is set will the descriptor follow. The pattern length contains the pointer, which points to the end of the descriptor. The defect list length together with the pattern length points to the end of the entire parameter list. In the defect list format field of the FORMAT UNIT command is the value 000b, indicating 4-byte long defect descriptors.

Defect descriptors

Defect descriptors are used by the commands FORMAT UNIT, READ DEFECT DATA, SEND DIAGNOSTIC and RECEIVE DIAGNOSTIC RESULTS. The various formats are selected using a 3-bit code.

Block format (000b)

The four bytes of the descriptor contain the LBN of the block in which the defect is located (Table 13.6). When using the block format the list must be constructed in ascending order. An LBN may correspond to more than one sector.

Index format (100b)

The index pulse indicates the beginning of every track on the disk. The first four bytes of the index format contain the cylinder and head number of the defect (Table 13.7).

Table 13.6 Defect descriptor in block format.

0	(MSB)
1	Block number of
2	defective block
3	(LSB)

Table 13.7   Defect descriptor in index format.

0	(MSB)	Cylinder number of	
1		defective block	
2			(LSB)
3		Head number	
4	(MSB)		
5		Position of defect as	
6		bytes after index	
7			(LSB)

The remaining four bytes contain the defect position measured in bytes from the index. If FFFFFFFFh is given here the entire track should be regarded as defective. For drives that support variable sector lengths, only the index format may be used for the manufacturer's defect list (PList).

Note that numbers such as FFFFFFFFh are often referred to as −1, which corresponds to their signed integer interpretation. Although this is easier to pronounce, the width of the number is no longer apparent.

Sector format (101b)

The sector format is in structure exactly like the index format except that bytes 4 through 7 contain the sector number of the defect. Here too a sector number of FFFFFFFFh indicates that the entire track is defective (Table 13.8).

Commands for cache management

In addition to the commands that implicitly modify the cache, there are a number of SCSI-2 commands that configure the cache directly.

The command LOCK/UNLOCK CACHE allows certain regions in the cache to be locked. Locked blocks will not be overwritten by other data. The command is structured like a READ(10) command. Byte 1, bit 1 is the lock bit. When set, a region is

Table 13.8   Defect descriptor in sector format.

0	(MSB)	Cylinder number of	
1		defective block	
2			(LSB)
3		Head number	
4	(MSB)		
5		Defective	
6		sector	
7			(LSB)

locked; otherwise it is freed. Only those regions that are in the cache at the time of the command are affected. The command PRE-FETCH is also structured like READ(10). It instructs the target to read the specified blocks from the medium into the cache. No transfer across the SCSI bus takes place.

Finally, SYNCHRONIZE CACHE causes the target to write the specified region of the cache to the medium. This makes sense when a target has been allowed to respond to WRITE commands immediately with GOOD status before actually writing the medium.

13.3   Mode parameter pages for disk drives

The following mode parameter pages are defined for disk drives (Table 13.9):

Format page (03h)

The format page contains the information necessary to format the medium (Table 13.10). In particular it contains information concerning replacement sectors and tracks. The terms interleave, track skew and cylinder skew were already covered in Chapter 2.

A new term is introduced here, however, which has special meaning in the SCSI world. With respect to SCSI, a zone refers to a group of tracks to which a certain number of replacement sectors or tracks are allocated.

Outside the world of SCSI the term zone is often used in the context of zone-bit recording. Zone-bit recording refers to a recording technique whereby the outer cylinders are written with a higher bit density, and therefore more sectors, than the inner cylinders. In SCSI the regions with a constant number of sectors are called notches. It is unfortunate that the terminology is inconsistent here.

A look at the format page reveals that many values vary with each notch. It is possible for a target to define some or all mode parameter pages separately for each

Table 13.9   Mode parameter pages for disk drives.

Page code	Name	Page	SCSI-2	SCSI-3 (SBC)
01h	Read/write error page		8.3.3.6	7.1.3.6
02h	Disconnect/reconnect page	145	7.3.3.2	SPC
03h	Format page	168	8.3.3.3	7.1.3.3
04h	Disk drive geometry page	170	8.3.3.7	7.1.3.7
05h	Floppy disk page		8.3.3.2	7.1.3.2
07h	Verify error page		8.3.3.8	7.1.3.8
08h	Cache page	172	8.3.3.1	7.1.3.1
09h	Peripheral device page	146	7.3.3.3	SPC
0Ah	Control mode page	147	7.3.3.1	SPC
0Bh	Medium type page		8.3.3.4	7.1.3.4
0Ch	Notch page	174	8.3.3.5	7.1.3.5
0Dh	Power condition page		–	7.1.3.6
1Ch	Informal exception page		–	SPC

Table 13.10 Format page.

	7	6	5	4	3	2	1	0
0	PS	Res	Format page (03h)					
1	Page length (16h)							
2	(MSB)	Tracks per zone						
3								(LSB)
4	(MSB)	Replacement sectors						
5		per zone						(LSB)
6	(MSB)	Replacement tracks						
7		per zone						(LSB)
8	(MSB)	Replacement tracks						
9		per LUN						(LSB)
10	(MSB)	Sectors						
11		per track						(LSB)
12	(MSB)	Data bytes						
13		per sector						(LSB)
14	(MSB)	Interleave						
15								(LSB)
16	(MSB)	Track skew						
17								(LSB)
18	(MSB)	Cylinder skew						
19								(LSB)
20	SSEC	HSEC	RMB	SURF	Reserved			
21	Reserved							
22								
23								

notch. A special notch page contains the number of active notches influenced by the MODE commands:

- **Tracks per zone**: The entire medium is divided into zones consisting of this number of tracks per zone. The last zone may have fewer tracks. A value of zero treats the entire medium as a single zone.

- **Replacement sectors per zone**: A zero instructs the target to use its default value. However, a notch page, if implemented, can be used to achieve zero sectors per zone.

- **Replacement tracks per zone**: Alternate tracks make it possible to replace an entire track that contains many defects. A value of zero is interpreted as such in this field.

- **Replacement tracks per LUN**: Corresponds to the above fields with respect to a LUN.

- **Sectors per track**: This is the number of physical sectors including alternates per track.

- **Bytes per sector:** This is the number of data bytes per physical sector. This is not necessarily equal to the number of bytes per logical block.

- **Interleave**: This field is only valid for MODE SENSE. It reflects the value defined by FORMAT UNIT.

- **Track skew**: Specifies the number of physical sectors between the last logical block of one track and the next logical block of the next track (see also Chapter 2).

- **Cylinder skew**: Specifies the number of physical sectors between the last logical block of one cylinder and the next logical block of the next cylinder (see also Chapter 2).

- **SSEC** (soft sector): Specifies that the drive should use soft sectoring.

- **HSEC** (hard sector): Specifies that the drive should use hard sectoring.

The target must support either hard or soft sectoring or both.

- **RMB** (removable): The target uses removable medium. This must reflect the information returned by the INQUIRY command.

- **SURF** (surface): When this bit is zero logical blocks are allocated progressively to the sectors of a cylinder before those of the next cylinder. When SURF is set logical blocks are allocated progressively to the sectors of a surface before those of the next surface. Most hard disks have this bit clear; most diskette drives have it set.

It is obvious that alternate sectors reduce the space available for user data. If too many alternate sectors are allocated then storage is sacrificed unnecessarily. On the other hand, the medium is unusable as soon as all alternate sectors have been exhausted. The answer is to find a compromise somewhere in between these two extremes.

In practice this is achieved in the following way: for simplicity, assume a medium with constant geometry; that is, without notches. A zone is defined as being a single track. For each zone one alternate sector is allocated. When necessary this alternate sector can be read with almost no delay. If additional sectors of the track are defective the entire track is reallocated. An alternate cylinder should be set aside for every 200 cylinders. This rule of thumb allocates between 3% and 5% of the drive capacity to replacement sectors.

Disk drive geometry page (04h)

Hard disks and diskettes use different geometry pages. In this book, however, only the hard disk geometry page is discussed. This page pertains to hard drives with removable medium as well. With the exception of spindle synchronization, the

Table 13.11 Mode commands: geometry page.

	7	6	5	4	3	2	1	0
0	PS	Res	Geometry page (04h)					
1	Page length (16h)							
2	(MSB)							
3	Number of cylinders							
4								(LSB)
5	Number of heads							
6	(MSB)		Start cylinder					
7	for							
8	write compensation							(LSB)
9	(MSB)		Start cylinder					
10	for							
11	reduced write current							(LSB)
12	(MSB)		Step rate					
13								(LSB)
14	(MSB)		Cylinder number					
15	of							
16	landing zone							(LSB)
17	Reserved						RPL	
18	Rotational offset							
19	Reserved							
20	(MSB)		Medium					
21	rotation rate							(LSB)
22	Reserved							
23								

parameters deal strictly with fixed geometry information (Table 13.11). Changeable parameters such as the number of sectors and sector length belong to the format page. For most fields, the relevant background terminology is explained in Chapter 2.

The rotational position locking field is used to synchronize the spindles of two or more individual disk drives. Synchronization makes it possible to read and write blocks from different drives at precisely the same time without latency delays by ensuring that these blocks rotate underneath the heads of their respective drives in unison. The drives must not only have the same rotational speed but must also synchronize the relative positions of the heads with respect to the medium. This is accomplished by declaring one drive the master and the remaining drives slaves, which govern their speed relative to the master. Here additional signals are needed that are not provided by the SCSI bus. Spindle synchronization is employed in RAID arrays, which achieve very high throughput by accessing drives in parallel while eliminating latency delays.

- **RPL** (rotational position locking): 00b disables synchronization; 01b instructs the drive to act as a slave, and 10b as a master.

- **Rotational offset**: This byte reflects the amount of rotational offset a slave will have to its master measured in 1/256th of a rotation. This allows a staggering of the individual disks.

Cache page (08h)

Table 13.12 shows the cache parameter page for the MODE commands. In SCSI-3, the cache page is complemented with several parameters and bits which make its length grow from 12 to 19 bytes. First, we will describe the elements which exist both in SCSI-2 and in SCSI-3.

- **WCE** (write cache enable): When set the target replies with a GOOD status as soon as all of the data has been received into the cache. Otherwise this status may not be returned until the data has been successfully written to the medium. Be aware that when WCE is set the target decides when to write the data to the medium. There may be a substantial delay here if a large number of I/O processes must be processed. The command SYNCHRONIZE CACHE forces all cache data yet to be secured to be written to the medium.

- **MF** (multiplication factor): Normally the values for pre-fetch maximum and minimum reflect a certain number of blocks. However, when MF is set these values represent scalars which are to be multiplied with the transfer length to obtain their meaning.

- **RCD** (read cache disable): Causes the medium to be read even if the data resides in the cache.

- **Read retention priority and write retention priority**: Specify with what priority the data either read or written into the cache is to be maintained. The priority given is with respect to data resulting from pre-fetch operations. 0h means that all data should be treated equally; 1h gives the data a lower priority than pre-fetch data; Fh gives the data higher priority than pre-fetch data.

- **Disable pre-fetch transfer length**: This field specifies the maximal transfer length for which a pre-fetch should occur. Zero disables pre-fetch.

- **Pre-fetch minimum**: This field specifies the minimum number of blocks that should be pre-fetched regardless of whether other commands are impeded.

- **Pre-fetch maximum**: This field specifies the maximum number of blocks that should be pre-fetched.

The interpretation of the above two fields is independent of the MF bit. If both values are equal pre-fetch will occur regardless of other pending commands. If there is a difference between minimum and maximum, a pre-fetch will be broken off inside this interval if otherwise another command would be delayed.

Table 13.12   Mode parameter cache page.

	7	6	5	4	3	2	1	0
0	PS	Res	Cache page (08h)					
1	Page length (0Ah, SCSI-3: 12h)							
2	IC	ABPF	CAP	DISC	SIZE	WCE	MF	RCD
3	Read retention priority				Write retention priority			
4	(MSB)			Disable pre-fetch				
5				transfer length				(LSB)
6	(MSB)			Pre-fetch minimum				
7								(LSB)
8	(MSB)			Pre-fetch maximum				
9								(LSB)
10	(MSB)			Absolute pre-fetch maximum				
11								(LSB)
12	FSW	LBCSS	DRA	VS	VS	Reserved		
13	Number of cache segments							
14	(MSB)			Cache segment size				
15								(LSB)
16	Reserved							
17 ...	Size of segment							
... 19	not reserved for cache							

- **Absolute pre-fetch maximum**: This field only has meaning when MF is set. It limits the pre-fetch length resulting from the multiplication factor.

  In SCSI-3, the following new parameters are introduced:

- **IC** (initiator control): When set, the device server must adjust its cache size according to the parameters in bytes 13 to 19. Otherwise, it can use its own algorithm to determine the size.

- **ABPF** (abort pre-fetch): The device server must abort pre-fetch processes when it is selected.

- **CAP** (caching analysis permitted): The device server may perform an analysis of the cache processes in order to optimize its strategy, even if the throughput may momentarily suffer. When CAP is not set, this is prohibited.

- **DISC** (discontinuity): The device server should pre-fetch also across discontinuities and track changes, until the buffer is full.

- **SIZE** (size enable): The value in bytes 14 and 15 is valid and should be used.

- **FSW** (force sequential write): The device server should write logical blocks in the cache in ascending sequential order. When FSW is not set, the device server can determine the order itself.

- **LBCSS** (logical block cache segment size): When set, the cache segment size is specified in logical blocks, otherwise in bytes.
- **DRA** (disable read ahead): Read-ahead is prohibited.
- **VS:** Vendor specific.

Notch page (0Ch)

The notch page describes the regions of the disk with a constant number of sectors per track (so-called notches). This optional page does not even have to be implemented for drives that do, in fact, contain regions of varying number of sectors (Table 13.13). If notch pages are implemented then each notch will have its own page (Figure 13.6).

- **ND** (notched drive): Only when this bit is set is the notch page valid. Otherwise the drive has no notches and the rest of the page is empty.
- **LPN** (logical or physical notch): When set this bit indicates that the boundaries of the active notches are expressed as logical blocks. Otherwise they are

Table 13.13 Mode commands: notch page.

	7	6	5	4	3	2	1	0
0	PS	Res	Notch page (0Ch)					
1	Page length (16h)							
2	ND	LPN	Reserved					
3	Reserved							
4	(MSB)	Maximum number						
5	of notches							(LSB)
6	(MSB)	Active notch						
7								(LSB)
8	(MSB)							
9	Beginning of							
10	active notch							
11								(LSB)
12	(MSB)							
13	End of							
14	active notch							
15								(LSB)
16	3Fh	3Eh	3Dh	...				
...	Mode pages							
...	with notches							
23	...			04h	03h	02h	01h	00h

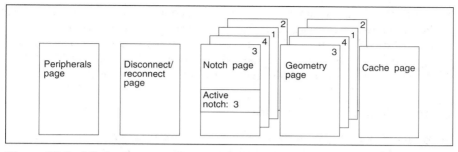

Figure 13.6   Mode parameter pages with notches.

expressed as physical addresses. Here the three most significant bytes hold the cylinder number and the lowest byte the head number.

- **Active notch**: This field contains the number of the notch to which this page and other MODE SELECT pages refer. This number is valid until it is changed by MODE SELECT. A zero means that subsequent mode commands pertain to those parameters that apply across all notches.

- **Mode pages with notches**: This field is 8 bytes long or a total of 64 bits. Each bit represents one of the MODE pages from 00h to 3Fh. The most significant bit corresponds to page 3Fh, the least significant to page 00h. A set bit means that the corresponding MODE page contains parameters that may be different for different notches. A zero means that the page applies to all notches.

13.4   The SCSI model of optical storage and WORM drives

The SCSI model of optical storage is very similar to that of regular disk drives. We will use magnetic disk drives as a basis for comparison and discuss the differences as they become relevant.

One difference between the two is that optical storage has the potential for much greater storage capacity. For this reason 12-byte commands have been defined for medium access commands. These have a 32-bit logical number field, like the 10-byte version, but also a 32-bit wide transfer length.

The device type for optical storage is very diverse. It includes read-only media (like CD-ROM), media that can be written only once (WORM drives) and media that can be rewritten indefinitely. CD-ROM and WORM drives, however, each have their own device type. Except for the audio dimension of CDs, these device types represent subclasses of the optical storage device type presented here.

Optical storage drives are often capable of working with all three types of medium. For this reason an initiator must use a MODE SENSE to determine what type of medium is involved when working with a device of this class. Naturally, this must occur whenever the medium is replaced.

Optical storage has physical characteristics that are foreign to magnetic disk drives. These differences are accounted for in the command set. For example, for WORM drives, there is the MEDIUM SCAN command that allows the seeking to locations that have not been written. Many rewritable optical medium drives require that data be erased before being written again. There is also a command for this purpose.

WORM drives have their own device type, which is a proper subclass of optical storage. Both of these are covered here. We postpone the discussion of CD-ROM at this point since its audio capabilities make it worthy of a separate chapter.

Generations of a logical block

Many optical storage devices are capable of emulating the rewriting of a block. The UPDATE command writes the modified logical block to another location on the medium and makes it available via a pointer to the new location. The original logical block remains unchanged and represents an earlier generation of the data. Older generations are identified with a lower generation number, starting with zero. The older generations of a logical block are accessible using the READ UPDATED BLOCK command.

The model of a SCSI WORM drive

WORM drives are also a subclass of optical storage. Since the medium can only be written once some commands are dispensable. For example, the ERASE command has no meaning here. Also missing is the FORMAT command because a WORM medium is already formatted.

13.5 Commands for optical storage and WORM drives

Table 13.14 lists the commands defined for optical storage and WORM drives. You will notice that all mandatory commands are either disk drive commands or commands for all SCSI classes. This allows us to concentrate on only those commands that are unique to optical storage devices.

Table 13.14 Commands for optical storage devices.

Op-code	Name	OS	WD	Page	SCSI-2	SCSI-3 (SBC)	Description
00h	TEST UNIT READY	M	M	131	7.2.16	SPC	Reflects whether or not the LUN is ready to accept a command
01h	REZERO UNIT	O	O		8.2.13	6.1.3	Seek track 0
03h	REQUEST SENSE	M	M	132	7.2.14	SPC	Returns detailed error information
04h	FORMAT UNIT	O	O	163	8.2.1	6.1.1	Formats medium
07h	REASSIGN BLOCKS	O	O		8.2.10	6.1.10	Defective blocks reassigned
08h	READ(6)	O	O	159	8.2.5	6.1.5	Read. Limited addressing
0Ah	WRITE(6)	O	O	159	8.2.5	6.1.20	Write. Limited addressing
0Bh	SEEK(6)	O	O		8.2.15	6.1.15	Seek to a logical block
12h	INQUIRY	M	M	128	7.2.5	SPC	Returns LUN specific information
15h	MODE SELECT(6)	O	O	140	7.2.8	SPC	Set device parameters
16h	RESERVE UNIT	M	M	136	8.2.12	6.1.12	Make LUN accessible only to certain initiators

Table 13.14 Commands for optical storage devices (*continued*).

Op-code	Name	OS	WD	Page	SCSI-2	SCSI-3 (SBC)	Description
17h	RELEASE UNIT	M	M	136	8.2.11	6.1.11	Make LUN accessible to other initiators
18h	COPY	O	O		7.2.3	SPC	Autonomous copy from/to another device
1Ah	MODE SENSE(6)	O	O	140	7.2.10	SPC	Read device parameters
1Bh	START/STOP UNIT	O	O		8.2.17	6.1.17	Load/unload medium
1Ch	RECEIVE DIAGNOSTIC RESULTS	O	O		7.2.13	SPC	Read self-test results
1Dh	SEND DIAGNOSTIC	M	M	138	7.2.1	SPC	Initiate self-test
1Eh	PREVENT/ALLOW MEDIUM REMOVAL	O	O		8.2.4	6.1.14	Lock/unlock medium
25h	READ CAPACITY	M	M		8.2.7	6.1.7	Read number of logical blocks
28h	READ(10)	M	M	159	8.2.6	6.1.6	Read logical block
29h	READ GENERATION	O	O	179	15.2.6	6.2.6	Read maximum generation address of LBN
2Ah	WRITE(10)	M	M	159	8.2.6	6.2.13	Write logical block
2Bh	SEEK(10)	O	O		8.2.15	6.1.15	Seek to a logical block
2Ch	ERASE	O	O	181	15.2.1	6.2.1	Erase
2Dh	READ UPDATED BLOCK	O	O	179	15.2.7	6.2.7	Read specific version of changed block
2Eh	WRITE AND VERIFY	O	O		15.2.15	6.2.15	Write logical block, verify success
2Fh	VERIFY	O	O		15.2.11	6.2.11	Verify data on medium
30h	SEARCH DATA HIGH(10)	O	O		8.2.14	6.1.14	Search logical blocks for data pattern
31h	SEARCH DATA EQUAL(10)	O	O		8.2.14	6.1.14	Search logical blocks for data pattern
32h	SEARCH DATA LOW(10)	O	O		8.2.14	6.1.14	Search logical blocks for data pattern
33h	SET LIMITS(10)	O	O		8.2.16	6.1.16	Define logical block boundaries
34h	PRE-FETCH	O	O		8.2.3	6.1.3	Read data into buffer
35h	SYNCHRONIZE CACHE	O	O		8.2.8	6.1.18	Write cache to medium
36h	LOCK/UNLOCK CACHE	O	O		8.2.2	6.1.2	Hold data in cache
37h	READ DEFECT DATA(10)	O	O		8.2.8	6.1.8	Read list of defective blocks
38h	MEDIUM SCAN	O	O	179	15.2.3	6.2.3	Search for free area
39h	COMPARE	O	O		7.2.2	SPC	Compare data
3Ah	COPY AND VERIFY	O	O		7.2.4	SPC	Autonomous copy from/to another device, verify success
3Bh	WRITE BUFFER	O	O		7.2.17	SPC	Write the data buffer
3Ch	READ BUFFER	O	O		7.2.12	SPC	Read the data buffer
3Dh	UPDATE BLOCK	O		178	15.2.10	6.2.10	Substitute block with an updated one
3Eh	READ LONG	O	O	161	8.2.9	6.1.9	Read data and ECC
3Fh	WRITE LONG	O	O	161	8.2.23	6.1.23	Write data and ECC
40h	CHANGE DEFINITION	O	O	139	7.2.1	SPC	Set SCSI version
4Ch	LOG SELECT	O	O		7.2.6	SPC	Read statistics
4Dh	LOG SENSE	O	O		7.2.7	SPC	Read statistics
55h	MODE SELECT(10)	O	O	140	7.2.9	SPC	Set device parameters
5Ah	MODE SENSE(10)	O	O	140	7.2.10	SPC	Read device parameters
A8h	READ(12)	O	O		15.2.4	6.2.4	Read logical block
AAh	WRITE(12)	O	O		15.2.4	6.2.14	Write logical block
ACh	ERASE(12)	O			15.2.2	6.2.4	Erase logical block
AEh	WRITE AND VERIFY	O	O		15.2.16	6.2.16	Write logical block, verify success
AFh	VERIFY(12)	O	O		15.2.12	6.2.12	Verify data on medium
B0h	SEARCH DATA HIGH(12)	O	O		15.2.8	6.2.8	Search logical blocks for data pattern

Table 13.14   Commands for optical storage devices (*continued*).

Op-code	Name	OS	WD	Page	SCSI-2	SCSI-3 (SBC)	Description
B1h	SEARCH DATA EQUAL(12)	O	O		15.2.8	6.2.8	Search logical blocks for data pattern
B2h	SEARCH DATA LOW(12)	O	O		15.2.8	6.2.8	Search logical blocks for data pattern
B3h	SET LIMITS(12)	O	O		15.2.9	6.2.9	Set logical block boundaries
B7h	READ DEFECT DATA(12)	O	O		15.2.5	6.2.5	
B8h	READ ELEMENT STATUS	O	O	220	16.2.5	SMC	Read element status

Note: Commands added to this command set in SCSI-3 are shaded light gray; mandatory commands are shaded dark gray.

At this point I would also like to skip the 12-byte versions of the READ and WRITE commands. Here the parameters and control bits are identical to the 6- and 10-byte versions.

UPDATE BLOCK (3Dh)

This command is used to substitute a logical block with an updated one (Table 13.15). The new logical block lies in an alternative area outside the normal user data. Therefore, the command does not change the number of free blocks on the medium as reported by READ CAPACITY. When the alternative blocks are used up, the command aborts with a CHECK CONDITION status and the sense code NO DEFECT SPARE LOCATION AVAILABLE.

The new data is written to a new location on the medium, leaving the old data intact. In fact, the older version can still be accessed using READ UPDATED BLOCK. READ will, of course, always read the current version of the logical block. This command always operates on one logical block at a time, thus there is no transfer length.

Table 13.15   The UPDATE BLOCK command.

	7	6	5	4	3	2	1	0
0	UPDATE BLOCK (3Dh)							
1	(LUN)			Reserved				Rel
2	(MSB)							
3	Logical							
4	block number							
5								(LSB)
6	Reserved							
7								
8								
9	Control byte							

Table 13.16   The READ GENERATION command.

	7	6	5	4	3	2	1	0
0	READ GENERATION (29h)							
1	LUN			Reserved				Rel
2	(MSB)							
3	Logical							
4	block number							
5								(LSB)
6	Reserved							
7								
8	Transfer length (04h)							
9	Control byte							

Table 13.17   READ GENERATION parameter block.

	7	6	5	4	3	2	1	0
0	(MSB)			Most recent				
1				generation				(LSB)
2	Reserved							
3								

READ GENERATION (29h)

The READ GENERATION command returns the current generation number of a logical block (Table 13.16). The reply is contained in the first two bytes of a 4-byte long parameter block (Table 13.17).

READ UPDATED BLOCK(10) (2Dh)

This command is very much like a normal READ command. Even the control bits in byte 1 have the same meaning. However, there is no transfer length because the command reads exactly one block (Table 13.18).

Bytes 6 and 7 hold the generation of the block to be read. When the Latest bit is set then the most recent generation is numbered zero and the numbers incremented for older generations. Otherwise it is the oldest version that is numbered zero and the numbers incremented for newer generations. If the requested generation does not exist the command will return a CHECK CONDITION status.

MEDIUM SCAN (38h)

This command searches for a continuous region of written or unwritten medium after the start address. The command uses a parameter block containing the length of the region and the length of area to be searched (Table 13.19).

Table 13.18   The READ UPDATED BLOCK command.

	7	6	5	4	3	2	1	0
0	READ UPDATED BLOCK(10) (2Dh)							
1	(LUN)			DPO	FUA	Reserved		Rel
2	(MSB)							
3	Block address (LBN)							
4								
5								(LSB)
6	Latest	(MSB)		Generation				
7								(LSB)
8	Reserved							
9	Control byte							

A number of parameter bits are used (Table 13.20). When the WBS (written block search) bit is set then the target will search for a written region; when clear, an unwritten region. The PRA (partial results acceptable) bit indicates that the largest of those regions found should be returned in lieu of a qualifying region. The ASA bit specifies that the written or unwritten region should be continuous. The RSD bit

Table 13.19   The MEDIUM SCAN command.

	7	6	5	4	3	2	1	0
0	MEDIUM SCAN (38h)							
1	(LUN)			WBS	ASA	RSD	PRA	Rel
2	(MSB)							
3	Start							
4	address							
5								(LSB)
6	Reserved							
7								
8	Parameter list length (08h)							
9	Control byte							

Table 13.20   MEDIUM SCAN parameter block.

	7	6	5	4	3	2	1	0
0 ...	(MSB)			Number of				
... 3				blocks requested				(LSB)
4 ...	(MSB)			Number of				
... 7				blocks to scan				(LSB)

Table 13.21   The ERASE command for optical storage.

	7	6	5	4	3	2	1	0
0	ERASE (2Ch)							
1	(LUN)			Reserved		ERA	Res	Rel
2	(MSB)							
3	Start							
4	address (LBN)							
5								(LSB)
6	Reserved							
7	(MSB)			Number				
8								(LSB)
9	Control byte							

instructs the target to search from the end of the medium backwards. The result of the search process is a status. CONDITION MET indicates that a region meeting the specifications was found. Then REQUEST SENSE will return the sense key EQUAL or NO SENSE with the LBN of the region in the information bytes. If no qualifying region is found then GOOD status is returned with the sense key set to NO SENSE.

ERASE(10) (2Ch)

The ERASE command instructs the target to erase a number of logical blocks beginning with a start address (Table 13.21). This command is important for rewritable optical drives which require erasure before writing. Although erasure is already implemented within WRITE commands, for performance reasons it is more effective to erase large regions with a single ERASE command.

When the ERA bit is set the Number field must contain a zero, and all of the medium after the start address will be erased. Otherwise Number holds the number of blocks to be erased.

13.6   Mode parameters for optical storage and WORM drives

Mode parameter header

The medium type (byte 1) and the device type specific parameter (byte 2) have the interpretations shown in Table 13.22.

For a MODE SENSE command WP indicates that the medium is write protected. A set Cache bit indicates that the target has a cache and that cache control is possible using the DPO and FUA bits of the WRITE command.

The EBC (enable blank check) bit causes sectors to be verified as unwritten before a write is executed. When the checking is enabled an attempt to write an already written sector will result in a CHECK CONDITION.

Table 13.22 Mode parameter header byte 1 and byte 2.

Code	Medium type
00h	Default
01h	Read-only medium (R/O)
02h	WORM medium (W-O)
03h	Rewritable medium (R/W)
04h	R/O or W-O
05h	R/O or R/W
06h	W-O or R/W

Bit	7	6	5	4	3	2	1	0
	WP	Reserved		Cache	Reserved			EBC

Mode parameter pages

The mode parameter pages are defined in Table 13.23.

The optical device page (06h)

The optical device page (Table 13.24) contains precisely one parameter: the RUBR (report updated block read) bit. When set this bit causes the target to reply with CHECK CONDITION to a read of a block updated with an UPDATE command. In this way the host will know that the block being accessed does not represent the most recent version of the data.

Table 13.23 Mode parameter pages for optical storage.

Page code	Name	Page	SCSI-2	SCSI-3 (SBC)
01h	Read/write error page		8.3.3.6	7.1.3.6
02h	Disconnect/reconnect page	145	7.3.3.2	SPC
06h	Optical device page	182	15.3.3.1	7.2.3.1
07h	Verification error page		8.3.3.8	7.1.3.8
08h	Cache page	172	8.3.3.1	7.1.3.1
09h	Peripheral device page	146	7.3.3.3	SPC
0Ah	Control mode page	147	7.3.3.1	SPC
0Bh	Medium type page		8.3.3.4	7.1.3.4
0Dh	Power condition page		–	7.1.3.6
1Ch	Informal exception page		–	SPC

Table 13.24 Optical storage page.

	7	6	5	4	3	2	1	0
0	PS	Res	Page code (06h)					
1	Page length (02h)							
2	Reserved							RUBR
3								

14 Stream-oriented devices

The SCSI-3 document SSC (SCSI Stream Commands) summarizes the device models, commands and parameters for stream-oriented devices. It contains the device types of tape drives (sequential access devices), printer devices and communication devices.

14.1 The model of a SCSI tape drive

SCSI tape drives belong to the sequential access device type of the ANSI standard. I am not aware of any devices other than tape drives belonging to this class.

The data in a sequential access device is organized on the medium as a linear sequence of blocks. In order to access the data of a certain block the medium must be moved from the current position through all intervening positions to the desired block. It is easy to see that this is precisely the situation described by a tape drive.

At present, there have been almost no changes from SCSI-2 to SCSI-3. The READ POSITION command has become mandatory and is therefore included in this book. Furthermore, a new parameter page, the COMPRESSION page, has been added. Strangely enough, it seems that the current SSC proposal does not contain attached medium changers for tape drives.

The drive

The SCSI model of a tape drive differentiates between the drive itself and the exchangeable medium. The drive is either in ready condition or not ready. The drive is in ready condition when it is able to execute all possible commands. For example, the drive is not ready when no medium is present or when an online switch is de-activated.

The drive can also find itself in the write protected state. Although the write protection mechanism is usually implemented on the removable medium, many drives have a write protection switch as well.

The recording medium

The recording medium for sequential devices consists of a tape of various widths and lengths coated with magnetic material. This tape may be wound onto single reels or packaged in a cartridge or cassette format. When the medium is loaded in the device and data access is possible the medium is said to be mounted. During loading and unloading the medium is demounted. This terminology corresponds to that of replaceable medium drives.

The usable length of a tape has a beginning and end, which are marked BOM (beginning of medium) and EOM (end of medium), respectively. These do not necessarily correspond to the physical ends of the tape. The length beyond these marks is used to secure the tape to the reels.

Many recording formats include an additional EW (early warning) marking. This mark is placed at a position prior to the EOM mark. It allows the target enough time to warn the initiator of the end of the tape and write any data that may already be in its buffer.

Recording formats

The range of recording formats for magnetic tape is almost endless (Figure 14.1). Fortunately, it is of little consequence for the discussion of SCSI tape drives which format is used on the medium itself. The format is strictly a matter of concern for the drive, not the SCSI controller. When a drive is compatible with a number of different formats, the MODE SELECT command is used to choose among them.

Nevertheless, as background information three basic recording formats are mentioned here. The first of these is parallel storage format. Here multiple tracks are recorded simultaneously in the same direction. This is the method traditional reel-to-reel devices employ, using nine tracks, eight data and parity, on ½ inch wide tape. The parallel recording technique leads to a relatively high throughput at moderate tape speeds. Common specifications are 6250 bits per inch (BPI) at 125 inches per second (IPS). These values multiplied together yield a data throughput of 780 Kbytes per second. The disadvantage of this method is the necessity of a relatively complex and therefore expensive read/write head.

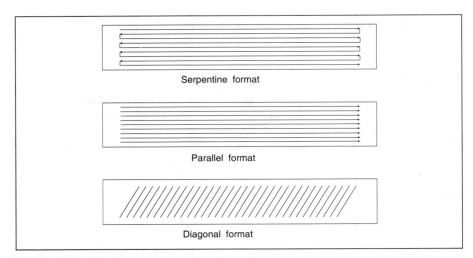

Serpentine format

Parallel format

Diagonal format

Figure 14.1 Various tape recording formats.

The second technique uses a simple read/write head and only a single track. The data are written and read serially. When one end of the tape is reached the head is moved slightly so that the track can be continued in the opposite direction. This is repeated until the result is a serpentine track running back and forth across the tape. This method is used mainly in cassette devices following the QIC standard.

The helical scan technique originally came from video cassette recording. Here a rotating head is used to write short diagonal tracks across the width of a relatively slow moving tape. This method is used by the EXABYTE drive and is also similar to the technique used in 4 mm DAT drives.

Many recording formats use preformatted media. These methods make possible the use of physical blocks in organizing data. The physical block structure, which is largely hidden from the SCSI interface, can be accessed directly using the LOCATE command.

Partitions

A tape can be divided into one or more partitions. Partition 0, which always exists, is called the default partition. Every partition has its own identification for beginning, end, and EW, and they are called BOPx, EOPx and EWx, where x stands for the number of the partition. Commands for tape devices always pertain to the active partition. The active partition can be changed using either the device configuration page of MODE SELECT or the LOCATE command.

Objects within a partition

Within a partition data blocks and tape marks are used to segment the medium. These are organized hierarchically, with data blocks at the lowest level followed by filemarks and at the highest level setmarks.

The EOD (end of data) mark is special in that its implementation is dependent on the type of recording format. In general, this mark is generated when a certain length of unwritten tape has gone past the read head.

Data blocks

To an initiator a tape, like a disk drive, looks like a sequence of logical blocks, and as with a disk drive logical blocks may or may not correspond one-to-one with physical blocks on the tape. The blocks themselves are either fixed or of variable size up to 16 Mbytes. This is more than adequate. Extremely long blocks should be avoided since a block must be read and written as a single unit without interruption.

Tape marks

A tape drive may also employ the use of tape marks among the logical blocks holding user data. Tape marks make it possible to locate specific places on the tape without having to read the intervening data. Moreover, tape marks can be identified on higher tape speeds than are used to read actual data. This further decreases the access time. There are two types of tape mark: the filemark and the setmark. Setmarks represent the higher level division of a partition, filemarks the lower level.

Buffered and unbuffered modes

The role of data buffers with respect to disk I/O was covered earlier in this book. Such a buffer is realized as onboard RAM and its contents are volatile. The buffer is used to store data temporarily before it is written to the medium or passed on to the initiator, as the case may be.

SCSI tape devices support both buffered and unbuffered modes of operation. The modes relate to the way in which write operations are performed; that is, all commands that write either data blocks or tape marks. In addition, some commands include an Immed (immediate) control bit which overrides the mode for a given command.

Tape devices without a data buffer always operate in the unbuffered mode. In this mode any write operation will conclude with a status phase only after a write to the medium has occurred. However, when Immed is set, commands that do not write to the medium (like, for instance, REWIND) are allowed to return GOOD status immediately after the command is received.

Tape devices with a data buffer can be configured to operate in either mode. This configuration is accomplished using the appropriate parameter page of the MODE SELECT command.

The data buffer of a SCSI tape device may hold tape marks as well as data. In the buffered mode a tape device is allowed to return GOOD status as soon as write data has been received into the buffer. Commands with the Immed bit set are allowed to respond in the same manner. When Immed is clear this forces a command to be executed in the unbuffered mode.

14.2　Commands for tape devices

Tape device commands (Table 14.1) differ greatly from those of disk drives in many respects but this is especially so with regard to READ and WRITE commands and their derivatives. These commands do not make use of logical block numbers but only a transfer length. A command begins its reading or writing at the current position of the tape.

REWIND (01h)

The REWIND command causes the target to position the medium to the beginning of the active partition (Table 14.2). However, before doing so the target must write to the medium all data, filemarks, and setmarks that may reside in the buffer.

The only parameter is the Immed bit in byte 1. When set the target will return status after any buffered data has been written to the medium but before command execution has begun. When clear status will be returned only after the medium has been fully rewound.

Table 14.1 SCSI tape drive commands.

Op-code	Name	Type	Page	SCSI-2	SCSI-3 (SCC)	Description
00h	TEST UNIT READY	M	131	7.2.16	SPC	Reflects whether or not the LUN is ready to accept a command
01h	REWIND	M	186	9.2.11	5.2.10	Rewinds tape
03h	REQUEST SENSE	M	132	7.2.14	SPC	Returns detailed error information
04h	FORMAT MEDIUM	O	189	9.2.11	5.2.2	Prepare medium for use
05h	READ BLOCK LIMITS	M	192	9.2.5	5.2.6	Returns possible block lengths
08h	READ	M	188	9.2.4	5.2.5	Read
0Ah	WRITE	M	189	9.2.14	5.2.13	Write
0Fh	READ REVERSE	O	188	9.2.7	5.2.8	Read backwards
10h	WRITE FILEMARKS	M	191	9.2.15	5.2.14	Write filemarks
11h	SPACE	M	190	9.2.12	5.2.11	Advance tape
12h	INQUIRY	M	128	7.2.5	5.2.12	Returns LUN specific information
13h	VERIFY	O		9.2.13	SPC	Verify data
14h	RECOVER BUFFERED DATA	O		9.2.8	5.2.9	Recover data from buffer
15h	MODE SELECT(6)	M	140	7.2.8	SPC	Set device parameters
16h	RESERVE UNIT	M	136	9.2.10	SPC	Make LUN accessible only to certain initiators
17h	RELEASE UNIT	M	136	9.2.9	SPC	Make LUN accessible to other initiators
18h	COPY	O		7.2.3	SPC	Autonomous copy from/to another device
19h	ERASE	M	191	9.2.1	5.2.1	Erase tape
1Ah	MODE SENSE(6)	M	140	7.2.10	SPC	Read device parameters
1Bh	LOAD/UNLOAD	O	195	9.2.2	5.2.3	Load/unload medium
1Ch	RECEIVE DIAGNOSTIC RESULTS	O		7.2.13	SPC	Read self-test results
1Dh	SEND DIAGNOSTIC	M	138	7.2.1	SPC	Initiate self-test
1Eh	PREVENT/ALLOW MEDIUM REMOVAL	O		8.2.4	SBC	Lock/unlock door
2Bh	LOCATE	O	193	9.2.3	5.2.4	Seek LBN
34h	READ POSITION	(M)	193	9.2.6 M	5.2.7 P	Read current tape position
39h	COMPARE	O		7.2.2	SPC	Compare data
3Ah	COPY AND VERIFY	O		7.2.4	SPC	Autonomous copy from/to another device, verify success
3Bh	WRITE BUFFER	O		7.2.17	SPC	Write the data buffer
3Ch	READ BUFFER	O		7.2.12	SPC	Read the data buffer
40h	CHANGE DEFINITION	O	139	7.2.1	SPC	Set SCSI version
4Ch	LOG SELECT	O		7.2.6	SPC	Read statistics
4Dh	LOG SENSE	O		7.2.7	SPC	Read statistics
55h	MODE SELECT(10)	O	140	7.2.9	SPC	Set device parameters
5Ah	MODE SENSE(10)	O	140	7.2.10	SPC	Read device parameters

Note: Commands added to this command set in SCSI-3 are shaded light gray; mandatory commands are shaded dark gray. (M) means that the command is classified differently in SCSI-2 and SCSI-3. The corresponding classification is indicated after the reference to the standard.

SCSI-1 compatible devices do not necessarily write buffered data to the medium before the execution of this command. In order to make SCSI-2 and SCSI-1 devices compatible one can make use of the WRITE FILEMARKS command with the Immed bit set before issuing a REWIND command.

Table 14.2 The REWIND command.

	7	6	5	4	3	2	1	0
0	REWIND (01h)							
1	(LUN)			Reserved				Immed
2	Reserved							
3								
4								
5	Control byte							

READ (08h) and READ REVERSE (0Fh)

The READ command is structured differently to the disk drive version (Table 14.3). There is no field for the logical block number since the tape READ command always begins with the next logical block. The next block is the first block reached as the tape moves toward the EOP mark. Lacking the LBN field, the 6-byte version has ample room for the transfer length, making a 10- or 12-byte version of this command unnecessary.

In addition to the LUN number byte 1 contains two further parameters. The Fixed bit indicates whether fixed or variable length blocks are expected. This also defines how the transfer length is to be interpreted.

The SILI (suppress incorrect length indicator) bit specifies how the target should react when a logical block is read with an unexpected length. When the SILI bit is clear the target will abort any command leading to length error with a CHECK CONDITION status. Otherwise, such length errors will be more or less tolerated.

Bytes 2 to 4 contain the transfer length. When the Fixed bit is set then the transfer length reflects the number of blocks of fixed length to be read. The fixed block length can be read using MODE SELECT. If Fixed is clear then a block of variable length will be read and the transfer length indicates how much space the initiator has reserved for the data. The 24-bit transfer length is sufficient for block lengths up to 16 Mbytes, which should be adequate for years to come. When the transfer length is zero the tape will not be moved, nor will data be transferred.

The read reverse command functions in exactly the same way, except that the reading process is carried out in the reverse direction. Thus, the logical blocks and the

Table 14.3 The READ command for tape drives.

	7	6	5	4	3	2	1	0
0	READ (08h) or READ REVERSE (0Fh)							
1	(LUN)			Reserved			SILI	Fixed
2	(MSB)							
3	Transfer length							
4								(LSB)
5	Control byte							

bytes within the logical blocks are transferred to the initiator in reverse order. Not all tape technologies support reverse reading which originates from ½ inch reel devices. This command is optional.

If a tape mark is found during the reading of a block a CHECK CONDITION status will be returned. The precise behavior in such a case can be modified using the mode parameters.

WRITE (0Ah)

The WRITE command is analogous to the READ command and functions analogously as well (Table 14.4). Byte 1 contains the LUN number and Fixed bit with the same interpretation they have with the READ command.

The WRITE command is executed in either the buffered or unbuffered mode depending on how the MODE SELECT parameters have been set. In the buffered mode the status phase takes place as soon as the target receives all data into its data buffer. The advantage here is that the I/O process completes more quickly. On the other hand a nonrecoverable write error may occur after GOOD status has been returned. SCSI accommodates such a deferred error using the mechanism already described on page 133. The data not yet written to the medium can be recovered using the optional command RECOVER BUFFER DATA. In the unbuffered mode the data must be written to the medium before the status phase takes place. The latter approach is preferred by many system administrators because it avoids such problems.

If an EW mark is found during a WRITE command the device will attempt to finish writing the data and will, in any case, return a CHECK CONDITION status to the initiator. It can be determined whether the data was accommodated in the partition by examining the sense key.

FORMAT MEDIUM (04h)

The FORMAT MEDIUM command (Table 14.5) prepares the magnetic tape for use, as the SCC document states, albeit not too clearly. There are some recording formats that use formatted or preformatted media which can be reformatted with this command. Many common media do not need any formatting, such as ½ inch tapes, 4 mm tapes and 8 mm Exabyte. The command is new in SCSI-3 and it is optional.

Table 14.4   The WRITE command for tape drives.

	7	6	5	4	3	2	1	0
0	WRITE (0Ah)							
1	(LUN)			Reserved				Fixed
2	(MSB)							
3	Transfer length							
4								(LSB)
5	Control byte							

Table 14.5 The FORMAT MEDIUM command.

	7	6	5	4	3	2	1	0
0	FORMAT MEDIUM (04h)							
1	Reserved						Verify	Immed
2	Reserved				Format			
3	(MSB)			Transfer length				
4								(LSB)
5	Control byte							

The Format field can assume the following values: 0h denotes the default format, 1h to 7h are reserved, and 8h to Fh denote vendor-specific values. When the transfer length is greater than 0, the command can be passed a parameter list whose meaning is vendor specific.

SPACE (11h)

The SPACE command is used to advance or rewind the tape a certain number of data blocks or tape marks (Table 14.6). The rewind capability is optional.

The parameter Count in bytes 2 through 4 indicates the number of objects to be advanced. Negative numbers (in two's complement) indicate rewinding.

In addition to the LUN number byte 1 contains the Code field which specifies what is to be counted. The possible codes are given in Table 14.7. Two of these, filemarks and setmarks, are worth explaining. When sequential filemarks are to be counted then the tape is advanced until Count consecutive filemarks are found. This means that for Count n, the tape will be positioned after the nth filemark when the command completes. Sequential setmarks are handled in the same way.

The hierarchy of objects plays an important role in error and event handling for the SPACE command. The details can be found in the ANSI specification in Section 9.2.12. However, a generalization can be made: if a higher level object is encountered during spacing than is being counted, then the command will be broken off at that point with a CHECK CONDITION status. For example, if filemarks are being counted a setmark will lead to command termination.

Table 14.6 The SPACE command.

	7	6	5	4	3	2	1	0
0	SPACE (11h)							
1	(LUN)			Reserved		Code		
2	(MSB)							
3	Count							
4								(LSB)
5	Control byte							

Table 14.7   Meaning of the Code field.

Code	Description	M/O
000b	Blocks	M
001b	Filemarks	M
010b	Sequential filemarks	O
011b	End-of-data	O
100b	Setmarks	O
101b	Sequential setmarks	O

In addition, reaching either the beginning or the end of a partition during a space command will cause the command to be terminated with CHECK CONDITION status.

WRITE FILEMARKS (10h)

This command writes to the current position the number of tape marks given in the transfer length field (Table 14.8). When the WSmk bit is 1 then setmarks are written; when 0 filemarks are written. The Immed bit specifies that the target should reply with GOOD status as soon as the command is recognized. Otherwise all buffered data and tape marks must be written before the execution of the command begins. WRITE FILEMARKS with transfer length zero can be used to cause the data buffer to be written to tape.

If an EW mark is encountered during or before the write filemarks command the target will attempt to finish writing the requested number of tape marks. In either case it concludes the command with CHECK CONDITION status. The sense data reveal whether or not the tape marks were successfully written.

ERASE (19h)

This command erases the medium starting at the current position (Table 14.9). Just how this is carried out is device dependent. However, afterwards a data pattern should be in place where previously data blocks and tape marks were found.

When the Long bit is set, the remainder of the tape starting at the current position will be erased. Otherwise a gap will be erased on the tape whose length is specified in the device configuration parameter page as gap length. The Immed bit has its standard interpretation.

Table 14.8   The WRITE FILEMARKS command.

	7	6	5	4	3	2	1	0
0	WRITE FILEMARKS (10h)							
1	(LUN)			Reserved			WSmk	Immed
2	(MSB)							
3				Transfer length				
4								(LSB)
5	Control byte							

Table 14.9 The ERASE command.

	7	6	5	4	3	2	1	0
0	ERASE (19h)							
1	(LUN)			Reserved			Immed	Long
2	Reserved							
3								
4								
5	Control byte							

READ BLOCK LIMITS (05h)

This command (Table 14.10) returns the maximum and minimum block size of the device. There are no parameters.

The block size information is returned in a parameter block where bytes 1 through 3 contain the maximum block length, and bytes 4 through 5 the minimum block length (Table 14.11).

A maximum block length of zero indicates that there is no block length limit. When the maximum and minimum lengths are equal the device supports only a fixed block length. In this case the READ and WRITE commands must always have the Fixed bit set and the block length must reflect the value returned by this command.

Table 14.10 The READ BLOCK LIMITS command.

	7	6	5	4	3	2	1	0
0	READ BLOCK LIMITS (05h)							
1	(LUN)			Reserved				
2	Reserved							
3								
4								
5	Control byte							

Table 14.11 Block limits parameter block.

	7	6	5	4	3	2	1	0
0	Reserved							
1	(MSB)							
2	Maximum block length							
3								(LSB)
4	(MSB)			Minimum				
5				block length				(LSB)

Table 14.12   The LOCATE command.

	7	6	5	4	3	2	1	0
0	LOCATE (2Bh)							
1	(LUN)			Reserved		BT	CP	Immed
2	Reserved							
3	(MSB)							
4	Block							
5	number							
6								(LSB)
7	Reserved							
8	Partition							
9	Control byte							

LOCATE (2Bh)

The LOCATE command is optional but is, nonetheless, a very useful command (Table 14.12). On the one hand, it makes it possible to search the tape for a specific logical or physical block. Additionally, the command can be used to change the active partition.

Since in general tape can hold an enormous number of blocks LOCATE is a 10-byte command. The block number is contained in bytes 3 through 6, allowing 4 giga-blocks to be addressed. When the BT bit is set the block address is interpreted as a device specific physical address, otherwise as SCSI LBN.

Byte 8 contains the number of the Partition to become active before positioning to the block number. This byte is ignored when the CP bit in byte 1 is not set.

READ POSITION (34h)

The READ POSITION command (Table 14.13) determines the current position of the medium and possible blocks in the buffer. No access to the medium is made. This command was optional in SCSI-2 and has become mandatory in SCSI-3.

Table 14.13   The READ POSITION command.

	7	6	5	4	3	2	1	0
0	READ POSITION (34h)							
1	(LUN)			Reserved		TCLP	LONG	BT
2 ...	Reserved							
...								
... 8								
9	Control byte							

Table 14.14   READ POSITION short data format.

	7	6	5	4	3	2	1	0
0	BOP	EOP	BCU	BYCU	Reserved	BPU	PERR	Reserved
1	Partition number							
2–3	Reserved							
4 ...	(MSB)		Position of first block					
... 7								(LSB)
8 ...	(MSB)		Position of last block					
... 11								(LSB)
12	Reserved							
13 ...	(MSB)		Number of blocks in buffer					
... 15								(LSB)
16 ...	(MSB)		Number of bytes in buffer					
... 19								(LSB)

In SCSI-2 and SCSI-3 the short data format (Table 14.14) applies when the TCLP bit is not set. This format contains information about the data present in the buffer. Positions are indicated in SCSI blocks when the BT bit is not set; otherwise they are manufacturer specific. When the TCLP bit is not set, the LONG bit must not be set either.

The BOP and EOP bits indicate that the tape has reached a BOP or EOP mark.

The BPU (block position unknown) bit indicates that the position of the first or last block is unknown. If it is not set, the corresponding fields contain valid values.

New in SCSI-3 are the following bits. The BCU (block count unknown) bit indicates that the value of number of blocks in the buffer is invalid. BYCU (byte count

Table 14.15   READ POSITION long data format (SCSI-3 only).

	7	6	5	4	3	2	1	0
0	BOP	EOP	Reserved		MPU	BPU	Reserved	
1 ...	Reserved							
... 3								
4 ...	(MSB)		Partition number					
... 7								(LSB)
8 ...	(MSB)		Block number					
... 15								(LSB)
16 ...	(MSB)		File mark number					
... 23								(LSB)
24 ...	(MSB)		Record mark number					
... 32								(LSB)

unknown) is the corresponding bit for the number of bytes in the buffer. The PERR (position error) bit indicates that owing to a counter overflow one or all values may be invalid.

When the TCLP (total current logical position) bit is set, the LONG bit must be set too. Then the long data format (Table 14.15) applies, and the numbers of the current partition, the block, the filemark and the setmark are returned as well. This variation only exists since SCSI-3.

The BOP, EOP and BPU bits have the same meaning as in the short data format. The MPU (mark position unknown) bit means that the values for filemark and setmark numbers are invalid.

LOAD/UNLOAD (1Bh)

This command loads or unloads the medium (Table 14.16). In addition, the tape can be re-tensioned by spooling the entire tape from one reel to the other.

The command has no parameters but a few control bits in bytes 1 and 4. The Immed bit works as usual, allowing the target to return a status GOOD immediately rather than after the command has been completed. When the Load bit is set the tape is to be loaded and positioned to the BOT mark.

If the Load bit is clear the tape will be unloaded. All buffered data and tape marks are written to the medium prior to unloading. If the EOT bit is set the tape will be positioned to the EOT mark, otherwise the BOT mark will be sought. In either case the medium is dismounted and any subsequent command calling for medium access will cause a CHECK CONDITION status with the sense key NOT READY.

Finally, the ReTen control bit causes the tape to be re-tensioned before the action described by the Load bit is performed.

Table 14.16   The LOAD/UNLOAD command.

	7	6	5	4	3	2	1	0
0	LOAD/UNLOAD (1Bh)							
1	(LUN)			Reserved				Immed
2	Reserved							
3								
4						EOT	ReTen	Load
5	Control byte							

14.3   Mode parameters for tape devices

Mode parameter header

The device type specific byte of the mode parameter header (Table 14.17) returned by the MODE SENSE command contains the following information:

Table 14.17   Device-specific parameter byte in header.

Bit	7	6	5	4	3	2	1	0
0	WP	Buffer mode			Speed			

- The WP bit indicates that the medium is write protected.
- Buffer mode is defined for three values. These pertain to commands that write either data or tape marks to the medium, which together are referred to as write operations.
- 000b is the unbuffered mode. For all write operations the target must wait until the medium has actually been written before returning status.
- 001b: The target may return GOOD status as soon as all data has been received into the data buffer.
- 010b: The target may return GOOD status as soon as all data has been received into the data buffer *and* all buffered data from other initiators has been written to the medium.
- In the Speed field a 0 represents the device's default tape speed. The values 1h through Fh reflect speeds from slowest to fastest.

Block descriptor

Byte 0 of the block descriptor contains a device type specific code for the write density. The most important of these are given in Table 14.18.

Mode parameter pages

The mode parameter pages in Table 14.19 are defined for tape devices.

The data compression page (0Fh)

The data compression page (Table 14.20) is new in SCSI-3. It contains information on the data compression used.

Table 14.18   Write density for tape drives.

Code	Width	Tracks	BPI	Format	Type
01h	½ inch	9	800	NRZI	Reel-to-reel
02h	½ inch	9	1600	PE	Reel-to-reel
03h	½ inch	9	6250	GCR	Reel-to-reel
0Fh	¼ inch	15	10 000	GCR	QIC-120 cassette
10h	¼ inch	18	10 000	GCR	QIC-150 cassette
11h	¼ inch	26	16 000	GCR	QIC-320 cassette
13h	4 mm	1	61 000	DDS	4 mm DAT
14h	8 mm	1	54 000		EXABYTE
00h			Default density		

Table 14.19 Mode parameter pages for tape devices.

Page code	Name	Page	SCSI-2	SCSI-3 (SSC)
01h	Read/write error page		9.3.3.4	5.3.3.5
02h	Disconnect/reconnect page	145	7.3.3.2	SPC
09h	Peripheral device page	146	7.3.3.3	SPC
0Ah	Control mode page	147	7.3.3.1	SPC
0Fh	Data compression page	196	–	5.3.3.1
10h	Device configuration page	198	9.3.3.1	5.3.3.2
11h	Partitions page 1	198	9.3.3.3	5.3.3.3
12h	Partitions page 2	198	9.3.3.3	5.3.3.4
13h	Partitions page 3	198	9.3.3.3	5.3.3.4
14h	Partitions page 4	198	9.3.3.3	5.3.3.4
1Ch	Informal exception page		–	SPC

The DCE (data compression enabled) bit activates data compression. The DDE (data decompression enabled) bit activates data decompression. The DCC (data compression capable) bit indicates that the device supports data compression.

The RED field specifies how the device behaves when it passes borders between data of different compression. When data appears that has been compressed with an unsupported compression algorithm, the drive must report a CHECK CONDITION status with a MEDIUM ERROR sense code. When a change occurs between two supported algorithms, a simple warning may be sufficient.

The fields for the compression and decompression algorithms contain a code. Up to now, only 10h for IBM IDRC compression and 20h for DCLZ compression have been established.

Table 14.20 Data compression page (SCSI-3 only).

	7	6	5	4	3	2	1	0
0	PS	Res	Data compression page (0Fh)					
1	Page length (0Eh)							
2	DCE	DCC	Reserved					
3	DDE	RED						
4 ...	(MSB)							
...	Data compression algorithm							
... 7								(LSB)
8 ...	(MSB)							
...	Data decompression algorithm							
... 11								(LSB)
12 ...	Reserved							
...								
... 15								

Table 14.21   Device configuration page for tape devices.

	7	6	5	4	3	2	1	0
0	PS	Reserved		Page code (10h)				
1	Page length (0Eh)							
2	Reserved	CAP	CAR	Active format				
3	Active partition							
4	Write buffer empty ratio							
5	Read buffer empty ratio							
6	(MSB)			Write				
7				delay				(LSB)
8	DBR	BIS	RSmk	AVC	SOFC		RBO	REW
9	Gap size							
10		EOD		EEG	SEW		Reserved	
11	(MSB)							
12	Buffer size at EW							
13								(LSB)
14	Data compression							
15	Reserved							

The device configuration page (10h)

The device configuration page contains various configuration information for the tape drive (Table 14.21). Only the more important details will be covered here. Refer to Section 9.3.3 of the ANSI specification for further information.

Byte 3 contains the active partition. This can be modified using MODE SELECT when the CAP (change active partition) bit of byte 2 is set.

Partition pages 1 through 4 (11h, 12h, 13h, 14h)

Partition page 1 has an 8-byte header followed by up to 64 partition size descriptors of 2 bytes each. If more partitions are needed pages 2 through 4 can be used, each of which accommodates 64 partitions. This allows SCSI-2 devices to support up to 256 partitions. Partition page 1 is shown in Table 14.22. Each descriptor contains the length of its partition. The unit of measure for length is defined by the PSUM field. Here the value 00h means bytes, 01h Kbytes, and 02h Mbytes.

In SCSI-3 the value 03h is defined. It indicates that the partition size unit field specifies the exponent 10 to the power of n of the partition size.

Unlike page 1, partition pages 2 through 4 consist of only descriptors (Table 14.23).

Table 14.22   Partition page 1 for tape devices.

	7	6	5	4	3	2	1	0
0	PS	Reserved			Page code (11h)			
1	Page length							
2	Maximum number of partitions							
3	Number of partitions (n+1)							
4	FDP	SDP	IDP	PSUM		Reserved	CLEAR	ADDP
5	Format recognition							
6	Reserved				Partition size unit			
7	Reserved							
8...n	Partition descriptors							
n+1	(MSB)			Partition				
n+2				size				(LSB)

Table 14.23   Partition page 2 for tape devices.

	7	6	5	4	3	2	1	0
0	PS	Reserved			Page code (12h – 14h)			
1	Page length							
2...n	Partition descriptors							
n+1	(MSB)			Partition				
n+2				size				(LSB)

14.4   The model of a SCSI printer

The degree to which the various device types are defined in SCSI-2 varies greatly. Up until this point we have seen very detailed specifications for disk and tape drive devices. This is not the case for printers, as will become apparent in the description of the device model.

According to the current draft proposals, SCSI-3 too will not change anything fundamental. However, the draft document is far from being finished, and there might be some changes in the final standard.

The model of a SCSI printer represents to some extent an exception among SCSI device models (Figure 14.2). Here the design is of a bridge controller connected to a printer mechanism. Of course, there is nothing preventing the integration of the controller into the printer itself. We will see that one advantage of this approach is that the MODE SELECT command can be used to manipulate the physical printer interface.

The command set basically treats the printer as a black box that accepts data. No page description language is defined here, rather the data format is left up to the initiator. Nevertheless, this 'black box' does allow internal configuration to some

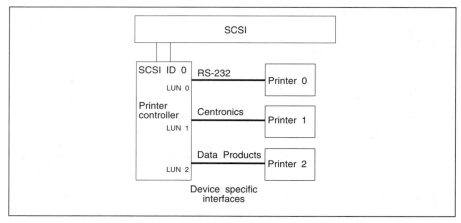

Figure 14.2   Model of a SCSI printer.

degree using SCSI commands. For instance, there is the optional control of printer fonts and forms. The printer itself may be equipped with a data buffer, making a buffered mode possible.

The standard does not specify what the printer must do when it receives a particular character. While a typical dot-matrix printer will simply print any printable character, a PostScript compatible printer will use the page description language PostScript to interpret the character. To make things even more complicated there are also a number of printer manufacturers that have developed unique printer control languages. Some of these have become de facto standards, which are often emulated by other printers. For example, many printers provide HP Laserjet emulation as well as Epson or Diablo emulations. Unfortunately, none of these emulations is defined in the SCSI-2 standard. If this were the case one could simply buy a SCSI printer and plug it in (Figure 14.3). As a result the software must be informed of the printer's emulation in order to function properly.

In summary, one can say that the SCSI-2 command set for printers is limited to data transfer and the control of certain parameters. With reference to the interface model this leaves the top level not completely defined.

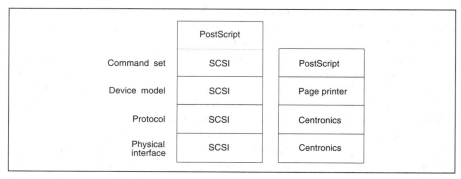

Figure 14.3   SCSI printer interface.

14.5 Printer commands

Table 14.24 lists all of the commands defined for SCSI printers. Printers have a relatively large number of commands that are completely vendor unique. These opcodes are 01h, 02h, 05h, 06h, 07h, 08h, 09h, 0Ch, 0Dh, 0Eh, 0Fh, 11h, 13h, 19h and C0h to FFh. All other opcodes are reserved.

PRINT (0Ah)

The PRINT command sends the number of bytes contained in Transfer length to the printer (Table 14.25). Depending on buffer mode the status phase will occur either immediately after the data transfer or after the printing has actually taken place.

Table 14.24 SCSI commands for printers.

Op-code	Name	Type	Page	SCSI-2	SCSI-3 (SCC)	Description
00h	TEST UNIT READY	M	131	7.2.16	SPC	Reflects whether or not the LUN is ready to accept a command
03h	REQUEST SENSE	M	132	7.2.14	SPC	Returns detailed error information
04h	FORMAT	(M)	203	10.2.1M	6.2.1 O	Font or form control
0Ah	PRINT	M	201	10.2.2	6.2.2	Print data
0Bh	SLEW AND PRINT	(M)	202	10.2.4M	6.2.4 O	Advance and print
10h	SYNCHRONIZE BUFFER	(M)	203	10.2.6M	6.2.6 O	Print contents of buffer
12h	INQUIRY	M	128	7.2.5	SPC	Returns LUN specific information
14h	RECOVER BUFFERED DATA	O		10.2.3	6.2.3	Retrieve data from the data buffer
15h	MODE SELECT(6)	M	140	7.2.8	SPC	Set device parameters
16h	RESERVE UNIT	M	136	9.2.10	SPC	Make LUN accessible only to certain initiators
17h	RELEASE UNIT	M	136	9.2.9	SPC	Make LUN accessible to other initiators
18h	COPY	O		7.2.3	SPC	Autonomous copy from/to another device
1Ah	MODE SENSE(6)	M	140	7.2.10	SPC	Read device parameters
1Bh	STOP PRINT	O	202	10.2.5	6.2.5	Interrupt printing
1Ch	RECEIVE DIAGNOSTIC RESULTS	O		7.2.13	SPC	Read self-test results
1Dh	SEND DIAGNOSTIC	M	138	7.2.1	SPC	Initiate self-test
39h	COMPARE	O		7.2.2	SPC	Compare data
3Ah	COPY AND VERIFY	O		7.2.4	SPC	Autonomous copy from/to another device, verify success
3Bh	WRITE BUFFER	O		7.2.17	SPC	Write the data buffer
3Ch	READ BUFFER	O		7.2.12	SPC	Read the data buffer
40h	CHANGE DEFINITION	O	139	7.2.1	SPC	Set SCSI version
4Ch	LOG SELECT	O		7.2.6	SPC	Read statistics
4Dh	LOG SENSE	O		7.2.7	SPC	Read statistics
55h	MODE SELECT(10)	O	140	7.2.9	SPC	Set device parameters
5Ah	MODE SENSE(10)	O	140	7.2.10	SPC	Read device parameters

Note: Mandatory commands are shaded dark gray. (M) means that the command is classified differently in SCSI-2 and SCSI-3. The corresponding classification is indicated after the reference to the standard.

Table 14.25   The PRINT command.

	7	6	5	4	3	2	1	0
0	PRINT (0Ah)							
1	(LUN)			Reserved				
2	(MSB)							
3	Transfer length							
4								(LSB)
5	Control byte							

Table 14.26   The SLEW AND PRINT command.

	7	6	5	4	3	2	1	0
0	SLEW AND PRINT (0Bh)							
1	(LUN)			Reserved				Channel
2	Slew value							
3	(MSB)			Transfer length				
4								(LSB)
5	Control byte							

SLEW AND PRINT (0Bh)

This command works just like the PRINT command except that it allows a certain number of lines to be skipped before printing, as well as a choice of forms channel (Table 14.26). When the Channel bit is set the number of the forms channel is given in Slew value. Otherwise, this byte is interpreted as the number of lines to be skipped before printing.

STOP PRINT (1Bh)

This command halts printing (Table 14.27). If the Retain bit is clear then the data remaining in the buffer is discarded. Otherwise, it is held and a subsequent PRINT command or a SYNCHRONIZE BUFFER will allow printing to continue.

Table 14.27   The STOP PRINT command.

	7	6	5	4	3	2	1	0
0	STOP PRINT (1Bh)							
1	(LUN)			Reserved				Retain
2	Manufacturer specific							
3	Reserved							
4								
5	Control byte							

Table 14.28   The FORMAT command.

	7	6	5	4	3	2	1	0
0	FORMAT (04h)							
1	(LUN)			Reserved				Type
2	(MSB)							
3	Transfer length							
4								(LSB)
5	Control byte							

Table 14.29   The SYNCHRONIZE BUFFER command.

	7	6	5	4	3	2	1	0
0	SYNCHRONIZE BUFFER (10h)							
1	(LUN)							
2								
3	Reserved							
4								
5	Control byte							

FORMAT (04h)

This command makes it possible to send form or font data to the printer (Table 14.28). The value 00b in the Type field chooses form control, the value 01b font control.

SYNCHRONIZE BUFFER (10h)

This command causes the printer to print the contents of the data buffer (Table 14.29). This is used to make sure that all data has been printed. Page printers sometimes need a form feed in this case. This command waits until after printing to return status. If for any reason printing cannot take place a CHECK CONDITION is returned.

14.6   Mode parameters for printers

Mode parameter header

The device type specific byte in the mode parameter header has the following form (Table 14.30):

- Buffer mode is defined for two values and is relevant for PRINT and SLEW AND PRINT commands. All other values are reserved.

Table 14.30   Device-specific parameter byte in MODE header.

Bit	7	6	5	4	3	2	1	0
0	Reserved	Buffer mode			Reserved			

Table 14.31   Mode parameter pages for printers.

Page code	Name	Page	SCSI-2	SCSI-3 (SSC)
02h	Disconnect/reconnect page	145	7.3.3.2	SPC
03h	Parallel interface page	204	10.3.3.1	6.3.3.1
04h	Serial interface page	205	10.3.3.3	6.3.3.3
05h	Printer options page		10.3.3.2	6.3.3.2
09h	Peripheral device page	146	7.3.3.3	SPC
0Ah	Control mode page	147	7.3.3.1	SPC

- 000b is for unbuffered mode. The printer controller will not return status until the data has actually been printed.

- 001b is the buffered mode. Here the controller is allowed to return GOOD status as soon as all data has been received into the buffer.

Mode parameter pages

Table 14.31 shows the mode parameter pages defined for printers.

Parallel interface page (03h)

This parameter page controls the characteristics of a parallel printer interface (Table 14.32). The parameter Parity assumes the values 00b for no parity, 01b for even parity and 10b for odd parity. The meaning of byte 2 is explained in detail in section 10.3.3.1 of the ANSI standard.

Table 14.32   Parallel interface page.

	7	6	5	4	3	2	1	0
0	PS	Reserved	Page code (03h)					
1	Page length (02h)							
2	Parity		PIPC	Reserved	VCBP	VCBS	VES	Autofeed
3	Reserved							

Table 14.33   Serial interface page.

	7	6	5	4	3	2	1	0
0	PS	Reserved	Page code (04h)					
1	Page length (06h)							
2	Reserved		Stop bit length					
3	Parity		Reserved	Bits per character				
4	RTS	CTS	Reserved		Protocol			
5	(MSB)							
6	Baud rate							
7								(LSB)

Table 14.34 Parameters of the serial interface.

Code	Parity	Code	Protocol
000b	No parity	0000b	No protocol
001b	Mark	0001b	XON / XOFF
010b	Space	0010b	ETX / ACK
011b	Odd	0011b	DTR
100b	Even		

Serial interface page (04h)

This parameter page controls the characteristics of a serial RS-232C interface. The fields are more or less self explanatory (Table 14.33). Section 2.1 is a good source of background information on the serial interface (Table 14.34). The RTS bit specifies that the printer controller should activate the RTS signal of the interface. If the CTS bit is clear the controller will ignore the RTS signal altogether. Otherwise output is stopped as long as RTS is inactive.

14.7 The model of a SCSI communications device

SCSI communications devices closely resemble processor devices. Here too data is received and sent across the bus. While processor devices may locally process the data, communications devices send it further. An important distinction is that communications make possible an additional level of addressing. The channel number allows the addressing of different logical channels. These might be connected to various physical communications ports within the device. On the other hand, these might be used to address different LAN protocols. The channel number is 16 bits long, making 64 000 logical channels available. As always, a communications device may have up to eight LUNs, which explodes this number to half a million. Examples of SCSI communications devices are shown in Figure 14.4.

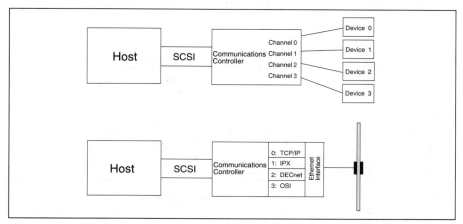

Figure 14.4 Examples of SCSI communications devices.

As with processor devices, the SCSI bus is used strictly as a physical interface since the SCSI-2 standard does not specify the contents of data packets. For this reason communications devices lack device-specific parameter pages.

At the current editorial state of the SSC document there seem to be hardly any differences between SCSI-2 and SCSI-3.

14.8 Commands for SCSI communications devices

Table 14.35 lists the commands defined for SCSI communications devices. For SCSI communications devices there are two additional commands defined, each with a 6-, 10-, and 12-byte version. Since the GET MESSAGE and SEND MESSAGE commands are identical except for the opcode they are discussed here in pairs.

GET MESSAGE(6) (08h) and SEND MESSAGE(6) (0Ah)

These versions of the commands are the only ones that are mandatory. In SCSI-3 only the send message command is mandatory. Neither of the two commands offers support for logical channels (Table 14.36).

Table 14.35 Commands for SCSI communications devices.

Op-code	Name	Type	Page	SCSI-2	SCSI-3 (SCC)	Description
00h	TEST UNIT READY	M	131	7.2.16	SPC	Reflects whether or not the LUN is ready to accept a command
03h	REQUEST SENSE	M	132	7.2.14	SPC	Returns detailed error information
08h	GET MESSAGE(6)	(M)	206	17.2.1M	7.2.1O	Receive
0Ah	SEND MESSAGE(6)	M	206	17.2.4	7.2.4	Send
12h	INQUIRY	M	128	7.2.5	SPC	Returns LUN specific information
15h	MODE SELECT(6)	O	140	7.2.8	SPC	Set device parameters
1Ah	MODE SENSE(6)	O	140	7.2.10	SPC	Read device parameters
1Ch	RECEIVE DIAGNOSTIC RESULTS	O		7.2.13	SPC	Read self-test results
1Dh	SEND DIAGNOSTIC	M	138	7.2.1	SPC	Initiate self-test
28h	GET MESSAGE(10)	O	207	17.2.2	7.2.2	Receive
2Ah	SEND MESSAGE(10)	O	207	17.2.5	7.2.5	Send
3Bh	WRITE BUFFER	O		7.2.17	SPC	Write the data buffer
3Ch	READ BUFFER	O		7.2.12	SPC	Read the data buffer
40h	CHANGE DEFINITION	O	139	7.2.1	SPC	Set SCSI version
4Ch	LOG SELECT	O		7.2.6	SPC	Select statistics
4Dh	LOG SENSE	O		7.2.7	SPC	Read statistics
55h	MODE SELECT(10)	O	140	7.2.9	SPC	Set device parameters
5Ah	MODE SENSE(10)	O	140	7.2.10	SPC	Read device parameters
A8h	GET MESSAGE(12)	O	207	17.2.3	7.2.3	Receive
AAh	SEND MESSAGE(12)	O	207	17.2.5	7.2.3	Send

Note: Mandatory commands are shaded dark gray. (M) means that the command is classified differently in SCSI-2 and SCSI-3. The corresponding classification is indicated after the reference to the standard.

Table 14.36 The GET MESSAGE(6) and SEND MESSAGE(6) commands.

	7	6	5	4	3	2	1	0
0	GET MESSAGE(6) (08h) or SEND MESSAGE(6) (0Ah)							
1	(LUN)			Reserved				
2	(MSB)							
3	Transfer length							
4								(LSB)
5	Control byte							

GET MESSAGE(10) (28h) and SEND MESSAGE(10) (2Ah)

The 10-byte version has no support for logical channels but does have a 16-bit wide transfer length field. The maximum length of a data packet is limited to 64 Kbytes (Table 14.37).

GET MESSAGE(12) (A8h) and SEND MESSAGE(12) (AAh)

Finally, the 12-byte version supports logical channels and a transfer length field of 32 bits wide (Table 14.38).

14.9 Mode parameter pages for communications devices

There are no device type specific mode parameter pages for communications devices. Table 14.39 shows the parameter pages relevant to this class.

Table 14.37 The GET MESSAGE(10) and SEND MESSAGE(10) commands.

	7	6	5	4	3	2	1	0
0	GET MESSAGE(10) (28h) or SEND MESSAGE(10) (2Ah)							
1	(LUN)							
2	Reserved							
3								
4	(MSB)			Channel				
5				number				(LSB)
6	Reserved							
7	(MSB)			Transfer				
8				length				(LSB)
9	Control byte							

Table 14.38   The GET MESSAGE(12) and SEND MESSAGE(12) commands.

	7	6	5	4	3	2	1	0
0	GET MESSAGE(12) (A8h) or SEND MESSAGE(12) (AAh)							
1	(LUN)			Reserved				
2								
3								
4	(MSB)			Channel				
5				number				(LSB)
6	(MSB)							
7				Transfer				
8				length				
9								(LSB)
10	Reserved							
11	Control byte							

Table 14.39   Mode parameter pages for communications devices.

Page code	Name	Page	SCSI-2	SCSI-3 (SSC)
02h	Disconnect/reconnect page	145	7.3.3.2	SPC
09h	Peripheral device page	146	7.3.3.3	SPC
0Ah	Control mode page	147	7.3.3.1	SPC

15 Graphics devices

In SCSI-3, scanners have got their own document. At the moment, they are the only device type in the SGC (SCSI Graphical Commands) document. Otherwise, nothing has really changed. As far as we currently know, commands and parameters are the same in SCSI-2 and SCSI-3.

15.1 The model of a SCSI scanner

A scanner is a device capable of converting pictures and text to an electronic representation made up of rows of pixels. Pixels can be black and white, color, or gray scale. The number of bits needed to represent a pixel is dependent on which of these three possibilities is chosen. As a result there are different data formats for storing scanned images. These formats are not specified in the SCSI standard; many are vendor unique. Similar to the printer definition, the SCSI standard is limited to the exchange of data and the control of the scanner.

A SCSI scanner uses the coordinate system shown in Figure 15.1. The units of the coordinate system can be specified using the measuring units page of the MODE

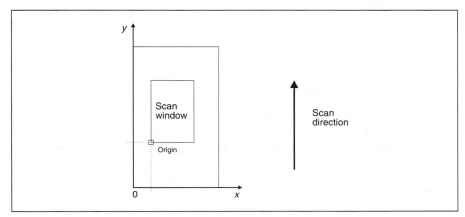

Figure 15.1 Coordinate system and scan window.

Table 15.1　Window descriptor.

	7	6	5	4	3	2	1	0
0	Window identifier							
1	Reserved							Auto
2–3	X-axis resolution							
4–5	Y-axis resolution							
6–9	X-axis upper left							
10–13	Y-axis upper left							
14–17	Window width							
18–21	Window length							
22	Brightness							
23	Threshold							
24	Contrast							
25	Image composition							
26	Bits per pixel							
27–28	Halftone pattern							
29	RIF	Reserved				Padding type		
30–31	Bit ordering							
32	Compression type							
33	Compression argument							
34–39	Reserved							
40–n	Vendor specific							

SELECT command. The available units are inches, millimeters or points (1/72 inch) or fractions thereof. The unit of measure chosen does not affect the resolution of the scanner.

A SCSI scanner can be configured such that the scanning surface is broken up into one or many windows. These windows may differ in size and location as well as scanning method. Each window is described by a separate window descriptor, an example of which is shown in Table 15.1.

The window descriptor

In order to save space, parameters that occupy more than one byte are represented in a single line in the table. As is usually the case for SCSI the length of the parameter block is contained within the parameter block itself.

Most fields here are self-explanatory. The Auto bit specifies that the scanner may create subwindows automatically. When reading the window parameter data this bit reflects whether the window was automatically created. The RIF bit indicates that the image is a negative. The image composition, halftone pattern and compression fields are essentially vendor specific.

15.2   SCSI scanner commands

Table 15.2 lists all of the commands defined for SCSI scanners. Out of these, there are only six commands that are specific for SCSI scanners. Two of these, namely READ and SEND, are quite similar to the READ(10) and WRITE(10) commands. They share the same opcode, but are structured in a slightly different way.

SET WINDOW (24h)

The SET WINDOW command creates one or more scanning windows (Table 15.3). Here the data phase contains a window list made up of a list header and one or more window descriptors, as in Table 15.1. The header contains only the total length of the window descriptors (Table 15.4). Individual descriptors must all be the same length.

Table 15.2   Commands for scanners.

Op-code	Name	Type	Page	SCSI-2	SCSI-3 (SGC)	Description
00h	TEST UNIT READY	M	131	7.2.16	SPC	Reflects whether or not the LUN is ready to accept a command
03h	REQUEST SENSE	M	132	7.2.14	SPC	Returns detailed error information
12h	INQUIRY	M	128	7.2.5	SPC	Returns LUN specific information
15h	MODE SELECT(6)	M	140	7.2.8	SPC	Set device parameters
16h	RESERVE UNIT	M	136	9.2.10	SPC	Make LUN accessible only to certain initiators
17h	RELEASE UNIT	M	136	9.2.9	SPC	Make LUN accessible to other initiators
18h	COPY	O		7.2.3	SPC	Autonomous copy from/to another device
1Ah	MODE SENSE(6)	M	140	7.2.10	SPC	Read device specific parameters
1Bh	SCAN	O	213	14.2.5	6.1.5	Scan
1Ch	RECEIVE DIAGNOSTIC RESULTS	O		7.2.13	SPC	Read self-test results
1Dh	SEND DIAGNOSTIC	M	138	7.2.1	SPC	Initiate self-test
24h	SET WINDOW	M	211	14.2.6	6.1.7	Set scan window
25h	GET WINDOW	O		14.2.2	6.1.2	Read window properties
28h	READ	M	212	14.2.4	6.1.4	Read
2Ah	SEND	O	212	14.2.7	6.1.6	Write
31h	OBJECT POSITION	O		14.2.3	6.1.3	Set object position
34h	GET DATA BUFFER STATUS	O		14.2.1	6.1.1	Read data buffer subdivision and filling rate
39h	COMPARE	O		7.2.2	SPC	Compare data
3Ah	COPY AND VERIFY	O		7.2.4	SPC	Autonomous copy from/to another device, verify success
3Bh	WRITE BUFFER	O		7.2.17	SPC	Write the data buffer
3Ch	READ BUFFER	O		7.2.12	SPC	Read the data buffer
40h	CHANGE DEFINITION	O	139	7.2.1	SPC	Set SCSI version
4Ch	LOG SELECT	O		7.2.6	SPC	Select statistics
4Dh	LOG SENSE	O		7.2.7	SPC	Read statistics
55h	MODE SELECT(10)	O	140	7.2.9	SPC	Set device parameters
5Ah	MODE SENSE(10)	O	140	7.2.10	SPC	Read device parameters

Note: Mandatory commands are shaded dark gray.

Table 15.3   The SET WINDOW command.

	7	6	5	4	3	2	1	0
0	SET WINDOW (24h)							
1	(LUN)			Reserved				
2 ...	Reserved							
... 5								
6	(MSB)							
7	Transfer length							
8								(LSB)
9	Control byte							

Table 15.4   Window header data.

	7	6	5	4	3	2	1	0
0	Reserved							
...								
5								
6	(MSB)			Window descriptor				
7	length							(LSB)

READ (28h) and SEND (2Ah)

The READ and SEND commands have the same opcodes as the normal READ(10) and WRITE(10) commands, but they have a slightly different structure.

The READ command reads data from the scanner (Table 15.5). Here different types of data are possible. Data type code 00h stands for image data, 02h for half tone

Table 15.5   The READ command for scanners.

	7	6	5	4	3	2	1	0
0	READ (28h)							
1	(LUN)			Reserved				
2	Data type code							
3	Reserved							
4	(MSB)			Data type				
5	qualifier							(LSB)
6	(MSB)							
7	Data length							
8								(LSB)
9	Control byte							

Table 15.6 The SCAN command.

	7	6	5	4	3	2	1	0
0	SCAN (1Bh)							
1	(LUN)							
2	Reserved							
3								
4	Data length							
5	Control byte							

masks and 03h for gamma curves. The data type qualifier is a vendor specific parameter, which is required for some data types. The data length is measured in blocks whose size has been specified using the mode parameter block descriptor.

In the same way, you can use the SEND command to send half tone masks and gamma curves to the scanner.

SCAN (1Bh)

The scan command initiates the scanning process (Table 15.6). This command is optional because this is done manually for many scanners. The data length specifies the length of the window list supplied in the data phase of the command. The window list is composed of one or many window numbers previously defined.

15.3 Mode parameters for scanners

Mode parameter pages

Table 15.7 shows the Mode parameter pages defined for SCSI scanners.

Measurement units page (03h)

This page is very straightforward (Table 15.8). Byte 2 specifies the basic unit of measure, where 00h stands for inches, 01h for millimeters, and 02h for points (1/72 inch). Bytes 4 and 5 contain the number of units that should make up a basic measurement unit. This means that when byte 2 contains 01h and byte 5 contains 64h the measurement unit is 1/100 of a millimeter.

Table 15.7 Mode parameter pages for scanners.

Page code	Name	Page	SCSI-2	SCSI-3 (SGC)
02h	Disconnect/reconnect page	145	7.3.3.2	SPC
03h	Measurement units page	213	14.3.3.1	7.1.3.1
09h	Peripheral device page	146	7.3.3.3	SPC
0Ah	Control mode page	147	7.3.3.1	SPC

Table 15.8 Measurement units page.

	7	6	5	4	3	2	1	0
0	Page code (03h)							
1	Page length (06h)							
2	Measurement unit							
3	Reserved							
4	(MSB)			Divisor				
5								(LSB)
6	Reserved							
7								

16 Medium-changer devices

16.1 The model of a SCSI medium-changer device

A SCSI medium-changer device is like a juke-box, allowing many individual media to be stored, loaded, unloaded, and accessed just like single media drives (Figure 16.1). There are four basic components or elements of this juke-box: the medium transport element (MTE), the storage element (SE), the import/export element (IOE), and the data transfer element (DTE). A device may, however, contain more than one of any of these elements. Each element is capable of being empty or holding a single medium. All elements are identified using a 16-bit address. The addresses of the various elements are consecutive and do not overlap, so that elements can be implicitly accessed by their address. In SCSI-2 all media must be of the same type. The SCSI-3 model of a medium changer, however, also allows a device that distributes different media such as cassette tape and optical disks across different drives.

Independent and attached medium changers

The medium changer as an independent device as it is defined in SCSI-2 is complemented in SCSI-3 with the variation of the attached medium changer. The independent medium changer is a separate SCSI device or a separate LUN and understands the entire SMC command set. The attached medium changer is part of the LUN of the principal device. It understands only two commands, namely MOVE MEDIUM and READ ELEMENT STATUS. The attached medium changer belongs to the model of all SCSI devices and is described in the SPC document.

Elements of the medium-changer device

The medium transport element

The MTE is the mechanism that moves media from one location to another. When a double-sided medium is being used the element contains the machinery necessary to turn the medium over. Since the transport element may contain a medium, it has an element address. Large devices contain more than one MTE.

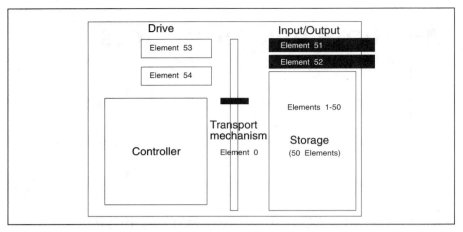

Figure 16.1   Model of a SCSI medium-changer device.

The storage element

Media is held in the SE until it is needed for access. From here individual media are moved by the MT element to other elements of the device.

The import/export element

The IOE allows an operator to load media into and remove media from the device. Therefore, when a medium unit is to be removed from the device the MTE moves it from its current position into the IOE. The IOE does not necessarily have to be implemented since many devices allow direct hand access to storage. Large medium-changers, on the other hand, may have several IOEs.

The data transfer element

Obviously, media can be accommodated within the DTE, the place where data is ultimately accessed. For this reason it also is addressed in the element address space. Large medium-changers may employ a number of these DTEs.

From the SCSI perspective the DTE and the medium-changer are completely separate entities. No data transfer commands are contained in the medium-changer command set. In fact, the DTE may not even be SCSI compatible. One possibility is that the DTE is connected to the host using an interface other than SCSI. Another possibility is for it to be connected to the very same SCSI bus but at a different SCSI ID; in other words, the DTE is a separate target. The latter is the standard case (Figure 16.2). Finally, the two might be implemented as individual LUNs of the same SCSI target. This configuration is the least likely since the LUNs belong to different device types.

Volume tags

Volume tags are used to identify a particular piece of medium. These tags, which are optional, are written on the medium itself and remain with it from element to element. Double-sided media have a primary volume tag for the default side and an alternate volume tag for the reverse side.

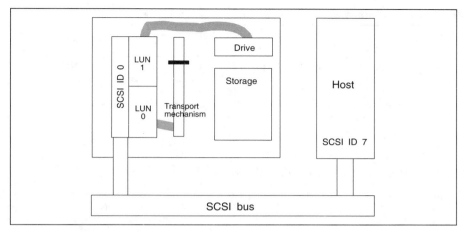

Figure 16.2   SCSI medium-changer configuration.

Tags are assigned either using a bar code reader or with the aid of a special command. Table 16.1 shows the format of a volume tag just as it is used by the commands READ ELEMENT STATUS and SEND VOLUME TAG.

The volume identification field contains ASCII characters. In order to be compatible with most operating systems you should use only numbers, capital letters and the underscore character. In particular, question marks and asterisks, which are wildcards in many systems, should be avoided.

The volume sequence number is 16 bits long and is used, for example, to keep track of the individual pieces of medium that belong to a single volume.

Table 16.1   Format of a medium volume tag.

	7	6	5	4	3	2	1	0
0								
...				Volume identification field				
31								
32				Reserved				
33								
34	(MSB)			Volume sequence number				
35								(LSB)

16.2   Commands for medium-changers

The major change from SCSI-2 to SCSI-3 is that the READ ELEMENT STATUS command has become mandatory. Since it must also be supported by attached medium-changers, it has been included in this edition of the book. Table 16.2 lists the commands defined for medium-changers.

Table 16.2   Commands for medium-changer devices.

Op-code	Name	Type	Page	SCSI-2	SCSI-3 (SBC)	Description
00h	TEST UNIT READY	M	131	7.2.16	SPC	Reflects whether or not the LUN is ready to accept a command
01h	REZERO UNIT	O		8.2.13	SPC	Seek track 0
03h	REQUEST SENSE	M	132	7.2.14	SPC	Returns detailed error information
07h	INITIALIZE ELEMENT STATUS	O		16.2.2	6.2	Initialize element
12h	INQUIRY	M	128	7.2.5	SPC	Returns LUN specific information
15h	MODE SELECT(6)	O	140	7.2.8	SPC	Set device parameters
16h	RESERVE	M	136	16.2.8	6.8	Make LUN accessible only to certain initiators
17h	RELEASE	M	136	16.2.6	6.6	Make LUN accessible to other initiators
1Ah	MODE SENSE(6)	O	140	7.2.10	SPC	Read device parameters
1Ch	RECEIVE DIAGNOSTIC RESULTS	O		7.2.13	SPC	Read self-test results
1Dh	SEND DIAGNOSTIC	M	138	7.2.1	SPC	Initiate self-test
1Eh	PREVENT/ALLOW MEDIUM REMOVAL	O		8.2.4	SPC	Lock/unlock door
2Bh	POSITION TO ELEMENT	O		16.2.4	6.4	Position to element
3Bh	WRITE BUFFER	O		7.2.17	SPC	Write data buffer
3Ch	READ BUFFER	O		7.2.12	SPC	Read data buffer
40h	CHANGE DEFINITION	O	139	7.2.1	SPC	Set SCSI version
4Ch	LOG SELECT	O		7.2.6	SPC	Select statistics
4Dh	LOG SENSE	O		7.2.7	SPC	Read statistics
55h	MODE SELECT(10)	O	140	7.2.9	SPC	Set device parameters
5Ah	MODE SENSE(10)	O	140	7.2.10	SPC	Read device parameters
A5h	MOVE MEDIUM	M	218	16.2.3	6.3	Move medium
A6h	EXCHANGE MEDIUM	O	219	16.2.1	6.1	Exchange medium
B5h	REQUEST VOLUME ELEMENT ADDRESS	O		16.2.7	6.7	Request volume element address
B6h	SEND VOLUME TAG	O		16.2.9	6.9	Assign volume name
B8h	READ ELEMENT STATUS	(O)	220	16.2.5 O	6.5 M	Read element status

Note: Mandatory commands are shaded gray. (M) means that the command is classified differently in SCSI-2 and SCSI-3. The corresponding classification is indicated after the reference to the standard.

MOVE MEDIUM (A5h)

In SCSI-2 this is the only mandatory command that is device specific. It causes the target to move a piece of medium from one element to another (Table 16.3). The element addresses of the MTE, the source and the destination are parameters of the command. The Invert bit indicates that the medium should be flipped.

If the source element is empty or the destination element is full the command will abort with a CHECK CONDITION status. This is also the case when an MTE is called for that is not supported in the mode parameter pages.

Table 16.3 The MOVE MEDIUM command.

	7	6	5	4	3	2	1	0
0	MOVE MEDIUM (A5h)							
1	(LUN)			Reserved				
2	(MSB)			Element address of				
3				transport device				(LSB)
4	(MSB)			Source address				
5								(LSB)
6	(MSB)			Destination address				
7								(LSB)
8								
9				Reserved				
10								Invert
11	Control byte							

EXCHANGE MEDIUM (A6h)

This command goes one step further than the MOVE MEDIUM command. The medium in the source element is moved to the destination 1 element and the medium previously in the destination 1 element is moved to the destination 2 element. The source element and the destination 2 element may or may not be the same. When they are the two media are exchanged (Table 16.4).

Table 16.4 The EXCHANGE MEDIUM command.

	7	6	5	4	3	2	1	0
0	EXCHANGE MEDIUM (A6h)							
1	(LUN)			Reserved				
2	(MSB)			Element address of				
3				transport device				(LSB)
4	(MSB)			Source address				
5								(LSB)
6	(MSB)			First destination address				
7								(LSB)
8	(MSB)			Second destination address				
9								(LSB)
10							Inv1	Inv2
11	Control byte							

READ ELEMENT STATUS (B8h)

This command allows you a detailed overview of the configuration of the entire medium-changer (Table 16.5). It supplies the data of all elements or of individual elements of the device, on demand. As described further above, these are the medium transport element, the storage element, the import/export element and the data transfer elements. The function unit code (see Table 16.6) specifies which elements are to be listed. The first element and the number of elements describe the range on which the command works. Thus, in order to get all elements, you specify 0h as function unit code, 0h as the first element address, and FFFFh as number of elements, together with a data length of FFFFFFh.

The element status data (Figure 16.3) consists of an eight byte header (Table 16.7) which is followed by the element pages. The element pages themselves contain an eight byte header (Table 16.8) and one or more element descriptors. The element descriptors are structured differently for the four function group types.

Table 16.5 The READ ELEMENT STATUS command.

	7	6	5	4	3	2	1	0
0	READ ELEMENT STATUS (B8h)							
1	(LUN)			VTag	Function unit type			
2	(MSB)	First element address						
3								(LSB)
4	(MSB)	Number of elements						
5								(LSB)
6	Reserved							
7	(MSB)							
8	Data length							
9								(LSB)
10	Reserved							
11	Control byte							

Table 16.6 Function unit types.

Code	Name
0h	All elements
1h	Medium transport element
2h	Storage element
3h	Import/export element
4h	Data transfer elements
5h – Fh	Reserved

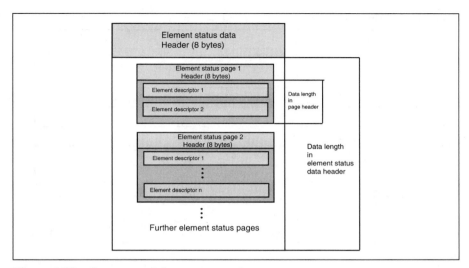

Figure 16.3 Structure of element status data.

Table 16.7 Element status data header.

	7	6	5	4	3	2	1	0
0	(MSB)			First element				
1				in the following list				(LSB)
2	(MSB)			Number of elements				
3				in the list				(LSB)
4	Reserved							
5	(MSB)							
6				Length of list in bytes				
7								(LSB)

Table 16.8 Element status page header.

	7	6	5	4	3	2	1	0
0	Function unit type							
1	PVT	AVT	Reserved					
2	(MSB)			Length of the individual				
3				element descriptors				(LSB)
4	Reserved							
5	(MSB)							
6				Length of descriptor data in bytes				
7								(LSB)

Table 16.9   The medium transport element descriptor.

	7	6	5	4	3	2	1	0
0	(MSB)			Element address				
1								(LSB)
2			Reserved			Excpt	Reserved	Full
3				Reserved				
4				Sense code				
5				Extended sense code				
6 ... 8				Reserved				
9	SVId	Invert			Reserved			
10	(MSB)			Last storage address				
11				of the medium in this element				(LSB)
12 ... 47				Primary title (n/a if PVT=0)				
48 ... 83				Secondary title (n/a if AVT=0)				
84 ... 87				Reserved (shifts upwards when a field is not applicable)				
88 ... z–1			Manufacturer specific (shifts upwards when a field is not applicable)					

The medium transport element (MTE) descriptor

The element address is the address of the medium-changer function unit whose status is described in Table 16.9.

The Excpt bit indicates that the unit is in an exceptional state. In this case, the Sense code and the Extended sense code apply and supply further information on the unit. Both sense data values are interpreted in the usual way.

The Full bit indicates that the function unit contains a medium. SVId indicates that the data field that holds the last storage address of the medium contains a valid value. The Invert bit indicates that the medium has been flipped since it was removed from the last storage position.

The storage element descriptor

The storage element descriptor looks exactly like the MTE descriptor, except for the additional Access bit in byte 2 (Table 16.10). It indicates whether the transport element can access the storage element.

The import/export element descriptor

With the exception of byte 2, the import/export element descriptor looks exactly like the MTE descriptor (Table 16.11). The ImEna and ExEna indicate whether this

Table 16.10 Storage element descriptor, byte 2.

2	Reserved	Access	Excpt	Reserved	Full

Table 16.11 Import/export element descriptor, byte 2.

2	Reserved	ImEna	ExEna	Access	Excpt	ImEx	Full

Table 16.12 Data transfer element descriptor, bytes 6 and 7.

6	NoBus	Reserved	IDvld	LUvld	Reserved	LUN
7	SCSI ID					

element supports import or export processes. When the ImEx bit is set, the medium in the element comes from a user, otherwise it comes from the MTE.

The data transfer element descriptor

This drive descriptor looks exactly like the storage descriptor, with the exception that bytes 6 and 7 supply information on the SCSI bus of the drive (Table 16.12). When the NoBus bit is set, the drive is not on the same bus as the medium-changer. When IDvld is set, the SCSI ID contains a valid value. LUvld indicates that the LUN contains a valid value.

16.3 Mode parameter pages for medium-changers

No device-independent mode parameter pages are defined for medium-changers. Not even the disconnect/reconnect page exists. There are, however, three device-specific pages, listed in Table 16.13.

The device capabilities page (1Fh)

Bits 0 through 3 in byte 2 specify whether the corresponding element is capable of independently storing a piece of medium. Bytes 4–7 contain a matrix of possible sources and destinations for the MOVE MEDIUM command (Table 16.14). A 1 indicates that a transfer between source and destination is supported. Often a direct transfer is not possible between the import/export element and the transfer element. This transfer

Table 16.13 Mode parameter pages for medium-changer devices.

Page code	Name	Page	ANSI
1Dh	Element address page	225	16.3.3.2
1Eh	Drive group page	224	16.3.3.3
1Fh	Device capabilities page	223	16.3.3.1

Table 16.14   The device capabilities page.

	7	6	5	4	3	2	1	0
0	PS	Reserved			Device capabilities page (1Fh)			
1	Page length (0Eh)							
2	Reserved				StorDT	StorI/E	StorST	StorMT
3	Reserved							
4	Reserved				MT→DT	MT→I/E	MT→ST	MT→MT
5	Reserved				ST→DT	ST→I/E	ST→ST	ST→MT
6	Reserved				I/E→DT	I/E→I/E	I/E→ST	I/E→MT
7	Reserved				DT→DT	DT→I/E	DT→ST	DT→MT
8 ... 11	Reserved							
12	Reserved				MT↔DT	MT↔I/E	MT↔ST	MT↔MT
13	Reserved				ST↔DT	ST↔I/E	ST↔ST	ST↔MT
14	Reserved				I/E↔DT	I/E↔I/E	I/E↔ST	I/E↔MT
15	Reserved				DT↔DT	DT↔I/E	DT↔ST	DT↔MT

is accomplished by first moving through the storage element. Bytes 12–15 contain a similar matrix for the command EXCHANGE MEDIUM.

The drive group page (1Eh)

Often a number of DTEs are grouped together in order to take advantage of a single MTE. If there are several MTEs each one is assigned a single DTE. The drive group (transport geometry) page contains information about the assignment of DTEs to MTEs and whether the latter has the capability to flip a medium (Table 16.15).

Table 16.15   The drive group page.

	7	6	5	4	3	2	1	0
0	PS	Reserved			Drive group page (1Eh)			
1	Page length							
	Drive group descriptors							
0	Reserved							Rot
1	Number in group							

The element address page (1Dh)

The element address assignment page contains the mapping of the various functional elements to their respective element addresses (Table 16.16).

Table 16.16 The element address page.

	7	6	5	4	3	2	1	0
0	PS	Reserved	Element address page (1Dh)					
1	Page length (12h)							
2	(MSB)	Medium transport						
3	element address							(LSB)
4	(MSB)	Number of medium						
5	transport elements							(LSB)
6	(MSB)	First storage						
7	element address							(LSB)
8	(MSB)	Number of						
9	storage elements							(LSB)
10	(MSB)	First import/export						
11	element address							(LSB)
12	(MSB)	Number of import/						
13	export elements							(LSB)
14	(MSB)	First data transfer						
15	element address							(LSB)
16	(MSB)	Number of data						
17	transfer elements							(LSB)
18	Reserved							
19								

17 Storage array controllers

The command set for storage array controllers (SCSI Controller Commands SCC) is new in SCSI-3. When you think of storage arrays, names like RAID arrays (Redundant Array of Independent Disks) come to mind. Indeed, RAID arrays can be implemented in many ways as SCSI storage arrays. There is obviously quite a large number of array controllers already on the market, in particular for RAID arrays. Mostly, they also use the SCSI bus for internal and external communication. However, most of them present themselves externally as a normal, maybe rather big SCSI-2 disk. Currently, I know of no implementation of a SCSI-3 array controller. For the remainder of this chapter, we will therefore be talking about future devices.

17.1 The model of the SCSI storage array

Generally speaking, SCSI storage arrays are several disk drives and other devices that can be accessed under a common SCSI address. The model of the SCSI storage array defines different objects, how they are configured, and how they interact to form the storage array.

This model encompasses such easy constructions as the combination of two physical drives into one logical drive up to complicated RAID-5 storage arrays. A linear volume set is defined as a combination of several drives in such a way that they form a single address space of logical block numbers. RAID arrays are various complex constructions which in addition offer some form of redundancy. However, they too map the logical block numbers of the different drives in the array into one single address space.

The SACL

Thus, all SCSI storage arrays share a mechanism that maps the physical block addresses of the individual drives into the address space of the array. This mechanism is called Storage Array Conversion Layer (SACL). A typical I/O subsystem consists of the operating system, the software driver, the host adapter, a device controller and a drive. The operating system requests a service, and the drive provides it. Each of the three levels between operating system and drive can represent the SACL.

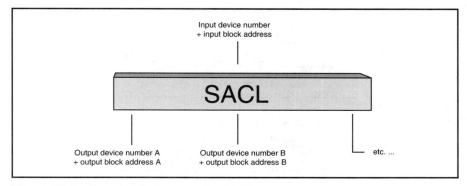

Figure 17.1   Functional diagram of a SACL.

A SACL is a formal function group (Figure 17.1) and as such is present in every storage array, even before SCSI-3. An example of a SACL at driver level is the Micropolis Raidion. SACLs at host adapter level are represented by the Vortex (ICP) SCSI array controllers. At SCSI bridge controller level we find, for example, devices produced by Mylex and CMD.

Software SACL

Each of these solutions has its advantages and disadvantages. An important point in favor of software drivers is that no additional hardware is needed, which can lead to a lower cost. On the other hand, such a storage array is tied to a particular operating system, in most cases even to a particular version. It also needs system resources on the host, which can be a negative factor for the overall performance of the system.

Host adapter SACL

Here, the SACL is located in a dedicated host adapter. This host adapter has its own processor, buffer and usually several SCSI buses for the drives to be connected. The separate processor uses less resources of the host operating system. However, such a device is normally tied to a determined host bus, and usually special software drivers are needed.

Controller SACL

A SACL constructed as a bridge controller is a board or an external device which has a SCSI bus as a connection to the host and one or more SCSI buses to connect the drives (Fingure 17.2). Externally, in SCSI-2 it presents itself as one single normal SCSI hard disk. Therefore, the subsystem functions with any SCSI host adapter and with any operating system. You can take such a system with you from one computer platform to another. You will only have to consider that the data structure obviously varies with the operating system and therefore reformatting may be indicated. The only real disadvantage of such systems is their relatively high cost.

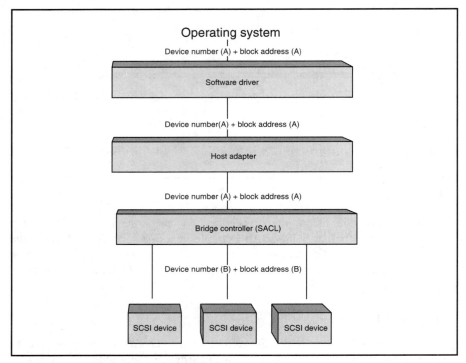

Figure 17.2   SACL controller model.

Please note, however, that the restrictions on the biggest possible disk which vary with the different operating systems also apply to storage arrays. Otherwise it can happen that even with a SACL controller you depend on driver software that is difficult to obtain. Please consult Chapter 7 for the 528-Mbyte limit of DOS and the 8-Gbyte limit of PC INT13.

Objects

A storage array is constructed by configuring objects. This configuration must not necessarily happen online. It can also be permanently set by the manufacturer, but in any case it must be reported correctly. Therefore, in the SCSI storage array specific commands, the report commands are mandatory, whereas the configuration commands are optional.

Objects can be added to a storage array. Then they are available to the application client and can be addressed. Objects combined into redundancy groups or volume sets are called associated. Objects can be attached to a component or covered by identical objects. Thus, for example, a hard disk can be available as a spare in a storage array and thus cover the other hard disks. Objects can be protected. Protected objects can handle the failure of one or more objects without loss of user data or a failure of the storage array as a whole.

Table 17.1 Component device types.

Code	Description
00h	Controller representing a SACL
01h	Non-volatile cache
02h	Power supply
03h	UPS power supply
04h	Display
05h	Keyboard
06h	Cooling fan

Components

The objects that constitute SCSI storage arrays are combined out of two fundamental categories. A component device is a physically addressable object which is not identified as a SCSI-3 device type, such as a power supply or a cooling fan. Table 17.1 shows a list of defined component devices. Application clients can only access component devices by means of commands addressed to the basis address (LUN 0) of the storage array.

Devices

Devices are the physically addressable objects that can be identified by a SCSI-3 device type, such as disk or tape drives or CD-ROMs. Application clients can physically address devices directly. Please note, however, that user data may be distributed arbitrarily across different devices combined into a volume set.

The remaining objects are constructed out of these two categories or they are part of an object of one of these categories.

P_Extent

A P_Extent is the entire area addressable by the host in a device or a continuous part of it. P_Extents are used by the application client to create redundancy groups and spares. P_Extents configured into a redundancy group are called assigned P_Extents.

Redundancy group

A redundancy group is the combination of protected user data and their check data into a single LUN. The P_Extents that form the redundancy group can be located on different devices. The check data can also be empty, that is, they can effectively be omitted.

PS_Extent

A PS_Extent is the entire protected data area in a redundancy group of a device or a continuous part of it. PS_Extents are used by the application client to create volume sets.

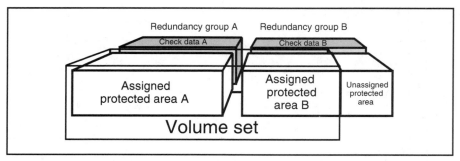

Figure 17.3 Volume set with several redundancy groups.

Volume set

A volume set is a group of one or more P_Extents combined into a LUN_V (Figure 17.3). Volume sets are created by the application client in order to create a continuous area of logical blocks of user data in a storage array. Volume sets must not overlap.

Spare

A spare is a replacement part. Spares exist for P_Extents, devices or components. Spares are associated with redundancy groups or devices. How the replacement of a faulty P_Extent, device or component is to be carried out is, however, left to the manufacturer's discretion.

17.2 Commands for storage array controllers

Besides several of the primary commands, the SCSI array commands contain a group of four command pairs, one each for the input and the output direction.

All these commands share one peculiarity: they use the least significant five bits of byte 1 to specify a service action. Depending on the service action, command structures and parameter lists are different, so that one might really talk about different commands with a common opcode. This technique is not (yet) used anywhere else in the SCSI standards.

Each of these commands has substantial parameter lists. I will, however, omit these and simply present some commands with their service actions and a brief explanation. This command set is too recent for the presentation of further details, and it still remains to be seen whether it succeeds and gets accepted.

MAINTENANCE(IN) (A3h)

The fundamental structure of the MAINTENANCE(IN) command is shown in Table 17.3.

Table 17.4 lists the corresponding service actions.

Table 17.2 Commands for storage array controllers.

Op-code	Name	Type	Page	SCSI-3 (SCC)	Description
00h	TEST UNIT READY	M	131	SPC	Reflects whether or not the LUN is ready to accept a command
03h	REQUEST SENSE	M	132	SPC	Returns detailed error information
12h	INQUIRY	M	128	SPC	Returns LUN specific information
15h	MODE SELECT(6)	O	140	SPC	Set device parameters
16h	RESERVE(6)	O	136	6.8	Make LUN accessible only to certain initiators
17h	RELEASE(6)	O	136	6.6	Make LUN accessible to other initiators
1Ah	MODE SENSE(6)	O	140	SPC	Read device parameters
1Bh	START/STOP UNIT	O		SPC	Load/unload medium
1Ch	RECEIVE DIAGNOSTIC RESULTS	O		SPC	Read self-test results
1Dh	SEND DIAGNOSTIC	O	138	SPC	Initiate self-test
3Bh	WRITE BUFFER	O		SPC	Write data buffer
3Ch	READ BUFFER	O		SPC	Read data buffer
4Ch	LOG SELECT	O		SPC	Select statistics
4Dh	LOG SENSE	O		SPC	Read statistics
55h	MODE SELECT(10)	O	140	SPC	Set device parameters
56h	RESERVE(10)	O		SPC	Make LUN accessible only to certain initiators
57h	RELEASE(10)	O		SPC	Make LUN accessible to other initiators
5Ah	MODE SENSE(10)	O	140	SPC	Read device parameters
A3h	MAINTENANCE(IN)	M	230	6.1	
A4h	MAINTENANCE(OUT)	O		6.2	
BAh	REDUNDANCY GROUP(IN)	M	232	6.3	
BBh	REDUNDANCY GROUP(OUT)	O		6.4	
BCh	SPARE(IN)	M	232	6.7	
BDh	SPARE(OUT)	O		6.8	
BEh	VOLUME SET(IN)	M	232	6.5	
BFh	VOLUME SET(OUT)	O		6.6	

Note: Commands added to this command set in SCSI-3 are shaded light gray; mandatory commands are shaded dark gray.

Table 17.3 The MAINTENANCE(IN) command.

	7	6	5	4	3	2	1	0
0	MAINTENANCE(IN) (A3h)							
1	Reserved			Service action				
2 ... 3	Reserved							
4	(MSB)			LUN_x				
5								(LSB)
6 ...	(MSB)			Transfer				
... 9				length				(LSB)
10	Varies with service action							
11	Control byte							

Table 17.4 Service actions for MAINTENANCE(IN).

Action	Type	Service name
00h	M	REPORT ASSIGNED/UNASSIGNED P_EXTEND
01h	M	REPORT COMPONENT DEVICE
02h	M	REPORT COMPONENT DEVICE ATTACHMENTS
03h	M	REPORT PERIPHERAL DEVICE
04h	M	REPORT PERIPHERAL DEVICE ASSOCIATIONS
05h	M	REPORT PERIPHERAL DEVICE/COMPONENT DEVICE IDENTIFIER
06h	M	REPORT STATES

REDUNDANCY GROUP(IN) (BAh)

This command reports on the properties of the redundancy groups of the target. Its fundamental structure is shown in Table 17.5.

Table 17.6 shows the corresponding service actions.

VOLUME SET(IN) (BEh)

This command reports on volume sets. It has the same structure as REDUNDANCY GROUP(IN), except for the value LUN_V in bytes 4–5. The command has only one service action, namely REPORT VOLUME SETS, which has the code 00h.

SPARE(IN) (BCh)

This command too is structured similarly to REDUNDANCY GROUP(IN), except that bytes 4–5 now contain the value LUN_S. Table 17.7 shows the possible service actions.

Table 17.5 The REDUNDANCY GROUP(IN) command.

	7	6	5	4	3	2	1	0
0	REDUNDANCY GROUP(IN) (BAh)							
1	Reserved			Service action				
2 ... 3	Reserved							
4	(MSB)			LUN_R				
5								(LSB)
6 ...	(MSB)			Transfer				
... 9				length				(LSB)
10	Reserved							RPTS
11	Control byte							

Table 17.6 Service actions for REDUNDANCY GROUP(IN).

Action	Type	Service name
00h	M	REPORT REDUNDANCY GROUPS
01h	M	REPORT UNASSIGNED REDUNDANCY GROUP SPARE

Table 17.7   Service actions for SPARE(IN).

Action	Type	Service name
00h	M	REPORT P_EXTENT SPARE
01h	M	REPORT PERIPHERAL DEVICE/COMPONENT DEVICE SPARE

17.3   Mode parameter pages for storage array controllers

For storage array controllers, four parameter generic pages are defined, together with one device type specific parameter page. Table 17.8 lists these parameter pages.

LUN mapping page (1Bh)

The LUN mapping page (Table 17.9) specifies to which physical device a command is addressed. When the Active bit is set, the mapping is used that is associated with the LUN in the IDENTIFY message. Otherwise, mapping is disabled.

Table 17.8   Mode parameter pages for storage array controllers.

Page code	Name	Page	SCSI-2	SCSI-3 (SCC)
02h	Disconnect/reconnect page	145	7.3.3.2	SPC
09h	Peripheral device page	146	7.3.3.3	SPC
0Ah	Control mode page	147	7.3.3.1	SPC
0Dh	Power condition page		–	SBC
1Bh	LUN mapping page	233	–	6.9.1.1

Table 17.9   The LUN mapping page.

	7	6	5	4	3	2	1	0
0	PS	Reserved		LUN mapping page (1Bh)				
1	Page length (FAh)							
2	Reserved							
3	Reserved							Active
4 ...	(MSB)			Mapping for				
... 11				LUN 1				(LSB)
...				Mappings for				
...				LUN 2 to LUN 30				
244 ...				Mapping for				
... 251				LUN 31				

Table 17.10   IDENTIFY message for SCC devices.

	7	6	5	4	3	2	1	0
	1	Disc-Priv	VOLSET	LUN				

The IDENTIFY message has a special format which substantially corresponds to the SCSI-3 format (Table 17.10). Besides the 5-bit LUN number, there is also the VOLSET bit. When this bit is set, the LUN number specifies a volume set and the LUN mapping page should not be used.

18 Multi-media devices

Currently, the SCSI-3 multi-media command set document (MMC) contains only one device type, namely the CD-ROM. In the near future, CD recorders will be added. Some commands for these devices are already contained in the latest MMC proposal.

The MMC is still very much under development. Thus, the indications given in this chapter are to be taken as highly provisional and subject to changes.

CD-ROM

CD-ROM is a wide and varied topic, worthy of an entire book. A number of books have, in fact, been written on the subject. For the purposes of this discussion, however, we will concentrate on those aspects of CD-ROM that are relevant to the SCSI bus. Because of this I will only be able to touch on topics like the recording format and the organization of the medium.

18.1 The model of a SCSI CD-ROM drive

SCSI CD-ROM drives can read data that conforms to the standards laid down in the yellow book and the red book (IEC 908). These CDs may hold audio information in addition to other forms of digital data. One major aspect of CD-ROM is that data can only be written with a device dedicated to the function; typical CD-ROM drives do not write (Figure 18.1).

The recording format demands that the data be written at a constant linear velocity (CLV). This means that the transfer rate is the same over the entire medium; in other words, there is no zone-bit recording. Nevertheless, the bit density is kept constant by rotating the disk more quickly for outer tracks and more slowly for inner tracks.

Normally the read head of a CD-ROM drive is parked as long as no data access is taking place. However, a CD-ROM drive can assume a HOLD state, in which the head remains in the area of the last read. A timeout is defined among the mode parameters, which specifies how long after an access the head should be kept in the HOLD state.

With respect to data access a CD-ROM drive does not differ significantly from other types of drives. Of course, as mentioned, no write commands have been

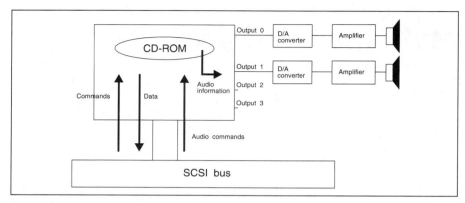

Figure 18.1   Model of a CD-ROM drive.

implemented. On the other hand, in addition to logical blocks CD-ROM drives also employ other forms of data addressing.

Many SCSI CD-ROM drives can also read the audio format. This is accomplished using a separate channel that is not defined within the SCSI standard. However, audio commands and mode parameters are included. Therefore a SCSI CD-ROM drive with audio capabilities can be used as a CD player and be controlled across the SCSI bus.

The CD medium (Red Book)

In terms of the organization of the medium, the CD is fundamentally different from the other types of disks discussed thus far. Data is recorded sequentially in the form of a spiral; this spiral is read with constant linear velocity (CLV). This is the only way to play back audio information without expensive intermediate storage. The CLV method requires that the rotating speed of the CD drive changes constantly during the reading process. On the outer tracks, it is about 210 rpm, on the inner ones about 539 rpm. The recording format for audio CDs is defined in the so-called Red Book which was published by Sony and Philips way back in 1980.

The smallest addressable unit is a physical sector (block, large frame), which in turn consists of 98 frames (small frames) of 24 bytes each. A sector is 1/75 of a second long and contains 2352 bytes of data.

The address of a sector is specified in terms of minutes, seconds, and sectors (or large frames) in the form MM:SS:FF. This is referred to as the MSF format. When an MSF address is used in a SCSI command it is given as shown in Table 18.1. The individual fields are encoded as a binary coded decimal. A CD can contain up to 99 titles (tracks).

Table 18.1   CD-ROM address in MSF format.

0	Reserved
1	M field
2	S field
3	F field

CD-ROM (Yellow Book)

The Yellow Book, published in 1983, defines the CD-ROM as an extension of the CD standard for data applications. Here, embedded into the large frames of 2352 bytes, sector lengths of 2048 (Mode 1) or 2336 (Mode 2) user data bytes are possible. Usually, Mode 1 is chosen for computer applications, because it contains enough space for an excellent error correction with 272 ECC bytes and because 2048 is a multiple of 512.

Mixed mode CDs

A mixed mode CD is divided into up to 99 CD-ROM titles. A CD-ROM title (track) is a continuous sequence of sectors of the same type. Thus, a mixed mode CD-ROM can contain a mixture of both data and audio tracks. A transition area must lie between tracks of differing types, but these areas too must be formatted. CD-ROM tracks can contain up to 99 indexes.

The mapping from physical sectors to logical blocks is done linearly. This also takes into account the transition areas in between tracks. This results in the situation where not all logical blocks are accessible by all commands. For instance, the logical blocks containing audio information can only be read with the audio commands, not with the regular read commands. The logical blocks that map to transition areas cannot be read at all.

CD-ROM/XA (Extended Yellow Book)

The CD-ROM/XA (extended architecture) allows you to mix computer data and audio sectors within one track. This is important for multi-media applications. In order to read these CD-ROMs, the drive must be XA capable.

Multi-session (Orange Book)

A session is a continuous sequence of tracks enclosed by a lead-in and a lead-out area. Traditional CDs and CD-ROMs contain a single session. With the arrival of CD recorders, the need arose for the possibility of writing CD-ROMs in several steps. In order for such a CD to be read, each session must be written completely, together with its lead-in and lead-out area. Thus, every time new data is to be added, a new session must be written.

18.2 Commands for CD-ROMs

For the most part the mandatory CD-ROM commands have already been introduced in previous chapters. An exception is READ CD-ROM CAPACITY which is a variation of the disk drive version. The commands unique to CD-ROMs are all optional (Table 18.2). Examples would include the command to read the disk table of contents and the audio commands. Of the latter, if any are implemented, then they must all be implemented.

Table 18.2   CD-ROM commands.

Op-code	Name	Type	Page	SCSI-2	SCSI-3 (SBC)	Description
00h	TEST UNIT READY	M	131	7.2.16	SPC	Reflects whether or not the LUN is ready to accept a command
01h	REZERO UNIT	(O)		8.2.13 O	SBC M	Seek track 0
03h	REQUEST SENSE	M	132	7.2.14	SPC	Returns detailed error information
08h	READ(6)	(O)	159	8.2.5 O	SBC M	Read. Limited addressing
0Bh	SEEK(6)	(O)		8.2.15 O	SBC M	Seek to LBN
12h	INQUIRY	M	128	7.2.5	SPC	Returns LUN specific information
15h	MODE SELECT(6)	(O)	140	7.2.8 O	SPC M	Set device parameters
16h	RESERVE	M	136	8.2.12	SPC	Make LUN accessible only to certain initiators
17h	RELEASE	M	136	8.2.11	SPC	Make LUN accessible to other initiators
18h	COPY	O		7.2.3	SPC	Autonomous copy from/to another device
1Ah	MODE SENSE(6)	(O)	140	7.2.10 O	SPC M	Read device parameters
1Bh	START/STOP UNIT	(O)		8.2.17 O	SBC M	Load/unload medium
1Ch	RECEIVE DIAGNOSTIC RESULTS	O		7.2.13	SPC	Read self-test results
1Dh	SEND DIAGNOSTIC	M	138	7.2.1	SPC	Initiate self-test
1Eh	PREVENT/ALLOW MEDIUM REMOVAL	(O)		8.2.4 O	SBC M	Lock/unlock door
25h	READ CD-ROM CAPACITY	M	239	13.2.8	4.2.12	Read number of logical blocks
28h	READ(10)	M	159	8.2.6	SBC	Read
2Bh	SEEK(10)	O		8.2.15	4.2.16	Seek LBN
2Fh	VERIFY(10)	O		15.2.11	SBC	Verify
30h	SEARCH DATA HIGH(10)	O		8.2.14	SBC	Search data pattern
31h	SEARCH DATA EQUAL(10)	O		8.2.14	SBC	Search data pattern
32h	SEARCH DATA LOW(10)	O		8.2.14	SBC	Search data pattern
33h	SET LIMITS(10)	O		8.2.16	SBC	Define logical block boundaries
34h	PRE-FETCH	O		8.2.3	SBC	Read data into buffer
35h	SYNCHRONIZE CACHE	O		8.2.8	SBC	Re-read data into cache
36h	LOCK/UNLOCK CACHE	O		8.2.2	SBC	Lock/unlock data in cache
39h	COMPARE	O		7.2.2	SPC	Compare data
3Ah	COPY AND VERIFY	O		7.2.4	SPC	Autonomous copy from/to another device, verify success
3Bh	WRITE BUFFER	O		7.2.17	SPC	Write data buffer
3Ch	READ BUFFER	O		7.2.12	SPC	Read data buffer
3Eh	READ LONG	O	161	8.2.9	SBC	Read data and ECC
40h	CHANGE DEFINITION	O	139	7.2.1	SPC	Set SCSI version
42h	READ SUBCHANNEL	O		13.2.10	4.2.14	Read subchannel data and status
43h	READ TOC	O	240	13.12.11	4.2.15	Read contents table
44h	READ HEADER	O		13.2.9	4.2.13	Read LBN header
45h	PLAY AUDIO(10)	O*	241	13.2.2	4.2.3	Audio playback
47h	PLAY AUDIO MSF	O*	241	13.2.4	4.2.5	Audio playback
48h	PLAY AUDIO TRACK/INDEX	O*	243	13.2.5	4.2.6	Audio playback
49h	PLAY AUDIO TRACK RELATIVE(10)	O*		13.2.6	4.2.8	Audio playback
4Bh	PAUSE/RESUME	O	241	13.2.1	4.2.2	'Pause' key of the drive

Table 18.2 CD-ROM commands (*continued*).

Op-code	Name	Type	Page	SCSI-2	SCSI-3 (SBC)	Description
4Ch	LOG SELECT	O		7.2.6	SPC	Select statistics
4Dh	LOG SENSE	O		7.2.7	SPC	Read statistics
4Eh	STOP PLAY/SCAN	O		–	4.12.18	Terminate audio playback
55h	MODE SELECT(10)	O	140	7.2.9	SPC	Set device parameters
5Ah	MODE SENSE(10)	O	140	7.2.10	SPC	Read device parameters
A5h	PLAY AUDIO(12)	O*	241	13.2.3	4.2.4	Audio playback
A8h	READ(12)	O		15.2.4	SBC	Read
A9h	PLAY TRACK RELATIVE(12)	O*		13.2.7	4.2.9	Audio playback
AFh	VERIFY(12)	O		15.2.12	SBC	Verify data
B0h	SEARCH DATA HIGH(12)	O		15.2.8	SBC	Search data pattern
B1h	SEARCH DATA EQUAL(12)	O		15.2.8	SBC	Search data pattern
B2h	SEARCH DATA LOW(12)	O		15.2.8	SBC	Search data pattern
B3h	SET LIMITS(12)	O		15.2.9	SBC	Set block limits
B8h	SELECT CD-ROM SPEED	O		–	4.2.17	Set data rate
B9h	READ CD MSF	O		–	4.2.11	Read CD information (all formats, MSF addresses)
BAh	AUDIO SCAN	O		–	4.2.1	Fast audio playback
BCh	SEND CD-ROM XA ADDCM DATA	O		–	?	
BDh	PLAY CD-ROM XA(12)	O		–	?	
BEh	READ CD	O		–	4.2.10	Read CD information (all formats, MSF addresses)

Note: Commands added to this command set in SCSI-3 are shaded light gray; mandatory commands are shaded dark gray. (M) means that the command is classified differently in SCSI-2 and SCSI-3. The corresponding classification is indicated after the reference to the standard.

READ CD-ROM CAPACITY (25h)

This command works just like the corresponding command for disk drives (Table 18.3).

Table 18.3 The READ CD-ROM CAPACITY command.

	7	6	5	4	3	2	1	0
0	READ CD-ROM CAPACITY (25h)							
1	(LUN)			Reserved				Rel
2	(MSB)							
3	Logical							
4	block number							
5								(LSB)
6	Reserved							
7								
8								PMI
9	Control byte							

When the PMI bit is clear the logical block number must be zero. In this case the logical block address and the length of the last valid block will be returned. For CD-ROMs, this value can vary by ±75 sectors because it is taken from the TOC.

If, on the other hand, the PMI bit is set then the command will return the address and the length of the logical block, after which a substantial delay in access time occurs relative to the block provided in the command. For CD-ROMs this means that the command returns the address of the last logical block of the track containing the logical block provided in the command.

The command returns an 8-byte long parameter block. The first 4 bytes contain the logical block number, the last 4 bytes the block length.

READ TOC (43h)

This command reads the table of contents of the medium (Table 18.4). Track zero is where the table of contents begins. The MSF bit indicates that the CD-ROM address should be returned in MSF format, otherwise a logical block number is returned.

The command returns a data block containing the table of contents with the structure shown in Table 18.5. It consists of a header and a track descriptor for each track.

Table 18.4   The READ TOC command.

	7	6	5	4	3	2	1	0
0	READ TOC (43h)							
1	(LUN)			Reserved			MSF	Rel
2					Format			
3	Reserved							
4								
5								
6	Track or session number							
7	(MSB)	Transfer						
8	length							(LSB)
9	Control byte							

Table 18.5   READ TOC data format (SCSI-2 format).

	7	6	5	4	3	2	1	0
0	(MSB)			Transfer length				
1								(LSB)
2	First track number							
3	Last track number							
	The following bytes contain the track descriptors							

Table 18.5 READ TOC data format (SCSI-2 format) (*continued*).

	7	6	5	4	3	2	1	0
0	Reserved							
1	ADR				Attribute			
2	Track number							
3	Reserved							
4 ...	(MSB)		Logical block number					
...7			of the first block of this track					(LSB)

In SCSI-3 further data formats have been added. The new Format field indicates which of these is going to be used. A value of 0h means SCSI-2 format. 4h stands for the new session format, and 8h indicates the new Q subcode format.

In byte 6 of the command, it is now possible to specify the track or session number from which the TOC is to be read.

18.3 Audio commands for CD-ROMs

The audio commands make it possible to control a SCSI CD-ROM drive across the SCSI bus like a remote-controlled CD player. Audio information is transmitted via the audio output ports.

PAUSE/RESUME (4Bh)

This 10-byte command simulates the pause button of a CD player. No parameters are involved except the Resume bit (byte 8, bit 0). When this bit is clear, playing should stop; otherwise it should continue.

PLAY AUDIO(10) (45h) and PLAY AUDIO(12) (A5h)

The PLAY AUDIO commands cause the playing of audio data. The data to be played is specified by the Start address and Transfer length fields. In addition, the SOTC bit of the CD-ROM audio page has influence on these commands.

The 10-byte version of the command is shown in Table 18.6. The 12-byte version uses no additional parameters and follows the usual format.

If the start address is not found or the data specified is not audio information, or if the data type changes during playing, the command will abort with a CHECK CONDITION status.

PLAY AUDIO MSF (47h)

This command also initiates playback of audio data but uses the MSF addressing format (Table 18.7). The data to be played is specified using the starting and ending address.

Table 18.6 The PLAY AUDIO(10) command.

	7	6	5	4	3	2	1	0
0	PLAY AUDIO(10) (45h)							
1	(LUN)		Reserved					Rel
2	(MSB)							
3	Start address							
4	(logical block)							
5								(LSB)
6	Reserved							
7	(MSB)	Transfer						
8	length							(LSB)
9	Control byte							

Table 18.7   The PLAY AUDIO MSF command.

	7	6	5	4	3	2	1	0
0	PLAY AUDIO MSF (47h)							
1	(LUN)		Reserved					
2	Reserved							
3	Start address, M field							
4	Start address, S field							
5	Start address, F field							
6	End address, M field							
7	End address, S field							
8	End address, F field							
9	Control byte							

Table 18.8   The PLAY AUDIO TRACK/INDEX command.

	7	6	5	4	3	2	1	0
0	PLAY AUDIO TRACK/INDEX (48h)							
1	(LUN)		Reserved					
2	Reserved							
3								
4	Start address, track							
5	Start address, index							
6	Reserved							
7	End address, track							
8	End address, index							
9	Control byte							

PLAY AUDIO TRACK/INDEX (48h)

This variant of PLAY AUDIO uses tracks and indexes to specify the data to be played (Table 18.8). Both of these parameters assume values between 0 and 99.

18.4 Mode parameters for CD-ROMs

Mode parameter header

The mode parameter header contains two parameters for CD-ROM. The field with the medium type assumes the values shown in Table 18.9.

The device-specific byte contains only a single parameter. Bit 4 is the Cache bit and is only defined for MODE SENSE. When set it indicates that the target is equipped with a cache and that the DPO and FUA bits of the WRITE command are supported.

Mode parameter block descriptor

The write density parameter in the mode parameter block descriptor takes on the values shown in Table 18.10.

Mode parameter pages

The mode parameter pages in Table 18.11 have been defined for CD-ROM devices.

Table 18.9 CD-ROM medium types.

Code	Medium type	Code	Medium type
00h	Default	04h	Reserved
01h	120 mm CD-ROM, data only	05h	80 mm CD-ROM, data only
02h	120 mm CD-ROM, audio only	06h	80 mm CD-ROM, audio only
03h	120 mm CD-ROM, audio and data	07h	80 mm CD-ROM, audio and data

Table 18.10 CD-ROM write density.

Code	Write density	Code	Write density
00h	Default	03h	2340 bytes/sector
01h	2048 bytes/sector	04h	Audio information
02h	2336 bytes/sector		

Table 18.11 Mode parameter pages for CD-ROM devices.

Page code	Name	Page	SCSI-2	SCSI-3 (MMC)
01h	Read/write error page		13.3.3.3	4.3.3.3
02h	Disconnect/reconnect page	145	7.3.3.2	SPC
07h	Verify error handling page		–	4.3.3.4
08h	Cache page	172	–	SBC
09h	Peripheral device page	146	7.3.3.3	SPC

Table 18.11   Mode parameter pages for CD-ROM devices (*continued*).

Page code	Name	Page	SCSI-2	SCSI-3 (MMC)
0Ah	Control mode page	147	7.3.3.1	SPC
0Bh	Medium type page		8.3.3.4	SBC
0Dh	CD-ROM page	244	13.3.3.2	4.3.3.2
0Eh	CD-ROM audio page	244	13.3.3.1	4.3.3.1

The CD-ROM page (0Dh)

The CD-ROM page is valid for all medium types (Table 18.12). The inactivity timeout (Inactive) specifies how long the head should remain in the hold state before being parked. A key to timeout values is shown in Table 18.13.

The parameter MSF seconds per MSF minute is self-explanatory. The default value here is 60; the default value for MSF frames per MSF second is 75.

The CD-ROM audio page (0Eh)

The Immed bit has the usual meaning. When set a status is returned immediately. When the SOTB (stop on track boundaries) bit is set the target will stop the playback at a track boundary. Otherwise playback will continue until the transfer length has been exhausted, even if it extends across several CD-ROM tracks (Table 18.14).

Table 18.12   The CD-ROM page.

	7	6	5	4	3	2	1	0
0	PS	Reserved			CD-ROM page (0Dh)			
1	Page length (06h)							
2	Reserved							
3	Reserved				Inactive			
4	(MSB)			Number of				
5	MSF seconds per MSF minute							(LSB)
6	(MSB)			Number of				
7	MSF frames per MSF second							(LSB)

Table 18.13   Timeout values.

Code	Timeout	Code	Timeout
00h	Vendor specific	08h	16 seconds
01h	125 ms	09h	32 seconds
02h	250 ms	0Ah	1 minute
03h	500 ms	0Bh	2 minutes
04h	1 second	0Ch	4 minutes
05h	2 seconds	0Dh	8 minutes
06h	4 seconds	0Eh	16 minutes
07h	8 seconds	0Fh	32 minutes

Table 18.14 The CD-ROM audio page.

	7	6	5	4	3	2	1	0
0	PS	Reserved		CD-ROM audio page (0Eh)				
1	Page length (0Eh)							
2						Immed	SOTB	Reserved
3	Reserved							
4								
5	APRV	Reserved			LBA factor			
6	(MSB)	Number of						
7	LBAs per second							(LSB)
8	Reserved				Output port 0 select			
9	Port 0 volume							
10	Reserved				Output port 1 select			
11	Port 1 volume							
12	Reserved				Output port 2 select			
13	Port 2 volume							
14	Reserved				Output port 3 select			
15	Port 3 volume							

A set APRV (audio playback rate valid) bit indicates that the LBA factor and the number of LBAs per second is valid.

The Number of LBAs per second field specifies the rate at which data is to be played back. The LBA factor is a multiplier that allows greater resolution for the setting of the LBAs per second. A 0h in this field causes Number of LBAs per second to be multiplied by 1 and a value of 8h multiplies by 1/256.

The end of the parameter page consists of settings for the four output channels. The Output port n select enables channels to port n. For instance, 0000b will mute the port, 0001b will connect channel 1, 0010b will connect channel 2, and so on. The value for Port n volume can range from 00h for very quiet to FFh for very loud.

18.5 CD recorders

The CD recorder is a new device in SCSI-3. Only 22 pages are dedicated to it in the 3.0 proposal for the MMC document of 27.9.1995. They mostly contain a description of the specific commands and some diagrams supposed to document the writing of a CD-ROM. The diagrams show that a CD recorder is a rather complex device. This, however, is not yet reflected in the text of the MMC proposal.

Thus, I will only briefly outline this still ongoing development. You should also be aware that the following information will be subject to changes.

18.6   Commands for CD recorders

Besides the commands for all SCSI devices, CD recorders must be able to handle some specific commands which are listed in Table 18.15.

WRITE SESSION (51h)

This command (Table 18.16) sends the data for writing a whole CD or a whole track. The structure of this command is completely different from the normal WRITE command. Although it is only a 10-byte command, it has a transfer length field of 32 bits in bytes 2 to 5. Except for the control byte, the command has no further parameters.

FORMAT/RESERVE TRACK (53h)

This command (Table 18.17) reserves the space for a data track on the CD, that is, it writes start and end address into the program memory area (PMA). No space can be reserved for audio tracks.

Table 18.15   Specific commands for CD recorders.

Op-code	Name	Type	Page	SCSI-3 (SCC)	Description
2Ah	WRITE(10)	M	159	SBC	Write
35h	SYNCHRONIZE CACHE	M		SBC	Write cache to medium
51h	WRITE SESSION	M	246	5.1.1.1	Writing of a whole CD or a whole track
53h	FORMAT/RESERVE TRACK	M	246	5.1.1.2	Reserve a data track
59h	READ MASTER CUE	O		5.1.2.1	Read master information from a master CD
5Bh	CLOSE SESSION/TRACK	M	247	5.1.1.3	Write the lead-in and lead-out areas of a session
5Ch	READ BUFFER STATUS	O		5.1.2.2	Read buffer status
5Fh	RECOVER TRACK	O		5.1.2.3	Repair damaged track

Table 18.16   The WRITE SESSION command.

	7	6	5	4	3	2	1	0
0	WRITE SESSION (51h)							
1	Reserved							
2	(MSB)							
3	Transfer length							
4	in bytes							
5								(LSB)
6	Reserved							
7								
8								
9	Control byte							

Table 18.17 The FORMAT/RESERVE TRACK command.

	7	6	5	4	3	2	1	0
0	FORMAT/RESERVE TRACK (53h)							
1 ...	Reserved							
... 4								
5	(MSB)							
6	Number of logical blocks							
7	to be reserved							
8								(LSB)
9	Control byte							

The next free track automatically becomes the new track number. Bytes 5 to 8 contain the length in blocks of the data track to be reserved. The track must at least be 4 seconds long, and there must obviously be enough space left on the medium to accommodate the required length.

CLOSE SESSION/TRACK (FINALIZE) (5Bh)

It does not seem clear as yet how the command (Table 18.18) will be finally called. In any case, the command finishes all unfinished titles and writes the lead-in and lead-out areas of the session. With audio or single-session CDs, or with multi-session CDs where no further session is permitted, byte 8 contains the value 00h. A value of 01h allows you to append further sessions to multi-session CDs.

Table 18.18 The CLOSE SESSION/TRACK command.

	7	6	5	4	3	2	1	0
0	CLOSE SESSION/TRACK (5Bh)							
1								
2 ...								Padding
...	Reserved							
... 7								
8	Next session							
9	Control byte							

19 The parallel SCSI interface

Up to SCSI-2, the only SCSI interface was the parallel interface. Only with SCSI-3 are other interface alternatives being introduced. Each of these new interfaces – SSA, Fibre Channel and Fire Wire – has some good arguments in its favor. How and whether any of these new interfaces will succeed is difficult to say.

But the parallel SCSI interface has seen some innovations with SCSI-3. Thus, the P cable was introduced, which allows 16-bit wide SCSI with only one cable. This cable is already widely used with devices that otherwise adhere to the SCSI-2 standard. Furthermore, SCSI-3 allows devices on the wide SCSI bus to have IDs up to 15 or even 31. Finally, a separate document defines Fast-20 (also known as Ultra-SCSI), a transfer mode with a speed of 20 Megatransfers per second.

19.1 Overview

The parallel SCSI interface exists in many variations. Each new generation of the SCSI standard has brought more or less drastic additions which have, however, always maintained backward compatibility with the previous standards.

Single-ended/differential

Since SCSI-1 and up to today there are two basic variations of the parallel SCSI interface which are electrically incompatible with each other: the single-ended and the differential interface. These two interface variations cannot be used together on the same SCSI bus. There are, however, some reliable converters on the market which allow the transition from single-ended SCSI to differential SCSI.

The single-ended interface is the most widely used. It is usually fully sufficient for connections inside a cabinet. In the best case, it allows a cable length of up to 6 m. With higher data rates and long external connections, the single-ended interface becomes extremely critical. SCSI-3 states that a single-ended SCSI bus should not be longer than 3 m. Only if no use is made of fast SCSI, are up to 6 m allowed. Ultra-SCSI (Fast-20) limits this to a further degree: when up to four devices are connected, 3 m of cable may be used, otherwise the length of the bus must be limited to 1.5 m.

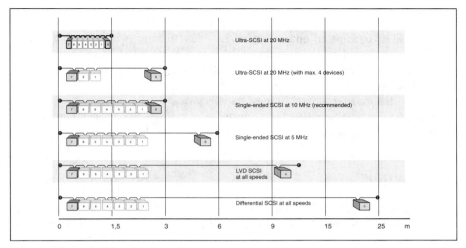

Figure 19.1   SCSI cable lengths.

These problems are not shared by the differential interface. It is far more resistant against external interferences and allows cable lengths of up to 25 m. Because of the high power consumption, however, the differential drivers cannot be integrated into the SCSI protocol chip. For this reason, they are more expensive and not widely available. Figure 19.1 summarizes the allowable cable lengths.

Low voltage differential (LVD)

The new low voltage differential interface is supposed to bring the advantage of single-ended and differential interfaces, namely low cost and high stability combined with long cable length. Its power consumption is so low that it can be integrated into the SCSI chip; on the other hand, it is so immune to interferences that cable lengths of up to 12 m will be possible. Standardization is practically finished, so that the first devices will be on the market before the end of 1997.

Narrow and Wide SCSI

Originally, the SCSI bus was 8 bits wide. With SCSI-2, 16-bit and 32-bit wide SCSI buses were introduced. The additional B cable for bits 8 to 31 has never been a success. Wide SCSI uses the 68-pin P and Q cables now standardized in SCSI-3. The P cable carries the data bits 0 to 15 and the control signals, the Q cable carries the data bits 16 to 31.

There is, however, an important difference between wide SCSI-2 and wide SCSI-3: while a wide SCSI-2 bus can principally handle only eight devices, a wide SCSI-3 bus can serve up to 16 or 32 devices, depending on the bus width.

Narrow and Wide SCSI can be mixed on the same bus. More details follow later in this chapter.

Speed

SCSI-1 had two transfer options: asynchronous transfer with about 1.5 to 3 Mbytes/sec and synchronous transfer with up to 5 Mbytes/sec. SCSI-2 introduced fast synchronous transfer with up to 10 megatransfers/sec (for 8-bit width). Finally, as an addition to the SPI document, SCSI-3 defines the Fast-20 (Ultra-SCSI) standard with a transfer rate of 20 megatransfers/sec.

Since SCSI devices negotiate their transfer rates as a function of their capabilities, devices of different speeds can be used together on one bus.

19.2   SCSI signals

The standard 8-bit wide SCSI-2 bus has 18 signals, nine data signals and nine control signals. In Wide SCSI, additional data signals are added, plus two further control signals for a second cable.

In this book all timing diagrams show signals as active-high; in other words, a logic 1 is represented by a high signal. In reality, however, signals are either active-low or differential for SCSI. In either case they must be driven into the active state. Termination resistors negate the signals, holding them nonactive until bus drivers drive the signal active. This makes it possible to leave devices on the bus whose power has been turned off. With the introduction of Ultra-SCSI, more and more devices use active negation with time-critical signals, that is, the devices even actively drive the signals to nonactive level.

Three of the SCSI signals, BSY, SEL, and RST, must be implemented as wired-or. This allows more than one driver to activate the signal at a given time. Of course, only one driver is necessary to make it active. All other signals need not be wired-or and are usually implemented with tri-state drivers.

Figure 19.2 shows a wired-or signal implemented with open collector transistors. As long as the transistor is inactive, the terminator assures the high, inactive state.

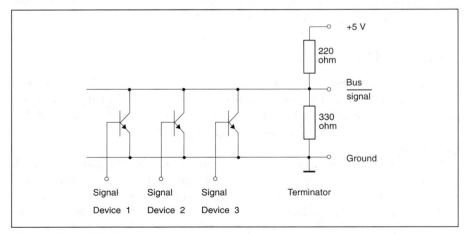

Figure 19.2   Wired-or bus signals.

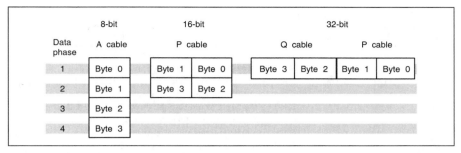

Figure 19.3   Byte ordering for Wide SCSI.

When the transistor turns on it pulls the voltage down to the active state. Even if more than one transistor becomes active simultaneously the result is the same.

Wide SCSI

Wide SCSI is a SCSI-2 option, which makes possible 16- or 32-bit wide data transfers. In order to handle the extra width an additional 29 signals are necessary. 16-bit wide SCSI fits on the P cable defined in SCSI-3 for the primary SCSI bus. For 32-bit wide SCSI a second cable, the Q cable, is needed, which accommodates the secondary SCSI bus. Physically, the P cable and the Q cable are identical: both have 68 pins. Figure 19.3 shows the ordering of bytes for 8-, 16- and 32-bit wide transfers.

The devices involved negotiate whether or not to use Wide SCSI. This is possible because commands and messages always take place across the 8-bit bus. It is even possible to mix devices using different data widths on the same bus. Figure 19.4 shows such a configuration.

Table 19.1 lists all SCSI signals along with their function. A look at the SCSI bus phase descriptions in Section 19.8 will make it easier to understand the role of each signal.

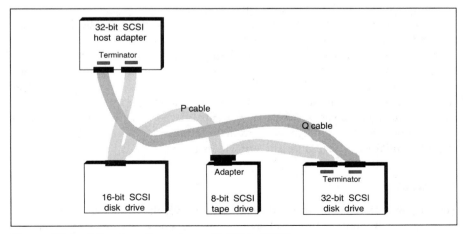

Figure 19.4   Mixed configuration with Wide SCSI.

Table 19.1   The SCSI signals.

Abbreviation	Name	Function
BSY	BUSY	Wired-or signal indicating that the bus is in use.
SEL	SELECT	Wired-or signal used during selection and reselection.
C/D	COMMAND/DATA	Used by the target to indicate the type of data transfer. When active, control information (commands or messages) is transferred.
I/O	INPUT/OUTPUT	Used by the target to indicate the direction of the data transfer (with respect to the initiator). When active the initiator receives data. Also differentiates selection from reselection.
MSG	MESSAGE	Used by the target during the MESSAGE phase.
REQ	REQUEST	Used by the target during the handshake sequence. This signal
REQQ		exists twice: REQ on the A and P cables, and REQQ on the Q cable.
ACK	ACKNOWLEDGE	Used by the initiator during the handshake sequence. This signal
ACKQ		also exists on the A and P cables and on the Q cable.
ATN	ATTENTION	Used by the initiator to indicate the ATTENTION condition.
RST	RESET	Wired-or signal that indicates the RESET condition.
DB(7) ...	DATA BUS	8 data bits and parity bit that comprise the data bus.
DB(0)		The data bits are also used during the arbitration
DB(P)		phase. Parity is odd.
DB(31) ...	DATA BUS	24 data bits and 3 parity bits that expand the data bus.
DB(8)		
DB(P3) ...		
DB(P1)		

Termination

Each end of the physical SCSI bus must be terminated with the appropriate resistors. These set the signals to inactive level and prevent reflections at the cable ends which would overlay the signal. Most SCSI devices have sockets for the terminating resistors or, even better, they have active terminator chips that can be switched on and off with a jumper or via software. The terminators in the two devices located at the ends of the bus should be left installed; the other devices should have their terminators removed or disabled. If a cable does not happen to end at a device then this loose end must be terminated with an external terminator.

A SCSI terminator must be supplied with +5 V. Leads in the SCSI cable are reserved for this purpose. These terminator power leads can be connected to the +5 V of any device by means of a jumper. Usually, only the host adapter supplies the terminator power. Thus, the terminators are powered as soon as the host is switched on. With very long cables (differential up to 25 m) the line drop of terminator power can become too high. In such cases, also the last device on the SCSI bus should supply terminator power. A diode in the supply lead ensures that switched-off devices do net get their supply voltage from the terminator power lead. Single-ended and differential SCSI need different terminators.

The data parity bit

The only way to detect a corrupted data byte sent over the SCSI bus is through the parity bit. Parity works as follows: the sender of a data byte sets the parity bit in such a way that the sum of all bits becomes odd. This is called odd parity. The receiver

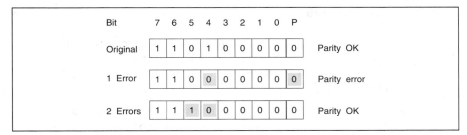

Figure 19.5 Shortcomings of SCSI parity.

then checks to see if the total number of 1s in the data and parity bits is odd. When this is the case the receiver assumes that the data is intact. The implementation of a parity bit went from optional in SCSI-1 to mandatory in SCSI-2. There is one parity bit for every eight data bits (that is, four for 32-bit Wide SCSI). If a SCSI device detects a parity error it will ask that the data be sent again. A detailed example of this can be found on page 301.

One deficiency in the parity bit approach is that only an odd number of 'bad' bits can be detected. This means that it is possible for corrupted data to go unnoticed (Figure 19.5). If an initiator sends a byte where two bits change their value on the bus, the parity bit will still be good. The target receives the byte and has no way of detecting the corrupted byte. When the target writes this data to the drive the error remains but the data is recorded as good. Although this is an obvious shortcoming, in practice it is extremely rare for an even number of bits to change their value.

Using a single parity bit as the sole method of error detection is not uncommon. Almost all memory buses, from PC to mainframe, share this design. Although I/O buses are generally exposed to noisier environments than internal buses, this simple method of ensuring data integrity proves to be effective here as well.

19.3 Cables and connectors

SCSI cables

As opposed to the ATA standard for the IDE interface, the SCSI standard primarily defines the SCSI bus cable, but not the power supply of the devices. An exception is the integrated SCA connection for hard disks which has been added to the SPI-2 document in the context of SCSI-3.

The single-ended and the differential pin assignments for SCSI are designed to make it possible to use the same cables. The A cable is a 50-pin cable while the P and Q cables are 68-pin. Either implementation may use either ribbon cable or twisted-pair, the latter being also allowed as shielded or unshielded round cable. For differential buses only twisted pair cable is recommended. Cables should have an impedance between 90 and 140 ohms.

When Fast SCSI is being used – that is, transfer rates above 5 MHz – the cable requirements are somewhat stricter. The cable should be shielded with an impedance between 90 and 132 ohms and a signal attenuation of less than 0.095 dB at 5 MHz.

SCSI-3 requires even stricter impedance values. At the same time, SCSI-3 defines a single-ended and a differential impedance measuring method. Especially for Ultra-SCSI (Fast-20), high-quality cables with Teflon isolation are recommended because their impedance comes nearest to the ideal value of 90 ohms.

For use of round cables with the single-ended SCSI bus, the SCSI-3 standard defines the following rules for the arrangement of lead pairs:

- Lead pairs 47/48 (ACK) and 57/58 (REQ) must be located in the cable core. If there are more than three lead pairs in the core, these two must not lie opposite to each other.

- The lead pairs for data signals must form the outer layer of the cable.

- Each lead pair must consist of the signal lead and the corresponding ground.

Since no lead pair assignment is defined for the differential bus, cables that meet the above requirements can be used for both interface variations.

Beware of pitfalls!

SCSI cables, in particular incorrectly wired round cables, are a frequent cause of malfunctioning SCSI configurations. The least critical is still ye goode olde ribbon cable. Thus, if you run into inexplicable problems, try to swap the external cables with a ribbon cable directly connected to the devices. And do not forget to check correct termination!

Internal cables and connectors

The most common choice for device internal SCSI connections are 50-pin ribbon cables with 1.27 mm (0.05 inch) conductor spacing. Ribbon cable connectors are directly crimped on. The device electronics typically use a 50-pin male header which fits the female ribbon cable connector. The contact numbers of connectors and cables match 1:1; see connector scheme 1 in Table 19.2 (page 259).

Wide SCSI too internally employs ribbon cable, but in a 68-pin high density version with a conductor spacing of 0.54 mm (0.025 inch). Thus an internal Wide SCSI cable is physically narrower than an internal narrow SCSI cable. Here the normal SCSI scheme is used: cables have male headers while devices have female connectors. The connectors used are unshielded high density connectors (Mini-Sub-D) with a contact distance of 1.27 mm (0.05 inch).

SCSI backplanes

RAID subsystems in particular employ SCSI backplanes which us the 80-pin SCA connector. The SCA-2 connection has been additionally incorporated into the SCSI-3 SPI-2 document.

SCA-2 contains not only all signals for Wide SCSI, but also the supply voltages and some additional signals, such as spindle synchronization of disk drives. In SCA-2 the contacts are of different length so that when plugging and unplugging the devices, power supply voltages and signals are connected in a specified sequence. This is a very simple way of exchanging devices during operation (hot swapping).

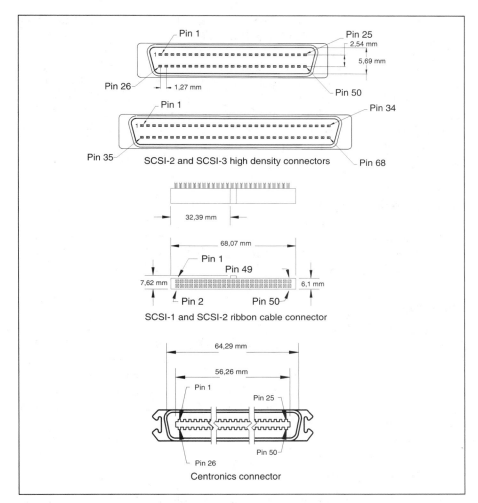

Figure 19.6   SCSI connectors.

External SCSI connections

For external connections shielded round cables are recommended, for which the SCSI-2 standard defines two basic connector variations. On the one hand, the 50-pin 'Centronics' connectors can be used which are already known from SCSI-1. Cables with such connectors are often, though not completely correctly, called SCSI-1 cables. On the other hand, the standard specifies shielded 50-pin high density connectors (Mini-Sub-D). These are commonly called SCSI-2 connectors, but they are also officially allowed in the SCSI-3 standard. For types, connector scheme 2 of Table 19.2 applies. Figure 19.6 gives detailed specifications.

Wide SCSI nearly exclusively uses the 68-pin high density connector (Mini-Sub-D) with the pin assignments defined in SCSI-3. This Wide SCSI cable is commonly called SCSI-3 cable, although Wide SCSI and SCSI-3 do not necessarily belong together.

New in the SPI-2 standard of SCSI-3 is the VHDCI connector (Very High Density Cable Interconnect). This Wide SCSI connector is so small that two of them will fit onto one PC slot cover.

Finally, there are some pin assignments that are not described in the SCSI specification. One of these comes from Apple and is also used in a number of inexpensive PC host adapters and devices. Here, the external connector is a DB-25 female connector. This solution is rather unsatisfactory and completely unusable for Fast-20 (Ultra-SCSI), because there is no separate ground lead for each signal. Obviously, differential and LVD will not work with this either. The pin assignment is shown under connector scheme 3 in Table 19.2 (page 259).

19.4   Single-ended SCSI

The vast majority of devices sold today are equipped with single-ended SCSI. The main reason for this is the extra cost in implementing differential and the cost of twisted-pair cabling. Most SCSI chips have single-ended drivers already built in.

Bus length

Single-ended SCSI allows a bus of up to 6 meters. When higher transfer rates than 5 Megatransfers per second are to be used, SCSI-2 limits the lengths to 3 m. The SCSI-3 Fast-20 option requires a further restriction: when more than four devices are connected, the bus must be only up to 1.5 m long. This is adequate for most applications within a single enclosure. Also allowed are short extensions from the bus, so-called stubs, of 10 cm or less. These must be kept at least 30 cm apart. Bear in mind that the distance from the protocol chip to the connector must be attributed to the stub length.

Signal levels and termination

Figure 19.7 shows the implementation of a typical single-ended SCSI signal. The output driver is a NAND gate. One input is for the signal and the other for enabling the output. The driver must meet the following specifications: 2.5–5.25 V (inactive); 0.0–0.5 V (active). It must be capable of sinking 48 mA at 0.5 V, of which 44 mA come from the termination. The input must recognize 0.0–0.8 V as active and 2.5–5.25 V as inactive. The input current for an active signal of 0.5 V must lie between 0.0 and –0.4 mA. For an inactive signal the current must lie between 0.0 and 0.1 mA at 5.25 V. The input hysteresis must be at least 0.2 V and the input capacitance at most 25 pF. These values must also hold for devices without power.

Passive termination

Also shown in the figure is the passive signal termination which in SCSI fulfills two tasks: it defines the inactive level of the signals and damps the signals at the bus end in order to prevent reflections. In SCSI-1 and SCSI-2 it consists of a pair of resistors

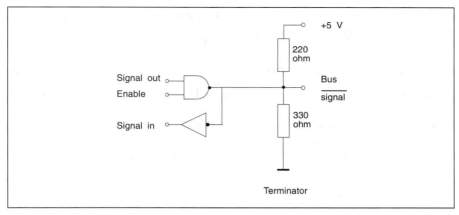

Figure 19.7 Typical single-ended SCSI.

for each signal of the SCSI bus. The 220 ohm resistor connects to +5 V while the 330 ohm connects to ground. Together the resistors bring the signal level to 3 V when no drivers are active. The resistors are allowed a tolerance of ± 5% although ± 1% is recommended. This passive termination scheme was introduced in SCSI-1.

Active termination

SCSI-2 introduces an alternative for terminating a single-ended bus which has meanwhile widely succeeded as the better one. The most important condition here is that the signal impedance lie between 100 and 132 ohms. This active termination circuit, which is shown in Figure 19.8, is less sensitive to noise than the passive termination. Active terminator chips also allow the termination to be switched on

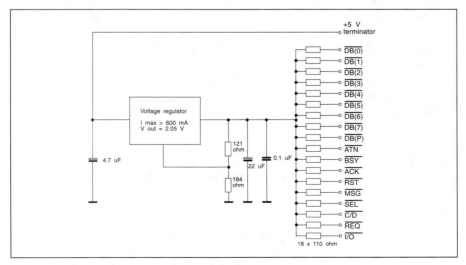

Figure 19.8 Alternative SCSI-2 termination.

and off via software. SCSI-3 defines a set of rules for correct termination which practically forces active termination.

Forced perfect termination

Forced perfect termination is a variation of active termination which works with an array of diodes and Zener diodes. It has often been praised as a possibility to run an overlong SCSI bus safely. However, since modern devices with fast SCSI interfaces use the active negation technique, use of forced perfect terminators should be strongly discouraged. In the worst case, it can lead to the destruction of SCSI driver chips through excessively high currents.

Active negation

In more recent SCSI chips, the active negation technique is employed in order to improve signal quality independently of terminators and, consequently, TERMPWR. In active negation, an active signal is not simply set to high resistance, but the driver actively sets it to a level of about 3 V. This is obviously possible only for signals for which the or-wiring is not needed. Usually, REQ and ACK and the data signals are operated with active negation. While the SCAM protocol is active, active negation must be disabled.

Improper termination

What happens when a single-ended bus is incorrectly terminated? I can give the following account from my own experience. If the bus has no termination at either end, there is no reference level for the signals and nothing will work. This rarely happens, however, because usually the host adapter has its termination installed. In general a SCSI bus with termination at only one end will work without problems over short lengths. However, if the bus is very long or is in a noisy environment then it will be susceptible to intermittent hanging. This is also true for other forms of improper termination. When the termination is not located at the physical end of the bus the problem will usually go unnoticed for quite some time. A bus with three terminators also tends to function without difficulties, in my experience.

This tolerant behavior is attractive but can lead to insidious problems. It is true that an incorrectly terminated bus will often work quite well. However, if the system is then moved or an additional device is added to the bus it may suddenly hang or show intermittent problems. When problems like this occur it always makes sense to begin looking for the problem bottom up by asking whether the bus is properly terminated.

Pin assignments

The various connectors defined in the SCSI standard were described in Section 19.3. There are at least three different pin layouts for the different connectors. The same connectors always use the same assignment. There are three schemes for this assignment:

- The A cable with 25 lead pairs for 'narrow' SCSI.
- The P cable with 34 lead pairs for 16-bit wide SCSI.
- The Q cable, again with 34 lead pairs, contains the higher 16 data bits and, in combination with the P cable, allows 32-bit wide SCSI.

Table 19.2 lists the pin assignments for the single-ended SCSI-2 A cable.

Wide SCSI

For Wide SCSI the SCSI-2 standard had defined an additional 68-pin B cable. It was, however, seldom employed in practice. Even the first Wide SCSI implementations used the P cable which is now defined as part of SCSI-3. It contains the control signals and the data bits 0 to 15 together with the two associated parity bits. These constitute the primary SCSI-3 bus.

For 32-bit wide SCSI, the SCSI-3 standard defines the additional Q cable for the secondary SCSI bus (Table 19.3). The Q cable contains data bits 16 to 31 together with the handshake signals REQQ/ACKQ. This doubling of handshake signals on the secondary bus is necessary because the primary and the secondary bus can be of different lengths and this leads to different signal transit times on the two cables.

Table 19.2   The A cable for single-ended SCSI.

Signal	Connector assignment 2	Cable and connector assignment 1		Connector assignment 2	Connector assignment 3	Signal
Ground	1	1	2	26	14	$\overline{DB(0)}$
Ground	2	3	4	27	2	$\overline{DB(1)}$
Ground	3	5	6	28	15	$\overline{DB(2)}$
Ground	4	7	8	29	3	$\overline{DB(3)}$
Ground	5	9	10	30	16	$\overline{DB(4)}$
Ground	6	11	12	31	4	$\overline{DB(5)}$
Ground	7	13	14	32	17	$\overline{DB(6)}$
Ground	8	15	16	33	5	$\overline{DB(7)}$
Ground	9	17	18	34	18	$\overline{DB(P)}$
Ground	10	19	20	35	19	Ground
Ground	11	21	22	36	13	Ground
Reserved	12	23	24	37	9	Reserved
Not connected	13	25	26	38	–	+5 V terminator
Reserved	14	27	28	39		Reserved
Ground	15	29	30	40	8	Ground
Ground	16	31	32	41	20	$\overline{ATN}$
Ground	17	33	34	42	6	Ground
Ground	18	35	36	43	23	$\overline{BSY}$
Ground	19	37	38	44	22	$\overline{ACK}$
Ground	20	39	40	45	10	$\overline{RST}$
Ground	21	41	42	46	21	$\overline{MSG}$
Ground	22	43	44	47	7	$\overline{SEL}$
Ground	23	45	46	48	11	$\overline{C/D}$
Ground	24	47	48	49	24	$\overline{REQ}$
Ground	25	49	50	50	12	$\overline{I/O}$

Table 19.3   The P cable for single-ended SCSI-3.

Signal	Connector	Cable		Connector	Signal
Ground	1	1	2	35	$\overline{DB(12)}$
Ground	2	3	4	36	$\overline{DB(13)}$
Ground	3	5	6	37	$\overline{DB(14)}$
Ground	4	7	8	38	$\overline{DB(15)}$
Ground	5	9	10	39	$\overline{DB(P1)}$
Ground	6	11	12	40	$\overline{DB(0)}$
Ground	7	13	14	41	$\overline{DB(1)}$
Ground	8	15	16	42	$\overline{DB(2)}$
Ground	9	17	18	43	$\overline{DB(3)}$
Ground	10	19	20	44	$\overline{DB(4)}$
Ground	11	21	22	45	$\overline{DB(5)}$
Ground	12	23	24	46	$\overline{DB(6)}$
Ground	13	25	26	47	$\overline{DB(7)}$
Ground	14	27	28	48	$\overline{DB(P)}$
Ground	15	29	30	49	Ground
Ground	16	31	32	50	Ground
+5 V terminator	17	33	34	51	+5 V terminator
+5 V terminator	18	35	36	52	+5 V terminator
Reserved	19	37	38	53	Reserved
Ground	20	39	40	54	Ground
Ground	21	41	42	55	$\overline{ATN}$
Ground	22	43	44	56	Ground
Ground	23	45	46	57	$\overline{BSY}$
Ground	24	47	48	58	$\overline{ACK}$
Ground	25	49	50	59	$\overline{RST}$
Ground	26	51	52	60	$\overline{MSG}$
Ground	27	53	54	61	$\overline{SEL}$
Ground	28	55	56	62	$\overline{C/D}$
Ground	29	57	58	63	$\overline{REQ}$
Ground	30	59	60	64	$\overline{I/O}$
Ground	31	61	62	65	$\overline{DB(8)}$
Ground	32	63	64	66	$\overline{DB(9)}$
Ground	33	65	66	67	$\overline{DB(10)}$
Ground	34	67	68	68	$\overline{DB(11)}$

Mixing narrow and wide SCSI

It has already been mentioned that you can mix narrow and wide SCSI on one bus. How does this look in practice? The simplest case is when you wish to connect a device with a narrow interface to a 68-pin internal bus. Then you simply need an adapter that connects the pins of an A cable socket with those of a corresponding P cable connector. You can, however, not use this adapter at the end of the bus because it does not terminate the superfluous data signals. By the way, the P cable uses the same assignments on leads 11 to 60 as the A cable on its 50 leads.

If you want to connect an external P cable with an external A cable, you need an adapter which not only connects the correct signals, but also terminates the super-fluous signals. Figures 19.9 and 19.10 show typical mixed configurations, while a circuit diagram of the cable adapter is shown in Figure 19.11. When mixing devices please note that an 8-bit SCSI device cannot see any IDs higher than 7!

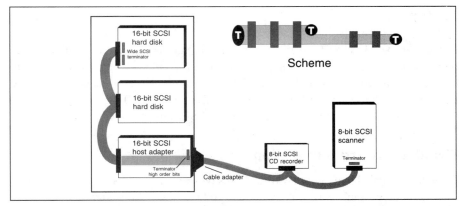

Figure 19.9 Typical mixed configuration of narrow and wide SCSI.

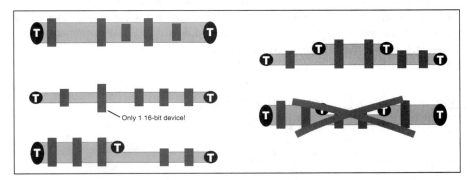

Figure 19.10 Various mixed configurations.

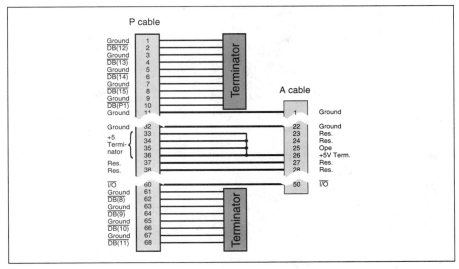

Figure 19.11 Circuit diagram of an A to P cable adapter for single-ended SCSI.

19.5   Differential SCSI

Differential SCSI is used mostly in applications that require cable lengths greater than 6 meters. The maximum length allowed here is 25 meters, independently of the speed. Stub lengths must be less than 20 cm. It is highly recommended that only twisted-pair cables be used for an external differential bus. Tables 19.4, 19.5 and 19.6 show the A, P and Q cables for differential SCSI, respectively.

Signal levels and termination

Each differential signal on the SCSI bus uses two wires, named +signal and −signal. The signal is recognized as active when the voltage of +signal is greater than that of −signal and inactive when the converse is true.

The sensor signal makes it possible to implement a circuit for protecting the differential drivers. The corresponding pin on the single-ended cable is connected to ground. In this way if a cable with a single-ended device attached is connected to a differential device the sensor signal becomes grounded, disabling the differential drivers.

Table 19.4   The A cable for differential SCSI.

Signal	Connector assignment 2	Cable and connector assignment 1		Connector assignment 2	Signal
Ground	1	1	2	26	Ground
+DB(0)	2	3	4	27	−DB(0)
+DB(1)	3	5	6	28	−DB(1)
+DB(2)	4	7	8	29	−DB(2)
+DB(3)	5	9	10	30	−DB(3)
+DB(4)	6	11	12	31	−DB(4)
+DB(5)	7	13	14	32	−DB(5)
+DB(6)	8	15	16	33	−DB(6)
+DB(7)	9	17	18	34	−DB(7)
+DB(P)	10	19	20	35	−DB(P)
Sensor line	11	21	22	36	Ground
Reserved	12	23	24	37	Reserved
+5 V terminator	13	25	26	38	+5 V terminator
Reserved	14	27	28	39	Reserved
+ATN	15	29	30	40	−ATN
Ground	16	31	32	41	Ground
+BSY	17	33	34	42	−BSY
+ACK	18	35	36	43	−ACK
+RST	19	37	38	44	−RST
+MSG	20	39	40	45	−MSG
+SEL	21	41	42	46	−SEL
+C/D	22	43	44	47	−C/D
+REQ	23	45	46	48	−REQ
+I/O	24	47	48	49	−I/O
Ground	25	49	50	50	Ground

Table 19.5 The P cable for differential Wide SCSI.

Signal	Connector	Cable		Connector	Signal
+DB(12)	1	1	2	35	−DB(12)
+DB(13)	2	3	4	36	−DB(13)
+DB(14)	3	5	6	37	−DB(14)
+DB(15)	4	7	8	38	−DB(15)
+DB(P1)	5	9	10	39	−DB(P1)
Ground	6	11	12	40	Ground
+DB(0)	7	13	14	41	−DB(0)
+DB(1)	8	15	16	42	−DB(1)
+DB(2)	9	17	18	43	−DB(2)
+DB(3)	10	19	20	44	−DB(3)
+DB(4)	11	21	22	45	−DB(4)
+DB(5)	12	23	24	46	−DB(5)
+DB(6)	13	25	26	47	−DB(6)
+DB(7)	14	27	28	48	−DB(7)
+DB(P)	15	29	30	49	−DB(P)
Sensor line	16	31	32	50	Ground
+5 V terminator	17	33	34	51	+5 V terminator
+5 V terminator	18	35	36	52	+5 V terminator
Reserved	19	37	38	53	Reserved
+ATN	20	39	40	54	−ATN
Ground	21	41	42	55	Ground
+BSY	22	43	44	56	−BSY
+ACK	23	45	46	57	−ACK
+RST	24	47	48	58	−RST
+MSG	25	49	50	59	−MSG
+SEL	26	51	52	60	−SEL
+C/D	27	53	54	61	−C/D
+REQ	28	55	56	62	−REQ
+I/O	29	57	58	63	−I/O
Ground	30	59	60	64	Ground
+DB(8)	31	61	62	65	−DB(8)
+DB(9)	32	63	64	66	−DB(9)
+DB(10)	33	65	66	67	−DB(10)
+DB(11)	34	67	68	68	−DB(11)

Differential termination

The differential SCSI bus needs different terminators than the single-ended bus. Differential terminators are always passive terminators. Figure 19.12 shows the differential interface for a signal along with its termination.

Beware of pitfalls!

While single-ended SCSI can also work with cables in which not all leads are wired, for differential SCSI you need practically all of the lead pairs. Cable adapters, for example from Mini-Sub-D to Centronics connectors, are often sloppily designed too. Developers often think only of single-ended SCSI and wire pins to ground which in differential (and LVD) SCSI carry signals. In case of doubt, please test the assignments with an ohmmeter.

Table 19.6 The Q cable for differential Wide SCSI.

Signal	Connector	Cable		Connector	Signal
+DB(28)	1	1	2	35	−DB(28)
+DB(29)	2	3	4	36	−DB(29)
+DB(30)	3	5	6	37	−DB(30)
+DB(31)	4	7	8	38	−DB(31)
+DB(P3)	5	9	10	39	−DB(P1)
Ground	6	11	12	40	Ground
+DB(16)	7	13	14	41	−DB(16)
+DB(17)	8	15	16	42	−DB(17)
+DB(18)	9	17	18	43	−DB(18)
+DB(19)	10	19	20	44	−DB(19)
+DB(20)	11	21	22	45	−DB(20)
+DB(21)	12	23	24	46	−DB(21)
+DB(22)	13	25	26	47	−DB(22)
+DB(23)	14	27	28	48	−DB(23)
+DB(P2)	15	29	30	49	−DB(P2)
Sensor line	16	31	32	50	Ground
+5 V terminator	17	33	34	51	+5 V terminator
+5 V terminator	18	35	36	52	+5 V terminator
Reserved	19	37	38	53	Reserved
Terminated	20	39	40	54	Terminated
Ground	21	41	42	55	Ground
Terminated	22	43	44	56	Terminated
+ACKQ	23	45	46	57	−ACKQ
Terminated	24	47	48	58	Terminated
Terminated	25	49	50	59	Terminated
Terminated	26	51	52	60	Terminated
Terminated	27	53	54	61	Terminated
+REQQ	28	55	56	62	−REQQ
Terminated	29	57	58	63	Terminated
Ground	30	59	60	64	Ground
+DB(24)	31	61	62	65	−DB(24)
+DB(25)	32	63	64	66	−DB(25)
+DB(26)	33	65	66	67	−DB(26)
+DB(27)	34	67	68	68	−DB(27)

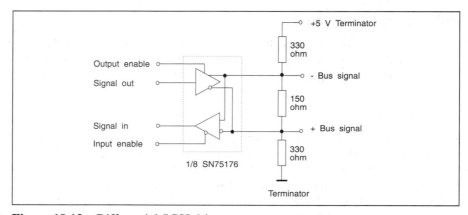

Figure 19.12 Differential SCSI driver.

19.6 Low voltage differential (LVD)

The disadvantages of traditional parallel SCSI interfaces have more and more developed into a serious obstacle for the further development of SCSI. Single-ended SCSI is interference-prone, the cable length is too short with fast speeds and Fast-20 (Ultra-SCSI) is how far this interface can go. Differential SCSI, on the other hand, is too expensive because of its high power consumption, so the drivers cannot be integrated into the protocol chip.

One way out of this dilemma is promised by the low voltage differential (LVD) interface. It is defined in the recent SCSI-3 SPI-2 document and a few of them will probably become available by the end of 1997. LVD is a differential interface with substantially reduced power requirements which allows it to be integrated into the SCSI protocol chip. This will place it more or less on the same price level as the single-ended interface, although it is slightly more expensive to manufacture: the chips need more contacts because each SCSI signal needs two leads.

Further – faster

Final specifications for operation of LDV are still outstanding, but it looks as though a cable length of 12 m will be supported for all speeds. At the same time there are

Table 19.7   The A cable for low voltage differential SCSI.

Signal	External connectors	Cable and internal connectors		External connectors	Signal
+DB(0)	1	1	2	26	−DB(0)
+DB(1)	2	3	4	27	−DB(1)
+DB(2)	3	5	6	28	−DB(2)
+DB(3)	4	7	8	29	−DB(3)
+DB(4)	5	9	10	30	−DB(4)
+DB(5)	6	11	12	31	−DB(5)
+DB(6)	7	13	14	32	−DB(6)
+DB(7)	8	15	16	33	−DB(7)
+DB(P)	9	17	18	34	−DB(P)
Ground	10	19	20	35	Ground
DIFFSENSE	11	21	22	36	Ground
Reserved	12	23	24	37	Reserved
+5 V terminator	13	25	26	38	+5 V terminator
Reserved	14	27	28	39	Reserved
Ground	15	29	30	40	Ground
+ATN	16	31	32	41	−ATN
Ground	17	33	34	42	Ground
+BSY	18	35	36	43	−BSY
+ACK	19	37	38	44	−ACK
+RST	20	39	40	45	−RST
+MSG	21	41	42	46	−MSG
+SEL	22	43	44	47	−SEL
+C/D	23	45	46	48	−C/D
+REQ	24	47	48	49	−REQ
+I/O	25	49	50	50	−I/O

Table 19.8 The P cable for low voltage differential Wide SCSI.

Signal	Connector	Cable		Connector	Signal
+DB(12)	1	1	2	35	−DB(12)
+DB(13)	2	3	4	36	−DB(13)
+DB(14)	3	5	6	37	−DB(14)
+DB(15)	4	7	8	38	−DB(15)
+DB(P1)	5	9	10	39	−DB(P1)
+DB(0)	6	11	12	40	−DB(0)
+DB(1)	7	13	14	41	−DB(1)
+DB(2)	8	15	16	42	−DB(2)
+DB(3)	9	17	18	43	−DB(3)
+DB(4)	10	19	20	44	−DB(4)
+DB(5)	11	21	22	45	−DB(5)
+DB(6)	12	23	24	46	−DB(6)
+DB(7)	13	25	26	47	−DB(7)
+DB(P)	14	27	28	48	−DB(P)
Ground	15	29	30	49	Ground
DIFFSENSE	16	31	32	50	Ground
+5 V terminator	17	33	34	51	+5 V terminator
+5 V terminator	18	35	36	52	+5 V terminator
Reserved	19	37	38	53	Reserved
Ground	20	39	40	54	Ground
+ATN	21	41	42	55	−ATN
Ground	22	43	44	56	Ground
+BSY	23	45	46	57	−BSY
+ACK	24	47	48	58	−ACK
+RST	25	49	50	59	−RST
+MSG	26	51	52	60	−MSG
+SEL	27	53	54	61	−SEL
+C/D	28	55	56	62	−C/D
+REQ	29	57	58	63	−REQ
+I/O	30	59	60	64	−I/O
+DB(8)	31	61	62	65	−DB(8)
+DB(9)	32	63	64	66	−DB(9)
+DB(10)	33	65	66	67	−DB(10)
+DB(11)	34	67	68	68	−DB(11)

already discussions about Fast-40, Fast-80 and more in connection with LVD. Thus, the parallel interface has definitely not yet reached its peak.

Universal drivers

The specific problem of the transition phase from single-ended to LVD has been solved quite cleverly: devices will be equipped with universal drivers (and terminators) which allow single-ended and LVD devices to work on the same bus. As long as any single-ended device is connected, the LVD devices switch into single-ended mode. At that moment the advantages of LVD are lost, but this strategy allows a smooth introduction of LVD without having to exchange all devices at one go.

You too can already make your provisions: from now on, only use cables in which all 25 or 34 lead pairs are wired through.

19.7 SCSI expanders

For quite some time various manufacturers have offered devices such as single-ended to differential SCSI converters or SCSI repeaters. These devices are, however, not covered by the SCSI standard. Presently, ANSI is working on a technical report under the title EPI (Enhanced Parallel Interface) which amongst others deals with these devices. A technical report is less than a standard. It describes marginal areas not covered by the standard itself, but it is not binding. On the other hand, it does not have to go through the complicated approval process.

The area covered by the EPI is defined as follows: 'This document is an ANSI technical report that provides guidance to experienced implementors and users of parallel SCSI beyond that contained in the formal standards.'

Segment

First, the EPI defines the term segment. A segment is a parallel SCSI connection terminated at both physical ends with a terminator. So far, this is more or less the common definition of the SCSI bus. The novelty is that several segments can be joined with expanders.

Each SCSI segment is electrically independent of the others. Thus, limits such as maximum length and bus load apply to each individual segment. Expanders can also connect segments with different interfaces, for example single-ended with differential.

Domain

All segments joined by expanders constitute a SCSI domain. This term is already known from the SAM (SCSI Architectural Model). All devices of a domain appear as logically connected. Thus, all devices of a domain share the available IDs and the bandwidth.

Expanders

An expander transparently connects two parallel SCSI segments. This means that it is invisible to the SCSI protocol and consequently has no SCSI ID. It cannot arbitrate by itself and it cannot send out its own messages. The signal delay must be as short as possible.

In reality, an expander will obviously cause signal delays. These limit the number of expanders that can be used in one SCSI domain. PARALAN, for example, specifies that at most two of their expanders may lie between any two devices.

Applications

A simple application is the connection of a single-ended SCSI segment with a differential one. Thus, you can connect a subsystem with differential devices via a 25-m cable and a single-ended/differential expander to a single-ended host adapter (see Figure 19.13).

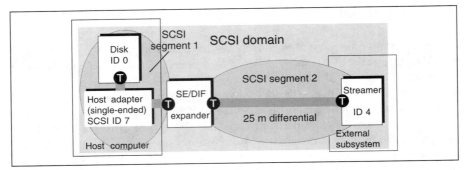

Figure 19.13   Single-ended/differential expander.

Another important application is the extension of a SCSI bus. Especially with Ultra-SCSI, the limit of 1.5 m for more than four devices is quickly reached. Here one can often not only reach an overall length of 2×1.5 m, but with a smart application of an expander, the bus can be divided into two segments in such a way that

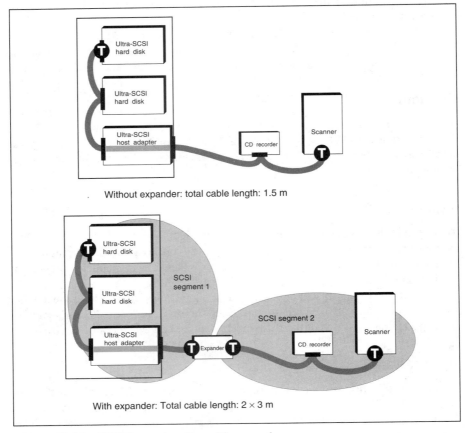

Figure 19.14   SCSI bus extension with expanders.

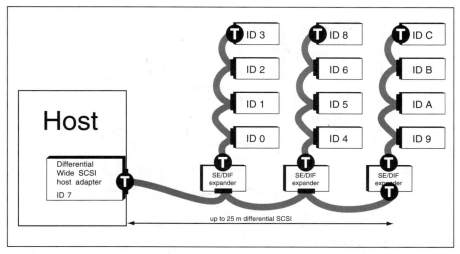

Figure 19.15   SCSI 'backbone'.

neither of the two segments contains more than four devices, which allows the total length to be increased to 6 m (see Figure 19.14).

Some manufacturers of SCSI expanders go even further. In a point-to-point connection of the expanders, that is, without any further devices in between, they allow much longer connections between the expanders than specified by the standard. Thus, with two differential expanders connected 'back to back' it is possible to cover a distance of 50 m.

Expanders cannot only be employed at the end of a SCSI segment; they can also branch off in the middle of a segment. This allows you to build configurations in which single-ended segments branch off a differential backbone segment (Table 19.15). Thus, all kinds of chain or tree structures are legal as long as the maximum number of expanders between two elements is not exceeded. Obviously, there are also illegal configurations with expanders. All kinds of loops are prohibited, which also excludes all configurations that contain alternative access paths to SCSI elements.

Serial expanders

Serial expanders consist of two expander parts that are connected via a serial cable (see Figure 19.16). The cables can be twisted pair, coax or fiber optical cables. Serial expanders can connect much longer distances than parallel expanders. There are devices available on the market that cover distances between 100 m and several kilometers. Owing to the high signal transit times with long distances, it is not sufficient to serialize and deserialize the parallel signals. Instead, data and commands must be buffered; this makes such devices extremely expensive and also causes them not to work properly in highly complex applications. Here, we can only recommend proper consultancy and a trial installation under real-life operating conditions.

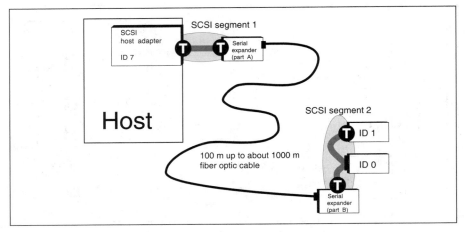

Figure 19.16   Serial expanders.

19.8   SCSI bus phases

All transactions on the SCSI bus are composed from eight distinct bus phases. SCSI-3 even defines one more bus phase. However, the emphasis of the SCSI-3 documentation is no longer on the bus phases, but on the description of service requests and service responses, in correspondence with the SAM architecture model. Therefore, you will also find no more timing diagrams in the SPI document. In spite of this fundamental change in the documentation it must still be said that from SCSI-2 to SCSI-3 nothing substantial has changed in the transactions, mainly because downward compatibility must be ensured.

Therefore, in our present description of SCSI-2, we shall stay with bus phases and timing diagrams. Only towards the end of the section will the new representation in SCSI-3 briefly be sketched.

Phase sequences

Everything begins and ends with the BUS FREE phase. BUS FREE describes the situation where no device is in control of the SCSI bus.

Three phases deal exclusively with bus protocol. During the ARBITRATION phase one or more initiators will indicate their wish to use the bus. If more than a single

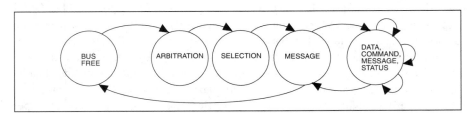

Figure 19.17   Simplified SCSI phase diagram.

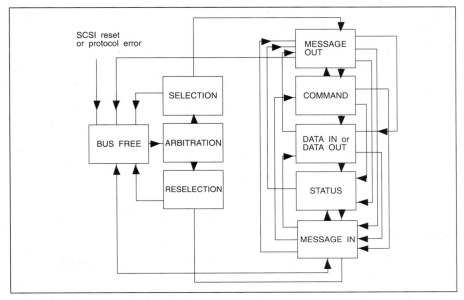

Figure 19.18 Complete SCSI phase diagram.

initiator arbitrates, the one with the highest SCSI ID wins. The successful initiator then uses the SELECTION phase to choose a target with which to communicate. The RESELECTION phase fulfills a similar function: after successfully arbitrating, a target that released the bus to execute a command re-establishes the connection to its initiator.

Finally, there are four phases for exchanging data. The COMMAND phase is used for transferring command opcodes, the DATA phase for data bytes. During a MESSAGE phase a target sends or receives information concerning the protocol itself. Finally, using the STATUS phase the target concludes a SCSI command and informs the initiator of its success or failure.

At any given time the SCSI bus can be in only one specific bus phase. The succession of phases is restricted; it is not possible for any phase to follow any other phase. Figure 19.17 shows a simplified phase diagram of the normal progression of a command. After BUS FREE follows ARBITRATION, SELECTION and a MESSAGE OUT phase. After these come the COMMAND and DATA phases, followed by a STATUS phase. The rules governing phase changes have evolved between SCSI-1 and SCSI-2. While ARBITRATION and the MESSAGE OUT phase were optional after a selection in SCSI-1, these have become mandatory in SCSI-2.

Figure 19.18 shows the complete SCSI phase diagram for SCSI-2. The arrows between the phases indicate that a transition from one phase to another is allowed. Thus, for example, in SCSI-2, COMMAND and DATA phases can only occur after a MESSAGE phase has taken place. Likewise, a MESSAGE phase must also conclude these phases.

At first glance this phase diagram can be very confusing; much more so than the average SCSI command. Figure 19.19 depicts an actual TEST UNIT READY command

```
Seq.     Phase         Data     Text
no.      symbol        hex      comment

 0       BUS FREE
 1       ARBITRATION   C0       ID 7 and ID 5, ID 7 wins
 2       SELECT        81       Target ID 0
 3       MESSAGE OUT   80       IDENTIFY
 4       COMMAND       00       TEST UNIT READY
 5       COMMAND       00
 6       COMMAND       00
 7       COMMAND       00
 8       COMMAND       00
 9       COMMAND       00
10       STATUS        00       GOOD
11       MESSAGE IN    00       COMMAND COMPLETE
12       BUS FREE      00
```

Figure 19.19   Phase sequence for TEST UNIT READY.

as captured by a SCSI analyzer. It begins with BUS FREE. After the typical sequence ARBITRATION, SELECTION, MESSAGE (IDENTIFY) comes a COMMAND phase of six bytes. Since no data is transferred with this command, the succession concludes immediately with the STATUS phase and the MESSAGE (COMMAND COMPLETE).

SCSI bus timing

When electrical signals change their value, they never do so as cleanly and abruptly as is shown in a timing diagram. In reality edges are much rounder, and – as is the case with the SCSI bus, where relatively long cables are used – reflections lead to 'ringing' and other distortions. In order to prevent these phenomena from causing ill effects, a number of delays have been built into the protocol. These delays allow the signal enough time to settle on the new value. Tables 19.9 and 19.10 list and briefly explain all of the timing values defined in the SCSI protocol. More detailed explanations follow in the sections on the individual bus phases.

Table 19.9   SCSI-3 timing values for Fast SCSI.

Name	Fast-20	Fast	Description
Fast assertion period	11 ns	22 ns	Minimum time that REQ (REQB) and ACK (ACKB) must be active for fast synchronous transfers
Fast cable skew delay	3 ns	4 ns	Maximum time for skew between any two signals on a SCSI cable for fast transfers
Fast deskew delay	15 ns	20 ns	Minimum time required for deskew of certain signals for fast synchronous transfers
Fast hold time	16.5 ns	33 ns	Minimum time required for fast synchronous transfers for data to remain on the bus after REQ (REQB) or ACK (ACKB) so that the receiver can safely store them
Fast negation period	15 ns	30 ns	Minimum time for fast transfers between the two REQ (REQB) pulses of a target. The same holds for the ACK (ACKB) pulses of an initiator

Table 19.10 SCSI-2 timing values (SCSI-3 values in parentheses).

Name	Time	Description
Arbitration delay	2.4 µs	During arbitration
Assertion period	90 ns (80 ns)	REQ (REQB) and ACK (ACKB) must be active at least this amount of time
Bus clear delay	800 ns	A device must release all signals within this amount of time after it has detected a BUS FREE phase
Bus free delay	800 ns	After detecting a BUS FREE phase a device must wait at least this long before arbitrating for the bus
Bus set delay	1.8 µs	Maximum time a device may activate BSY and its ID during arbitration
Bus settle delay	400 ns	Minimum time a device must wait in order that all bus signals settle to their new values
Cable skew delay	10 ns (4 ns)	Maximum difference in propagation time for any two signals of the SCSI cable
Data release delay	400 ns	Maximum time for an initiator to release DB(X) active after I/O goes false
Deskew delay	45 ns	Minimum time necessary to deskew certain signals
Disconnection delay	200 µs	When a target has freed the bus due to a DISCONNECT message it should wait at least this long before taking part in arbitration
Hold time	45 ns (53 ns)	For synchronous transfers the data must be set at least this long after the activation of REQ (REQB) or ACK (ACKB)
Negation period	90 ns (80 ns)	Minimum time that target must negate REQ (REQB) for synchronous transfers. The same holds for ACK (ACKB) for the initiator
Power on to selection	10 s	Recommended maximum time that a target should need after power-up to reply to commands like TEST UNIT READY
Reset to selection	250 ms	Recommended maximum time that a target should need after a SCSI reset to reply to commands like TEST UNIT READY
Reset hold time	25 µs	Minimum time that RST must be active
Selection abort time	200 ms	Maximum time for a device to activate BSY after being selected
Selection timeout delay	250 ms	Recommended minimum time that device should wait for a busy response during a SELECTION
Transfer period	progr.	Minimum time between two REQ or ACK pulses for synchronous transfers

The BUS FREE phase

When the SCSI bus is not being used by a device it remains in the BUS FREE phase. The bus is defined to be in this phase when the signals BSY and SEL have been inactive for longer than a bus settle delay of 400 ns. After power has been turned on or a SCSI reset has occurred the bus enters the BUS FREE phase.

In normal operation there are two standard cases in which the BUS FREE phase is entered. The first occurs after a command has been executed and the message COMMAND COMPLETE has been sent. The other normal case occurs when a target releases the bus after first sending a DISCONNECT message.

In addition to those just mentioned, there are exceptional cases, which the initiator can bring about by sending a message to the target. In response to these messages the target releases the bus. These messages are ABORT, BUS DEVICE RESET, RELEASE RECOVERY, ABORT TAG and CLEAR QUEUE. If an initiator detects a BUS FREE during the execution of a command that did not follow from one of these messages, it treats this as an error.

This error is called unexpected disconnect. The initiator then attempts to determine the reason for the error by sending a REQUEST SENSE command to the target. Another error situation that results in a BUS FREE occurs when a device does not respond after selection or reselection.

The ARBITRATION phase

The ARBITRATION phase is used to determine which device obtains control of the bus after a BUS FREE. If a device wishes to arbitrate for the bus it simultaneously activates the BSY signal along with the data bit that corresponds to its SCSI ID. All other signals must be left alone. Figure 19.19 shows the data bus with C0h during an ARBITRATION phase. Since DB(7) and DB(5) are set this means that the devices with SCSI IDs 7 and 5 are competing for the bus.

At this point each device arbitrating for the bus must wait for at least an arbitration delay of 2.4 µs. The device then looks at the data bus to see if a SCSI ID greater than its own has been asserted. The device with the higher ID, in this example ID 7, wins the arbitration and in response asserts the SEL signal. This indicates to all other devices that they should release BSY and remove their ID bit from the data bus within a bus clear delay of 800 ns. The delay concludes the ARBITRATION phase. The successful device now commences with either a SELECTION or RESELECTION phase.

Wide SCSI in SCSI-3 allows 16 or 32 devices to be present. For the lower eight IDs the old scheme remains: ID 7 has the highest priority (1) and ID 0 the lowest priority (8). This scheme is now transferred to the higher order bytes: ID 15 has priority 9 and ID 8 has priority 16; ID 23 has priority 17 and ID 16 has priority 24; and, finally, ID 31 has priority 25 and ID 24 the lowest of all priorities, namely 32.

When you connect buses of different width, you can only use IDs that are allowed by the narrowest bus segment. Otherwise, the devices on the narrow bus cannot recognize devices with higher IDs and arbitration will not work.

As opposed to SCSI-1, arbitration is mandatory in SCSI-2 even when the configuration includes only one initiator. In fact, targets also must arbitrate for the bus. This occurs after disconnecting from an initiator to execute a command. When the target is ready it arbitrates for the bus and reselects the initiator. This means that even in a configuration with a single initiator and a single target true competition for the bus can take place, for example when a target wants to reconnect to the initiator at the same time as the initiator wants to send the target another command.

The SELECTION phase

A selection phase takes place after an initiator wins the arbitration phase. If a target wins arbitration then the reselection phase follows. Selection and reselection differ in the state of the I/O signal. For reselection I/O is asserted; for selection it is not. A device can therefore identify itself as an initiator by not asserting I/O during the selection phase.

During the selection phase a connection is established with the desired target. BSY, SEL, and the initiator ID are all still active from arbitration. Now the initiator asserts the data signal corresponding to the ID of the desired target along with the ATN signal. The attention signal indicates that a MESSAGE OUT phase will follow selection. In the example in Figure 19.19, the value 81h is on the data bus during selection. This means that the initiator with ID 7 wishes to establish a connection with the target with ID 0. After at least two deskew delays the initiator releases BSY.

At this point all devices look to see whether their SCSI ID bit is asserted on the data bus. The selected device identifies the initiator by the other set data bit on the bus. Before a select abort time of 200 ms has elapsed the selected device must assert BSY and take over control of the SCSI bus. This is an important moment. From this point on the target has complete control over the sequencing of SCSI bus phases. It decides when to receive messages, command bytes or data from the initiator and when to send status. The target also decides whether or not to disconnect during a command and when to reconnect. Although the initiator controls what commands the target executes, the target alone is in charge of the bus protocol.

No more than two deskew delays after the target's assertion of BSY, the initiator must release the SEL signal. With this the selection phase is completed. SCSI-2 now calls for a MESSAGE OUT phase.

A selection phase is unsuccessful if the target device never responds to the initiator. In this case the initiator waits at least a selection abort time, after which it has two options. The initiator can either assert the RST signal, causing a transition to the BUS FREE phase, or it can release first the data signals then SEL and ATN in order to get back to BUS FREE.

An additional word on the effect of SCSI timing on throughput: the selection abort time of 200 ms is very long. In 200 ms a disk drive can perform around 10 I/O operations. For this reason it is very important for a target to react as quickly as possible to selection. A slow target that requires, for example, 5 ms to react to a selection not only reduces its own throughput, but also blocks the bus for all other devices during this time and degrades the overall throughput of the SCSI bus.

Figure 19.20 shows a schematic timing diagram of an ARBITRATION and SELECTION phase. Delay times have been omitted in the interest of simplicity. Actual timing diagrams that reflect precisely what has taken place on a bus can look very different. Figure 19.21 shows such a sequence recorded by a logic analyzer.

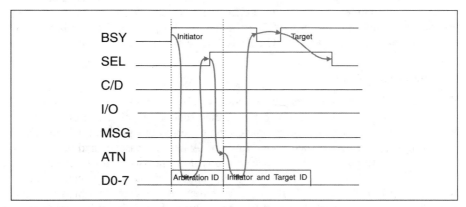

Figure 19.20 ARBITRATION and SELECTION.

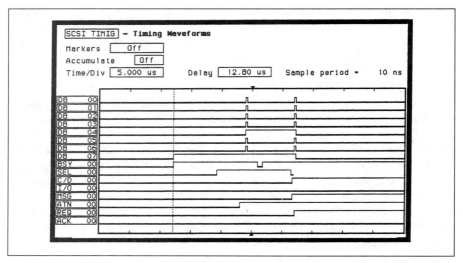

Figure 19.21   ARBITRATION and SELECTION as seen on a logic analyzer.

Some explanations of the figures showing logic analyzer output is called for. In the line directly above the timing diagram, you see 'Time/Div 5.000 µs'. This is the length of time (in µs) per division shown on the upper and lower edges of the diagram. 'Sample period = 10 ns' tells you that measurements are made every 10 ns. On the left-hand side you see the names of all of the signals.

In this example it is easy to see that during the SELECTION phase the BSY signal is inactive for about 1 µs; this moment represents the transfer of control from the initiator to the target. A glitch can be seen on the data lines during the SELECTION phase. This is caused by the toggling of the target's SCSI ID on the data bus. Such glitches are the reason why delays are built into the protocol.

The RESELECTION phase

The RESELECTION phase allows a target to reconnect to the initiator after having disconnected to complete a command. Following a successful arbitration the target reselects the initiator that sent it a SCSI command. This phase is differentiated from selection by the active I/O signal. Otherwise, these phases are identical.

The MESSAGE phase

The phase following a successful selection is always a MESSAGE OUT phase. A message phase is used by the target to either send or receive a message byte. Message bytes contain information concerning the SCSI bus protocol, where IN and OUT are interpreted with respect to the initiator. A list of messages and their meanings is given in Chapter 20. A message can consist of one, two or a variable number of bytes. The first byte tells which of these three types of messages is being sent. A variable length message is referred to as an extended message, in which case the length of the message is contained in the second byte. What follows is a description of the timing and protocol of the message phase.

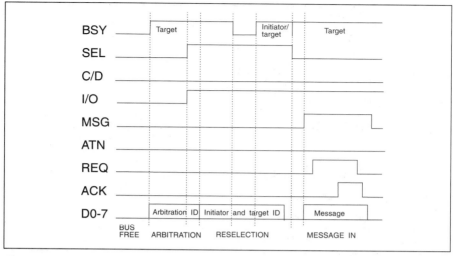

Figure 19.22   RESELECTION and MESSAGE IN.

A look at the phase diagram in Figure 19.22 shows that a MESSAGE IN phase can take place after each information transfer phase as well as after a RESELECTION. Following the flow of the message phase in Figure 19.22 we see that the BSY signal is still set from the SELECTION phase. The target then activates MSG, I/O and C/D in order to proceed to the MESSAGE IN phase.

Now the message byte is put on the data bus. After deskew and cable deskew delays the target sets the REQ signal. In response the initiator reads in the message byte and sets ACK. The target can now remove the byte from the bus and release REQ. Finally, the initiator responds by releasing ACK. Such an exchange is known as an asynchronous request/acknowledge handshake or REQ/ACK sequence. This method of transfer is used for the command, data, and status phases as well.

At this point the bus is still in the MESSAGE IN phase. If additional bytes are to be sent, that number of REQ/ACK sequences take place to transfer them. To end the message phase the target releases the MSG signal.

The target receives a message from the initiator during a MESSAGE OUT phase. An extra step is needed here since the initiator must inform the target of its intention to send a message. To do this the initiator activates the ATN signal, which is permitted during any phase except BUS FREE or ARBITRATION. During data and command phases it is up to the target whether to receive the message byte immediately or wait until the end of the phase. ATN during a selection, message or status phase calls for immediate transfer of the message byte after the current REQ/ACK sequence.

This transfer unfolds almost identically to the REQ/ACK sequence described above. The target activates REQ. In response to this the initiator places the message byte onto the data bus and after the proper delays activates ACK. The target then reads the byte and releases REQ. Finally, the initiator releases ACK and the transfer is complete. The target knows whether additional bytes will follow by examining the first message byte. The initiator releases ATN when it has sent all of its message bytes. The target ends the MESSAGE phase by releasing the MSG signal.

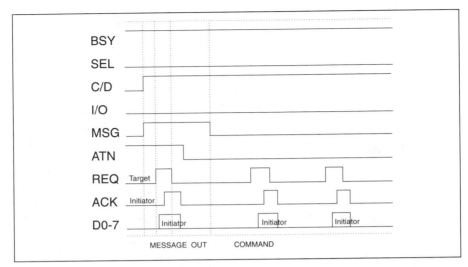

Figure 19.23   MESSAGE OUT and COMMAND.

Afterwards, if a command phase takes place the signals I/O and C/D are already in the proper state, as Figure 19.23 shows.

The COMMAND phase

The COMMAND phase is used by the target to receive the actual SCSI commands from the initiator. It is important to remember that the target has taken control of the bus since the end of the SELECTION phase. First it finishes the MESSAGE OUT phase, which the initiator brought about using ATN. Immediately thereafter is the beginning of the COMMAND phase.

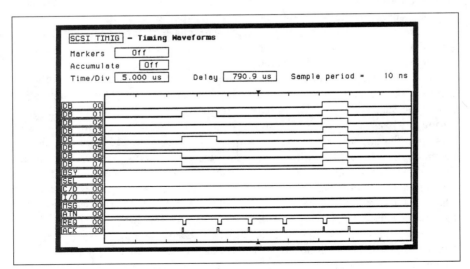

Figure 19.24   COMMAND phase as seen on a logic analyzer.

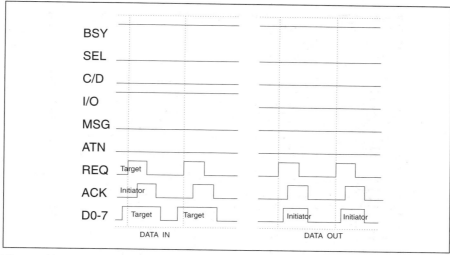

Figure 19.25   DATA IN and DATA OUT.

A command phase is characterized by the C/D line being active while I/O and MSG are inactive. The command phase proceeds with REQ/ACK sequences in the same manner as a MESSAGE OUT phase until all command bytes have been transferred.

On the leftmost side of the timing diagram (Figure 19.24) you can see the target already waiting with active REQ signal. After the first ACK little time is needed for the target to read the first byte and release REQ. Almost immediately after the initiator releases ACK the target is requesting the second byte. The initiator needs a relatively long time to prepare the bytes, as indicated by the distance between REQ/ACK sequences. This command happens to be an INQUIRY command (12 00 00 00 FF 00), which is covered in greater detail in Chapter 12.

By examining the first command byte the target can tell how many additional bytes will follow. It collects all bytes from the initiator and releases C/D, thus ending the COMMAND phase.

The DATA IN and DATA OUT phases

Almost all command sequences contain a data phase. This is how control information and user data are exchanged between target and initiator. The target begins a data phase by de-asserting C/D and MSG. At this point either asynchronous or synchronous transfers may take place, depending on a previous agreement between the two devices. The asynchronous method will be described here, while synchronous transfer is covered in Section 19.10.

If the target wishes to send data to the initiator it asserts the I/O signal, indicating a DATA IN phase. On the other hand, when the target wishes to receive data it de-asserts I/O for a DATA OUT phase. Figure 19.25 depicts a single DATA IN and DATA OUT transfer, and Figure 19.26 shows the DATA phase as seen on a logic analyzer. The REQ/ACK sequences proceed as described in the message phases.

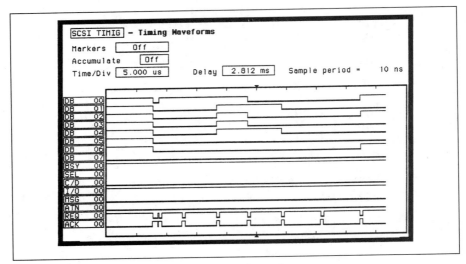

Figure 19.26   DATA phase as seen on a logic analyzer.

The STATUS phase

A target uses the status phase to send status information to an initiator. In contrast to a message, which can be sent at any time during a command sequence, a status phase only takes place when a command has completed, been interrupted or been refused by the target. In this phase C/D and I/O are asserted while MSG remains de-asserted. Status information, always one byte in length, is transferred in a single REQ/ACK sequence. A list of status bytes and their meanings can be found in Section 11.2.

Figure 19.27 shows the status phase and subsequent MESSAGE IN phase of an average SCSI command. The COMMAND COMPLETE message tells the initiator that this command is finished. Afterwards the target releases the bus completely and BUS FREE results.

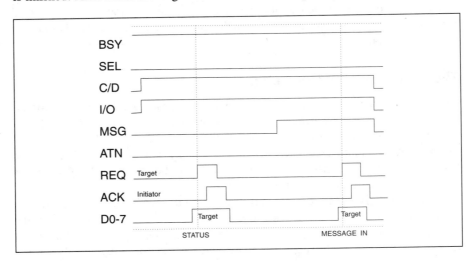

Figure 19.27   STATUS and MESSAGE IN.

19.9   The service model

The SAM (SCSI Architectural Model) of SCSI-3 introduces the client–server model. This is also followed by the SPI insofar as it defines the services that the parallel interface supplies as connection system to the upper level protocols.

Confirmed and unconfirmed services

There are confirmed and unconfirmed services. A confirmed service consists of request, indication, response and confirmation. An unconfirmed service consists only of a request and an indication. Figure 19.28 shows the model of a confirmed service. Thus, an SPI service has the following steps. First, the service is started by the client with a request of the upper level protocol (ULP) to the parallel interface agent (PIA). The transport system forwards it to the server PIA. At the server's side, the PIA triggers an indication to the ULP. The ULP answers with a response to the PIA. This response is forwarded via the transport system to the client PIA which terminates the service with a confirmation to the client ULP.

There are ten different services which in part directly correspond to the bus phases. They are listed in Table 19.11.

Example: command service

The command service is a confirmed service which transports a command byte from the initiator to the target. If you compare the following description with the SCSI-2 command phase and the timing diagram you will soon notice the correspondence.

- **Command request**: The command request does not contain parameters. When the target PIA receives a command request, it must set the C/D signal, negate the MSG and I/O signals and start a REQ/ACK cycle by setting REQ.

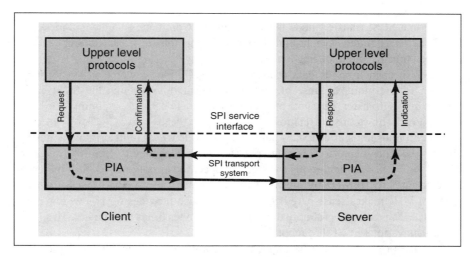

Figure 19.28   Confirmed services.

Table 19.11   SCSI protocol services.

Service	Type
Bus free service	Unconfirmed
Reset service	Unconfirmed
Selection service	Confirmed
Reselection service	Confirmed
Command service	Confirmed
Data out service	Confirmed
Data in service	Confirmed
Status service	Confirmed
Message out service	Confirmed
Message in service	Confirmed

- **Command indication**: The command indication contains no parameters. When the initiator PIA detects the C/D signal, sees that the MSG and I/O signals are negated and that a REQ/ACK cycle has begun, then it must generate a command indication.

- **Command response**: The command response contains the command byte and the attention flag as parameters. When the initiator PIA receives a command response, it must put the command byte on the data lines, set the ATN signal in accordance with the attention flag and terminate the REQ/ACK cycle.

- **Command confirmation**: The command confirmation contains the command byte together with the attention flag and parity flag as parameters. When the target PIA detects the termination of the REQ/ACK cycle, it must read the command byte from the data lines, and set the parity flag in accordance with the parity check and the attention flag in accordance with the ATN signal. With these parameters, it then generates the command response.

19.10 Synchronous transfers and Fast SCSI

The normal SCSI transfer mode is asynchronous. Commands, status and messages are always transmitted asynchronously. Only for data transfer can an alternative synchronous transfer mode be negotiated.

In SCSI, asynchronous data transfer is by definition slower than synchronous transfer. Furthermore, because of the signal transit time through the SCSI cable, asynchronous transfer depends on the distance between the individual devices. Figure 19.29 shows this correlation.

Synchronous transfer is a SCSI data transfer mode which in its original definition allows data rates of up to 5 Mbytes per second, independently from the distance. Already in SCSI-1, synchronous transfer was specified as optional. SCSI-2 increases the data rates to 10 MHz by offering what is known as Fast SCSI. Measuring the speed in MHz makes sense here because SCSI-2 also provides for bus widths of up to 4 bytes. The data rate is simply the bus width in bytes times the rate in MHz. Table 19.12 lists various SCSI throughputs.

Both the original and the Fast synchronous transfers use the same bus protocol. For Fast SCSI, however, the built-in delays are shorter and the overall times are

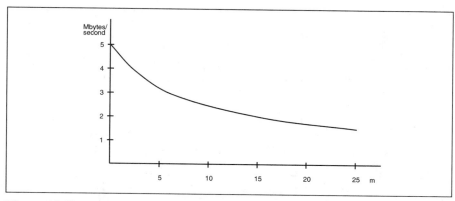

Figure 19.29 Asynchronous data rates relative to the distance.

faster. The method with which a target and initiator negotiate transfer parameters has also remained the same for Fast SCSI. Because of their similarity, the general term 'synchronous transfers' will be used for both methods.

The use of synchronous transfers is negotiated between the initiator and the target using messages. Chapter 20 covers this aspect in greater detail.

Synchronous DATA IN and DATA OUT phases

When a target uses the synchronous method of data transfer it is allowed to send a certain maximum number of REQ pulses without waiting for ACK pulses. The pulses occur at a fixed period, called the synchronous transfer period. The maximum number of REQ pulses without receiving an ACK is called the REQ/ACK offset. Another way to look at the offset is this: given that at the end of a transfer an equal number of REQ and ACK pulses must occur, the offset is the maximum number of outstanding ACK pulses. If the offset is reached then the target must wait until the initiator sends an ACK before it sends further REQs. The result of this approach is that cable delays – the time it takes signals to traverse the length of the SCSI cable – are effectively eliminated from the transfer speed. For asynchronous transfers the transfer rate is directly dependent on the cable length. For each byte sent there is a delay equal to the following: the time it takes the leading edge of the REQ to travel from target to initiator, plus the time it takes the leading edge of the ACK to travel back to the host, plus the time it takes for the trailing edge of the REQ to reach the initiator, plus the time it takes for the trailing edge of the ACK to make it back to the host. The synchronous method eliminates the interlocking handshaking and with it the cable delays.

Table 19.12 Various SCSI throughputs.

| Transfer rate | Bandwidth | | |
Transfer width	8-bit	16-bit	32-bit
Asynchronous (approximately 3 MHz)	3 Mbytes/sec	6 Mbytes/sec	12 Mbytes/sec
Synchronous	5 Mbytes/sec	10 Mbytes/sec	20 Mbytes/sec
Fast	10 Mbytes/sec	20 Mbytes/sec	40 Mbytes/sec
Fast-20	20 Mbytes/sec	40 Mbytes/sec	80 Mbytes/sec

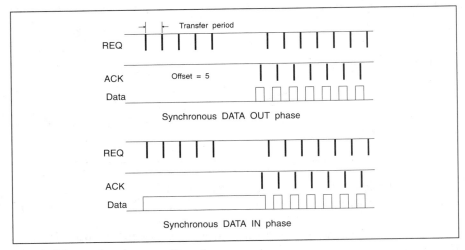

Figure 19.30   Synchronous data phases.

Figure 19.30 shows synchronous DATA IN and DATA OUT phases. Here a REQ/ACK offset of five is being used. Let us look first at the DATA OUT phase. The target sends five REQ pulses at a fixed frequency determined by the synchronous transfer period. It must then wait since the offset of five outstanding ACK pulses has been reached. Finally, the ACK pulses come along with the data from the initiator at the same frequency. With the arrival of the first ACK pulse the number of outstanding pulses has dropped below the offset and the target responds by sending data continually at the defined frequency. In this way the transfer proceeds with maximum efficiency.

The synchronous DATA IN phase looks very much the same. Here, however, the target places a byte on the data bus before the first REQ pulse. The byte is held there

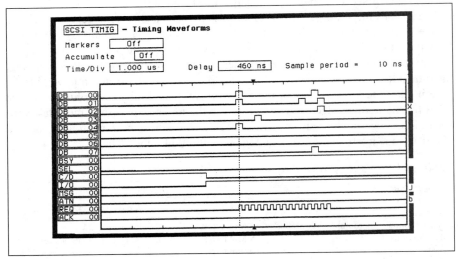

Figure 19.31   Synchronous data phase as seen on a logic analyzer (part 1).

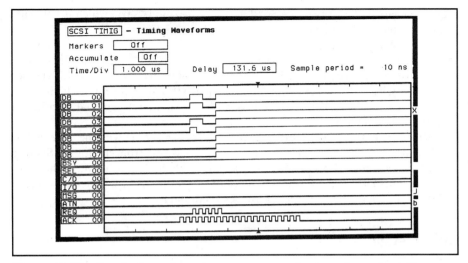

Figure 19.32 Synchronous data phase as seen on a logic analyzer (part 2).

until the first ACK signal has been read. Afterwards the transfer takes place at the rate determined by the transfer period.

Figures 19.31 and 19.32 show this phase once again, this time as seen by a logic analyzer. These are DATA IN phases as they occur in the real world. The target sends 15 REQ pulses and the accompanying data bytes, then all is still because no ACKs are returned. It is safe to assume that the transfer offset is 15. In the second diagram, which occurs approximately 130 μs later, the ACK pulses are returned by the initiator. After the second REQ the target proceeds to send the remaining five data bytes. The ACK pulses continue until a total of 20 have been sent.

19.11 Ultra-SCSI or Fast-20

Fast-20 is an extension of the SCSI-3 SPI document frequently called Ultra-SCSI by the industry. Depending on the bandwidth used, it allows a data rate of 20, 40 or 80 Mbytes/second. Fast-20 works in the same way as Fast SCSI, with the exception that some timing values are slightly tighter (see Table 19.9). The bus length of the single-ended bus is limited too: when up to four devices are connected, the bus length can be up to 3 m. From four devices up to the maximum of eight devices, the bus can only be 1.5 m long. For differential buses and LVD there is no length restriction: here the usual 25 or 12 m are allowed.

19.12 Ultra-2 SCSI or Fast-40 and more?

At least on the marketing side, the competition of the serial interface alternatives has put supporters of the parallel SCSI interface under severe pressure. As a reaction they organized themselves in the SCSI Trade Association (STA) which has the aim of pushing the development of ever faster parallel transfer modes.

As a first result, the standardization of the Fast-40 (Ultra-2) transfer mode is expected, and there are already speculations about Fast-80. Fast-40 works with 40 Megatransfers per second, that is 40 Mbytes/sec with narrow and 80 Mbytes/sec with 16-bit wide transfer. However, it must be noted that all transfer rates higher than 20 Megatransfers per second can only be realized with the differential interface or with the new LVD interface.

Neither the differential nor the LVD interface is compatible with the wide-spread single-ended interface. In order to facilitate the transition from traditional SCSI to LVD, LVD devices will supposedly be equipped with dual-mode drivers. These bus drivers use the DIFFSENSE signal to detect whether they are connected to a single-ended bus or a LVD bus and set themselves accordingly.

19.13   Wide SCSI

Wide SCSI uses the same hardware protocol as the 8-bit transfers. The most widely spread is the 16-bit wide transfer because the additional nine signals needed for this fit on the 68-pin P cable of SCSI-3 (see Section 19.2). The SCSI-2 B cable is practically never used. Often Wide SCSI is thought to be equivalent to 16-bit wide transfer; however, the SCSI-3 SPI document defines 32-bit wide transfer as well.

In 32-bit wide SCSI, the data signals are distributed across two cables. In order to prevent signal skewing problems resulting from different cable lengths, an additional REQ and ACK are included on the second cable. This allows an independent REQ/ACK sequence for each cable. During all but the DATA IN and DATA OUT phases the second cable is unused.

Just as is the case with Fast SCSI, the use of Wide SCSI is negotiated between devices using the message system.

19.14   SCAM

SCAM stands for SCSI configured automatically or, as marketing buffs prefer to read, 'automagically'. This term hides a relatively complicated protocol which allows SCSI devices to have their SCSI ID dynamically assigned during initialization of the SCSI bus. The idea behind this concept is to make the SCSI bus plug-and-play capable, so that the user must no longer carry out any manual configuration when he/she adds or removes devices to or from the bus. There is even a specification for plug-and-play SCSI which will be presented in Section 19.15. It builds on SCAM but contains additional specifications, for example for cables and connectors.

SCAM is mere child's play

Maybe one could best compare the phases of the SCAM protocol with the preparations for a fictitious children's game. The game only works when each participant (device) has a unique number (ID). These numbers are distributed after the following scheme.

First it is determined who of the participants is a suitable leader (dominant initiator). If there is more than one candidate, the best one is selected following certain rules. Under the leader's direction, the preparation proper begins. First, the leader assigns participants that can only work with a determined number (SCAM tolerant devices) exactly that number. All other participants (SCAM devices) have a name (ID string). In each round, the participants put the letters of their names one after the other on the table. Whose letter is lower in the alphabet than that of any other participant stops playing. Thus, after each round only those remain whose names are the same up to that point and whose names are 'high'. (When names are identical, it is dad's car registration plate that counts.) When only one player is left, he/she/it is assigned a number and no longer participates in the game. Then, the next game starts, and so on, until all players have got their number (ID). Now the SCSI game can begin. By the way, each morning (after powering up) and after accidents (SCSI resets) the numbers are distributed anew.

The SCAM protocol is described in Appendix B of the SCSI-3 SPI document. Its implementation is optional, but when it is implemented it must comply with the specifications. The author knows lots of children's games. Maybe they will be the subject of another book.

Conformity levels

There are three levels of conformity with SCAM. Devices which completely refuse to function under SCAM are SCAM intolerant.

The first level is constituted by SCAM tolerant devices. They do not support the SCAM protocol, but their functioning is not affected by SCAM and they do not affect the SCAM protocol. This conformity level is only defined for targets.

The second level is constituted by devices that support SCAM level 1. They can participate in the SCAM protocol but do not support some further-reaching capabilities of level 2, such as more than one initiator and the hot-plug capability. For home and office use this will play practically no role, for which reason I regard SCAM level 1 as absolutely sufficient. Furthermore, SCAM level 1 can be realized with traditional SCSI chips provided they satisfy two conditions: first, the SCSI signals must be software controllable independently from each other. Oldtimers such as the NCR 53C80 obviously support this feature, but even more recent chips mostly have at least a maintenance mode in which the individual signals can be controlled separately. The second condition is that either the chip does not use active negation or that it can be disabled.

The complete implementation of SCAM is SCAM level 2. Level 2 devices can carry out a SCAM configuration even when the bus is operating. Furthermore, level 2 supports more than one host adapter on the bus. However, SCAM level 2 cannot be implemented without hardware support, that is, the capability must already exist in the chip.

SCAM IDs

The SCAM protocol distinguishes between different states of SCSI IDs.

The SCSI ID with which a SCSI port is working at the moment is called current ID. This can be an ID set via firmware, switches of jumpers, or an ID assigned via SCAM. The current ID reflects the view of the device.

From the point of view of the SCAM protocol there exist assigned and unassigned IDs. An assigned ID is the ID assigned to a device by the SCAM protocol. As soon as the assignment has been carried out, the assigned ID is also the current ID. SCAM tolerant devices are always assigned their current ID. An unassigned ID is the current ID of a SCAM device which has not yet been assigned an ID in the course of the SCAM protocol.

SCAM initiators

Even in a configuration with several SCAM initiators, only one of them has the task to assign IDs to the devices on the bus. This initiator is called the dominant SCAM initiator. Initiators that are not dominant are called subordinate SCAM initiators. If there is more than one initiator on the bus, they first have to negotiate which of them will become the dominant initiator. This capability is, however, reserved to level 2 initiators. When level 1 initiators find another initiator on the bus, they assume that they are subordinate initiators. Therefore there must be only one level 1 initiator on any one SCSI bus.

After power-on or a reset, a dominant initiator first builds a table of the SCSI IDs and marks all entries as unassigned. During a selection, SCAM tolerant devices must report after 2 ms, whereas SCAM devices are implicitly assigned their current ID when they are selected for more than 4 ms. Therefore the dominant initiator selects each device, for more than 2 ms but less than 4 ms. When a device answers, the initiator has found a SCAM tolerant device and enters it into the table. In order to return in an orderly way to a bus free phase, the initiator should follow the selection with an INQUIRY command. In this way, the initiator goes through all IDs and finds the SCAM tolerant devices.

Afterwards it initiates the SCAM protocol, isolating all SCAM devices one after the other and assigning them their IDs. Once this process is finished, the initiator sends a function sequence CONFIGURATION PROCESS COMPLETE and terminates the SCAM protocol.

The SCAM target state diagram

After power-on or a reset, SCAM level 1 targets (Figure 19.33) first go into the SCAM monitor state, where they wait either for a normal or for a SCAM selection.

The simplest case occurs when a SCAM target already has a current ID which is, for example, set via firmware or jumpers. When the device is selected under this ID for at least 4 ms, the ID becomes an assigned ID. This simplified procedure without the complicated SCAM protocol is called implicit assignment.

Until the next power-on or bus reset, a target with assigned ID behaves like a SCAM tolerant device. In particular, it no longer participates in the SCAM protocol.

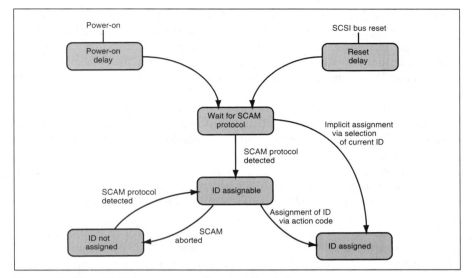

Figure 19.33 SCAM target state diagram (level 1).

When a target in the monitor state detects a SCAM initiation, it passes into an ID assignable state in which the ID can be assigned via the SCAM protocol. Now the device participates in the SCAM protocol until it has been assigned an ID or the protocol is terminated. When the target is assigned its ID via a SCAM action, it behaves like a SCAM tolerant device and no longer participates in the SCAM protocol.

Once all IDs are assigned, the SCAM protocol is terminated with the SCAM function CONFIGURATION PROCESS COMPLETE and the dominant initiator releases the c/D signal. However, the SCAM protocol can also end before the device is assigned an ID, for example when the protocol is aborted because the c/D signal changes to false in the middle of the process. In this case the device passes into a state without ID and does not answer any SCSI selection. However, it continues to monitor the bus and when it detects another SCAM protocol, the device passes again into the assignable state.

The state diagram of a level 2 SCAM target differs only by the fact that it initiates the SCAM protocol after power-on. Depending on whether a SCAM initiator answers or not, it passes into the monitor state or the assignable state. Owing to this capability, SCAM level 2 devices can also be added to an operating bus (hot plug).

SCAM initiation

The SCAM protocol makes extensive use of the wired-or of the SCSI signals. Remember that a single-ended SCSI signal is active when it is low. In the inactive state, the signals are set to high by the terminator. A signal is activated by shorting a device to ground. When several devices activate different signals, the bus carries the wired-or of all signals. In order to make this function, devices that use single-ended drivers with active negation must disable their active negation while the SCAM protocol is running.

Only those devices participate in the SCAM protocol that still have no assigned ID. Thus, neither SCAM tolerant devices participate because their fixed ID is always immediately their assigned ID, nor do the SCAM targets that had their current ID implicitly assigned by way of a selection. One after the other, the remaining devices receive their IDs via the SCAM protocol and do not participate in it until the next power-on or bus reset.

A device initiates the SCAM protocol by first arbitrating and then executing a SCAM selection. One peculiarity is that in this case a device without ID is allowed to arbitrate. This leads to the requirement for SCAM tolerant devices that they must not be affected in their functioning by arbitration without ID.

When the device has won the arbitration, the BSY and SEL signals are set. Then it must free all data lines and set MSG. Shortly after, it must release BSY. Thus the device waits at least one SCAM response delay and then also releases MSG. Then it waits until all other devices have released MSG.

Devices that are still participating in the SCAM protocol recognize a SCAM selection by the fact that SEL and MSG are set, but not BSY. After a certain delay they release the MSG signal and wait until all other devices have done the same. Then each participating SCAM device sets BSY and waits for a moment until it sets several other signals.

Now a SCAM target sets the signals I/O, DB(6) and DB(7); a SCAM initiator also sets C/D. Then the devices release the SEL signal. When the SEL signal is inactive on the bus, then because of the wired-or it means that the signal has been released by all devices. Now all SCAM devices release the signal DB(6) and monitor the bus.

When C/D is not set, no SCAM initiator is participating and all devices release the bus. In such a case, the SCAM protocol has not been initiated successfully. When, however, C/D is set, the participating devices set SEL and the SCAM protocol is initiated.

SCAM configuration rules

From what has been said up to now, it follows that the following conditions must be satisfied in order for a SCAM configuration to work:

- No SCAM intolerant devices must be installed on the bus. In particular, older targets may be SCAM intolerant, and this is obviously not mentioned in the owner's manual when the device was built before SCAM was developed.
- Each initiator on the bus must be a SCAM initiator. Only one initiator may be of SCAM level 1; all other initiators that might be present must support level 2.
- SCAM tolerant targets and those with level 1 must be powered on before or together with the SCAM initiator. The same holds for all targets when the initiator only supports level 1.

SCAM transfer cycles

All SCAM devices participate in the SCAM protocol that have not yet been assigned an ID. During this process, some devices send data to all other devices. One peculiar

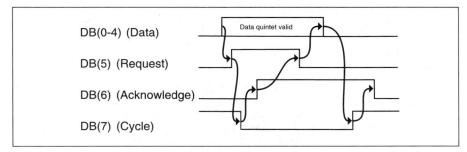

DB(0-4) (Data)

DB(5) (Request)

DB(6) (Acknowledge)

DB(7) (Cycle)

Data quintet valid

Figure 19.34   SCAM transfer cycles.

feature is that more than one device is allowed to send and that the data on the bus results in a wired-or of all data sent. In most cases the participating devices must not only send their data but also at the same time evaluate the data on the bus. Thus, there are no read and write cycles, but as in some networks data is read by all devices and written by one or more of them.

Data is sent over asynchronous transfer cycles (Figure 19.34). Only the data lines are used. DB(0) to DB(4) are user data, DB(7) is used for cycle control, DB(5) as request signal and DB(6) as acknowledge signal.

- A transfer cycle begins when DB(7) is active, but DB(5) and DB(6) are inactive.

- All devices that have to send data put this on signals DB(0) to DB(4) and all devices set DB(5) as request signal.

- All devices release DB(7) and wait until all other devices have done the same.

- All devices read the data from DB(0) to DB(4) and set DB(6) as acknowledge signal.

- All devices release the request signal DB(5) and wait until all other devices have done the same.

- Sending devices now release data lines DB(0) to DB(4). All devices set DB(7).

- All devices release the acknowledge signal DB(6) and wait until all other devices have done the same. This ends the transfer cycle.

SCAM function sequences

The stream of SCAM transfer cycles consists of one or more SCAM function sequences. A function sequence always starts with a synchronization transfer cycle in which the data lines DB(0) to DB(4) are all set. Also when this data pattern occurs in the middle of a current function sequence, a new function sequence starts immediately after this pattern.

The second transfer cycle contains the function code (Table 19.13). The CONFIGURATION PROCESS COMPLETE function which terminates the SCAM protocol has no further parameters.

The two ISOLATE functions are followed by an isolation stage in which one after the other all targets but one are eliminated from the function sequence. Eliminated devices wait for the next synchronization cycle.

Table 19.13　SCAM function codes.

Function code DB(4) to DB(0)	Description
00000b	ISOLATE
	Isolation of a device
00001b	ISOLATE AND SET PRIORITY FLAG
	Isolate with priority
00011b	CONFIGURATION PROCESS COMPLETE
	Configuration terminated
01111b	DOMINANT INITIATOR CONTENTION
	Determination of the dominant initiator
11111b	SYNCHRONIZATION
	Synchronization

In the following transfer cycles, all targets that participate in the isolation process send values on data lines DB(0) to DB(4) which derive bitwise from their identification string (Table 19.14). At the same time they read from the same data lines the value that results from the wired-or of all values sent. A target that reads a higher value than it has sent itself or whose identification string is terminated is eliminated and waits for the next synchronization cycle. Thus, in the end the target remains whose identification string was the highest in bitwise comparison.

The identification string is composed of a type code, the SCSI manufacturer identification (as in the INQUIRY command) and a manufacturer specific code. This last code is needed to distinguish between identical devices of the same manufacturer and will therefore contain something like a serial number. The priority code consists of the priority mark of the device, followed by a zero. This priority mark is immediately set after switching the device on. The code of the maximum ID is 10b for 'narrow' SCSI devices (ID 0–7), 01b for 16-bit wide SCSI (ID 0–F) and 00b for 32-bit wide SCSI (ID 0–1F). The 'ID valid' field contains 00b when the field is not valid. Code 01b means that the ID field contains the current ID of the device, but that it is not yet assigned. Code 11b, finally, means that the ID field contains the assigned ID. The SNA (serial number available) field indicates whether the entire ID string is currently available. Some devices have their serial number recorded on the medium and can only read it when they are READY.

Table 19.14　The SCAM identification string.

	7	6	5	4	3	2	1	0
0	Priority code		Max ID code		Reserved	ID valid		SNA
1	Reserved			ID				
2 ...	Manufacturer identification							
...								
... 9								
10 ...	Manufacturer specific code							
...								
... 30								

Table 19.15 SCAM action codes.

First quintet	Second quintet	Description
11000b	ccnnnb	Assign ID 00nnnb
10001b	ccnnnb	Assign ID 01nnnb
10010b	ccnnnb	Assign ID 10nnnb
01011b	ccnnnb	Assign ID 11nnnb
	11000b	Delete priority mark
10100b	10010b	Localize off
	01011b	Localize on

After the isolation process, the initiator sends an action code (Table 19.15) which consists of two consecutive transfer cycles. The action code is always addressed to all devices that are still participating in the current function sequence.

Most action codes assign the device its ID. One action code deletes the priority mark of a device, which automatically gives its identification string a rather low value so that the device is isolated only late. Localizing is an action with which a device attracts attention, for example with a blinking LED. In certain situations this action is meant to help the operating personnel find a determined device.

Termination of the SCAM protocol

After initiation the SCAM protocol consists of a sequence of transfer cycles during which the C/D signal is always kept set by the dominant initiator. Release of the C/D signal terminates the SCAM protocol in any case, no matter in which state the devices are. All devices must release all signals, so that the bus changes into a normal bus free phase. Normally, after having assigned an ID to all devices, the dominant initiator will send the SCAM function sequence CONFIGURATION PROCESS COMPLETE and then release the C/D signal.

19.15 Plug-and-Play SCSI

Plug-and-Play (PnP) SCSI is supposed to make SCSI easier for the user. This is achieved in two ways. On the one hand, the options offered by SCSI are severely restricted to ensure, for example, that connectors and cables of all Plug-and-Play SCSI systems fit together. On the other hand, the SCAM protocol is used to assign the SCSI IDs. Together with appropriate operating system software, this is meant to ensure that a user must only switch his/her computer off, connect a new SCSI device, and switch the computer back on. The host adapter automatically assigns the new device its ID and, if needed, the operating system installs the corresponding drivers.

Less is more: restrictions on options

PnP SCSI devices have a single-ended interface and must have parity implemented. The only external connector allowed is the 50-pin high density connector. External

Table 19.16   Plug-and-Play SCSI default IDs.

SCSI ID	PnP SCSI default ID
7	Host adapter
6	Magnetic disk drive
5	
4	Tape drive or rewritable optical disk
3	CD-ROM
2	Scanner or printer
1	
0	

connectors must be identified with the symbol for single-ended SCSI. Only active terminators are permitted. Devices that supply TERMPWR must employ an automatic fuse which after having been activated must close the circuit at the next power-up of the device.

PnP SCSI devices must support SCAM level 1. In addition, the PnP document suggests default IDs for certain devices. The dominant initiator should preferably assign devices their default ID (Table 19.16); if this is not possible, the next smaller free ID.

System configurations

PnP configurations can only contain internal devices, external devices or a mixture of both internal and external devices. PnP host adapters that support external devices must possess a terminator at the external port that switches on and off automatically depending on whether a device is connected or not. PnP SCSI devices must not terminate the bus. Instead, external PnP subsystems must be terminated by an external terminator which is plugged into the output socket of the last external subsystem.

For the internal SCSI bus, coded sockets and connectors must be used to ensure that cables cannot be connected erroneously. The internal SCSI bus is terminated by an internal terminator on the cable and not, as usual, on a device. When the host adapter is integrated on the mother board, it terminates the bus. The internal cable leads from the host adapter to the internal devices and from there possibly to a socket that leads to the outside world. This socket must contain an automatic terminator that switches off when an external cable is connected.

Software considerations

A common compatibility problem with hard disks can occur when a disk has been formatted using an adapter of manufacturer 'A' and is then connected to an adapter of manufacturer 'B'. When the mapping, that is, the assignment of logical blocks to the sectors of PC interrupt INT13h, is handled differently by both adapters, disks formatted with one adapter cannot be used with the other one.

Mind you, mapping of physical sectors to logical SCSI blocks is the disk's business and independent from the host adapter and transparent to the outside. Here we are talking of the conversion of SCSI logical blocks to the CHS values of the PC BIOS interrupt INT13h. PnP SCSI specifies that this mapping must follow the documentation of Microsoft's INT13 extensions.

Chapter 9 of the PnP SCSI specification lists some more general points that PnP SCSI devices must adhere to.

- The READ CAPACITY command must indicate the capacity value effectively available to the user (without spare sectors).

- After power-on, the device should react without great delay to the INQUIRY command, that is, possibly before it is READY.

- Each device must tolerate negotiation of synchronous transfer, that is, it must either accept it or refuse it correctly.

- Host adapter manufacturers should supply software for one or more of the driver levels ASPI, CAM or Miniport (WIN 95, NT).

- A host adapter should be software-configurable. This applies both to hardware resources such as address and interrupt and to SCSI options such as synchronous transfer.

- A host adapter should assign the SCSI IDs via SCAM in a reproducible way. Thus, as long as the configuration does not change, the devices should be assigned the same IDs at every system start.

20 SCSI interlock protocol

The SCSI interlock protocol (SIP) is the protocol of the parallel SCSI interface. It has been called SIP only since SCSI-3; before, it was simply the SCSI protocol. It has practically not changed from SCSI-2 to SCSI-3 and consists mainly of the SCSI message system. One important change has been made, however, to the IDENTIFY message which now supports 32 LUNs.

20.1 The message system

In the previous chapter we went over the workings of the MESSAGE phase in detail. We saw that during the course of a normal SCSI command at least two MESSAGE phases occur: after SELECTION or RESELECTION and before the final BUS FREE phase. SCSI messages represent the lowest level of bidirectional communication on the SCSI bus.

We now take a closer look at the SCSI message system. SCSI messages are used for a number of different purposes. Messages are the only means by which an initiator can inform a target of a problem. As an example, consider a parity error on the data bus (see Section 20.3). In general, a message can interrupt the normal flow of phases at any time. The initiator simply sets the ATN signal, completely asynchronously, and the target then collects the message.

The target also uses messages to inform the initiator of events that the initiator cannot foresee. An example of this is when the target wishes to free the bus during a running command. In this case it tells the initiator to secure certain information vital to the I/O process and also informs it of the imminent release of the bus.

Table 20.1 SCSI message format.

Value	Message format
00h	One-byte message (COMMAND COMPLETE)
01h	Extended messages
02h–1Fh	One-byte messages
20h–2Fh	Two-byte messages
30h–7Fh	Reserved
80h–FFh	One-byte message (IDENTIFY)

Table 20.2 Extended message format.

Byte	Value	Description
0	01h	Extended message
1	n	Number of following message bytes
2	Ext. Code	Extended message code
3−n+1		Message arguments

Finally, messages are used to negotiate the parameters of the various options such as synchronous or Wide transfers. Here either the target or initiator sends a number of messages indicating the desired option and parameters. The other device then returns messages either echoing these parameters or values corresponding to its capabilities.

SCSI messages consist of one, two or an arbitrary number of bytes. The first byte, known as the message code, determines the format of a message. Table 20.1 shows the message format. In the case of an extended message the second byte gives the length and the third byte contains the extended message code. Table 20.2 depicts the general structure of an extended message.

The following discussions of the individual messages are grouped by function. Table 20.3 is an overview of all SCSI messages ordered by message code.

Table 20.3 SCSI message codes.

Code	Ini	Tar	Name	Page	Direction	ATN neg.
00h	M	M	COMMAND COMPLETE	300	In	
01, xx, 00h	O	O	MODIFY DATA POINTER	301	In	
01, xx, 01h	O	O	SYNCHRONOUS DATA TRANSFER REQUEST	303	In/Out	Yes
01, xx, 03h	O	O	WIDE DATA TRANSFER REQUEST	304	In/Out	Yes
02h	O	O	SAVE DATA POINTERS	301	In	
03h	O	O	RESTORE POINTERS	301	In	
04h	O	O	DISCONNECT	302	In/Out	Yes
05h	M	M	INITIATOR DETECTED ERROR	300	Out	Yes
06h	O	M	ABORT	307	Out	Yes
07h	M	M	MESSAGE REJECT	308	In/Out	Yes
08h	M	M	NO OPERATION	300	Out	Yes
09h	M	M	MESSAGE PARITY ERROR	308	Out	Yes
0Ah	O	O	LINKED COMMAND COMPLETE	300	In	
0Bh	O	O	LINKED COMMAND COMPLETE (WITH FLAG)	300	In	
0Ch	O	M	BUS DEVICE RESET	307	Out	Yes
0Dh	O	O	ABORT TAG	307	Out	Yes
0Eh	O	O	CLEAR QUEUE	307	Out	Yes
0Fh	O	O	INITIATE RECOVERY		Out	Yes
10h	O	O	RELEASE RECOVERY		Out	Yes
11h	O	O	TERMINATE I/O PROCESS	307	Out	Yes
12h	O	O	CONTINUE TASK		Out	Yes
13h	O	O	TARGET TRANSFER DISABLE		Out	Yes
14h	O	(M)	BUS DEVICE RESET OTHER PORT		Out	Yes
16h	M	M	CLEAR ACA	308	Out	
20h	O	O	SIMPLE QUEUE TAG	306	In/Out	No
21h	O	O	HEAD OF QUEUE TAG	306	Out	No
22h	O	O	ORDERED QUEUE TAG	306	Out	No
23h	O	O	IGNORE WIDE RESIDUE	305	In	
24h	M	M	ACA QUEUE TAG	306	Out	
80h+	M	M	IDENTIFY	299	In/Out	No

20.2　I/O processes (tasks)

I/O process and nexus

The terms 'nexus' and 'I/O process', as described in the SCSI standard, are loosely defined. In SCSI-3 an I/O process is called a task. Since this book is based on SCSI-2, I will continue to use the term I/O process. An I/O process begins with the initial selection of a target by an initiator and extends through all bus free phases and reselections until a final bus free is reached. The I/O process may consist of a single SCSI command or a series of linked commands. The process normally ends with the BUS FREE phase which follows the final COMMAND COMPLETE message. A process can be terminated in response to a number of different messages, a SCSI reset or a protocol error.

The initiator maintains an area in memory of the host for each I/O process to store COMMAND, DATA, and STATUS information. For each area, or so-called buffer, there exist two pointers: the current and saved pointers. At the start of the process all three current pointers point to the beginning of their respective buffers. As the process progresses these pointers advance through memory. When a disconnect takes place another process may start up and use the bus, so prior to this the active pointers need to be saved. This is actually accomplished by the target, which sends a SAVE POINTERS message to the initiator. Later when the process becomes active again the saved pointers are copied back to the active pointers and the process continues to completion.

Nexus is the term used to describe the relationship between an initiator and a target during an I/O process. As soon as the selection of a target takes place an initiator–target nexus (I_T nexus) is established. However, an I_T nexus alone is not enough to carry out an I/O process.

SCSI commands sent by an initiator are not executed by a target itself, but rather by one of its LUNs or target routines. As we saw earlier, LUNs are the physical devices connected to the target. Target routines are a set of very particular programs that run on the target. These routines are optional and mainly used for diagnostic purposes. They are, however, only seldom implemented and have therefore been omitted in SCSI-3. A closer look at target routines is taken in Section 12.1.

With the sending of an IDENTIFY message to the target, either a LUN or a target routine is addressed. This replaces the existing I_T nexus with an initiator–target–LUN nexus (I_T_L nexus) or an initiator–target–routine nexus (I_T_R nexus), respectively. The SCSI standard speaks of an I_T_x nexus when referring to either of these. An I_T_x nexus is sufficient to carry out an I/O process.

Tagged queues, which are optionally supported by targets, are an ordered stack for SCSI commands. They allow a target to store up to 256 commands from various initiators. Tagged queues do not exist for target routines. When supported, a QUEUE TAG message follows immediately after the IDENTIFY message. The existing I_T_L nexus is thereby replaced by an initiator–target–LUN–queue nexus (I_T_L_Q nexus). The SCSI standard speaks of an I_T_x_y nexus when referring to either an I_T_x or an I_T_L_Q nexus (Figure 20.1). We will see more on queues later in this chapter.

Without a tagged queue a target can accept only one command per LUN for each initiator on the SCSI bus. In this case only I_T_L nexuses are ever established.

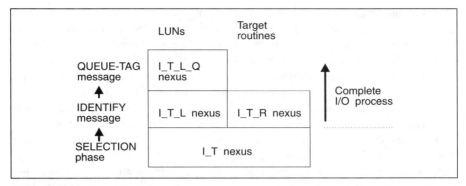

Figure 20.1   Structure of a nexus.

IDENTIFY (80h–FFh)

The IDENTIFY message is used to establish a connection, or nexus, between a device and a LUN or target routine. For the initial SELECTION of an I/O process it is an initiator that establishes this so-called I_T_x nexus. For any subsequent RESELECTION the target then uses an IDENTIFY message to identify a particular I_T_x nexus and thus which I/O process to activate.

The IDENTIFY message itself, which is one byte long, is shown in Table 20.4. As you can see IDENTIFY messages have a variable field within this single byte of information. Bit 7 is always set. In effect this reserves all messages from 80h to FFh as IDENTIFY messages. The remaining seven bits carry the variable information:

- DiscPriv (disconnect privilege): This bit may only be set by an initiator. It allows a target to use its own discretion to disconnect from the initiator and thus free the bus for others to use.
- LUNTAR (LUN/target routine): When this bit is set a target routine is addressed, otherwise a LUN is addressed. (Note that the name implies otherwise!)
- LUNTRN (LUN/target number): The LUN or target routine number.

In SCSI-2, target routines were intended for maintenance and diagnostic purposes. They were, however, seldom implemented and have disappeared with SCSI-3.

In SCSI-3, the structure of the IDENTIFY message is slightly different. Since target routines no longer exist, bit 5 is now reserved. On the other hand, since SCSI-3 now supports up to 32 LUNs, bits 0 to 4 are used for this purpose (Table 20.5).

Table 20.4   IDENTIFY message in SCSI-2.

	7	6	5	4	3	2	1	0
	1	DiscPriv	LUNTAR	Reserved	Reserved	LUNTRN		

Table 20.5   IDENTIFY message in SCSI-3.

	7	6	5	4	3	2	1	0
	1	DiscPriv	Reserved	LUN				

Since most SCSI devices have embedded controllers – that is, they recognize only LUN 0 – the most common IDENTIFY message is C0h. This means IDENTIFY, LUN 0 with disconnect privilege. If the target is not allowed to release the bus during command execution the message becomes 80h.

An initiator is allowed to send multiple IDENTIFY messages during a single I/O process. However, only the disconnect privilege may be modified. Should an initiator attempt to change the LUN or target routine number this will cause the target to bring about BUS FREE. Such an unexpected disconnect terminates the I/O process.

There are many ways in which an IDENTIFY message will be considered invalid. The simplest case is when either of the two reserved bits is set. Also, a message addressing a target routine is invalid when no such routines are implemented. Here the target may respond with either a MESSAGE REJECT message or a CHECK CONDITION status.

A reselection to an I/O process that does not exist is called an unexpected reselection. In this situation the proper response is an ABORT message.

COMMAND COMPLETE (00h)

The target uses this message to inform the initiator that the I/O process has completed. Afterwards a BUS FREE phase is brought about by the target.

LINKED COMMAND COMPLETE (0Ah) and
LINKED COMMAND COMPLETE (WITH FLAG) (0Bh)

These messages are sent instead of COMMAND COMPLETE for linked commands of a command chain. LINKED COMMAND COMPLETE (WITH FLAG) is used when the control byte of the command had its flag bit set. The last command of a chain uses the regular COMMAND COMPLETE message.

NO OPERATION (08h)

This dummy message, as the name implies, does nothing. As an example of when it might be useful, consider an initiator that has asked to send a message by setting ATN. In the time it takes the target to switch to the message phase the initiator may eliminate the need for the message. In this case it sends a NO OPERATION in order to use up the message phase and allow the command to continue.

INITIATOR DETECTED ERROR (05h)

An initiator uses this message when it encounters an internal problem but believes it can continue with the process. Since it is possible that the active pointers have become defective the target must either send a RESTORE POINTERS message or cause BUS FREE (without SAVE DATA POINTERS) and then reselect the initiator.

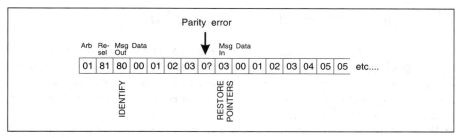

Figure 20.2   Parity error.

20.3   SCSI pointers

As mentioned earlier, each initiator manages a set of three pointers for each I/O process. These pointers keep track of the current position in the COMMAND, DATA and STATUS buffers. The target can influence these pointers using the message system.

SAVE DATA POINTERS (02h)

This message causes the initiator to save the active data pointer to the saved data pointer. It is sent before every BUS FREE phase change.

RESTORE POINTERS (03h)

RESTORE POINTERS causes the initiator to copy the saved pointers to the current pointers. This mechanism is put to use, for example, when a target detects a parity error in a COMMAND, DATA or STATUS byte (see Figure 20.2). As soon as such an error is discovered the target sends a RESTORE POINTERS message to the initiator. Afterwards the next DATA OUT phase starts the transfer at the beginning of the data buffer.

MODIFY DATA POINTER (01h, 05h, 00h, byte 3 ... byte 6)

This message allows the target to directly modify the value of the data pointer (Table 20.6). The 4-byte argument is interpreted as a signed integer, which is added to the current value of the data pointer.

Table 20.6   MODIFY DATA POINTER.

Byte	Value	Description		
0	01h	Extended message		
1	05h	Length of extended message		
2	00h	MODIFY DATA POINTER		
3	n	(MSB)		
4	n		Argument	
5	n			
6	n		(LSB)	

20.4 Disconnect/reconnect: freeing the bus

One of the most important characteristics of the SCSI bus is the ability to interrupt a running I/O process in order to free the bus for other devices. This opportunity arises frequently for targets that must access data from a physical medium. Hard drives typically require in the order of 20 ms to access their data, while tape drives sometimes need several minutes.

When and under what conditions a device should free the bus can be programmed into the target using the MODE SELECT command. An entire parameter page, the disconnect/reconnect page, is dedicated to this purpose. In addition, the DiscPriv (disconnect privilege) bit in the IDENTIFY message tells the target whether it may disconnect for the current I/O process. Besides the DISCONNECT message, which will now be introduced, the SAVE DATA POINTERS message of the previous section plays an important role in freeing the bus.

DISCONNECT (04h)

Using the disconnect/reconnect parameters supplied by the initiator, the target decides when to free the SCSI bus. It then sends the messages SAVE DATA POINTERS and DISCONNECT, and brings about the BUS FREE phase. It is important to remember that the DISCONNECT message does not cause the data pointer to be saved. DISCONNECT indicates only that the target intends to switch to the BUS FREE phase.

The initiator may also send the DISCONNECT message, which is understood by the target as an ultimatum. In this case the target switches to the MESSAGE IN phase and sends the SAVE DATA POINTERS and DISCONNECT messages. The target must wait for at least a disconnect delay of 200 µs after BUS FREE before arbitrating again for the bus.

Let us turn now to Figure 20.3. Time runs from left to right in the figure. I/O process 1 frees the bus after only a short time. During this disconnect time two other processes take the opportunity to use the bus. The numbers in the boxes represent the data (in hex) on the SCSI bus during the various bus phases, while the details are explained above.

At the left-hand side the initiator with SCSI ID 7 arbitrates for the bus. We see bit 7 set in the data byte or 80h. It wins the arbitration and starts the first I/O process. During the SELECTION phase it chooses the target with ID 0. The 81h on the data bus reflects the addition of bit 0 to the initiator's own bit 7. Following selection comes a MESSAGE OUT phase, which the initiator uses to send an IDENTIFY message with DiscPriv set for LUN 0 (C0h). Now comes a READ(6) command with the opcode (08h), logical block number (00000h), number of blocks (01h), and control byte (00h). After accepting the command the target decides to release the bus. It sends the message SAVE DATA POINTER (02h) and DISCONNECT (04h) and frees the bus for other devices.

A little later, after two other processes have been active, I/O process 1 again takes control of the bus. It first arbitrates with ID 0 (01h) and reselects the initiator by adding ID 7 to its own (81h). At this point it could very well be the case that the target and initiator have several active I/O processes. Using an IDENTIFY message, the

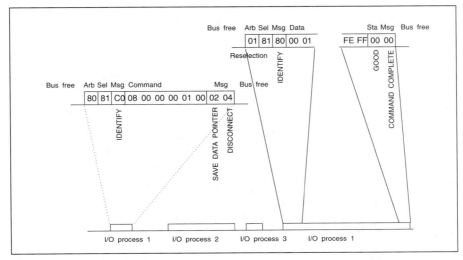

Figure 20.3 Freeing the bus and reselection.

target indicates the specific LUN and therefore I/O process. With this established the target sends the actual data of the requested logical blocks. Finally, a GOOD status (00h) and COMMAND COMPLETE message (00h) conclude the I/O process.

20.5 Transfer options

SYNCHRONOUS DATA TRANSFER REQUEST (01h, 03h, 01h, mm, nn)

The target and initiator negotiate whether to use synchronous transfers using the message system. Bear in mind that such transfers apply only to the data phases. Commands, messages, and status are always sent asynchronously.

A SCSI device that wishes to use synchronous transfers sends the message SYNCHRONOUS DATA TRANSFER REQUEST to the other device. Contained in this extended message are the desired transfer period and offset. The value in byte 3 times 4 ns equals the transfer period, while byte 4 equals the offset (Table 20.7). An exception to this rule is the value 12h, 50 ns, which is needed for Fast-20.

The other device, either initiator or target, replies immediately with its own SYNCHRONOUS DATA TRANSFER REQUEST. This message either echoes the first request or contains less demanding parameters, such as longer period, less offset. If the device

Table 20.7 SYNCHRONOUS DATA TRANSFER REQUEST.

Byte	Value	Description
0	01h	Extended message
1	03h	Number of message bytes after byte 2
2	01h	SYNCHRONOUS DATA TRANSFER REQUEST
3	n	Transfer period
4	n	REQ/ACK offset

```
Seq.      Phase         Data      Text
No.       symbol        hex       comment

0         BUS FREE
1         ARBITRATION   C0        ID 7 and ID 5, ID 7 wins
2         SELECT        81        Target ID 0
3         MESSAGE OUT   80        IDENTIFY
4         MSG OUT       01        Extended Message
5         MSG OUT       03        Extended Message Length
6         MSG OUT       01        SYNCHRONOUS TRANSFER REQUEST
7         MSG OUT       34        Wants transfer period 136nS
8         MSG OUT       0F        Wants REQ/ACK offset 15
9         MSG IN        01        Extended Message
10        MSG IN        03        Extended Message Length
11        MSG IN        01        SYNCHRONOUS TRANSFER REQUEST
12        MSG IN        32        Gets transfer period 128nS
13        MSG IN        0F        Gets REQ/ACK offset 15
14        COMMAND       00
15        COMMAND       00
16        COMMAND       00
```

Figure 20.4   Synchronous transfer request.

does not support synchronous data transfer at all it can send either a MESSAGE REJECT
or a SYNCHRONOUS DATA TRANSFER REQUEST with the offset set to zero. In both cases
the result is asynchronous transfers for the data phases. Figure 20.4 shows a relevant
sequence taken from a SCSI analyzer.

In principle, either target or initiator can request synchronous transfers. In practice,
however, the initiator or in general the host adapter is the one that initiates this negotiation. Some older host adapters were known to have difficulty with a SYNCHRONOUS
DATA TRANSFER REQUEST from a target. For this reason some target devices allow the
synchronous transfer option to be disabled by jumper.

This negotiation does not take place for every I/O process. Rather the agreement
holds between devices until the next SCSI reset or a BUS DEVICE RESET message. Of
course, either device may decide to negotiate new parameters should a reason arise.

WIDE DATA TRANSFER REQUEST (01h, 02h, 03h, nn)

A device that wishes to uses Wide SCSI sends its partner device a WIDE DATA TRANS-
FER REQUEST. This message contains the desired bus width encoded in byte 3. Here

Table 20.8   WIDE DATA TRANSFER REQUEST.

Byte	Value	Description
0	01h	Extended message
1	02h	Number of message bytes after byte 2
2	03h	WIDE DATA TRANSFER REQUEST
3	n	Transfer width 2^{3+n}

00h means 8-bit, 01h 16-bit and 02h 32-bit wide transfers (Table 20.8). Just as with the synchronous negotiation, the partner device replies immediately with its own WIDE DATA TRANSFER REQUEST message here either echoing the width or sending a smaller value. If Wide SCSI is not supported then it either replies with a width of zero or sends the MESSAGE REJECT message.

This agreement also holds until a SCSI reset or BUS DEVICE RESET message. Likewise, the negotiation does not take place before each I/O process. Such an implementation would increase the overhead of the SCSI protocol unnecessarily.

Of course, it can also occur that the total number of bytes to be sent is not divisible by the transfer width. Here the valid bytes of the final transfer are padded with one or more dummy bytes. In this case a message is sent immediately following the transfer indicating how many bytes to ignore.

IGNORE WIDE RESIDUE (23h, nn)

IGNORE WIDE RESIDUE indicates which bytes of a final wide transfer to ignore. Table 20.9 shows the structure of the message and the meaning of byte 1.

20.6   Tagged queues

We took a first look at tagged queues during the definition of a nexus. Tagged queues are a SCSI-2 option which allows each LUN to queue up to 256 I/O processes per initiator. The main advantage of this approach is that it makes optimization possible.

For targets that support tagged queues, implementing the QUEUE TAG message is obligatory. An initiator enters a command into the queue by sending QUEUE TAG immediately following IDENTIFY. This action sets up an I_T_L_Q nexus replacing the I_T_L nexus previously established.

There are three types of QUEUE TAG messages. All contain a reference number for the I/O process or queue tag in byte 1 (Table 20.10). This same tag is sent in a QUEUE TAG message at reselection time to identify which process is resuming.

Table 20.9   IGNORE WIDE RESIDUE.

Byte	Description
0	IGNORE WIDE RESIDUE (23h)
1	Byte mask

	Invalid bits	
Byte mask	32-bit transfers	16-bit transfers
00h	Reserved	Reserved
01h	DB(31–24)	DB(15–8)
02h	DB(31–16)	Reserved
03h	DB(31–8)	Reserved
04h–FFh	Reserved	Reserved

Table 20.11   The QUEUE TAG messages.

Byte	Description
0	Message (20h, 21h, 22h)
1	Number

Using the QUEUE TAG messages, an initiator also has the ability to influence the position of commands within the queue.

SIMPLE QUEUE TAG (20h)

This message causes the I/O process to be added to the command queue. It is up to the target to decide exactly when to process it (provided no ORDERED QUEUE TAGS have been received, which are discussed next). Commands with a SIMPLE QUEUE TAG allow, for example, disk drives to optimize time intensive seeks to the medium. Targets always use this message when reselecting an initiator for a tagged process.

HEAD OF QUEUE TAG (21h)

This message leads to placing the I/O process in question at the beginning of the queue. The currently active process is run until completion. Subsequent HEAD OF QUEUE TAG processes are placed ahead of older ones at the beginning of the queue. In this way multiple HEAD OF QUEUE TAG processes are executed in last-in, first-out order.

ORDERED QUEUE TAG (22h)

This message causes I/O processes to be executed in the order in which they were received. In other words, all processes that were already in the queue will be executed before this process and likewise all processes that arrive afterwards will be executed after this one. An exception to this is made for processes with the HEAD OF QUEUE TAG.

ACA QUEUE TAG (24h)

This message is new in SCSI-3 and causes a task to be entered into the queue as an ACA task (auto contingent allegiance). The device server handles this task according to the rules set forth in the SCSI architecture model.

Tagged queues and error handling

A target that does not support tagged queues will reply to a QUEUE TAG message with MESSAGE REJECT. If an initiator receives a command tagged with a number already in the queue the result is a so-called incorrect initiator connection. In response, the target terminates all I/O processes of this initiator and sends the CHECK CONDITION status. A subsequent request sense command would then return the sense key ABORTED COMMAND and the extended sense key OVERLAPPED COMMANDS ATTEMPTED.

If a target attempts to reselect with an incorrect number in the QUEUE TAG message, the initiator will respond with ABORT TAG.

20.7 Termination of I/O processes

There are a number of ways to terminate or kill I/O processes, for instance simple termination of all processes of a target or LUN. In tagged queues either all or only active processes can be halted. Additionally, an I/O process can be made to terminate 'as soon as possible'.

BUS DEVICE RESET (0Ch)

This message tells the target to kill all active and outstanding I/O processes. In reality, the target performs a soft reset. This action not only kills all I/O processes but also nullifies device reservations and causes device parameters to be reset to start-up values. The target enters unit attention condition, which means that it will reply to the next command with a CHECK CONDITION status. The sense key for the following REQUEST SENSE command will be UNIT ATTENTION (06h).

CLEAR QUEUE (0Eh)

This message is only implemented by devices supporting tagged queues. The CLEAR QUEUE message kills the active I/O processes and those waiting in the queue from any and all initiators for this LUN or target routine.

ABORT TAG (0Dh)

The ABORT TAG message allows I/O processes within ordered tagged queues to be terminated. This message kills only the currently active process. Neither status nor a final message will be sent for the terminated process. The I/O processes in the queue are unaffected. The state of the LUN remains unchanged in all other respects.

ABORT (06h)

The abort message terminates all running I/O processes and all those in the queue for this I_T_L nexus. As with the ABORT TAG message, the target skips the status and message phases and immediately brings about BUS FREE. All other I_T_L nexuses remain unaffected.

TERMINATE I/O PROCESS (11h)

This message tells the target to terminate the current I/O process as soon as possible. There are a few differences here with respect to the methods just described.

Firstly, it is up to the target's own discretion as to when to end the process. In this way it can see to it that, for example, the data structure of a tape is not damaged by continuing a write until the end of the record. If the write were immediately cut short a damaged record would result.

After the target has terminated the process the progression to the BUS FREE phase takes place normally. First, the status I/O PROCESS TERMINATED is sent followed by a COMMAND COMPLETE message. If by chance an error occurs when terminating the process the status byte will reflect this.

The message TERMINATE I/O PROCESS is intended for longer I/O processes that may delay the execution of more important tasks. A subsequent request sense command will return the sense key NO SENSE (00h) and the extended sense key I/O PROCESS TERMINATED (00h, 06h). The information field of the sense data will contain the difference between the amount of data requested and the amount transferred.

CLEAR ACA (16h)

This message is new in SCSI-3. The target terminates the auto contingent allegiance state and releases the bus.

20.8   Error handling in the message system

Two problems may occur when sending messages for which there is a means to recover. Since the message system represents the lowest level of communication on the SCSI bus, special messages exist to handle precisely these cases.

MESSAGE REJECT (07h)

This message is appropriate when a device does not support an optional message. After receiving the unsupported message the device responds immediately with MESSAGE REJECT.

If an initiator wishes to reject a message it must first assert ATN before de-asserting the ACK of the last REQ/ACK sequence.

In the case of a target, which can control bus phases directly, it simply brings about the MESSAGE IN phase and sends the message. If ATN is still active after the MESSAGE REJECT message the target switches back to MESSAGE OUT and collects the messages.

MESSAGE PARITY ERROR (09h)

The target responds to parity errors during COMMAND, DATA, and MESSAGE OUT phases with a RESTORE POINTERS message. This action makes it possible to retry the transfer with the same data.

However, parity errors during a MESSAGE IN phase require a special procedure. In this case the initiator sends the MESSAGE PARITY ERROR message. As always, it asserts ATN to inform the target of its desire to send a message. The target reacts to MESSAGE PARITY ERROR by resending the original message.

20.9 Asynchronous event notification

In addition to messages SCSI provides targets with an alternative method of informing an initiator of unforeseen difficulties. This optional mechanism is called asynchronous event notification (AEN).

To carry out AEN the initiator and target must be able to trade roles temporarily. The target (acting as an initiator) sends the initiator (acting as a target) the SEND command. The data within the command contains information describing the target's difficulties.

The SEND command and the AEN format for the data are described in Chapter 12.

There are a number of applications for AEN. For example, devices of the communications or processor class often have data for an initiator that is not the direct result of a command. AEN allows the target to inform the initiator of the situation, which in turn can request the data from the device.

Another application is the implementation of a write cache for a disk or tape drive. A write cache allows a device to send GOOD status and COMMAND COMPLETE immediately upon receiving the write data into its cache, effectively eliminating the access time from the command execution time. Of course, at this point the data has not been written to the medium and therefore a write error could still occur. AEN is used to inform the initiator of the problem by sending it the sense data describing the nature of the error (Figure 20.5).

There is a possible alternative to the above approach for devices that have write cache but do not implement AEN. Here the target simply responds with a CHECK CONDITION status for the next command. The disadvantage of this method is obvious: an initiator does not learn of the error until it sends that same device another command. Up until that point it goes on believing that the command was successful.

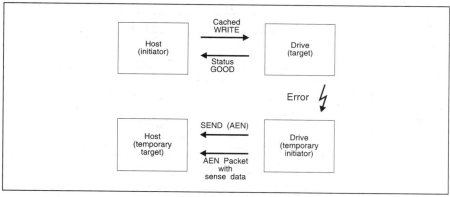

Figure 20.5   Asynchronous event notification.

21 The new SCSI-3 interfaces

Many expectations in connection with SCSI-3 are directed towards the new serial interfaces. They can and will remedy the fundamental problems of the parallel SCSI bus. Since at the same time an important part of SCSI, namely device models, commands and parameters, remains untouched, the higher level software drives can also remain unchanged. In other words, when someone builds a host adapter with a Fibre Channel interface, they must only supply an ASPI driver for this host adapter in order to make existing operating systems and application programs work with the new interface.

Three competing serial interfaces have been integrated into SCSI-3: Fibre Channel, Fire Wire and SSA (Figure 21.1). None of these interfaces has been invented by the SCSI committee. Fibre Channel is backed by an industrial consortium and, as SCSI, is standardized by ANSI. Fire Wire is a development initiated by Apple and an IEEE standard (P1394). SAA, finally, is an IBM development.

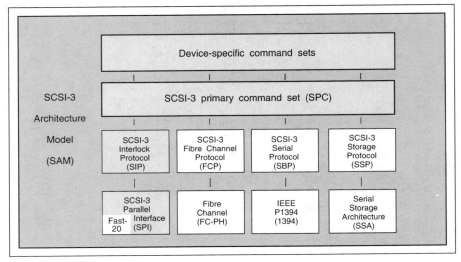

Figure 21.1 The new SCSI interfaces.

In spite of the enthusiasm shown by supporters of each of these interfaces, one fact should not be forgotten: although some of the standards have been ready for a fairly long time, there are still hardly any devices that implement them. This is exactly the opposite of how the successful SCSI standards have developed. They were always developed on the basis of such a popular demand that they were implemented into large numbers of devices even before the standard was finalized. All will depend on whether there is enough user demand for the features of one of the new interfaces before they have become obsolete.

Another important point of development and success of SCSI must not be forgotten: the parallel SCSI interface makes it possible to offer peripheral devices with only one interface for all computer systems, from home computers to PCs, to workstations and even mainframes. This means enormous cost savings for manufacturers and commerce and, in the end, the users. This is why the differential parallel interface, in spite of its undisputed advantages, has never had a broad success.

The new interfaces would once again mean stockpiling of different versions of the same device. And even worse, Fibre Channel comes in countless variations: twisted pair, coaxial cable, and several kinds of fiber optic cables. SSA too has defined twisted pair and fiber optic cables.

Thus, I hardly believe that all three serial interfaces will succeed on the market. Only one of them will probably make it. Personally, I think it even possible that none of these SCSI interfaces will actually succeed.

21.1 Fundamental problems of the parallel SCSI interface

The wish for other interface alternatives originates out of real deficiencies of the parallel SCSI interface. Some of these deficiencies can be remedied, others are fundamental and nothing can be done about them.

Cables

50-pin or 68-pin cables are relatively expensive and the voluminous connectors stand in the way of further miniaturization of the devices.

Serial interfaces are better off. Fire Wire only needs 6 leads, but the cable is relatively thick because it also carries a power supply voltage. Fibre Channel can use fiber optic, coaxial and 9-pin twisted pair cables. SSA too only needs a 9-pin cable.

Bus length

For many applications, the bus length is too short. Even though it is possible to reach up to 25 m with the differential interface, the problem remains that the differential interface is only available for a few devices. The single-ended interface allows a maximum of 6 m which is reduced by the new fast variation down to 3 or even 1.5 m.

Fire Wire can connect 16 devices that can be up to 4.5 m from one another. SSA allows a device distance of 20 m with twisted pair cables and 680 m with optical fiber cables. With up to 128 devices, this allows quite a distance to be covered. Things look similar with Fibre Channel. Distances of up to 50 m with twisted pair cables and up to 10 km with optical fiber are possible between two devices. The maximum number of devices lies between 127 and 16 million.

Data rate

The original data transfer rate of 10 Mbytes/sec was too low. Here, however, things have been changing. With SCSI-3 the propagation of 16-bit wide SCSI is growing, and at the same time Fast-20 was defined. In combination this results in a data rate of 40 Mbytes/sec. Most recent developments under discussion are Fast-40 and Fast-80. Should these developments succeed, the data rate of 160 Mbytes/sec will be higher than that of some serial alternatives. I would like, however, to remind you that command transfer is carried out in all parallel SCSI variations with a maximum of about 5 Mbytes/sec.

Fire Wire allows data rates of 3 to 50 Mbytes/sec and thus runs the risk of being surpassed by parallel SCSI. SSA goes up to 80 Mbytes/sec and Fibre Channel even up to 200 Mbytes/sec.

Real time/guaranteed bandwidth

With the widespread introduction of multi-media applications such as video, an old issue becomes important again. The parallel SCSI interface is not real-time capable and can also not provide a guaranteed bandwidth for a given device.

Fire Wire and Fibre Channel allow isosynchronous transfer. This is a transfer with guaranteed delivery of data in a specific time window. In the worst case, data is delivered incorrectly rather than too late. This is exactly the feature needed for multi-media. Applied to video, 'incorrect' means a (maybe only minimally) disturbed image, whereas 'too late' means a jerky image.

Data integrity

With only one parity bit per byte, the parallel SCSI interface is not particularly well protected against data errors.

Here, the serial interfaces promise remedy. Fibre Channel and SSA, which have error correction built in at hardware level, are excellent. Fire Wire is only mediocre with its error correction being carried out on the higher protocol levels.

21.2 Fibre Channel

Fibre Channel is a universal serial high-speed interface for computers and mass storage. In contrast to all other interfaces and buses discussed in this book, it possesses features of both an I/O channel and a local network. Indeed, Fibre Channel can serve as the transport medium for both application areas. However, the Fibre

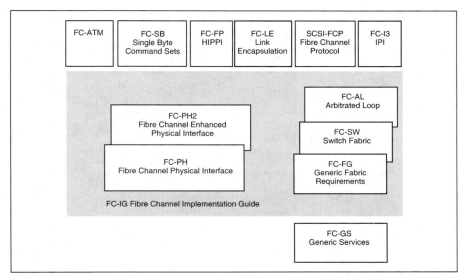

Figure 21.2 Fibre Channel protocol family.

Channel does not contain a higher protocol of its own, but protocols such as SCSI-3, IPI or IP build on Fibre Channel as their base (Figure 21.2).

Fibre Channel allows data rates from 12.5 to 100 Mbytes/sec; up to 400 Mbytes/sec are being planned. Fibre Channel allows point-to-point connection, a ring or a switch topology. The number of nodes is practically unlimited. Other than its name suggest, Fibre Channel can use twisted pair, coaxial and fiber optic cables as transport medium. Depending on speed and transport medium, distances from a few meters up to 10 km can be covered. With fiber optic cables, covering the maximum distance is even possible at 100 Mbits/sec.

Fibre Channel originates from the development of an improved physical interface for IPI. It was developed from 1988 by the ANSI committee X3T9, and it was clear from the beginning that Fibre Channel would also be used as a physical interface for other protocols. Wide industry support made this development possible. The main part of this support comes from IBM who contributed their experience with the ESCON channel and the patented 8B/10B coding. Outside ANSI there is the industrial Fibre Channel Association (FCA) whose aim is to promote marketing of the Fibre Channel. Meanwhile the X3T9 committee has been split, and now X3T11 is responsible for the Fibre Channel.

Fibre Channel protocol layers

The Fibre Channel main document is FC-PH and is available in Revision 4.3 of June 1994. Extensions to FC-PH are laid out in FC-PH2. FC-PH is divided into four layers, FC-0 to FC-4 (Figure 21.3).

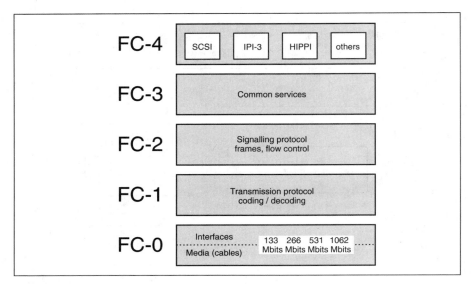

Figure 21.3 Fibre Channel protocol layers.

- **FC-0** describes the physical interface, that is transport media, connections, senders and receivers. All variations, such as twisted pair, coaxial and fiber optic cables are covered. In FC-PH2 the original definition is complemented with transfer rates of 2 and 4 Gigabits/sec.

- **FC-1** describes the 8B/10B coding method. This method is an IBM patent and is also used by the SSA interface (see Section 21.6).

- **FC-2** describes the signaling protocol. This contains all mechanisms needed to transport data from one node to another. FC-2 describes the addressing and the possible topologies. The protocols of FC-4 use these mechanisms.

- **FC-3** describes services that regard all ports of a node.

- **FC-4** contains the mappings of the various protocols, that is SCSI, IPI, HIPPI or IP.

Fibre Channel terminology

In the following pages, Fibre Channel is often abbreviated as FC. Devices that can be accessed via Fibre Channel are called nodes. FC nodes have at least one port. A node that initiates a transaction is called an originator; the node that answers it is called a responder.

Besides nodes, there are Fibre Channel switches. In a network constructed out of switches, the entirety of the switches is called the fabric. For the nodes, the fabric represents a kind of black box: nodes do not have to know what happens in the fabric and they also have nothing to tell the fabric. The fabric forwards data packets from a source to a destination. Connections between FC ports are called links.

Table 21.1 Fibre Channel interfaces.

		Sender	Medium	Throughput		Distance
				Mbaud	*Mbytes/sec*	
O p t i c a l		LED long-wave	62.5 µm Multimode	132.81	12.5	1 km
		Laser long-wave	Monomode	265.62	25	2 or 10 km
		LED long-wave	62.5 µm Multimode			1.5 km
		Laser short-wave	50 µm Multimode			2 km
		Laser short-wave	50 µm Multimode	531.25	50	1 km
		Laser long-wave	Monomode			2 or 10 km
		Laser short-wave	50 µm Multimode	1062.5	100	1 km
		Laser long-wave	Monomode			2 or 10 km
E l e c t r i c a l		ECL	CATV coax	132.81	12.5	100 m
			Submin coax			40 m
			Twisted pair			100 m
			CATV coax	265.62	25	75 m
			Submin coax			30 m
			Twisted pair			50 m
			CATV coax	531.25	50	50 m
			Submin coax			20 m
			CATV coax	1062.5	100	25 m
			Submin coax			10 m

Fibre Channel interfaces

Fibre Channel defines a large number of physical interfaces. Fiber optic, coaxial and twisted pair cables can be used as the transport medium. Speeds reach from 12.5 Mbytes/sec to 100 Mbytes/sec, in future even up to 400 Mbytes/sec. Distances reach from a few meters to 10 kilometers. Table 21.1 lists the variations.

This variety is a result of the attempt to find a compromise between cost, throughput and transfer distance for different applications. However, not all variations are compatible with each other. This will certainly lead to the effect that only a few variations will finally succeed. Furthermore, a whole new market might open up for adapter products with and without speed adaptation.

Fibre Channel topologies

Fibre Channel supports three fundamental topologies: the point-to-point connection, the ring (arbitrated loop) and the fabric (see Figure 21.4).

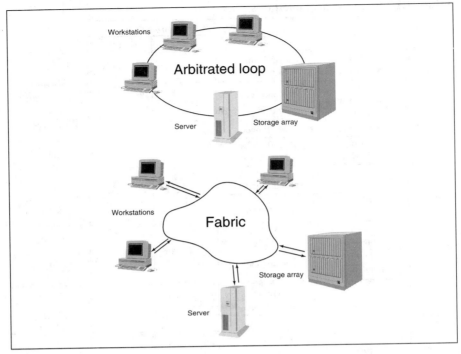

Figure 21.4　Fibre Channel topologies.

A ring can have 126 nodes. The address space of a fabric is only limited by the length of the ID (24 bits). This allows for about 16 million nodes.

FC frames

Data packets in Fibre Channel are called frames. A frame consists of a start mark, the header, the payload, a checksum and an end mark (Figure 21.5). The payload may contain further headers if they are required by the protocol. These additional headers, however, reduce the amount of transported user data.

A sequence consists of one or more frames and has a sequence ID (SEQ_ID). Within a sequence the frames are numbered by a sequence number (SEQ_CNT). A sequence always represents a unidirectional operation.

Several, even simultaneous sequences can be combined into an exchange. Exchanges can be bidirectional. An exchange has an ID on both the originator and the responder side.

4 bytes	24 bytes	0 - 2112 bytes	4 bytes	4 bytes
Start mark	Header	Payload (optional header and user data)	CRC	End mark

Figure 21.5　Structure of a Fibre Channel frame.

Table 21.2 Header of a Fibre Channel frame.

	Byte 0	*Byte 1*	*Byte 2*	*Byte 3*
	Bit 31			*Bit 0*
0	Routing	Destination ID		
4	Reserved	Source ID		
8	Type	Frame control		
12	Sequence ID	Data control	Sequence number	
16	Originator exchange ID		Responder exchange ID	
20	Parameters			

The FC header primarily (Table 21.2) contains the source and destination IDs. The routing field contains the routing information. The Type field specifies the contents of the payload. For SCSI FCP it contains the value 08h.

21.3 From Fibre Channel to SCSI-3: the Fibre Channel Protocol (FCP)

The Fibre Channel protocol defines the mapping of SCSI processes onto Fibre Channel. A SCSI task (SCSI-2: I/O process) corresponds to a FC exchange. SCSI requests and responses as defined in the SAM (they correspond to SCSI-2 bus phases) are mapped onto information units (IU).

The information units

All SCSI processes are combined out of four basic IU types: FCP_CMND (command), FCP_DATA (data), FCP_XFER_RDY (ready to transfer) and FCP_RSP (response). Table 21.3 shows, by way of example, the structure of the FCP_CMND information unit.

Table 21.3 Structure of a FCP_CMND IU.

		7	6	5	4	3	2	1	0
FCP_LUN	0 ... 7	LUN number							
	8	Reserved							
	9	Reserved					Task attributes		
FCP_CNTL	10	TRM TASK	CLR ACA	TRGT RESET	Reserved		CLR TSKST	ABRT TSKST	Reserved
	11	Reserved							
FCP_CDB	12 ...	SCSI command block							
	... 27	(CDB)							
FCP_DL	28 ... 31	Transfer length							

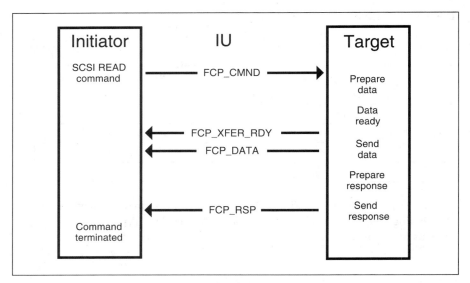

Figure 21.6   Execution of a SCSI READ command on the Fibre Channel.

Figure 21.6 shows the schematic execution of a SCSI READ command on the Fibre Channel.

21.4   Fire Wire (IEEE P1394)

Fire Wire is the marketing name given by the initiator Apple to the serial IEEE P1394 bus. Fire Wire has been especially designed for the requirements of multi-media applications. It supports arbitration and both asynchronous and isosynchronous transfer. Asynchronous transfer might be characterized by the motto 'better late than wrong', isosynchronous transfer by 'better wrong than late'.

P1394 was developed as a peripheral bus with the aim of low cost and appropriate transfer speed and delay. Its configuration is shown in Figure 21.7.

P1394 uses either the conductors of a backplane or a shielded cable with three wire pairs. Two of them are used for signal transmission; the third one carries the power supply voltage for the peripheral device. The signal lines employ differential CMOS transceivers with a signal voltage of 220 mV. Fire Wire allows devices to be connected or disconnected during normal operation.

Data transfer is carried out half duplex, that is, either one or the other device can send on one connection. The serial transfer rate for backplane buses is 24.5 or 49 Mbits/sec. For external P1394 it is a multiple of 98.304 Mbits/sec. The coding allows every device to determine the speed at which data is sent by itself.

P1394 devices are called nodes. On the cable, two nodes may be up to 4.5 m from each other. Since a P1394 cable bus can have 16 nodes, the total cable length can be 72 m. The total address space, however, is much higher. The node ID is 16 bits long. The higher 10 bits address the bus, the lower 6 bits the node. An entire system can thus have 64 449 nodes, 63 each on 1023 buses.

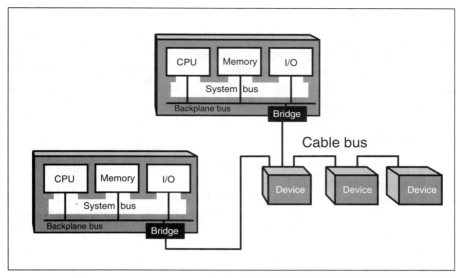

Figure 21.7   Fire Wire configuration.

Protocol structure

The P1394 protocols are divided into three layers: the transaction layer, the link layer and the physical layer (Figure 21.8).

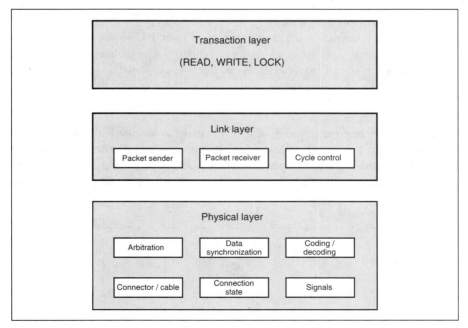

Figure 21.8   P1394 block diagram.

Transaction layer

The transaction layer defines a complete protocol in the form of request and response. It defines three transactions, namely READ, WRITE and LOCK. A READ transaction transfers data from an answering device, the responder, to the requesting device, called the requestor. Vice versa, a write transaction transfers data from a requestor to one or more responders. A LOCK transaction corresponds to the well-known read/modify/write cycle: data is sent from a requestor to a responder which processes it and sends it back to the requestor.

Link layer

The link layer provides half-duplex packet transmission. Two subactions are defined: one delivers an asynchronous packet, the other delivers an isosynchronous packet. Each subaction consists of three parts: arbitration, packet transmission and acknowledgment.

Physical layer

The physical layer obviously includes cables and connectors. P1394 uses a shielded twisted pair cable with two wire pairs for the signals and one for the power supply voltage. Figure 21.9 shows the connector plug.

The topology of the cable bus is tree-shaped. It has one root node, branching nodes and end nodes (leaves). This tree-like structure also implies that, as opposed to the parallel SCSI bus, the bus signals must be forwarded actively. Thus, at least the root and each branching node must be switched on.

Arbitration too belongs to the physical protocol layer. P1394 has three arbitration modes: fair, urgent and isosynchronous arbitration. Isosynchronous arbitration always has precedence. Only after all nodes that want to transfer isosynchronously have finished their transfers, a pause occurs which is long enough to begin an urgent or a fair arbitration. In this procedure, the distance between a node and the root has no influence on the arbitration.

Finally, a very important feature of P1394 belongs to the physical layer: the auto-configuration. In Fire Wire, no addresses must be configured. The bus configures itself as part of the initialization process. The bus also detects when a node is added or removed after initialization. Then it executes a reinitialization. Here a node may receive a new physical node address.

Figure 21.9   P1394 connector.

21.5   From P1394 to SCSI-3: the Serial Bus Protocol (SBP)

The task of the SBP is to map the elements defined by the SCSI architecture model onto the P1394 architecture. The main elements are SCSI commands, task management functions and error handling.

Initialization

First the P1394 bus must initialize itself. Then the SBP makes use of the transaction layer services to transmit commands, data and status. Each P1394 node contains a configuration ROM which stores a 64-bit long, worldwide unique node ID. Furthermore, it contains information on whether a node supports the SBP and with it the SCSI-3 protocol.

After initialization, an initiator scans the P1394 bus and logs in with the targets that support the SBP. Only then can normal SCSI commands be issued. An SBP target contains one or more command FIFOs for SCSI commands. A FIFO (first in first out) is a form of a waiting queue.

The CDS

The Command Data Structure (CDS) is a data structure that transports commands and control information from an initiator to a target (Table 21.4). When an initiator writes a CDS into a target, this is called a TAP operation. When a target gets a CDS from an initiator, this is called a FETCH operation.

Table 21.4   SCSI CDS.

Bytes	Description			
0–3	(MSQ)	Address of		
4–7		next CDS		(LSQ)
8–11	(MSQ)	Address of		
12–15		this CDS		(LSQ)
16–19	Reserved	Identifier	LUN	
20–23	CDS codes	Task codes	Reserved	Protocol flags
24–27	CDB 0	CDB 1	CDB 2	CDB 3
28–31	CDB 4	CDB 5	CDB 6	CDB 7
32–35	CDB 8	CDB 9	CDB 10	CDB 11
36–39	CDB 12	CDB 13	CDB 14	CDB 15
40–43	CDS transfer length			
44–47	Data transfer control		CDS sense length	
48–51	(MSQ)	Data buffer		
52–55		address		(LSQ)
56–59	(MSQ)	CDS status FIFO		
60–63		address		(LSQ)
64–67	(MSQ)	CDS sense data		
68–71		buffer address		(LSQ)

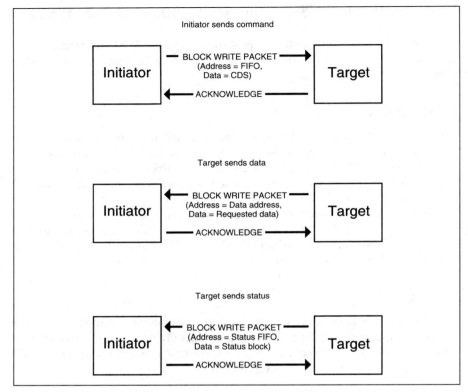

Figure 21.10　READ command execution.

Information is transferred on the P1394 bus in quadlets, that is four bytes, or octlets, that is eight bytes. The data structure of a CDS is divided into quadlets. The most significant quadlet is called MSQ, the least significant quadlet LSQ.

There are five different types of CDS: the login CDS, the SCSI CDS, the management CDS, the isosynchronous SCSI CDS and the isosynchronous control CDS. Table 21.4 shows a SCSI CDS. A SCSI CDS offers space for a SCSI-CDB up to 16 bytes long.

Command execution

Figure 21.10 shows the example of a READ command execution.

21.6 SSA

SSA stands for Serial Storage Architecture. It was originally developed by IBM as I/O channel 9444 and made available to the entire computer industry in 1991 as an alternative to the parallel SCSI-3 interface. Since 1994, the ANSI X3T10.1 committee is concerned with its standardization and documentation.

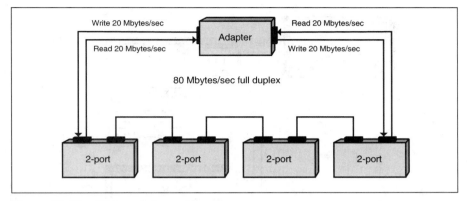

Figure 21.11   SSA sample configuration.

SSA is a high performance interface designed as an I/O bus from the very beginning. SSA builds on ports that are capable of transmitting 20 Mbytes/sec in full duplex mode. Dual port architecture allows a theoretical maximum speed of 80 Mbytes/sec to be reached.

The dual port architecture also allows fault-tolerant connections between host and I/O device to be established. Figure 21.11 shows one of the many possible SSA configurations.

Features

SSA has several features that are missing in the parallel SCSI interface. SSA cables and connectors are relatively small. For internal connections, a 6-pin cable with a minute connector is used. Externally, a shielded cable and Mini-DB9 connectors are employed. With copper wire cable, SSA can be transmitted over 20 m, with fiber optic cable a distance between two nodes of up to 680 m can be covered.

The reliability of the data connection is higher than with SCSI. Already at hardware level, CRC allows an error rate of one error per 10^{13} bytes to be reached. A further data check is carried out on the link layer.

SSA devices can be exchanged during normal operation. The dual port architecture allows you to configure fault-tolerant subsystems with high availability.

The modules

An SSA system consists of different basic modules. A node is a system, a controller or a peripheral device with one or more SSA connections. There are three types of node: single port nodes, dual port nodes and switch nodes.

A link is a dedicated connection between two individual ports of two nodes. When a link does not transmit data, synchronization characters are exchanged which allow you to establish whether the link is working or not.

The physical SSA connection is called a port. A port can be connected to exactly one link.

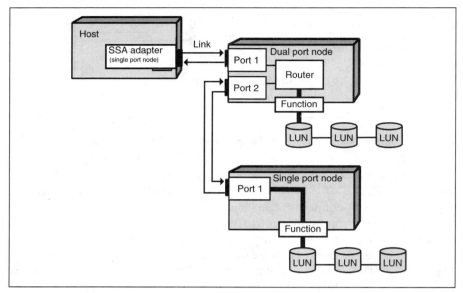

Figure 21.12   SSA modules.

A node can assume the role of an initiator or a target. As the SSA initiator, it issues requests to other nodes. At least one SSA node must be an initiator. This is the master node. An SSA target executes the requests of SSA initiators. Up to 128 SSA LUNs can be connected to an SSA target.

A logical unit (LUN) is a physical or logical device which can be accessed by a target. Figire 21.12 summarizes the configuration of SSA modules.

A router is a functional unit in a dual port node which decides whether an incoming frame is destined to this node or should be forwarded via the other port.

Topology

Three different topologies can be realized with SSA: the bus, the ring and the connection of several buses via switches. Figure 21.13 shows the different topologies.

A bus can have 129 nodes, a ring 128. The end of a bus can be a switch, whereas a ring cannot contain any switches. A switch can have up to 96 ports and be itself connected to other switches, which allows one to build very large SSA networks.

Data transfer

The SSA transport layer is defined in the SSA TL1 document (X3T10.1/0989D). Information transfer is carried out on the basis of frames. A frame consists of a control character, a one to six character address, between zero and 128 characters of data and four CRC characters (Figure 21.14).

Data bytes and protocol functions are coded as characters in the 8B/10B code, an IBM development. A particular feature of this code is that there are special characters

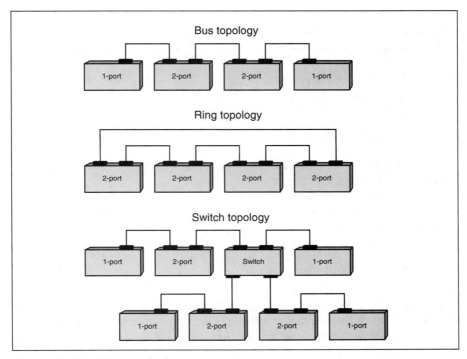

Figure 21.13   SSA topologies.

which can be found in a continuous data stream because they use bit sequences
which otherwise do not occur. These special characters are used for structuring the
data stream and for protocol functions.

There are three different types of frame. Application frames are used for data
transport and for all information of the higher protocol layers. SCSI commands, data
status and messages are transported in application frames. Privileged frames are

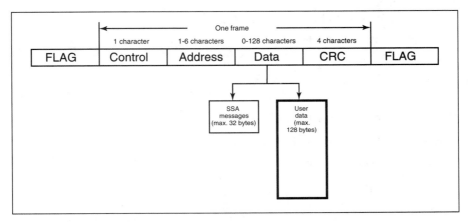

Figure 21.14   SSA frames.

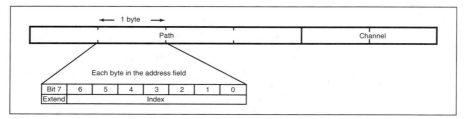

Figure 21.15   SSA address field.

used by the transport layer for configuration and error handling. Control frames are used by the transport layer to reset nodes or links.

The data field of an application frame is of particular interest. It can contain either user data or a SSA message structure (SMS). The latter contains, for example, SCSI messages, commands and status.

Addressing

The address of an application frame consists of six bytes (Figure 21.15). Four bytes address the path and two the channel. In each address byte, the most significant bit is the extend bit. When set, it means that this byte is complemented by the following byte. Thus, from left to right, the first byte with the extend bit not set is the end of the path, and the second one is the end of the channel.

The addressing itself, that is the structure of a path, is more than strange. It is optimized to make routing as easy as possible. It can best be understood by looking at the routing rules. By means of these simple rules, routing can be carried out entirely by the hardware, thus very fast.

Routing rules

The routing rules are represented in a syntax similar to that of the Pascal programming language.

A single port node follows this routing rule:

```
If FirstByte = 00h
then
      begin
           'Accept the frame';
           'Interpret the remainder of the address as channel';
      end
else 'Reject the frame';
```

A dual port node follows this routing rule:

```
If FirstByte = 00h
then
      begin
           'Accept the frame';
           'Interpret the remainder of the address as channel';
      end
```

```
else
    if FirstByte.Index 0
    then
        begin
            FirstByte.Index := FirstByte.Index - 1;
            'Forward frame via other port';
        end
    else 'Reject the frame';
```

Thus, in a frame that is forwarded, the index is decremented by 1. The frame is forwarded until the index is zero. Then it has reached its destination. The routing rules for a switch are only slightly more complicated.

21.7   From SSA to SCSI-3: the Serial Storage Protocol (SSP)

The task of the SSP is to map the elements defined by the SCSI architecture model onto the SSA architecture. The main elements are SCSI commands, task management functions and error handling. Task management is carried out by the SSP via SSA message structures (SMS). Although there are SSA message structures which correspond exactly to one SCSI message, this is not always the case. SSA message structures and SCSI-3 messages must not be confused.

The SCSI command SMS

As an example of SCSI SSA message structures, Table 21.5 shows you how a SCSI command is embedded in the SCSI command SMS. Table 21.6 lists the types of SCSI SMS.

Table 21.5   SCSI command SMS.

	7	6	5	4	3	2	1	0
0	SMS code (82h)							
1	SSP code (10h)							
2 ... 3	Tag							
4 ...	Initiator							
... 7	path							
8	LUN							
9	Reserved							
10	DDRM			Reserved			Queue Cntl	
11	Reserved							
12 ... 13	Initiator channel							
14 ... 15	Reserved							
16 ...	SCSI command							
...31	block (CDB)							

Table 21.6 Types of SCSI SMS.

SMS name	SMS code	SSP code	Sender	Receiver
SCSI RESPONSE	82h	03h	Target	Initiator
SCSI COMMAND	82h	10h	Initiator	Target
SCSI STATUS	82h	11h	Target	Initiator
ABORT TAG	82h	30h	Initiator	Target
ABORT	82h	31h	Initiator	Target
CLEAR QUEUE	82h	32h	Initiator	Target
DEVICE RESET	82h	33h	Initiator	Target
CLEAR ACA CONDITION	82h	34h	Initiator	Target

22 The ASPI software interface

It is fortunate that SCSI-2 defines devices so precisely on the target side. The result is that a SCSI-2 host adapter works well with all SCSI-2 targets. However, what about the relationship between the host and the host adapter? Here the operating system must understand which SCSI commands to send to the target.

For host adapters that emulate a standard disk drive controller this is no problem. The host adapter receives drive commands like any PC disk drive controller and then translates the actions to appropriate SCSI commands. However, this hardly takes advantage of the full functionality of the SCSI bus. Here the controller is dedicated to the disk and cannot, for example, control a scanner or printer on the same bus.

There is much more involved in supporting a so-called transparent host adapter, one capable of sending arbitrary commands to any SCSI target device. There is a large number of such host adapters and each of them is designed differently; each must be supported differently by the operating system.

Help comes in the form of an additional software layer between the host adapter and the operating system or application. This software is delivered with hardware (since it is hardware specific) and provides a standardized software interface to the operating system. The result is that from the operating system's point of view all host adapters using this software interface look the same.

Here there are a number of examples of such an approach in the industry. The VMS operating system for DEC VAX machines uses the concept of class and port drivers. These are already integrated into the system so that the interplay of subsystems is clearly defined. In the PC domain two important software interfaces have emerged specifically for SCSI: the ANSI CAM (Common Access Method) specification and the ASPI interface from Adaptec, Inc.

At the moment ASPI drivers are easier to come by than CAM drivers. In fact, the SCSI monitor program (with source code) included with this book sits on top of ASPI. This application represents a good example of an ASPI implementation and it makes sense to give an overview of ASPI at this time. We will go into just enough detail to understand how ASPI is used in the SCSI monitor. The complete documentation for ASPI under DOS, Windows, OS/2, Novell and UNIX is available from Adaptec.

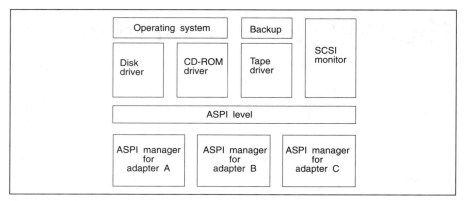

Figure 22.1   ASPI functional overview.

22.1   The concept of ASPI

ASPI stands for Advanced SCSI Programming Interface. Figure 22.1 depicts the functional layers of the interface. Different host adapters use different ASPI managers, and multiple managers can be installed simultaneously. The host software, whether device drivers or applications, talks to the SCSI bus through the ASPI interface. In this way the host software is isolated from the specific hardware details of a given host adapter.

In a DOS environment the ASPI manager is loaded at boot time by the system. Therefore, in order to use ASPI one must first obtain the entry point from DOS. When a call is made to ASPI using the entry point the address of a SCSI request block is put onto the stack. All the information necessary to carry out the SCSI procedure is contained in the request block. In the following section I show how this is done by way of short examples in Turbo Pascal (7.0).

22.2   SCSI request blocks

ASPI function calls

ASPI has a set of seven function calls, which are listed in Table 22.1. It is worth pointing out that no hard SCSI reset is included among these. This is certainly due

Table 22.1   ASPI function codes.

Code	Meaning
00h	HOST ADAPTER INQUIRY
01h	GET DEVICE TYPE
02h	EXECUTE SCSI COMMAND
03h	ABORT SCSI COMMAND
04h	RESET SCSI DEVICE
05h	SET HOST ADAPTER PARAMETERS
06h	GET DISK DRIVE INFORMATION

Table 22.2 ASPI status bytes.

Status	Description
00h	In progress
01h	OK
02h	SRB cancelled by host
04h	Error
80h	Invalid SRB
81h	Invalid host adapter
82h	SCSI target not found

to the fact that ASPI is capable of multi-tasking and allows many active SCSI processes to be active simultaneously. A SCSI reset would abort all of these processes in one fell swoop. On the other hand, a little experience with the SCSI monitor will show that an illegal command causes some host adapters to crash, and only a SCSI reset or system boot will correct this. The ASPI status bytes are shown in Table 22.2.

SCSI request block (SRB) fields either contain parameters to be set or they deliver information back and can only be read. In the SRBs depicted here the fields that contain information returned from ASPI have a gray background.

SRB header

An SRB always includes an 8-byte long header. Following the SRB come a certain number of parameter bytes, depending on the function. The SRB header is shown in Table 22.3:

- Function: One of the function codes given in Table 22.1.
- Status: This byte takes on the values given in Table 22.2.
- Host adapter: The ASPI number of the host adapter. This number is assigned by the ASPI manager. The first adapter is assigned zero.
- Flags: These flags are independent of the function.

HOST ADAPTER INQUIRY (00h)

This function call returns information on the installed host adapter (Table 22.4). The host adapter number must be provided to the call.

Table 22.3 Format of an SRB header.

	7	6	5	4	3	2	1	0
0	Function							
1	Status							
2	Host adapter							
3	Flags							
4 ... 7	Reserved							

Table 22.4   HOST ADAPTER INQUIRY.

	7	6	5	4	3	2	1	0
0	HOST ADAPTER INQUIRY (00h)							
1	Status							
2	Host adapter							
3	Reserved							
4 ... 7	Reserved							
8	Number of host adapters							
9	SCSI ID							
10 ... 25	SCSI manager name							
26 ... 41	Host adapter name							
42 ... 57	Host adapter specific							

The Host adapter ID field contains the SCSI ID of the host adapter. The Host adapter name and SCSI manager name fields are ASCII.

The function call GET DEVICE TYPE returns information on the SCSI device class. This can be accomplished using the INQUIRY command, so we skip it here.

EXECUTE SCSI COMMAND (02h)

This call is used to send an arbitrary SCSI command (Table 22.5). After the call the SRB status must be polled until a value other than zero appears. The Adaptec documentation describes an alternative to polling which uses a so-called POST routine. This is not recommended for application programs but is preferable for device drivers.

In byte 3 we are only concerned with the Direction bits. A value of 0 here means that the direction of the data transfer is determined by the SCSI command.

- Target ID: The SCSI ID of the target to receive the command.
- LUN: The LUN number sent in the IDENTIFY message.
- Data buffer length: The number of data bytes to be transferred.
- Sense data length: The number of bytes reserved for sense data at the end of this SRB. For the SCSI monitor this is set to 0 and the automatic requesting of sense data should be turned off at the host adapter.
- Data buffer: Segment and offset of the data buffer.
- SRB link pointer: Pointer to the next SRB in set of linked commands (its use should be avoided).
- SCSI command length: Length of SCSI command.
- Host adapter status: Here five status codes are defined.
  - 00h: OK
  - 11h: Target does not respond

Table 22.5   EXECUTE SCSI COMMAND.

	7	6	5	4	3	2	1	0
0	EXECUTE SCSI COMMAND (02h)							
1	Status							
2	Host adapter							
3	Reserved		Direction			Reserved	Link	Post
4 ... 7	Reserved							
8	Target ID							
9	LUN							
10 ... 13	Data buffer length							
14	Sense data length							
15 ... 16	Data buffer (offset)							
17 ... 18	Data buffer (segment)							
19 ... 20	SRB link pointer (offset)							
21 ...22	SRB link pointer (segment)							
23	SCSI command length							
24	Host adapter status							
25	Target status							
26 ... 27	POST routine (offset)							
28 ... 29	SRB routine (segment)							
30 ... 63	Reserved							
64...64+m	SCSI command							
64+m ... 64+m+n	Sense data							

- — 12h: Data overrun
- — 13h: Unexpected BUS FREE
- — 14h: Target bus phase error
- Target status: This is the byte returned during the SCSI status phase.
- SCSI command: The bytes of the SCSI command.
- Sense data: Reserved for sense data when the host adapter is set to automatically request sense.

ABORT SCSI COMMAND (03h)

This function call attempts to abort a SCSI command (Table 22.6). The call itself always returns with a GOOD status. Whether or not the command was actually aborted can be determined only by examining the status of the original SRB.

Table 22.6   ABORT SCSI COMMAND.

	7	6	5	4	3	2	1	0
0	ABORT SCSI COMMAND (03h)							
1	Status							
2	Host adapter							
3	Reserved							
4 ... 7	Reserved							
8 ... 9	SRB address (offset)							
10 ... 11	SRB address (segment)							

22.3   ASPI initialization and function calls

ASPI initialization

In order to call ASPI the entry point must be known. This is achieved using DOS interrupt 21h, as shown in the following program sample. First ASPI is opened and the entry point is determined; afterwards ASPI is closed.

ASPI open

```
function FileOpen(FileName:string):integer;

const DOS_OPEN_FILE = $3D;

var register: registers;

begin
 FileName:=FileName+chr(0);
 with register
 do
  begin
   ax := DOS_OPEN_FILE shl 8;
   bx:=0;
   cx:=0;
   ds := seg(FileName);
   dx := ofs(FileName)+1; { because Pascal strings
                            carry their length in byte 0 }
  end;
  MSDOS(register);
  if (register.flags and FCarry) 0
  then FileOpen:=-1
  else FileOpen:=register.ax;
end;
```

ASPI entry point

```
procedure GetASPIEntry(FileHandle:integer; var
AspiEntry:MemAdress);

const   ASPI_ENTRY_LENGTH = 4;
        DOS_IOCTL_READ  = $4402;

var register: registers;

begin
 with register
 do
  begin
   ax := DOS_IOCTL_READ;
   bx := FileHandle;
   cx := ASPI_ENTRY_LENGTH;
   ds := seg(AspiEntry);
   dx := ofs(AspiEntry);
  end;
  MSDOS(register);
end;
```

ASPI close

```
function FileClose(FileHandle:integer):integer;

const DOS_CLOSE_FILE = $3E;

var register: registers;

begin
 with register
 do
  begin
   ax := DOS_CLOSE_FILE shl 8;
   bx:=FileHandle;
  end;
  MSDOS(register);
  if (register.flags and FCarry) = 0
  then FileClose:=0
  else FileClose:=register.ax;
end;
```

And all together ...

```
function InitializeASPI(var
AspiEntrypoint:MemAdress):boolean;
```

```
const ASPI_NAME = 'SCSIMGR$';

var result: integer;
  AspiFileHandle: integer; begin
 AspiFileHandle:=FileOpen(ASPI_NAME);
 if AspiFileHandle-1
 then
  begin
   GetASPIEntry(AspiFileHandle,AspiEntryPoint);
   FileClose(AspiFileHandle);
   InitializeASPI:=true;
  end
 else   InitializeASPI:=false;
end;
```

Calling ASPI

The following function calls ASPI to execute an SRB. The variable AspiEntryPoint
is a global variable of the main program:

```
procedure SRBexecute(var SRB: SRBarray);
var SRBsegment, SRBoffset: integer;

begin
 SRBsegment:=seg(SRB);
 SRBoffset:=ofs(SRB);

 asm
 mov ax, SRBsegment
 push ax
 mov ax, SRBoffset
 push ax
 LEA BX, AspiEntryPoint
 call DWORD PTR [bx]
 add sp,4
 end;
end;
```

Afterwards the SRB status must be polled until it changes from 0 to another value:

```
Procedure HostInquire;

const
 SRB_STATUS      = $01;
 HA_SCSI_ID      = $09;
 ENTRY_LENGTH    = $10;
 MANAGER_NAME    = $0A;
 HA_NAME         = $1A;
```

```
var k: integer;
  Status: byte;
  SRB: SRBarray;
  DataBuffer  : DataBufferType;

begin
 for k:=0 to high(SRB) do SRB[k]:=0;

{What is the result of this ASPI call?
Right! HOST ADAPTER INQUIRY Host adapter number 0}

 SRBexecute(SRB);
 repeat until SRB[SRB_STATUS]0;
 if SRB[SRB_STATUS] = 1
 then
   begin
    writeln('Host Adapter SCSI ID:
         ',SRB[HA_SCSI_ID]);
    write ('Name of Host Adapter: ');
    for k:=0 to ENTRY_LENGTH-1 do
    write(char(SRB[HA_NAME+k]));
    writeln;
   end
 else writeln('SRB Execution Error!');
end;
```

In Appendix E and on the accompanying diskette you will find the source code to
SCANSCSI.PAS. The program is relatively easy to follow and provides a good
example using an ASPI interface call to execute a SCSI command.

23 The SCSI monitor program

Accompanying this book is a diskette containing a SCSI monitor program. This program allows you to send arbitrary SCSI commands to a SCSI device, including the sending and receiving of data. For users without the necessary SCSI host adapter the program includes a target simulator so that a bit of experimentation is still possible.

The program runs on an IBM PC compatible computer with at least 512 Kbytes of memory running DOS 3.3 or later. A hard disk is not required. Also necessary is a SCSI host adapter and ASPI (developed by Adaptec) manager software supporting the host adapter. It is also possible to integrate the driver software into the program itself. The hooks for this are included in the source code.

A list of tested host adapters is contained in the README.DOC file of the diskette. Please take note that Adaptec host adapters can be configured to send a REQUEST SENSE automatically upon a CHECK CONDITION status. This is not desirable for use with a monitor program since here the user wants to be in full control of the sequence of commands. This feature can be disabled by a switch or jumper on the host adapter board.

Warning

This program gives no warning or feedback concerning the outcome of SCSI commands on a target. It allows you to give any and all SCSI commands regardless of their effect. Be extremely careful when sending commands to a disk drive containing important information. A seemingly innocent write command could destroy valuable data.

The program is useful for familiarizing yourself with the many details of SCSI protocol and commands. In order to avoid undesired results reserve the test target using the RESERVE UNIT command.

And a bit of advice: if you aren't exactly sure what something will do, don't do it!

Program design

The SCSI monitor program is written in Borland Pascal 7.0. You should also be able to compile it using Turbo Pascal 7.0. It will definitely not run unmodified with Turbo

Pascal versions 6.0, 4.0 and earlier. In order to make the program easier to port to other systems it is written in standard Pascal. I have not made use of any special features unique to Turbo Pascal. However, a minimal amount of machine specific assembler code has been incorporated.

The user interface is simple but at first perhaps a little cryptic. After some practice, however, it is quick and easy to work with. Be careful not to confuse commands for the monitor program with SCSI commands.

The monitor program makes use of 10 command buffers and 10 data buffers for holding SCSI commands and SCSI data. Each data buffer is 4 Kbytes long. A command buffer has room for 12 command bytes as well as a status byte, a byte for the SCSI ID, a byte for the LUN, a byte for the command length, and finally a byte indicating the next command buffer to be used. Both the command and data buffers are numbered, respectively, from 0 to 9.

The current command and data buffer are displayed on the screen. The command buffer and data buffer are completely independent of each other. For example, command buffer 3 can be used with the data in data buffer 0.

The display

Figure 23.1 shows the display of the SCSI monitor. All values are in hexadecimal. At the top of the display you see the current command buffer along with ID, LUN, and status. Below this the current data buffer is shown in hexadecimal. To the right are the corresponding ASCII characters, which is useful for interpreting the data from commands such as INQUIRY. A value of 40h is added to control characters below 20h and displayed in inverse video.

```
SCSI Monitor V1.0 rev 024 11.3.93 (fs)
                                                   Id Lu St 1N nX
SCSI command  00: 00 00 00 00 00 00 00 00 00 00 00 00   00 00 ?? 00 FF
SCSI data buffer Nr. 00:

0000: 00 00 00 00 00 00 00 00 00 00 00 00 00 00 00 00
0010: 00 00 00 00 00 00 00 00 00 00 00 00 00 00 00 00
0020: 00 00 00 00 00 00 00 00 00 00 00 00 00 00 00 00
0030: 00 00 00 00 00 00 00 00 00 00 00 00 00 00 00 00
0040: 00 00 00 00 00 00 00 00 00 00 00 00 00 00 00 00
0050: 00 00 00 00 00 00 00 00 00 00 00 00 00 00 00 00
0060: 00 00 00 00 00 00 00 00 00 00 00 00 00 00 00 00
0070: 00 00 00 00 00 00 00 00 00 00 00 00 00 00 00 00
0080: 00 00 00 00 00 00 00 00 00 00 00 00 00 00 00 00
0090: 00 00 00 00 00 00 00 00 00 00 00 00 00 00 00 00
00A0: 00 00 00 00 00 00 00 00 00 00 00 00 00 00 00 00
00B0: 00 00 00 00 00 00 00 00 00 00 00 00 00 00 00 00
00C0: 00 00 00 00 00 00 00 00 00 00 00 00 00 00 00 00
00D0: 00 00 00 00 00 00 00 00 00 00 00 00 00 00 00 00
00E0: 00 00 00 00 00 00 00 00 00 00 00 00 00 00 00 00
00F0: 00 00 00 00 00 00 00 00 00 00 00 00 00 00 00 00

Command: H
Commands: Data, End, Go, Help, Id, Command, Lun, leNgth, dRiver
```

Figure 23.1   SCSI monitor with help information.

The command buffer

- Command nn: The current command buffer.
- Id (SCSI ID): The ID of the device to receive the command.
- Lu: LUN to which the command pertains.
- St: SCSI status of the last executed command. This value remains unchanged until another command is executed. Even if the command buffer, the LUN, or the SCSI ID is edited the status remains unchanged.

  Three special symbols are displayed in this field:

  ??   No command has been executed from this buffer.

  **   SCSI command is now being executed.

  ––   The target does not reply.
- lN: Length of the command. If this value is zero then the default command length defined for SCSI-2 command groups is used. Otherwise no command is sent. The behavior depends on the hardware employed (see README.DOC).
- nX: Next command buffer to be used when this command has completed.

Monitor commands

C (Command)

Syntax: C<Number>,<Offset>,<Count> <Byte1> <Byte2> ...

- Number: Number of the command buffer. The current command buffer changes to display this buffer. Default: the current buffer.
- Offset: Byte position in the buffer where the command should be placed. Default: 00h.
- Count: When this parameter is included then only one command byte can be given. This single command byte is then copied into the buffer 'Count' times. Default: 00h.
- Byte1 ... ByteN: The command bytes.

Examples

        C1 12 00 00 00 FF

This example writes '12 00 00 00 FF' starting at byte 0 into command buffer 1 and makes this the current command buffer.

        C3

This command makes command buffer 3 the current command buffer.

        C,3 AA

This command writes AAh into byte 3 of the current command buffer.

        C,,A 0

This command fills the current command buffer with zeros.

I (ID)

Syntax: I <ID>

- ID: The ID for the current command buffer is changed to this value.

L (LUN)

Syntax: L <LUN>

- LUN: The LUN for the current command buffer is changed to this value.

N (leNgth)

Syntax: N <Value>

- Value: The command length for the current command buffer is changed to this value.

X (neXt)

Syntax: X <CommandBuffer>

- CommandBuffer: The number of the command buffer, which should be executed automatically after the execution of the current command. The value FFh means that no command is to be executed afterwards. Looping on the current command buffer is allowed.

D (Data)

Syntax: D<Number>,<Offset>,<Count> <Byte1> <Byte2> …

This command, along with its arguments, works completely analogously to the 'C' command. It allows modification of the data buffer.

G (Go)

Syntax: G

This command starts the execution of the SCSI command in the current command buffer. When necessary the current data buffer is employed. During the execution time of the command the status will display '**'. The execution of a string of commands linked using the nX field can be aborted by hitting any key.

H or ? (Help)

Syntax: H

This causes a short command overview to be displayed.

R (dRiver)

Syntax: R <Driver>

- Driver: A for the ASPI driver or S for the target simulator. The target simulator emulates a target at ID 0, LUN 0. The target simulator is capable of executing TEST UNIT READY, INQUIRY and REQUEST SENSE.

Q (Quit)

Syntax: Q

Quit the program.

Getting started

Insure that the SCSI monitor is working by sending an INQUIRY command. INQUIRY will return a GOOD status even if an invalid LUN is addressed or if the target is in UNIT ATTENTION.

I assume here that a host adapter has been installed and that the ASPI manager has been successfully loaded. Connect a SCSI target device with ID 0 to the bus. You can easily determine whether your device is recognizable to the host adapter using the program SCANSCSI.EXE, which is also on the diskette.

Afterwards run the SCSI monitor and enter the following command:

Command: C 12 0 0 0 FF

You should now see this command in the current command buffer. The ID and LUN should both be zero, the default settings, which need not be modified. The status '??' indicates that a command has yet to be executed.

Now enter:

Command: G

Now a 00h should be seen in the status field. Furthermore, data returned from the target should now occupy the current data buffer. You should see the product name written to the right of the buffer in ASCII.

If status is '– –' then SCSI ID 0 did not reply. In general this means that the device was not properly installed.

Examples

When working with the SCSI monitor bear in mind that it is possible to send any arbitrary SCSI command, whether valid or not. Therefore, always check the status field after sending a command to see whether it has been successfully executed.

```
SCSI Monitor V1.0 rev 024 11.3.93 (fs)                     ID Lu St 1N nX
                                                           03 00 02 00 FF
SCSI command  00: 00 00 00 00 00 00 00 00 00 00 00 00

SCSI data buffer No. 00:

0000: 00 00 00 00 00 00 00 00 00 00 00 00 00 00 00 00
0010: 00 00 00 00 00 00 00 00 00 00 00 00 00 00 00 00
0020: 00 00 00 00 00 00 00 00 00 00 00 00 00 00 00 00
0030: 00 00 00 00 00 00 00 00 00 00 00 00 00 00 00 00
0040: 00 00 00 00 00 00 00 00 00 00 00 00 00 00 00 00
0050: 00 00 00 00 00 00 00 00 00 00 00 00 00 00 00 00
0060: 00 00 00 00 00 00 00 00 00 00 00 00 00 00 00 00
0070: 00 00 00 00 00 00 00 00 00 00 00 00 00 00 00 00
0080: 00 00 00 00 00 00 00 00 00 00 00 00 00 00 00 00
0090: 00 00 00 00 00 00 00 00 00 00 00 00 00 00 00 00
00A0: 00 00 00 00 00 00 00 00 00 00 00 00 00 00 00 00
00B0: 00 00 00 00 00 00 00 00 00 00 00 00 00 00 00 00
00C0: 00 00 00 00 00 00 00 00 00 00 00 00 00 00 00 00
00D0: 00 00 00 00 00 00 00 00 00 00 00 00 00 00 00 00
00E0: 00 00 00 00 00 00 00 00 00 00 00 00 00 00 00 00
00F0: 00 00 00 00 00 00 00 00 00 00 00 00 00 00 00 00

Command: G
```

Figure 23.2 SCSI monitor after TEST UNIT READY.

```
SCSI Monitor V1.0 rev 024 11.3.93 (fs)
                                                           Id Lu St 1N nX
SCSI command  00: 03 00 00 00 FF 00 00 00 00 00 00 00      03 00 02 00 FF

SCSI data buffer No. 00:

0000: 00 00 00 00 00 00 00 00 00 00 00 00 00 00 00 00
0010: 00 00 00 00 00 00 00 00 00 00 00 00 00 00 00 00
0020: 00 00 00 00 00 00 00 00 00 00 00 00 00 00 00 00
0030: 00 00 00 00 00 00 00 00 00 00 00 00 00 00 00 00
0040: 00 00 00 00 00 00 00 00 00 00 00 00 00 00 00 00
0050: 00 00 00 00 00 00 00 00 00 00 00 00 00 00 00 00
0060: 00 00 00 00 00 00 00 00 00 00 00 00 00 00 00 00
0070: 00 00 00 00 00 00 00 00 00 00 00 00 00 00 00 00
0080: 00 00 00 00 00 00 00 00 00 00 00 00 00 00 00 00
0090: 00 00 00 00 00 00 00 00 00 00 00 00 00 00 00 00
00A0: 00 00 00 00 00 00 00 00 00 00 00 00 00 00 00 00
00B0: 00 00 00 00 00 00 00 00 00 00 00 00 00 00 00 00
00C0: 00 00 00 00 00 00 00 00 00 00 00 00 00 00 00 00
00D0: 00 00 00 00 00 00 00 00 00 00 00 00 00 00 00 00
00E0: 00 00 00 00 00 00 00 00 00 00 00 00 00 00 00 00
00F0: 00 00 00 00 00 00 00 00 00 00 00 00 00 00 00 00

Command: K 3 0 0 FF
```

Figure 23.3　How REQUEST SENSE is set up.

The first example in Figure 23.2 shows a CHECK CONDITION status (02h) after a TEST UNIT READY command. Why was this status returned? To answer this question, the command REQUEST SENSE is set up in the command buffer. This is shown in Figure 23.3.

Finally, the example in Figure 23.4 shows the results of the REQUEST SENSE command. The error code is 70h, indicating that the error pertains to the last executed command. The sense key is 02h (NOT READY). The sense code 29h means POWER-ON OR RESET. This is just what is expected from a LUN receiving its first command after power-up.

In order to observe this with my configuration I had to turn the SCSI target off and on after the system had already booted. In this way I prevented the host adapter from clearing the UNIT ATTENTION when it scans the bus at boot time.

```
SCSI Monitor V1.0 rev 024 11.3.93 (fs)
                                                           ID Lu St 1N nX
SCSI command  00: 03 00 00 00 FF 00 00 00 00 00 00 00      03 00 00 00 FF

SCSI data buffer No. 00:

0000: 70 00 02 00 00 00 00 0B 00 00 00 00 29 00 00 00   p
0010: 00 00 00 00 00 00 00 00 00 00 00 00 00 00 00 00
0020: 00 00 00 00 00 00 00 00 00 00 00 00 00 00 00 00
0030: 00 00 00 00 00 00 00 00 00 00 00 00 00 00 00 00
0040: 00 00 00 00 00 00 00 00 00 00 00 00 00 00 00 00
0050: 00 00 00 00 00 00 00 00 00 00 00 00 00 00 00 00
0060: 00 00 00 00 00 00 00 00 00 00 00 00 00 00 00 00
0070: 00 00 00 00 00 00 00 00 00 00 00 00 00 00 00 00
0080: 00 00 00 00 00 00 00 00 00 00 00 00 00 00 00 00
0090: 00 00 00 00 00 00 00 00 00 00 00 00 00 00 00 00
00A0: 00 00 00 00 00 00 00 00 00 00 00 00 00 00 00 00
00B0: 00 00 00 00 00 00 00 00 00 00 00 00 00 00 00 00
00C0: 00 00 00 00 00 00 00 00 00 00 00 00 00 00 00 00
00D0: 00 00 00 00 00 00 00 00 00 00 00 00 00 00 00 00
00E0: 00 00 00 00 00 00 00 00 00 00 00 00 00 00 00 00
00F0: 00 00 00 00 00 00 00 00 00 00 00 00 00 00 00 00

Command: G
```

Figure 23.4　Results of the REQUEST SENSE command.

24 Measuring and testing

Two components are needed in order to test SCSI targets practically: a SCSI emulator capable of sending arbitrary SCSI commands, and a logic analyzer with which one can monitor the happenings on the SCSI bus. For testing initiators the same setup is needed except that the emulator must be capable of emulating a target.

24.1 SCSI analyzers

A SCSI analyzer permits the logging of SCSI bus activity and displaying it in a variety of formats. The most basic form of representation is the timing diagram. Such diagrams have been presented throughout this book in schematic form. Here we will see diagrams generated from an actual piece of measurement equipment (Figure 24.1).

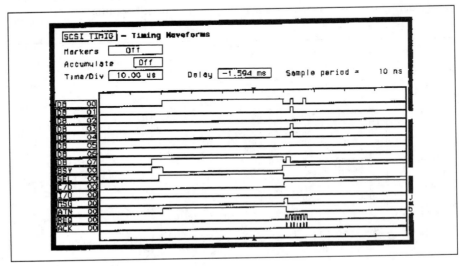

Figure 24.1 SCSI timing diagram.

Timing diagrams

Timing diagrams of the SCSI bus can, in principle, be made using any logic analyzer. However, the device should have a time resolution of at least 10 ns (that is, 100 MHz). For Fast SCSI this resolution is almost too low. The Fast hold time, the minimal time between the activation of REQ or ACK and the changing of the data lines, is defined to be 10 ns. If I were trying to track down Fast synchronous data transfer problems I would prefer the successor model with a resolution down to 1 ns.

If there are problems with phase sequencing on the SCSI bus there is no way to avoid the need for a timing analysis. Fortunately such problems have become very rare now that bus timing is controlled by protocol chips. Nevertheless, the potential for bus timing problems will always exist, no matter how reliable the protocol chips are.

Another application of a timing diagram is to gain an overview of longer time intervals. For example, how long does a target need from arbitration to the MESSAGE OUT phase? Here, there may be a world of difference in the behavior of different SCSI devices. Alternatively, how long are the gaps between bursts for fast synchronous transfers? Does a device disconnect from the bus and how long does it take to do so? All of these questions can be answered using the timing diagram.

Bus phase list

Another important representation of bus activity is in the form of a list of bus phases. Here the individual bus phases are listed one after another, usually stamped with a time mark. This representation is especially helpful for software development. Did the host adapter really send the command it was supposed to send? Why was nothing returned? Did the target answer? Was the correct LUN addressed in the MESSAGE OUT phase?

A number of logic analyzers equipped with a SCSI disassembler are capable of delivering a list of bus phases. However, most of these have very small buffers, holding 1 Kbyte or less. Here it becomes extremely important to trigger on an event close enough to the activity of interest, otherwise it will pass through and out of the shallow buffer.

Better still are a number of dedicated SCSI analyzers offered by various manufacturers. Although they may lack timing diagram capabilities, they possess buffers for the bus phase lists of 32 Kbytes and larger.

24.2   SCSI emulators

The SCSI monitor program

The SCSI monitor included with this book is an easy to use program (without rival as far as price is concerned) which allows arbitrary SCSI commands to be sent to any target on the SCSI bus. Although it is really intended as an educational device for the SCSI bus it can also be used for simple evaluation testing of SCSI peripherals.

With a little practice you can modify the MODE parameters and format a disk drive. Such tasks are a little cumbersome without the ability to execute a series of preprogrammed commands. The source code of the monitor is included on the diskette, so it is easy to modify and extend the original program (but note that this is not allowed for commercial purposes).

Commercial solutions

Commercial SCSI emulators have more flexibility. For example, these are often capable of generating SCSI bus errors and other conflicts that are extremely useful for evaluating SCSI devices. Moreover, they allow lengthy test sequences to be programmed and run, and often come delivered with tests designed for various devices. Target emulation is also possible with some equipment. This makes it possible to put initiators through tests that might be impossible using actual target devices. How do you get a normal target to return more data than was requested? A target emulator is designed to do just that.

24.3   Examples from industry

The intent here is not to give a comprehensive overview of products but rather a feeling for the variety of devices by way of a few examples.

Logic analyzers

Among the classic logic analyzers are the HP 1630 and HP 1650 machines. A SCSI bus adapter, the HP 10343B, is available for both of these. The adapter makes connecting to both single-ended and differential buses very simple. Wide SCSI support, however, is lacking. The adapter comes with SCSI disassembler software, which enables the analyzer to display output in the form of a bus phase list. The analyzer is capable of resolution down to 10 ns which is more than adequate for most situations. The only weak point is the very small event buffer of 512 bytes. The timing diagrams and bus phase lists in this book were generated using the HP 1650B together with the HP 10343B.

The successor to this product is the HP 16500 logic analyzer family. This device is capable of measuring down to 1 ns. The event buffer size has been increased to 16 Kbytes. There is also an HP E2423A SCSI preprocessor available. This adapter, like the HP 10343B, allows access to single-ended and differential SCSI buses. In addition, Wide SCSI is supported.

SCSI analyzers

Adaptec builds an entire family of SCSI analyzers (see Figure 24.2). These are all implemented as PC boards with associated software. The SDS-310 is designed for transfer rates up to 5 Mbytes per second (50 ns resolution) and 8-bit SCSI. The SDS-310F supports fast synchronous transfers (20 ns resolution) and 16-bit SCSI as

```
55.619_293_720  Bus_free                                       00032
56.611_335_080      Arb_win             7                      00034
56.612_463_240                          (Atn Assertion)     A  00035
56.612_886_480          Sel_start       5 7                 A  00036
56.612_899_440          Sel_end                             A  00037
56.614_185_340              Msg_out     C0 01 03 01 32          00038
56.615_214_460                          (Atn Deasset)          00039
56.615_227_600          Msg_out         07                     00040
56.615_459_880          Msg_in          01 03 01 3E 07          00041
56.623_041_840              Command     00 00 00 00 00 00       00042
56.623_470_080              Status      00                      00043
56.623_896_700          Msg_in          00                      00044
56.624_697_760  Bus_free                                       00045
62.382_979_060      Arb_start                           7      00046
62.382_981_460      Arb_win             7                      00047
62.384_108_860                          (Atn Assertion)     A  00048
62.384_530_060          Sel_start       5 7                 A  00049
62.384_543_260          Sel_end                             A  00050
62.385_669_740                          (Atn Deassert)         00051
```

Figure 24.2   Bus phase list of Adaptec analyzer.

well. Both devices have a 32 Kbyte buffer. A special adapter is required for differential buses.

I-Tech is a company that specializes in SCSI test systems. It makes the IPC-6500, an analyzer with 20 ns resolution for Fast and Wide SCSI. This device comes with a 64 Kbyte buffer and is capable of timing diagram as well as phase list output. I-Tech also makes SCSI emulators and pocket testers. The latter use LEDs and are useful for diagnosing bus problems, such as a differential device connected to a single-ended bus.

SCSI emulators

Ancot is another important name in the area of SCSI test systems. The INI-350 is a SCSI initiator capable of generating controlled errors. The device is able to test SCSI targets by putting them through strange phase sequences. It is important for a target to be able to recover from improper sequences and, above all, not to lock up the bus. For these reasons the INI-350 is valuable in the design verification process. Of course, it is also fully capable of normal operation and serves well as a SCSI compliant initiator. Ancot also offers the usual assortment of test equipment, with an emphasis on standalone devices.

SCSI development systems

The SDS-3F family of test equipment is ideal for testing the entire range of SCSI options including fast synchronous and 16-bit wide transfers. These products represent an integrated development system complete with SCSI analyzer and emulator. The analyzer component has a configurable event buffer of up to 256 Kbytes. Its time resolution, however, is only good down to 20 ns. Various configurations of the emulator are capable of playing both initiator and target roles.

Adaptec has also announced the SDS-5 series of equipment. Among the improvements are an event buffer of 2 Mbytes and resolution down to 10 ns.

Summary

If you are mainly interested in occasionally testing SCSI targets for overall functionality then the SCSI monitor should be more than adequate for you.

If, on the other hand, you really need to know what is happening on the SCSI bus then there is no way to avoid investing in either a logic analyzer or a dedicated SCSI analyzer. In general, logic analyzers have better time resolution than dedicated SCSI analyzers, but the latter are less expensive and have larger event buffers.

In most circumstances the combination of a powerful SCSI emulator together with a SCSI analyzer should suffice for the testing and evaluation of SCSI targets.

For professional design work an extensive SCSI development system is an invaluable tool, especially for work on initiators. What is more, targets supporting tagged queues are almost impossible to test without the aid of such a system.

25 SCSI chips

The development of SCSI followed closely the development of the SCSI protocol chips. Without an inexpensive, fast implementation of the bus interface SCSI would never have captured the market in the way it has. In this chapter I introduce three VLSI protocol chips which have helped to make this possible. In general, each of them is suited to a different application.

Chip characteristics

When choosing a protocol chip a number of criteria must be taken into consideration.

Initiator or target?

Most protocol chips are capable of playing either the initiator or the target role. Nevertheless, some chips are better suited to one application or the other. In particular, there are chips for host adapters that require no additional logic for use with the ISA bus. In addition, these chips have a lot of SCSI overhead built in.

SCSI features

By SCSI features I mean, above all, the support of (fast) synchronous transfers as well as Wide SCSI. Here the maximum REQ/ACK offset is of interest. For Wide SCSI, if the second 8-bit data path is not implemented on the chip then there should at least be provision for the REQB/ACKB signals of the B cable.

SCSI bus drivers

Whether or not SCSI line drivers are integrated into the chip represents an important cost consideration. Chips with integrated single-ended drivers are the norm, but they should also provide the control signals for additional differential circuitry.

CPU interface

The CPU interface is key to smooth integration of the SCSI chip into the device design. A SCSI chip designed for an Intel 286 microprocessor will not only require extra 'glue' logic to make it work with a Motorola 68000, but it will also work less efficiently. Since this information is sometimes lacking in the chip's data sheets, you should ask the manufacturer.

Host bus interface

Recently, more and more chips are entering the market that come with an integrated host bus interface, for example for the PCI bus. Often the same chip kernel is available with different host bus or CPU interfaces.

Architecture

The architecture of a chip includes various aspects of the hardware, including the data path width, and the number and kinds of registers. Another important point is to what extent the firmware of the SCSI device must intervene in the SCSI bus protocol. Ideally, the firmware should be responsible for setting up transfers, and the rest should be handled by the chip. With respect to this area, there are chips that cover the entire spectrum, beginning with those that need to be led by the firmware through every single bus phase.

Another important architecture issue is the presence of a buffer for SCSI transfers. The larger the buffer is on the chip, the more time the firmware has to react without slowing overall performance.

25.1   The NCR 5385

The NCR 5385 was the original single chip SCSI controller. Over the years it was succeeded by the 5385E and then the 5386. All three versions have fundamentally the same design. You would be hard pressed to find a 5385 in a newly developed product. The NCR chip business has since passed into the hands of the new Symbios Logic corporation which produces chips with latest state-of-the-art technology. Nevertheless, here we take a quick look at the very first NCR chip, in order to gain a perspective for the later generations.

The 5385 is equally suited to target and initiator applications. It supports exclusively asynchronous transfers with a maximum transfer rate of approximately 2 Mbytes per second. The 5385 even needs external SCSI line drivers. Additional logic is necessary for differential drivers as well.

Table 25.1   NCR 5385 registers.

Address	Type	Register
0h	R/W	Data register
1h	R/W	Command register
2h	R/W	Control register
3h	R/W	Target ID
4h	R	Extra status
5h	R	ID register
6h	R	Interrupt register
7h	R	Source ID
9h	R	Diagnostic status
Ch	R/W	(MSB)
Dh	R/W	Transfer counter
Eh	R/W	(LSB)

The 14 registers of the 5385 (Table 25.1) are selected using four address lines. It is up to the hardware designer whether to map the registers to the memory or I/O space of the processor.

The 5385 is not capable of linking together complex SCSI phase sequences. What is more, every phase change must be controlled by the firmware. Here the chip occupies three states: DISCONNECTED, INITIATOR, and TARGET. In each state only certain commands are possible. This keeps the firmware from initiating invalid bus phases. For example, the command RESELECT is only possible in the DISCONNECT state.

25.2   PC host adapters: FUTURE DOMAIN TMC-950

The TMC-950 is an example of a single chip SCSI host adapter (Figure 25.1). No additional components are necessary to build an ISA to SCSI adapter; only if you wish to integrate a BIOS will an EPROM and decode circuitry be required. This solution is seen on a number of low cost host adapters from the Far East. Because of its popularity we take a closer look now at the workings of the TMC-950. The chip on the Seagate ST01 and ST02 host adapters has a different name but is identical.

The chip comes in a JEDEC 68-pin PLCC package. It incorporates both single-ended SCSI drivers and an ISA bus interface. It supports only the initiator role and cannot be used for target applications. Only asynchronous SCSI transfers are possible, and this at a maximum rate of 2 Mbytes per second. Although such features put the chip at the lower end of the performance spectrum, its low cost and simplicity make it very attractive in many applications. It lends itself well to a system where access to a CD-ROM and perhaps a SCSI tape drive is necessary but speed is not crucial. If, on the other hand, access to a number of fast disk drives is called for, the TMC-950 is not recommended.

Programming the chip is very simple. For example, to cause the chip to arbitrate involves the sending of a single command. Afterwards one merely waits until the chip responds that it has succeeded.

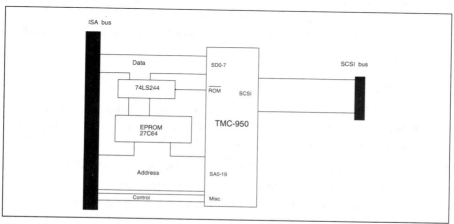

Figure 25.1   Three-chip PC host adaptor using TMC-950.

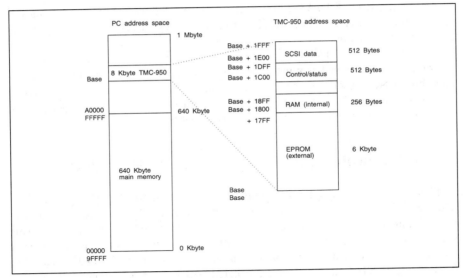

Figure 25.2   Address space of TMC-950.

Hardware model

The model of the TMC-950 is unusual and differs from those chips designed primarily for target applications (Figure 25.2). From the host's perspective the chip is an 8 Kbyte window in memory above the 640 Kbyte boundary. Four base addresses can be selected, the default of which is CA000h. The lower 6 Kbytes address the external ROM. The ROM holds disk BIOS routines. Above this at base+1800h comes 256 bytes of internal RAM. This is used to store BIOS variables and flags. The area from base+1C00h to base+1DFFh is the control/status register, regardless of which of the 512 bytes is addressed. The same is true for the area from base+1E00h to base+1FFFh, which addresses the SCSI data register. For the Seagate ST01 and ST02 the control/status register lies in memory between base+1A00h and base+1BFFh, and the SCSI data register lies between base+1C00h and base+1FFFh.

When read, the control/status register returns status information; when written, control bits are set or cleared (Table 25.2).

The control register

The bits RST, SEL, BSY and ATN activate the corresponding signals on the SCSI bus. It is the responsibility of the software to assure a proper sequence of bus phases. This allows for the generation of invalid phases in order to test the response of a target.

- Arb (start arbitration): When this bit is set the chip will begin arbitration.

- Par (SCSI parity enable): Turns on the generation of the SCSI parity bit.

- ISel: When this bit is set the chip will generate an interrupt when the SEL signal goes active.

Table 25.2   The control and status registers of the TMC-950.

Control register

7	6	5	4	3	2	1	0
Dri	ISel	Par	Arb	ATN	BSY	SEL	RST

Status register

7	6	5	4	3	2	1	0
ArbC	Par	SEL	RnA	C/D	I/O	MSG	BSY

- Dri (SCSI bus drivers enable): The SCSI line drivers of the TMC-950 are only enabled during arbitration or when this bit is set along with an active I/O signal.

The status register

The bits BSY, MSG, I/O, C/D and SEL reflect the state of the corresponding signals of the SCSI bus (Table 25.2).

- RnA (request and not acknowledge): This bit is set as long as REQ but not ACK is active. This is the precise moment when the data register must be written or read.
- Par: This bit is set when a SCSI parity error occurs.
- ArbC: This bit is set when the chip wins arbitration.

The SCSI data register

The SCSI data register is used to exchange data with the SCSI bus. By program control the signals I/O and REQ are monitored through the status register. As soon as REQ is active the value of I/O determines whether a read or a write is performed. Afterwards the chip activates the ACK signal.

Summary

The TMC-950 is a chip designed exclusively for use in PC host adapters. No additional components are necessary for integration in an ISA system. On the SCSI side the chip supports only asynchronous transfers. Single-ended SCSI drivers are incorporated in the chip. To a certain extent SCSI bus phases are handled by the chip autonomously. The lack of a data buffer for SCSI data transfers results in a slower transfer rate.

25.3   PCI bus to Fast-20: Symbios Logic SYM53C860

Symbios Logic was excorporated from NCR and has taken over the entire chips business of NCR. The SYM53C860 is a particularly advanced chip of the 53C8xx family. It has an 8-bit wide single-ended SCSI interface which besides asynchronous

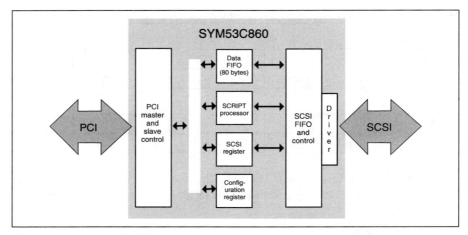

Figure 25.3   SYM53C860 block diagram.

and synchronous SCSI also supports Fast-20, that is synchronous transfer with up to 20 Mbytes/sec. The chip has a complete PCI interface as its system interface (Figure 25.3). The SYM53C860 can be programmed in two different ways. On the one hand, it contains a processor which interprets a special script language. For these scripts there is a complete development package which even contains ASPI and CAM drivers. On the other hand, as with first-generation chips, each SCSI signal can be accessed at register level. Thus, if you want to build a simple SCSI analyzer or tester yourself, the 53C860 is a possible candidate.

SCRIPTS

In first-generation SCSI chips, a microprocessor or the host CPU must control and monitor each individual bus phase. This results in a massive workload for the

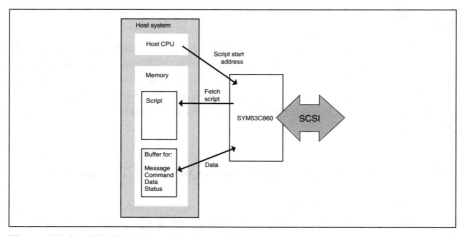

Figure 25.4   SCRIPTS functional overview.

```
;   Excerpt from: 8xxtarg.ss    Revision 2.0  10/31/95
;   available from Symbios Logic: ftp.symbios.com

;ABSOLUTE DECLARATIONS
ABSOLUTE non_handled_msg              = 0x06
ABSOLUTE bad_extended_msg             = 0x07

TABLE table_indirect \
    msg_out_buf = 1{??}, \
    cmd_buf = 12{??}, \

; ENTRY declarations
ENTRY msg_out_phase

msg_out_phase:
    return, if not atn ;return if atn gone
    move from msg_out_buf, with msg_out ;get message byte
    jump rel(extended_msg), if 0x01 ;jump if extended message
    jump rel(abort), if 0x06 ;jump if abort message
    jump rel(msg_out_phase), if 0x08    ;jump back if nop message
    int non_handled_msg ;interrupt if can<@146>t handle message

abort:
    move 0x20 to scntl1 ;turns off the halt on parity error or atn
    disconnect ;go to bus free
    int command_aborted ;int to notify driver that command was aborted
```

Figure 25.5 Sample SCRIPTS program.

processor and, if there is insufficient computing power, in a slow SCSI transfer. Modern chips reduce this workload by processing parts of SCSI sequences without the aid of the external processor.

The Symbios Logic chips go one step further. They contain their own RISC processor which executes instructions of the script language SCRIPTS which is specially targeted toward SCSI (Figure 25.4). The SCRIPTS processor itself fetches the instructions via DMA from main memory. Ready-made scripts for initiator and target applications are available as a development package from the chip manufacturer. The scripts themselves can be exchanged among the various chips of Symbios Logic.

SCRIPTS programs look like assembler programs (Figure 25.5). Also the programming technique is much the same and consists of creating data structure tables and writing routines for different initiator or target states. The different routines are accessed by jumps or by interrupts. Programmers familiar with any assembler should not have any difficulties with SCRIPTS.

Appendix A
SCSI-2 commands (by opcode)

Key:

M   Mandatory
O   Optional
V   Vendor specific

D	Disk drives	T	Tape drives
P	Printers	E	Processor drives
W	WORM drives	R	CD-ROM
S	Scanners	O	Optical storage
M	Medium-changers	C	Communication devices

Opcode	D	T	P	E	W	R	S	O	M	C	Command
00	M	M	M	M	M	M	M	M	M	M	TEST UNIT READY
01		M									REWIND
01	O		V		O	O		O	O		REZERO UNIT
02	V	V	V	V	V	V			V		
03	M	M	M	M	M	M	M	M	M	M	REQUEST SENSE
04			O								FORMAT
04	M							O			FORMAT UNIT
05	V	M	V	V	V	V			V		READ BLOCK LIMITS
06	V	V	V	V	V	V			V		
07									O		INITIALIZE ELEMENT STATUS
07	O	V	V		O			O	V		REASSIGN BLOCKS
08										M	GET MESSAGE(06)
08	O	M	V		O	O		O	V		READ(06)
08				O							RECEIVE
09	V	V	V	V	V	V			V		
0A			M								PRINT
0A										M	SEND MESSAGE(06)
0A				M							SEND(06)
0A	O	M			O			O	V		WRITE(06)
0B	O				O	O		O	V		SEEK(06)
0B			O								SLEW AND PRINT

Opcode	D	T	P	E	W	R	S	O	M	C	Command
0C	V	V	V	V	V	V			V		
0D	V	V	V	V	V	V			V		
0E	V	V	V	V	V	V			V		
0F	V	O	V	V	V	V			V		READ REVERSE
10		O			O						SYNCHRONIZE BUFFER
10	V	M		V	V	V					WRITE FILEMARKS
11	V	M	V	V	V	V					SPACE
12	M	M	M	M	M	M	M	M	M	M	INQUIRY
13	V	O	V	V	V	V					VERIFY(06)
14	V	O	O	V	V	V					RECOVER BUFFERED DATA
15	O	M	O		O	O	O	O	O	O	MODE SELECT(06)
16	M				M	M		M	O		RESERVE
16		M	M				M				RESERVE UNIT
17	M				M	M		M	O		RELEASE
17		M	M				M				RELEASE UNIT
18	O	O	O	O	O	O	O	O			COPY
19	V	M	V	V	V	V					ERASE
1A	O	M	O		O	O	O	O	O	O	MODE SENSE(06)
1B		O									LOAD/UNLOAD
1B							O				SCAN
1B			O								STOP PRINT
1B	O				O	O		O			START/STOP UNIT
1C	O	O	O	O	O	O	O	O	O	O	RECEIVE DIAGNOSTIC RESULTS
1D	M	M	M	M	M	M	M	M	M	M	SEND DIAGNOSTIC
1E	O	O			O	O		O	O		PREVENT/ALLOW MEDIUM
											REMOVAL
20	V				V	V		V	O		
21	V				V	V		V	O		
22	V				V	V		V	O		
23	V				V	V		V	O		
24	V				V	V	M				SET WINDOW
25							O				GET WINDOW
25	M				M			M			READ CAPACITY
25						M					READ CD-ROM CAPACITY
26	V				V	V					
27	V				V	V					
28										O	GET MESSAGE(10)
28	M				M	M	M	M			READ(10)
29	V				V	V		O			READ GENERATION
2A										O	SEND MESSAGE(10)
2A							O				SEND(10)
2A	M				M			M			WRITE(10)
2B		O									LOCATE
2B									O		POSITION TO ELEMENT
2B	O				O	O		O			SEEK(10)

Opcode	D	T	P	E	W	R	S	O	M	C	Command
2C	V							O			ERASE(10)
2D	V				O			O			READ UPDATED BLOCK
2E	O				O			O			WRITE AND VERIFY(10)
2F	O				O	O		O			VERIFY(10)
30	O				O	O		O			SEARCH DATA HIGH(10)
31							O				OBJECT POSITION
31	O				O	O		O			SEARCH DATA EQUAL(10)
32	O				O	O		O			SEARCH DATA LOW(10)
33	O				O	O		O			SET LIMITS(10)
34							O				GET DATA BUFFER STATUS
34	O				O	O		O			PRE-FETCH
34		O									READ POSITION
35	O				O	O		O			SYNCHRONIZE CACHE
36	O				O	O		O			LOCK/UNLOCK CACHE
37	O							O			READ DEFECT DATA(10)
38					O			O			MEDIUM SCAN
39	O	O	O	O	O	O	O	O			COMPARE
3A	O	O	O	O	O	O	O	O			COPY AND VERIFY
3B	O	O	O	O	O	O	O	O	O	O	WRITE BUFFER
3C	O	O	O	O	O	O	O	O	O	O	READ BUFFER
3D					O			O			UPDATE BLOCK
3E	O				O	O		O			READ LONG
3F	O				O			O			WRITE LONG
40	O	O	O	O	O	O	O	O	O	O	CHANGE DEFINITION
41	O										WRITE SAME
42						O					READ SUB-CHANNEL
43						O					READ TOC
44						O					READ HEADER
45						O					PLAY AUDIO(10)
47						O					PLAY AUDIO MSF
48						O					PLAY AUDIO TRACK INDEX
49						O					PLAY TRACK RELATIVE
4B						O					PAUSE/RESUME
4C	O	O	O	O	O	O	O	O	O	O	LOG SELECT
4D	O	O	O	O	O	O	O	O	O	O	LOG SENSE
55	O	O	O		O	O	O	O	O	O	MODE SELECT(10)
5A	O	O	O		O	O	O	O	O	O	MODE SENSE(10)
A5									M		MOVE MEDIUM
A5						O					PLAY AUDIO(12)
A6									O		EXCHANGE MEDIUM
A8										O	GET MESSAGE(12)
A8					O	O		O			READ(12)
A9						O					PLAY TRACK RELATIVE(12)
AA										O	SEND MESSAGE(12)
AA					O			O			WRITE(12)

Opcode	D	T	P	E	W	R	S	O	M	C	Command
AC								O			ERASE(12)
AE					O			O			WRITE AND VERIFY(12)
AF					O	O		O			VERIFY(12)
B0					O	O		O			SEARCH DATA HIGH(12)
B1					O	O		O			SEARCH DATA EQUAL(12)
B2					O	O		O			SEARCH DATA LOW(12)
B3					O	O		O			SET LIMITS(12)
B5									O		REQUEST VOLUME ELEMENT ADDRESS
B6									O		SEND VOLUME TAG
B7								O			READ DEFECT DATA(12)
B8									O		READ ELEMENT STATUS

Appendix B
SCSI-2 commands (alphabetically)

Command	Opcode	D	T	P	E	W	R	S	O	M	C
CHANGE DEFINITION	40	O	O	O	O	O	O	O	O	O	O
COMPARE	39	O	O	O	O	O	O	O	O		
COPY	18	O	O	O	O	O	O	O	O		
COPY AND VERIFY	3A	O	O	O	O	O	O	O	O		
ERASE	19	V	M	V	V	V	V				
ERASE(10)	2C	V							O		
ERASE(12)	AC								O		
EXCHANGE MEDIUM	A6									O	
FORMAT	04			O							
FORMAT UNIT	04	M							O		
GET DATA BUFFER STATUS	34							O			
GET MESSAGE(06)	08										M
GET MESSAGE(10)	28										O
GET MESSAGE(12)	A8										O
GET WINDOW	25							O			
INITIALIZE ELEMENT STATUS	07									O	
INQUIRY	12	M	M	M	M	M	M	M	M	M	M
LOAD/UNLOAD	1B		O								
LOCATE	2B		O								
LOCK/UNLOCK CACHE	36	O				O	O		O		
LOG SELECT	4C	O	O	O	O	O	O	O	O	O	O
LOG SENSE	4D	O	O	O	O	O	O	O	O	O	O
MEDIUM SCAN	38					O			O		
MODE SELECT(06)	15	O	M	O		O	O	O	O	O	O
MODE SELECT(10)	55	O	O	O		O	O	O	O	O	O
MODE SENSE(06)	1A	O	M	O		O	O	O	O	O	O
MODE SENSE(10)	5A	O	O	O		O	O	O	O	O	O
MOVE MEDIUM	A5									M	
OBJECT POSITION	31							O			
PAUSE/RESUME	4B						O				
PLAY AUDIO MSF	47						O				
PLAY AUDIO TRACK INDEX	48						O				
PLAY AUDIO(10)	45						O				
PLAY AUDIO(12)	A5						O				

Command	Opcode	D	T	P	E	W	R	S	O	M	C
PLAY TRACK RELATIVE(10)	49						O				
PLAY TRACK RELATIVE(12)	A9						O				
POSITION TO ELEMENT	2B									O	
PRE-FETCH	34	O				O	O		O		
PREVENT/ALLOW MEDIUM REMOVAL	1E	O	O			O	O		O	O	
PRINT	0A			M							
READ BLOCK LIMITS	05	V	M	V	V	V	V			V	
READ BUFFER	3C	O	O	O	O	O	O	O	O	O	O
READ CAPACITY	25	M				M			M		
READ CD-ROM CAPACITY	25						M				
READ DEFECT DATA(10)	37	O							O		
READ DEFECT DATA(12)	B7								O		
READ ELEMENT STATUS	B8									O	
READ GENERATION	29	V				V	V		O		
READ HEADER	44						O				
READ LONG	3E	O				O	O		O		
READ POSITION	34		O								
READ REVERSE	0F	V	O	V	V	V	V			V	
READ SUB-CHANNEL	42						O				
READ TOC	43						O				
READ UPDATED BLOCK	2D	V				O			O		
READ(06)	08	O	M	V		O	O		O	V	
READ(10)	28	M				M	M	M	M		
READ(12)	A8					O	O		O		
REASSIGN BLOCKS	07	O	V	V		O			O	V	
RECEIVE	08				O						
RECEIVE DIAGNOSTIC RESULTS	1C	O	O	O	O	O	O	O	O	O	O
RECOVER BUFFERED DATA	14	V	O	O	V	V	V				
RELEASE	17	M				M	M		M	O	
RELEASE UNIT	17		M	M				M			
REQUEST SENSE	03	M	M	M	M	M	M	M	M	M	M
REQUEST VOLUME ELEMENT ADDRESS	B5									O	
RESERVE	16	M				M	M		M	O	
RESERVE UNIT	16		M	M				M			
REWIND	01		M								
REZERO UNIT	01	O		V		O	O		O	O	
SCAN	1B							O			
SEARCH DATA EQUAL(10)	31	O				O	O		O		
SEARCH DATA EQUAL(12)	B1					O	O		O		
SEARCH DATA HIGH(10)	30	O				O	O		O		
SEARCH DATA HIGH(12)	B0					O	O		O		
SEARCH DATA LOW(10)	32	O				O	O		O		
SEARCH DATA LOW(12)	B2					O	O		O		
SEEK(06)	0B	O				O	O		O	V	
SEEK(10)	2B	O				O	O		O		

Command	Opcode	D	T	P	E	W	R	S	O	M	C
SEND DIAGNOSTIC	1D	M	M	M	M	M	M	M	M	M	M
SEND MESSAGE(06)	0A										M
SEND MESSAGE(10)	2A										O
SEND MESSAGE(12)	AA										O
SEND VOLUME TAG	B6									O	
SEND(06)	0A				M						
SEND(10)	2A								O		
SET LIMITS(10)	33	O				O	O		O		
SET LIMITS(12)	B3					O	O		O		
SET WINDOW	24	V				V	V	M			
SLEW AND PRINT	0B			O							
SPACE	11	V	M	V	V	V	V				
STOP PRINT	1B			O							
START/STOP UNIT	1B	O				O	O		O		
SYNCHRONIZE BUFFER	10			O		O					
SYNCHRONIZE CACHE	35	O				O	O		O		
TEST UNIT READY	00	M	M	M	M	M	M	M	M	M	M
UPDATE BLOCK	3D					O			O		
VERIFY(06)	13	V	O	V	V	V	V				
VERIFY(10)	2F	O				O	O		O		
VERIFY(12)	AF					O	O		O		
WRITE AND VERIFY(10)	2E	O				O			O		
WRITE AND VERIFY(12)	AE					O			O		
WRITE BUFFER	3B	O	O	O	O	O	O	O	O	O	O
WRITE FILEMARKS	10	V	M		V	V	V				
WRITE LONG	3F	O				O			O		
WRITE SAME	41	O									
WRITE(06)	0A	O	M			O			O	V	
WRITE(10)	2A	M				M			M		
WRITE(12)	AA					O			O		

Appendix C
SCSI-2 sense codes

Sense code	Extended sense code	Meaning
00	00	NO ADDITIONAL SENSE INFORMATION
00	01	FILEMARK DETECTED
00	02	END-OF-PARTITION/MEDIUM DETECTED
00	03	SETMARK DETECTED
00	04	BEGINNING-OF-PARTITION/MEDIUM DETECTED
00	05	END-OF-DATA DETECTED
00	06	I/O PROCESS TERMINATED
00	11	AUDIO PLAY OPERATION IN PROGRESS
00	12	AUDIO PLAY OPERATION PAUSED
00	13	AUDIO PLAY OPERATION SUCCESSFULLY COMPLETED
00	14	AUDIO PLAY OPERATION STOPPED DUE TO ERROR
00	15	NO CURRENT AUDIO STATUS TO RETURN
01	00	INDEX/SECTOR SIGNAL
02	00	SEEK COMPLETE
03	00	PERIPHERAL DEVICE WRITE FAULT
03	01	NO WRITE CURRENT
03	02	EXCESSIVE WRITE ERRORS
04	00	LOGICAL UNIT NOT READY
04	01	LOGICAL UNIT IS IN PROCESS OF BECOMING READY
04	02	LOGICAL UNIT NOT READY
04	03	LOGICAL UNIT NOT READY
04	04	LOGICAL UNIT NOT READY
05	00	LOGICAL UNIT DOES NOT RESPOND TO SELECTION
06	00	REFERENCE POSITION FOUND
07	00	MULTIPLE PERIPHERAL DEVICES SELECTED
08	00	LOGICAL UNIT COMMUNICATION FAILURE
08	01	LOGICAL UNIT COMMUNICATION TIME-OUT
08	02	LOGICAL UNIT COMMUNICATION PARITY ERROR
09	00	TRACK FOLLOWING ERROR
09	01	TRACKING SERVO FAILURE
09	02	FOCUS SERVO FAILURE
09	03	SPINDLE SERVO FAILURE

Sense code	Extended sense code	Meaning
0A	00	ERROR LOG OVERFLOW
0C	00	WRITE ERROR
0C	01	WRITE ERROR RECOVERED WITH AUTO REALLOCATION
0C	02	WRITE ERROR − AUTO REALLOCATION FAILED
10	00	CRC OR ECC ERROR
11	00	UNRECOVERED READ ERROR
11	01	READ RETRIES EXHAUSTED
11	02	ERROR TOO LONG TO CORRECT
11	03	MULTIPLE READ ERRORS
11	04	UNRECOVERED READ ERROR − AUTO REALLOCATE FAILED
11	05	L-EC UNCORRECTABLE ERROR
11	06	CIRC UNRECOVERED ERROR
11	07	DATA RESYNCHRONIZATION ERROR
11	08	INCOMPLETE BLOCK READ
11	09	NO GAP FOUND
11	0A	MISCORRECTED ERROR
11	0B	UNRECOVERED READ ERROR − RECOMMEND REASSIGNMENT
11	0C	UNRECOVERED READ ERROR − RECOMMEND REWRITE THE DATA
12	00	ADDRESS MARK NOT FOUND FOR ID FIELD
13	00	ADDRESS MARK NOT FOUND FOR DATA FIELD
14	00	RECORDED ENTITY NOT FOUND
14	01	RECORD NOT FOUND
14	02	FILEMARK OR SETMARK NOT FOUND
14	03	END-OF-DATA NOT FOUND
14	04	BLOCK SEQUENCE ERROR
15	00	RANDOM POSITIONING ERROR
15	01	MECHANICAL POSITIONING ERROR
15	02	POSITIONING ERROR DETECTED BY READ OF MEDIUM
16	00	DATA SYNCHRONIZATION MARK ERROR
17	00	RECOVERED DATA WITH NO ERROR CORRECTION APPLIED
17	01	RECOVERED DATA WITH RETRIES
17	02	RECOVERED DATA WITH POSITIVE HEAD OFFSET
17	03	RECOVERED DATA WITH NEGATIVE HEAD OFFSET
17	04	RECOVERED DATA WITH RETRIES AND/OR CIRC APPLIED
17	05	RECOVERED DATA USING PREVIOUS SECTOR ID
17	06	RECOVERED DATA WITHOUT ECC − DATA AUTO-REALLOCATED
17	07	RECOVERED DATA WITHOUT ECC − RECOMMEND REASSIGNMENT
18	00	RECOVERED DATA WITH ERROR CORRECTION APPLIED
18	01	RECOVERED DATA WITH ERROR CORRECTION AND RETRIES APPLIED
18	02	RECOVERED DATA − DATA AUTO-REALLOCATED
18	03	RECOVERED DATA WITH CIRC
18	04	RECOVERED DATA WITH LEC
18	05	RECOVERED DATA − RECOMMEND REASSIGNMENT
19	00	DEFECT LIST ERROR
19	01	DEFECT LIST NOT AVAILABLE
19	02	DEFECT LIST ERROR IN PRIMARY LIST

Sense code	Extended sense code	Meaning
19	03	DEFECT LIST ERROR IN GROWN LIST
1A	00	PARAMETER LIST LENGTH ERROR
1B	00	SYNCHRONOUS DATA TRANSFER ERROR
1C	00	DEFECT LIST NOT FOUND
1C	01	PRIMARY DEFECT LIST NOT FOUND
1C	02	GROWN DEFECT LIST NOT FOUND
1D	00	MISCOMPARE DURING VERIFY OPERATION
1E	00	RECOVERED ID WITH ECC CORRECTION
20	00	INVALID COMMAND OPERATION MODE
21	00	LOGICAL BLOCK ADDRESS OUT OF RANGE
21	01	INVALID ELEMENT ADDRESS
22	00	ILLEGAL FUNCTION (SHOULD USE 20 00)
24	00	INVALID FIELD IN CDB
25	00	LOGICAL UNIT NOT SUPPORTED
26	00	INVALID FIELD IN PARAMETER LIST
26	01	PARAMETER NOT SUPPORTED
26	02	PARAMETER VALUE INVALID
26	03	THRESHOLD PARAMETERS NOT SUPPORTED
27	00	WRITE PROTECTED
28	00	NOT READY TO READ TRANSITION (MEDIUM MAY HAVE CHANGED)
28	01	IMPORT OR EXPORT ELEMENT ACCESSED
29	00	POWER ON
2A	00	PARAMETERS CHANGED
2A	01	MODE PARAMETERS CHANGED
2A	02	LOG PARAMETERS CHANGED
2B	00	COPY CANNOT EXECUTE SINCE HOST CANNOT DISCONNECT
2C	00	COMMAND SEQUENCE ERROR
2C	01	TOO MANY WINDOWS SPECIFIED
2C	02	INVALID COMBINATION OF WINDOWS SPECIFIED
2D	00	OVERWRITE ERROR ON UPDATE IN PLACE
2F	00	COMMANDS CLEARED BY ANOTHER INITIATOR
30	00	INCOMPATIBLE MEDIUM INSTALLED
30	01	CANNOT READ MEDIUM – UNKNOWN FORMAT
30	02	CANNOT READ MEDIUM – INCOMPATIBLE FORMAT
30	03	CLEANING CARTRIDGE INSTALLED
31	00	MEDIUM FORMAT CORRUPTED
31	01	FORMAT COMMAND FAILED
32	00	NO DEFECT SPARE LOCATION AVAILABLE
32	01	DEFECT LIST UPDATE FAILURE
33	00	TAPE LENGTH ERROR
36	00	RIBBON
37	00	ROUNDED PARAMETER
39	00	SAVING PARAMETERS NOT SUPPORTED
3A	00	MEDIUM NOT PRESENT
3B	00	SEQUENTIAL POSITIONING ERROR
3B	01	TAPE POSITION ERROR AT BEGINNING-OF-MEDIUM

Sense code	Extended sense code	Meaning
3B	02	TAPE POSITION ERROR AT END-OF-MEDIUM
3B	03	TAPE OR ELECTRONIC VERTICAL FORMS UNIT NOT READY
3B	04	SLEW FAILURE
3B	05	PAPER JAM
3B	06	FAILED TO SENSE TOP-OF-FORM
3B	07	FAILED TO SENSE BOTTOM-OF-FORM
3B	08	REPOSITION ERROR
3B	09	READ PAST END OF MEDIUM
3B	0A	READ PAST BEGINNING OF MEDIUM
3B	0B	POSITION PAST END OF MEDIUM
3B	0C	POSITION PAST BEGINNING OF MEDIUM
3B	0D	MEDIUM DESTINATION ELEMENT FULL
3B	0E	MEDIUM SOURCE ELEMENT EMPTY
3D	00	INVALID BITS IN IDENTIFY MESSAGE
3E	00	LOGICAL UNIT HAS NOT SELF-CONFIGURED YET
3F	00	TARGET OPERATING CONDITIONS HAVE CHANGED
3F	01	MICROCODE HAS BEEN CHANGED
3F	02	CHANGED OPERATING DEFINITION
3F	03	INQUIRY DATA HAS CHANGED
40	00	RAM FAILURE (SHOULD USE 40 NN)
40	NN	DIAGNOSTIC FAILURE ON COMPONENT NN (80H–FFH)
41	00	DATA PATH FAILURE (SHOULD USE 40 NN)
42	00	POWER-ON OR SELF-TEST FAILURE (SHOULD USE 40 NN)
43	00	MESSAGE ERROR
44	00	INTERNAL TARGET FAILURE
45	00	SELECT OR RESELECT FAILURE
46	00	UNSUCCESSFUL SOFT RESET
47	00	SCSI PARITY ERROR
48	00	INITIATOR DETECTED ERROR MESSAGE RECEIVED
49	00	INVALID MESSAGE ERROR
4A	00	COMMAND PHASE ERROR
4B	00	DATA PHASE ERROR
4C	00	LOGICAL UNIT FAILED SELF-CONFIGURATION
4E	00	OVERLAPPED COMMANDS ATTEMPTED
50	00	WRITE APPEND ERROR
50	01	WRITE APPEND POSITION ERROR
50	02	POSITION ERROR RELATED TO TIMING
51	00	ERASE FAILURE
52	00	CARTRIDGE FAULT
53	00	MEDIA LOAD OR EJECT FAILED
53	01	UNLOAD TAPE FAILURE
53	02	MEDIUM REMOVAL PREVENTED
54	00	SCSI TO HOST SYSTEM INTERFACE FAILURE
55	00	SYSTEM RESOURCE FAILURE
57	00	UNABLE TO RECOVER TABLE-OF-CONTENTS
58	00	GENERATION DOES NOT EXIST

Sense code	Extended sense code	Meaning
59	00	UPDATED BLOCK READ
5A	00	OPERATOR REQUEST OR STATE CHANGE INPUT (SPECIFIED)
5A	01	OPERATOR MEDIUM REMOVAL REQUEST
5A	02	OPERATOR SELECTED WRITE PROTECT
5A	03	OPERATOR SELECTED WRITE PERMIT
5B	00	LOG EXCEPTION
5B	01	THRESHOLD CONDITION MET
5B	02	LOG COUNTER AT MAXIMUM
5B	03	LOG LIST CODES EXHAUSTED
5C	00	RPL STATUS CHANGE
5C	01	SPINDLES SYNCHRONIZED
5C	02	SPINDLES NOT SYNCHRONIZED
60	00	LAMP FAILURE
61	00	VIDEO ACQUISITION ERROR
61	01	UNABLE TO ACQUIRE VIDEO
61	02	OUT OF FOCUS
62	00	SCAN HEAD POSITIONING ERROR
63	00	END OF USER AREA ENCOUNTERED ON THIS TRACK
64	00	ILLEGAL MODE FOR THIS TRACK

Appendix D
The SCSI bulletin board

The ANSI SCSI specification can also be acquired in an electronic format from the SCSI bulletin board (SCSI BBS) in the US. The telephone number (as of January 1997) is:

+1-719-533-7950

If you are calling for the first time, you will need to register for a user account. In general it takes a few days to set up the account and the permissions that allow you to access data on the BBS. The SCSI BBS offers access to the various X3T9 documents, among other important documentation and information. You can follow, for example, ongoing discussions concerning the SCSI-3 standard. It is also possible to access information on other X3T domains such as IPI, ATA, or HIPPI.

```
WILDCAT! Copyright (c) 87,95 Mustang Software, Inc.  All Rights Reserved.
   Registration Number: 92-3725.  v4.10 M10(MultiLine 10).  Node: 1.

   Connected at 14400 bps. Reliable connection. ANSI detected.

================================================================================
The SCSI Bulletin Board System
Provided by Symbios Logic Inc. (formerly NCR Microelectronics)
Using the WildCat! BBS Package Version 4.10 M10 Node 1

Modem.................USR Courier HST(tm) Dual Standard(tm)
Baud rates............300--14400 (+HST 16800)
================================================================================

You may either use your REAL name (which gives you more privileges AFTER I
upgrade your account) or the guest account (which lets you list and download
files without registering).

To use the guest account, log in as:

First Name? Guest
 Last Name?               (just press enter)
 Password? [         ]    (just press enter)
What is your first name? friedhelm
What is your  last name? schmidt
Looking up "FRIEDHELM SCHMIDT". Please wait...
Your name "FRIEDHELM SCHMIDT" was not found in the user data base.
Hello!  You are a new user to the system and we want to welcome you.
```

There are many features to discover, so please read the HELP files and
experiment with new choices.
Check the Bulletin menu and Newsletter file for additional information.
Welcome to The SCSI BBS.
For our BBS records we would like to get some additional information.
Please answer as correctly as possible to enable us to provide
the best service and support possible.

and so on ...
************************** Draft Standards **************************
While this BBS is called The SCSI BBS, there are other I/O interfaces covered
here as well. I have separated the files for these projects into different
file areas in a rather ad hoc fashion. Here is the map:

SCSI-1	File Area 7
SCSI-2	File Area 8
SCSI-3	File Area 20
ATA	File Area 15
CAM	File Area 13
ESDI	File Area 21
HIPPI	File Area 16
IPI	File Area 14
Fibre Channel	File Area 17

Please remember that these files are provided for review and comment purposes
only. The final ANSI-approved versions will not be posted here; if you
want an ANSI-approved standard, you must purchase the paper copy from ANSI
(or Global Engineering Documents). Ordering information is contained in
another bulletin.

Appendix E
Source code for SCANSCSI.PAS

SCANSCSI is a short utility program that also serves as a good example of an ASPI application. It checks all LUNs of all SCSI IDs to see whether a device is present. It does not rely on the ASPI internal table of devices but rather sends an INQUIRY command to each LUN. In this way devices that have been added to the bus after the loading of the ASPI manager are also discovered.

```
program scanscsi(input,output);

{*** Copyright Notice: This source code belongs to the book
  "The SCSI Bus and IDE Interface" from Addison-Wesley.

  It may be ported and modified for non-commercial
  purposes when this copyright notice is included.
  Authorization of the publisher is necessary for
  commercial purposes.

}

uses CRT, DOS;

const
  PNAM       : string='SCSI-Scanner V1.0 rev 003 25.2.93 (fs)';

{ASPI Specific Constants}

  ASPI_SRB_LENGTH = $7F;

  SRB_COMMAND_CODE = $00;
  SRB_STATUS       = $01;
  SRB_TARGET_ID    = $08;
  SRB_LUN          = $09;
  SRB_DATA_LENGTH  = $0A;
  SRB_BUFFER_OFS   = $0F;
  SRB_BUFFER_SEG   = $11;
  SRB_SCSI_LEN     = $17;
```

```
        SRB_HA_STATUS  = $18;
        SRB_TARGET_STATUS= $19;
        SRB_SCSI_CMD   = $40;

        SRB_X_SCSICMD  = $02;

    {SCSI Specific Constants}

    SCSI_CMD_LENGTH    = 11;

    {Program specific constants}

    DATA_LENGTH    = $FF;

    {Messages}

     ASPI_CONNECTED       ='ASPI loaded';
     ASPI_OPEN_ERROR          ='Error opening ASPI';

    type

    {Generic Types}
      MemAdress =   record
                      Offset: integer;
                      Segment: integer;
                    end;

    {ASPI-Types}

       SRBsize= 0..ASPI_SRB_LENGTH;
       SRBarray = array[SRBsize] of byte;

    {SCSI-Types}

       SCSICmdSize = 0..SCSI_CMD_LENGTH;
       SCSICmd = record
                   Command: array[SCSICmdSize] of byte;
                   Status: byte;
                   ID: byte;
                   LUN: byte;
                   Len: byte;
                   TimeOut: integer;
                 end;
       BufferLength = 0..DATA_LENGTH;
       DataBufferType = array[BufferLength] of byte;

    var
     CommandBuffer  : SCSICmd;
     DataBuffer     : DataBufferType;
     ID,LUN         : byte;
```

```pascal
AspiEntryPoint: MemAdress;
SRB: SRBarray;
SCSIConnected: string;

{**** Low Level Functions}

function FileOpen(FileName:string):integer;

const DOS_OPEN_FILE = $3D;

var register: registers;

begin
 FileName:=FileName+chr(0);
 with register
 do
  begin
   ax := DOS_OPEN_FILE shl 8;
   bx:=0;
   cx:=0;
   ds := seg(FileName);
   dx := ofs(FileName)+1; { because Pascal strings carry their
                            length in byte 0 }
  end;
  MSDOS(register);
  if (register.flags and FCarry) > 0
  then FileOpen:=-1
  else FileOpen:=register.ax;
end;


function FileClose(FileHandle:integer):integer;

const DOS_CLOSE_FILE = $3E;

var register: registers;

begin
 with register
 do
  begin
   ax := DOS_CLOSE_FILE shl 8;
   bx:=FileHandle;
  end;
  MSDOS(register);
  if (register.flags and FCarry) = 0
  then FileClose:=0
  else FileClose:=register.ax;
end;

{**** Miscellanous Generic Functions}
```

```
{**** SCSI generic functions}

function SCSICmdLen(Opcode: byte):byte;
begin
 SCSICmdLen:=0;
 if Opcode and $E0 = $00 then SCSICmdLen:=6;
 if Opcode and $E0 = $20 then SCSICmdLen:=10;
 if Opcode and $E0 = $40 then SCSICmdLen:=10;
 if Opcode and $E0 = $A0 then SCSICmdLen:=12;
end;

{**** ASPI-specific functions}

procedure GetASPIEntry(FileHandle:integer; var
 AspiEntry:MemAdress);

const ASPI_ENTRY_LENGTH = 4;
    DOS_IOCTL_READ  = $4402;

var register: registers;

begin
 with register
 do
  begin
   ax := DOS_IOCTL_READ;
   bx:=FileHandle;
   cx:=ASPI_ENTRY_LENGTH;
   ds := seg(AspiEntry);
   dx := ofs(AspiEntry);
  end;
  MSDOS(register);
end;

procedure SCSI2SRB(var SRB: SRBarray; Command: SCSICmd;
 var DataBuffer: DataBufferType);

var k:integer;
begin
 for k:=0 to High(SRB) do SRB[k]:=0;
 SRB[SRB_COMMAND_CODE]:=SRB_X_SCSICMD;
 with Command do
  begin
   SRB[SRB_TARGET_ID]:=ID;
   SRB[SRB_LUN]:=LUN;
   SRB[SRB_SCSI_LEN]:=SCSICmdLen(Command[1]);
   for k:=0 to SRB[SRB_SCSI_LEN]-1 do
SRB[SRB_SCSI_CMD+k]:=Command[k];
  end;
```

```
  SRB[SRB_DATA_LENGTH]:=lo(DATA_LENGTH);
  SRB[SRB_DATA_LENGTH+1]:=hi(DATA_LENGTH);
  SRB[SRB_BUFFER_SEG]:=lo(seg(DataBuffer));
  SRB[SRB_BUFFER_SEG+1]:=hi(seg(DataBuffer));
  SRB[SRB_BUFFER_OFS]:=lo(ofs(DataBuffer));
  SRB[SRB_BUFFER_OFS+1]:=hi(ofs(DataBuffer));

end;

procedure SRBexecute(var SRB: SRBarray);
var SRBsegment, SRBoffset: integer;

begin

 SRBsegment:=seg(SRB);
 SRBoffset:=ofs(SRB);

 asm
 mov ax, SRBsegment
 push ax
 mov ax, SRBoffset
 push ax
 LEA BX, AspiEntryPoint
 call DWORD PTR [bx]
 add sp,4
 end;
end;

function InitializeASPI(var AspiEntrypoint:MemAdress): boolean;

const ASPI_NAME = 'SCSIMGR$';

var result: integer;
  AspiFileHandle: integer;
begin
 AspiFileHandle:=FileOpen(ASPI_NAME);
 if AspiFileHandle>-1
 then
  begin
   GetASPIEntry(AspiFileHandle,AspiEntryPoint);
   FileClose(AspiFileHandle);
   InitializeASPI:=true;
  end
 else   InitializeASPI:=false;
end;

procedure initialize;

var ByteNbr : integer;
```

```
begin
  with CommandBuffer do
  begin
   for ByteNbr:=0 to SCSI_CMD_LENGTH do
    Command[ByteNbr]:=0;
   ID:=0;
   LUN:=0;
   Status:=$FF;
  end;
   for ByteNbr:=0 to DATA_LENGTH do DataBuffer[ByteNbr]:=0;
end;

Procedure Inquire(ID,LUN:byte);
const INQUIRY : array [SCSICmdSize] of byte =
($12,$0,$0,$0,$ff,$0,$0,$0,$0,$0,$0,$0);

var k: integer;
  Status: byte;
begin
 for k:=0 to SCSI_CMD_LENGTH do CommandBuffer.command[k]:=INQUIRY[k];
 CommandBuffer.ID:=ID;
 CommandBuffer.LUN:=LUN;
 If LUN=0 then writeln('SCSI-ID ',ID,': ');
 SCSI2SRB(SRB,CommandBuffer,DataBuffer);
 SRBexecute(SRB);
 repeat until SRB[SRB_STATUS]<>0;
 if SRB[SRB_STATUS] = 1 then
  if SRB[SRB_HA_STATUS]= 0 then
   begin
    Status:=DataBuffer[0] and $E0;
    if Status=0 then
     begin
      write('  LUN ',LUN,': ');
      for k:=8 to 35 do write(chr(DataBuffer[k]));
      writeln;
     end;
   end
  else if LUN=0 then writeln;
end;

begin
 writeln(PNAM);
 initialize;
 if InitializeASPI(AspiEntryPoint)
 then
  begin
   writeln(ASPI_CONNECTED);
   for ID:=0 to 7 do
   for LUN:=0 to 7 do Inquire(ID,LUN);
  end
 else writeln(ASPI_OPEN_ERROR);

end.
```

Appendix F
Addresses of manufacturers and organizations

Adaptec (SCSI host adapters and chips)

Adaptec, Inc.
691 South Milpitas Blvd.
Milpitas, CA 95035
USA
Tel.: +1-408-945-8600
Fax: +1-408-262-2533
http://www.adaptec.com

AdvanSys (SCSI host adapters and chips)

Advanced System Products, Inc.
1150 Ringwood Court
San Jose, CA 95131
USA
Tel.: +1-408-383-9400
Fax: +1-408-383-9612
http://www.advansys.com

Ancot (SCSI testers)

Ancot Corporation
115 Constitution Drive
Menlo Park, CA 94025
USA
Tel.: +1-415-322-5322
Fax: +1-415-322-0455
http://www.ancot.com

Apcon (SCSI expanders and switches)

APCON, Inc.
17938 SW Upper Boones Ferry Road
Portland, OR 97224
USA
Tel.: +1-503-639-6700
Fax: +1-503-639-6740
http://www.apcon.com

Buslogic (SCSI host adapters)

BusLogic, Inc. have been taken over by Mylex.

DTP (SCSI host adapters)

Distributed Processing Technology
140 Candace Drive
Maitland, FL 32751
USA
Tel.: +1-407-830-5522
Fax: +1-407-260-5366
http://ftp.dpt.com

Emulex (Fibre Channel)

Emulex Corporation
3545 Harbor Blvd
Costa Mesa, CA 92626
USA
http://www.emulex.com

ENDL (Documentation)

ENDL Inc.
14426 Black Walnut Court
Saratoga, CA 95070
USA
Tel.: +1-408-867-6630
Fax: +1-408-867-2115
dal_allan@mcimail.com

FCA (Fibre Channel)

FCA Fibre Channel Association
12407 MoPac Expressway North 100-357
P.O. Box 9700
Austin, TX 78766-9700
USA
Tel.: +1-512-328-8422
Fax: +1-512-328-8423
http://www.amdahl.com/ext/CARP/FCA/FCA.html

Future Domain (SCSI host adapters and chips)

Future Domain Corporation have been taken over by Adaptec.

Global Engineering (SCSI standards)

Global Engineering Documents
15 Iverness Way East
Englewood, CO 80112
USA
Tel.: +1-303-792-2181
Fax: +1-303-792-2192

I-Tech (SCSI testers)

I-Tech Corporation
6975 Washington Ave. SO.
Edina, MN 55439
USA
Tel.: +1-612-941-5905
Fax: +1-612-941-2386
http://www.i-tech.com

ICP (SCSI Raid)

Vortex Computersysteme GmbH
Falterstraße 51-53
D-74223 Flein
Tel.:+49-7131-59720
Fax: +49-7131-255063
sales@vortex.de

IntraServer (Host adapters)

IntraServer Technology, Inc.
125 Hopping Brook Park
Holliston, MA 01746
USA
Tel.: +1-508-429-0425
Fax: +1-508-429-0430
http://www.intraserver.com

Mylex (Host adapters, RAID controllers)

Mylex Corporation
34551 Ardenwood Blvd.
Fremont, CA 94555
USA
Tel.: +1-510-796-6100
Fax: +1-510-745-7521

Paralan (SCSI expanders)

Paralan Corporation
7875 Convoy Court
San Diego, CA 92111
USA
Tel.: +1-619-560-7266
Fax: +1-619-560-8929
http://www.paralan.com

Promise (SCSI host adapters)

Promise Technology, Inc.
1460 Koll Circle
San Jose, CA 95112
USA

Tel.: +1-408-452-0948
Fax: +1-408-452-1534
http://www.promise.com

QLogic (SCSI chips, Fibre Channel products)

QLogic Corporation
3545 Harbor Blvd
Costa Mesa, CA 92626
USA
Tel.: +1-714-668-5359
Fax: +1-714-668-5090
http://www.qlc.com

SSA

SSA Industry Association
http://www.ssaia.org

STA

SCSI Trade Association
c/o Technology Forums Ltd
3331 Brittan Avenue, Suite 4,
San Carlos, CA 94070
USA
Tel.:+1-415-631-7152
Fax: +1-415-631-7154
http://www.scsita.com

Symbios Logic (SCSI chips)

Symbios Logic
1635 Aeroplaza Drive
Colorado Springs, CO 80916
USA
Tel.: +1-719-573-3200
http://www.symbios.com

Western Digital (SCSI host adapters, chips and peripheral devices)

Western Digital Corporation
8105 Irvine Center Drive
Irvine, CA 92718
USA
Tel.: +1-714-932-5000
Fax: +1-714-932-4300
http://www.wdc.com

Glossary

Active high

An electrical signal is active high when it is interpreted as true for high voltage levels. *See also* Active low.

Active low

A signal that is interpreted as true in the low voltage state. Often such signals have a bar over the name, such as $\overline{DASP}$.

SCSI   Since all SCSI signals are active low they are not marked in any special way in the SCSI chapters.

IDE   Active low signals are marked with a bar in the IDE chapters.

SCSI-3   **Application client**

An application client is an abstract construction inside an initiator which handles exactly one SCSI command or task management request. The application client dies with the termination of the associated function.

FC   **Arbitrated loop**

A ring-shaped topology for Fibre Channel. It is less demanding on the hardware than the *Fabric* and thus less expensive.

SCSI, SSA, FC   **Arbitration**

The process used by the devices connected to the bus to determine which of them can use the bus next.

AT bus

Refers to either the system bus of IBM AT compatible computers, the ISA bus, or the IDE interface. The term AT bus is not used in this book but instead ISA bus and IDE interface are used.

ATA standard

The ANSI version of the IDE interface is called ATA. The name comes from AT Attachment. In this book ATA is used whenever the ANSI standard is meant.

Bandwidth

see Throughput.

SSA   **Bridge**

A connection from an internal backplane bus to the external cable bus.

SCSI   **Bridge controller**

A SCSI device controller which is not integrated into the device, but accesses the device via an additional I/O bus.

Cache

A small storage capable of very fast access. For disk drives such a cache is implemented as RAM, usually at least 1 Mbyte in size. All data read from the medium is stored here. Data that is already in the cache can be read up to 20 times faster. When the cache is full the oldest data is overwritten.

SCSI   **CAM**

The Common Access Method is a standard for the software interface between operating system and host adapter.

SCSI   **CCS**

The Common Command Set is an extension to SCSI-1 which defines the command set for magnetic disks much more precisely. The CCS looks very similar to the disk commands in SCSI-2.

SCSI   **Contingent allegiance condition**

This is created for an I_T_x nexus after a CHECK CONDITION or COMMAND TERMINATED status. In this condition a LUN holds sense data pertaining to the I_T_x nexus. If a LUN is only capable of holding data for a single I_T_x nexus then attempts by all other initiators to access the LUN will be met with BUSY status. In the event that a tagged queue is implemented for this LUN other commands will not be affected (*see* Extended contingent allegiance condition). The contingent allegiance condition ends when a new command is received from the same initiator or by an ABORT or BUS DEVICE RESET message.

Controller

In this book a controller is a system component that controls a peripheral device. A controller may reside on the peripheral itself or be integrated into the host system. The term is often used with reference to a subsystem that is actually a combination of a controller and host adapter. As an example, a disk drive controller allows for the attachment of disk drives to the host system.

SCSI   A SCSI controller allows the connecting of one or more peripheral devices to the SCSI bus. The device that connects the SCSI bus to the host system is called a host adapter.

CRC (cyclic redundancy check)

A checksum that is written in addition to the data to a sector. With the aid of CRC data errors can be detected with higher confidence than with a simple parity bit.

Data rate

see Throughput.

SCSI-3   **Device server**

Functional unit inside a SCSI LUN responsible for the management of the physical device.

DMA (direct memory access)

Refers to the ability of a host adapter to write and read host system memory without host intervention. This not only makes possible very fast data transfers but also frees the host processor to do other tasks. This is especially advantageous in multi-tasking systems where multiple tasks are the norm. Programmed I/O (PIO), on the other hand, is performed entirely by the host processor.

SCSI-3   **Domain**

An I/O subsystem in which all SCSI devices are connected via a common service delivery subsystem. In more practical terms: all SCSI devices that are connected to each other in such a way that they share the SCSI ID address space.

ECC (error correction code)

Additional bits written with the data that allow, to a certain degree, the recognition and correction of data errors. Disk drives always employ error correction codes.

SCSI   **Extended contingent allegiance condition**

This extends the normal contingent allegiance condition in that the execution of all commands in the tagged queue of this LUN is also suspended. This condition exists for an I_T_L nexus and is entered by the target in certain error situations. The target sends an INITIATE RECOVERY message after a CHECK CONDITION status. Afterwards the initiator should take appropriate measures to recover from the error. The extended contingent allegiance condition is ended when the initiator sends a RELEASE RECOVERY message.

FC   **Fabric**

An abstract construction in Fibre Channel topology which can be best imagined as an electronic cross bar distributor. FC devices connected to a fabric deliver their data packets to the fabric which then forwards them to the correct destination device.

Formatted capacity

As opposed to unformatted capacity, this is the amount of space available to store information on a disk drive. The replacement sectors are not included. The formatted capacity of a drive is usually between 10 and 30% less than the unformatted capacity.

Formatting

A hard disk or replaceable medium disk needs to be formatted before data can be stored on it. Here sectors for data storage are written to the medium. Since the sectors take up more room than just what is needed for data storage there arises a difference between formatted and unformatted drive capacity.

Full duplex

A communication mode which allows simultaneous sending and receiving.

Geometry

The geometry of a disk drive describes the format of the drive in terms of cylinders, heads, and sectors. For example, two drives with different geometries differ in the number of cylinders.

Hard sector

A type of disk drive formatting where the beginning of each sector is marked by a pulse generated by the head disk assembly. In comparison, the pulse from a soft sector format is generated from the read/write electronics and requires space on the medium.

Host adapter

A host adapter allows a controller to be connected to the I/O bus of the host. The host adapter may be integrated on the motherboard of the system or it may be implemented as a separate board.

IDE interface

A disk drive interface used primarily in the PC domain. The name comes from integrated disk electronics. Also known as ATA interface.

Index

A pulse indicating the beginning of a track on a rotating disk.

SCSI

Initiator

One of two possible roles a SCSI device can play. The initiator is the device that initiates the I/O process. As soon as the target device is selected it controls the I/O process as well as the SCSI protocol.

I/O bus

A computer bus for the attachment of peripheral devices.

SCSI

I/O process

Any logical connection between two SCSI devices is referred to as an I/O process. It begins with the selection of a target by an initiator. It exists during the entire command execution or command chain including all BUS FREE periods. Normally, the process ends after the message COMMAND COMPLETE with a BUS FREE phase. In SCSI-3, an I/O process is called task.

ISA bus

The original system bus of the IBM AT. The bus has since become a standard and is used by all AT compatible systems. The name comes from industry standard architecture.

SCSI

I_T_x Nexus

Either an I_T_L nexus or an I_T_L_Q nexus.

SCSI

LUN (logical unit)

Each SCSI target contains at least one and up to eight LUNs. A LUN is the actual physical device. For example a SCSI controller connected to three disk drives controls three LUNs.

Mapping

For disk drives, the correspondence between physical sectors and logical block numbers is accomplished through a mapping. A linear mapping refers to the approach where first sectors of a track, then tracks of a cylinder, and finally cylinders are exhausted for increasing LBN numbers. This approach insures that the access time for continuous logical blocks is minimal.

Master

When two devices or systems are in such a relationship that one of them has control over the other, the controlling device is the master and the other device the slave.

IDE   ## Master drive

For IDE, drive 0 is the master drive. The term derives from the fact that when spindle synchronization is used this drive supplies the clock for the second drive. Otherwise the drives are independent.

Mirrored drives

Two disk drives that are maintained to hold exactly the same information are said to be mirrored. Mirroring is the responsibility of a controller or special software and is transparent to the user. Mirrored drives are used for redundancy purposes in the event of a hardware failure.

FC   ## Originator

Device that initiates a Fibre Channel transaction. Corresponds to the SCSI initiator.

Parity bit

Simple error detection for a data byte. A parity bit transferred with the data byte allows the receiver to detect 1-bit errors. Multiple bit errors may not be detected.

FC   ## Payload

The part of a Fibre Channel data packet available for user data or data of higher protocol levels.

PIO (programmed I/O)

The exchange of data via a register or port by program control. In contrast to direct memory access (DMA), the processor moves each individual piece of data to memory, which is very time consuming.

Redundancy

Insurance against data loss or downtime through the use of duplicate components. In order to guarantee zero downtime some systems allow for replacements 'on-the-fly', or hot swaps.

SCSI-3   ## Request/response

Transaction model introduced with the SCSI-3 *SAM* architecture model.

FC   ## Responder

Device that executes a Fibre Channel transaction. Corresponds to the SCSI target.

Rotational position sensing (RPS)

A controller connected to multiple disk drives which monitors the relative rotational position of each drive is said to employ RPS. This is accomplished by monitoring the index pulses of the drives. When processing multiple I/O requests this allows the controller to choose the drive that can be accessed with minimal access time.

SSA   **Router**

Functional unit in a SSA node that decides whether a data packet is destined for this node or whether it must be forwarded.

SCSI-3   **SAM (SCSI Architectural model)**

A new document that describes the SCSI-3 architecture. All other SCSI-3 documents must meet the requirements of the SAM.

Slave

see Master.

IDE   **Slave drive**

see Master drive.

Soft sectoring

A method of formatting for a disk drive. Here the pulse marking the beginning of a sector is written to the medium during formatting and read from the medium during access to the sector, in contrast to hard sectoring, which uses slightly less space on the disk.

Spindle synchronization

Two or more disk drives that are synchronized for spindle speed and rotational position are said to employ spindle synchronization. This allows, for example, simultaneous writing of mirrored drives.

SCSI   **Status**

A byte sent from the target to the initiator at the end of a command sequence. This byte reflects the success or failure of the command execution. Afterwards the message COMMAND COMPLETE normally follows.

SCSI   **Status phase**

The SCSI bus phase where a status byte is transferred from the target to the initiator.

Target

One of two possible roles a SCSI device can play. The target is the device that executes commands for the initiator. After the selection phase the target takes control of bus protocol.

SCSI-3   **Task**

New name in SCSI-3 for the I/O process used in SCSI-2.

IDE   **Task file**

Another name for the command register block of an IDE controller.

SCSI   **Terminator**

A SCSI bus must be terminated at both ends by means of a terminator. Terminators are different for single-ended and differential SCSI. At higher transfer rates (Fast SCSI, Fast-20), single-ended SCSI needs active terminators.

Throughput (bandwidth, data rate)

Given in Mbytes per second, throughput relates how much data can be transferred over the bus in a given time. Throughput is the product of the transfer rate in MHz times the bus width in bytes. For example, a 32-bit wide SCSI bus with a transfer rate of 10 MHz results in a throughput of 40 Mbytes per second. As a further differentiation, there is also the peak transfer rate and sustained transfer rate. For example, a disk drive typically has a sustained transfer rate of 3 Mbytes per second. This is how fast the data can be read from the medium. However, a controller using Fast SCSI might be able to reach a peak data rate of 10 Mbytes per second.

Transfer rate

The speed at which a data transfer occurs measured in MHz. In the case of 8-bit transfers this is identical to throughput in Mbytes per second. It is often used to express serial rates like that of the data from the head of a drive. Here a transfer rate of 24 MHz corresponds to a throughput of 3 Mbytes per second.

Twisted pair cable

Cable built out of twisted wire pairs. Particularly suited for transmission of differential signals because they ensure that external interferences are received with nearly the same strength on both wires and therefore eliminate each other.

Unformatted capacity

The capacity of a disk drive or medium before formatting. Only the formatted capacity is important to the user. Unformatted capacity is approximately 10 to 30% higher than this. Manufacturers cite unformatted capacity since formatted capacity is a function of the exact method of formatting.

SCSI   **Unit attention condition**

This condition exists in a LUN relative to certain initiators when a status change has occurred in the LUN that the initiators did not cause. Examples of such status changes are the insertion of a medium in a replaceable medium drive, the setting of MODE parameters from a third-party initiator or a SCSI reset. As long as a unit attention condition exists the LUN will reply to all commands with a CHECK CONDITION status and status key UNIT ATTENTION, with the exception of INQUIRY and REQUEST SENSE, which will be executed normally. After this the LUN enters into a contingent allegiance condition. The unit attention condition ends for an initiator as soon as it receives the CHECK CONDITION status. Unit attention can also hold for all LUNs and all initiators. This occurs, for example, at power-up or after a SCSI reset.

Index

1/2-inch tape   184
6-byte command   124
10-byte command   125
12-byte command   175

A

A cable   19
ABORT   307
ABORT TAG   307
ABORT TASK   118
ABORT TASK SET   118
abort command   50
ACA   116
ACA bit   113
ACA QUEUE TAG   306
access time   18, 56
ACKNOWLEDGE MEDIA CHANGE   66
ACTIVE (status)   60
active negation   250, 258
active termination   257
address register   46, 49
address space   25
addressing
   logical   56
   physical   55
AEN   130, 147, 148, 150, 309
AER   148, 150
alternative status register   47, 48
ANSI   31
ANSI version   130
application client   107
ARBITRATION phase   274
arbitration   27, 274
architecture
   SCSI   101
ASPI   330

asynchronous   8
asynchronous event   309
asynchronous event notification   309
AT bus   31
AT task file   44
ATA interface   32
ATA-2   32
ATA-3   32
ATAPI   32, 73
ATAPI IDENTIFY DEVICE   81
ATAPI PACKET   77, 81
ATAPI SOFT RESET   82
ATAPI
   configuration word   81
   register   76
   task file   76
   transport protocol   77
audio   241
auto contingent allegiance   116
autosense   111

B

B cable   19
backplane   26
bandwidth   25
Bi-Tronics interface   12
BIOS   57
block descriptor   142
block format   166
BOM   184
BOOT - POST-BOOT   66
BOOT - PRE-BOOT   66
BPI   184
bridge controller   91, 106, 199
buffer   16, 156
buffer mode   186, 196, 203

BUS DEVICE RESET 307
BUS FREE phase 273
bus
    memory bus 27
    I/O bus 27
    universal bus 28

C

cache 133, 156, 157, 172
CAM 32, 329
capacity limits 57
capacity
    formatted 17
    net 17
CCS 96
CD recorder 245
CD-ROM 235
CD-ROM/XA 237
CDC 13
CDS 321
Centronics 10
CHANGE DEFINITION 139
CHECK POWER MODE 66
CHS mode 55
CLEAR ACA 118, 308
CLEAR QUEUE 307
client-server model 102, 281
CList 156
CLOSE SESSION/TRACK 247
CLV 235
command (SCSI)
    6-byte command 124
    10-byte command 125
    12-byte command 125
    16-byte command 126
    command descriptor block 111
    control byte 112
    group 112
    linked 113
    opcode 112
    status 114
    type of 126
command abortion 50
command chain 300
command class
    class 1 49
    class 2 50
    class 3 51
    class 4 51
    class 5 52

COMMAND COMPLETE 300
command descriptor block 110, 123
command model 110
COMMAND phase 278
command phase (IDE) 51
command phase (SCSI) 278
command register 48
command
    optional 66
    overlapping 117
communications device 205
Compaq 31
configuration sector 63
connector 254
Conner Peripherals 53
contingent allegiance 116
control byte 112
control mode page 147
controller 18, 91
CRC 15
cylinder 14, 55
cylinder number register 47
cylinder skew 17

D

DAT 185
DATA phase 279, 283
data phase (IDE) 51
data rate 25
data register 44
data separator 15, 18
defect descriptors 166
defect list 156
defect management 58, 155
deferred error 133, 157
device control register 48
device type 122
diagnosis 61
diagnostic pages 138
differential 93
direct memory access 42
DISCONNECT 302
disconnect
    unexpected 274
disconnect privilege 299
disconnect/reconnect page 145
DList 156
DMA 42, 51, 68, 71
DMA mode 40

domain 103, 267
DOOR LOCK 66
DOOR UNLOCK 66
double ported buffer 59
DOWNLOAD MICROCODE 67
Draft Proposal 88
drive synchronization 40
drive/head register 47
dualport 130

E

ECB bus 28
ECC 15, 16, 46, 69, 71, 72, 161
ECC error 65
EIA 7
EIDE 32
EISA bus 33
element 215
embedded controller 105
emulation 200
Enhanced Technical Report 267
EOD 185
EOM 184
EPI 267
ERASE 191
ERASE(10) 181
error code 61
error register 45, 61
ESDI interface 13
EXABYTE 185
EXCHANGE MEDIUM 219
EXECUTE DRIVE DIAGNOSTICS 61
expander 267
extended message 276
extent 154

F

fabric 314
Fast SCSI 282
Fast-20 248, 285
FCA 313
FCP 317
feature register 46
Fibre Channel 312
filemark 186
Fire Wire 318
flag bit 113
forced perfect termination 258
FORMAT 203
FORMAT MEDIUM 189

FORMAT TRACK 67
FORMAT UNIT 163
FORMAT/RESERVE TRACK 246
formatted capacity 17
formatter 15, 18
formatting 16, 58, 67, 163
formatting
    magnetic tape 189
frame
    Fibre Channel 316
freeing the bus 302

G

generations 176
geometry 14, 55, 64, 65, 170
GET MESSAGE(6) 206
GET MESSAGE(10) 207
GET MESSAGE(12) 207
GList 156
glitch 276
grown defects 156

H

handshake 11, 277
hard disk 13, 14
    geometry 14
hard sectoring 15
hardware reset 52
HDA 18
head 55
HEAD OF QUEUE TAG 306
header 15, 16
host adapter 18, 91, 105

I

I/O bus 27
I/O process 298, 307
ID 90
IDE
    adapter 33
    command 61
    command classes 49
    controller 44
    interface 31
    signals 38
IDENTIFY 299
IDENTIFY DEVICE 63
IDENTIFY DRIVE 63
IDLE 67
IDLE (status) 60, 66

IDLE IMMEDIATE   68
IGNORE WIDE RESIDUE   305
index   14
index format   166
information unit
    Fibre Channel   317
initialization pattern   164
INITIALIZE DRIVE PARAMETERS   65
initiator   91, 106
    SSA   324
INITIATOR DETECTED ERROR   300
INQUIRY   128
INQUIRY (ATAPI version)   82
INT 13   57
interface
    CMD   13
    ESDI   13
    peripheral interface   5, 7
    physical   5, 8, 10
    printer interface   5, 10
    serial   7
    ST506   13
interleave   16
interrupt request   47, 48
IPS   184
isosynchronous   318
I_T_ nexus   298

L

large frame   236
LBA mode   56
LBN   124, 152
linear mapping   56
link bit   112
link
    Fibre Channel   314
    SSA   323
LINKED COMMAND COMPLETE   300
linked commands   113
LOAD/UNLOAD   195
LOCATE   193
logic analyzer   345, 346
logical addressing   56
logical block   124, 152, 176
logical block (magnetic tape)   185
logical block number   56
logical unit   122
low voltage differential   249, 265
LUN   108, 122, 124, 298
    incorrect selection   117

SSA   324
LVD   249, 265

M

MAINTENANCE(IN)   230
mandatory command   61
mapping   153, 237
    linear   56
mass storage   4
master drive   34, 40, 53
measuring units   209
media changer
    attached   155, 15
MEDIA EJECT   68
medium   14
medium-changer devices   215
medium defects   155
MEDIUM SCAN   179
memory bus   27
message   118
message format   296
MESSAGE PARITY ERROR   308
MESSAGE phase   276
MESSAGE REJECT   308
message system   296, 308
MFM encoding   22
MFS format   236
mixed-mode CD   237
MMC   235
mode   40
mode parameter   122
mode parameter page   143
mode parameter pages
    for all device types   144
    for CD-ROMs   243
    for communications devices   207
    for disk drives   168
    for medium-changers   223
    for optical storage   181
    for printers   203
    for scanners   213
    for storage array controllers   233
    for tape devices   197
MODE SELECT   140
MODE SENSE   140
model
    of a hard disk   13
    of a peripheral device   5
    of a peripheral interface   5
    of an IDE hard disk   55

MODIFY DATA POINTER   301
mount   184
MOVE MEDIUM   218
multi-initiator   136
multi-session   237
multimedia devices   235

N

net capacity   17
net throughput   25
nexus   298
NO OPERATION   300
node
   Fibre Channel   314
   P1394   318
   SSA   323
NOP   68
notch   154, 168, 174

O

offset   283
opcode   112
open collector transistors   250
optical storage   175
ORDERED QUEUE TAG   306
originator   314

P

P cable   248, 259
P1394   318
parameter list   123, 139
parity error   253, 301, 308
partition   185
passive termination   256, 257
PAUSE/RESUME   241
PC host adapter   351
PCI bus   34
peak transfer rate   18
peripheral device page   146
peripheral device type   129
peripheral interface   5
peripheral qualifier   129
phase   270
physical addressing   55, 65
physical interface   5
pin assignments
   differential SCSI   262
   single-ended SCSI   258
PIO mode   40
PLAY AUDIO MSF   241

PLAY AUDIO TRACK/INDEX   243
PLAY AUDIO(10)   241
PLAY AUDIO(12)   241
PList   156
pointer   301
port
   Fibre-Channel   314
   SSA   323
PostScript   6
power conditions   60
power-up   52
pre-fetch   156
PRINT   201
printer   5, 10, 199
priority   104
processor devices   148
programmed I/O   41
protocol   12
   IDE   49
   XON/XOFF   9

Q

Q-22 bus   28
QIC   185
queue   298, 305

R

RAID   226
RAID array   92
RAM-Disk   155
READ   212
   tape drive   188
READ(6)   159
READ(10)   159
READ BLOCK LIMITS   192
READ BUFFER   68
READ CAPACITY   162
READ CD-ROM CAPACITY   239
READ DMA   68
READ DRIVE STATE   68
READ ELEMENT STATUS   220
READ GENERATION   179
READ LONG   69, 161
READ MULTIPLE   69
READ POSITION   193
READ REVERSE   188
READ SECTORS   65
READ TOC   240
READ UPDATED BLOCK(10)   179
READ VERIFY SECTORS   65

read/write head   14
ready condition   183
real time   25
RECALIBRATE   69
RECEIVE   150
reconnect   276, 302
recording format   184
Red Book   236
redundancy group   229
REDUNDANCY GROUP(IN)   232
register block   44
register model   44
relative addressing   130
RELEASE   136
removable medium drives   154
REQ/ACK offset   283
REQ/ACK sequence   277
REQUEST SENSE   115, 132
request/acknowledge   11
request/acknowledge handshake   277
reselection   302
    unexpected   300
RESELECTION phase   276
RESERVATION CONFLICT   136
RESERVE   136
reset   52
    hard   307
responder   314
REST (command)   69
RESTORE DRIVE STATE   69
RESTORE POINTERS   301
REWIND   186
RLL encoding   22
rotational latency   18
rotational position locking   172
router   324
RS-232   7

S

SACL   226
SASI   87
SAVE DATA POINTERS   301
SBC   152
SBP   321
SCA   254
SCAM   286
SCAN   213
scan window   210
scanner   209
SCC   226

SCSI
    architecture model   101
    device   90
    differential   262
    expander   267
    fast   303
    history   87
    priority   104
    segment   267
    single-ended   256
    synchronous   282, 303
    Wide   251, 286, 304
SCSI analyzer   344, 346
SCSI Bulletin Board   97
SCSI bus phase   270
    ARBITRATION   274
    BUS FREE   273
    COMMAND   278
    DATA   279, 283
    MESSAGE   276
    RESELECTION   276
    SELECTION phase   274
    STATUS   280
SCSI bus timing   272
SCSI cable   253
SCSI chip   349
SCSI configurations   108
SCSI controller   105
SCSI emulator   344, 345, 347
SCSI interlock protocol   296
SCSI message   296
SCSI pointer   301
SCSI signals   250
SCSI standard   97
SCSI transfer rates   94
SCSI-1   96
SCSI-2
    as opposed to SCSI-1   122, 140, 187, 271,
        274, 282
SCSI-3   89
SDI   104
Seagate   13
sector   14, 55
sector buffer   49, 59, 63, 67, 68, 71
sector count register   46
sector format   14, 16, 167
sector number register   47
sector skew   16
seek time   18
segment   267

SELECTION 274
selection phase 274
SEND 150, 212
SEND DIAGNOSTIC 138
SEND MESSAGE(6) 206
SEND MESSAGE(10) 207
SEND MESSAGE(12) 207
sense code 134
sense data 116, 133
sense key 134
sequential access 183
serial storage architecture 322
serial transmission 8
SERVICE 82
service delivery subsystem 104
service response 115
SET FEATURES 70
SET FEATURES (ATAPI) 82
SET MULTIPLE MODE 70
SET WINDOW 211
setmark 186
SFF 73
signal level 256, 262
SIMPLE QUEUE TAG 306
single ported puffer 59
single-ended 93
SIP 296
slave drive 34, 40, 53
SLEEP (command) 71
SLEEP (status) 60
SLEW AND PRINT 202
slot 26
Small Form Factor 32
SMD interface 13
SMS 326
soft sectoring 15, 22
SPACE 190
spare 230
SPARE(IN) 232
SPI 248
spiral offset 17
SRB 330
SSA 322
SSF8020 32
SSP 327
ST412 interface 13
ST506 interface 13
ST506 interface 19
STANDBY (command) 71
STANDBY (status) 60, 66

STANDBY IMMEDIATE 71
standby timer 67
status 114
    CHECK CONDITION 114
    RESERVATION CONFLICT 136
status byte 110
status codes 114
STATUS phase 280
status register 47
STOP PRINT 202
structural model 103
subordinate SCAM initiator 288
surface 14
sustained transfer rate 18
switch
    Fibre Channel 314
SYNCHRONIZE BUFFER 203
SYNCHRONOUS DATA TRANSFER REQUEST 303
synchronous SCSI 282
synchronous transfer 303
synchronous transfer period 283
synchronous transmission 9

T

tagged queue 298
tape drive 183
tape marks 185
target 91, 106, 121
    SSA 324
target emulator 346
TARGET RESET 118
target routine 122, 298
task 107, 115, 298
task attributes 120
task identifier 110
task management 118
task set 116
task set management 119
Technical Report 267
TERMINATE I/O PROCESS 308
TERMINATE TASK 118
termination 252, 256
    active and passive 257
    differential 263
    improper 258
terminator 20
TEST UNIT READY 131
third party reservation 137
throughput 9, 12, 16, 18, 25
timing 272

timing diagram   345
track   14, 237
track skew   17
transfer mode   70
transfer period   283
transfer rate   18

U

ULP   281
Ultra-SCSI   248, 250
unexpected disconnect   274
unexpected reselection   300
UNIT ATTENTION state   117
universal bus   28
UPDATE BLOCK   178
upper level protocol   281

V

Video-8   185
VME bus   28
volume set   230
VOLUME SET(IN)   232
volume tag   216

W

Western Digital   31
WIDE DATA TRANSFER REQUEST   304
Wide SCSI   286

WORM drive   176
WRITE
   tape drive   189
WRITE(6)   159
WRITE(10)   159
WRITE BUFFER   71
WRITE DMA   71
WRITE FILEMARKS   191
WRITE LONG   71, 161
WRITE MULTIPLE   71
write precompensation   46
write protection   183
WRITE SAME   71
WRITE SECTORS   66
WRITE SESSION   246
write splice   16
WRITE VERIFY   72
write-through cache   158

Y

Yellow Book   237

Z

ZBR   56, 154
zone   168
zone bit recording   56, 154